新世纪翻译本科R&D系列教材

总主编 陈 刚 卢巧丹

How to Prepare BTI & BA Translation Theses & Defense: A Basic Coursebook

翻译专业本科毕业论文写作与答辩教程

陈 刚 编著

ZHEJIANG UNIVERSITY PRESS
浙江大学出版社
·杭州·

图书在版编目（CIP）数据

翻译专业本科毕业论文写作与答辩教程 / 陈刚编著.
杭州：浙江大学出版社，2025.4. -- （新世纪翻译本科
R&D 系列教材 / 陈刚，卢巧丹总主编）. -- ISBN 978-7
-308-26091-6

Ⅰ. H059；G642.477

中国国家版本馆 CIP 数据核字第 2025ZL0280 号

新世纪翻译本科 **R&D** 系列教材（总主编　陈　刚　卢巧丹）

翻译专业本科毕业论文写作与答辩教程

How to Prepare BTI & BA Translation Theses & Defense:
A Basic Coursebook

陈　刚　编著

丛书策划	包灵灵
责任编辑	张颖琪
责任校对	田　慧
封面设计	周　灵
出版发行	浙江大学出版社
	（杭州天目山路 148 号　邮政编码 310007）
	（网址：http://www.zjupress.com）
排　版	浙江大千时代文化传媒有限公司
印　刷	杭州高腾印务有限公司
开　本	787mm×1092mm　1/16
印　张	18
字　数	648 千
版 印 次	2025 年 4 月第 1 版　2025 年 4 月第 1 次印刷
书　号	ISBN 978-7-308-26091-6
定　价	68.00 元

学好翻译的时代要求

——"三化"与国家、社会需求

"新世纪翻译本科 R&D 系列教材"总主编序

　　学好翻译，须与时俱进。时代的要求乃是也应是高校培养翻译人才的主要要求。

　　何为时代要求？答案是"三化"+国家、社会需求。前者指"专业化""职业化""专门化"；后者即国家需求和社会需求，包含战略面向和战术面向两个维度。翻译人才培养和翻译队伍建设应上升到国家战略高度[①]，应服务于国家战略；同时，翻译人才更多的是战术人才，活跃于国家建设各个领域：一是面向近（中）期百工百业，着眼于行业及市场需求；二是面向中长期未来，在重视行业及市场需求的同时着眼于国家深度开创、发展，让人类命运共同体的中国哲理引领人类的发展。具体而言，时代要求应包括中华民族复兴需求、国家发展战略需求（如中国文化/思想/经济"走出去"、共建"一带一路"倡议落实）、国家外交需求（如公共外交、民间外交）、国家政策需求（如思政教育、语言/翻译服务）、行业需求（如文旅、外贸、电商、传媒）、涉外单位需求（如国际化医院、各级外办、高档酒店）、区域发展需求（如各种国际/区域一体化经济文化会展、博览会）、地方建设需求（如招商引资、共同开发）、学校及教育/培训机构需求（如师资、研究人员）等。与此同时，我们肯定也要考虑满足译者和译员个人及个体发展的需求。

　　总而言之，不论涉及何种类型的翻译人才，高校及其翻译院系应该始终将培养热爱翻译事业的人才放在第一位，并且落实到位。当然，与其坐而论道，不如起而行之；与其纸上谈兵，不如面对世界。

一、继往开来

　　今天的世界，对翻译学科专业而言，就是要勇于并善于面对时代挑战、AI 挑战、发展挑战、战略挑战、战术挑战、市场挑战、产业挑战、转型挑战、升级挑战、社会挑战，乃至全球化挑战。简而言之，翻译学科专业<u>亟须改革、转型、发展、提升</u>。

　　浙江大学翻译专业已经走过十几年的历史征程。回顾历史，翻译人才的专业建设理念及行动远早于体制建制。如今作为教育部一流本科专业建设点（2020），浙江大学翻译专业的教师团队正继往开来，编写优势本科专业（群）系列教材。本系列教材与"新世纪翻译学 R&D 系列著作"（陈刚总主编、主审，2004—2005 年策划、设计，2007 年首

---

① 详见："中译外"高层论坛：呼唤翻译人才建设国家战略. (2007-04-10)[2022-03-10]. https://www.translators.com.cn/archives/2007/04/1110.

推《高级商务口笔译：口译篇》《高级商务口笔译：笔译篇》）有一共同和共通的撰写理念，即 R&D（Research & Development）——基于并超越中国传统译论和西方译论，在全球化语境下进行口笔译实践、教学、研究，努力走在翻译专业的前列[①]，但这一撰写理念应该也必须有自己的层次及其要求。"新世纪翻译学 R&D 系列著作"（以下简称"系列著作"）主要服务于本科层次的学生（即 BA[翻译方向]生和后来的 BTI[翻译专业]生）与研究生层次的学生（即 MA 生和后来的 MTI 生）。而"新世纪翻译本科 R&D 系列教材"（以下简称"系列教材"）主要服务于本科层次的 BTI & BA 生。编写该系列教材要跟上时代的发展，坚持"六化"原则：本科化、专业化、学术化、职业化、专门化、思政化。而 BTI & BA 生要学好翻译，则要强调"时代要求"，即"三化"+国家、社会需求。（请扫描二维码继续扩展阅读）

二、"三化"阐释

对"三化"的阐释离不开时代背景，"三化"的要求就是时代的要求。2007 年出版的"系列著作"总序中提及翻译时代，其重要性如今愈显："Translate or die"（Paul Engle 语）或"不译则亡"。国际著名翻译学家尤金·奈达（Eugene Nida）特别指出，翻译工作既复杂（complex）又引人入胜（fascinating），"事实上，I. A. 理查兹（I. A. Richards）在 1953 年就断言，翻译很可能是世界史上最为复杂的一种活动"[②]。一个不争的事实是，中英互译是世界诸语言互译中最为复杂、最为困难的一种。翻译几乎与语言同时诞生，是一项历史悠久的实践活动（old practice），又是不断焕发勃勃生机的有 AI 赋能的新专业和职业（new profession and occupation with AI empowerment）。（请扫描二维码继续扩展阅读）

三、"需求"阐释

编写本系列教材，就是以需求为导向，为解决国家、地方、学科、专业等诸多需求做点实事——一句话，为行业育人，为社会育才。我们要紧跟时代步伐，在竞争中处于较为优势的地位，必须在国家新的建设发展时期，好好**培育**并不断**提升**自己的翻译专业。（请扫描二维码继续扩展阅读）

本系列教材的设计与编写将针对（本校）BTI 生的需求和特点，内容深入浅出，亦包含挑战性译题，反映编写团队老中青成员各自的多元工作经历、生活阅历、研究领域特色和最新研究成果。有关编写和编排体例将采用国家及出版社的最新标准，坚持立德树人，以人为本；坚持中国立场、国际表达；力求专业、严谨；讲究科学、规范；力戒教条、死板；努力推陈出新，同时尊重分册编写者的差异性（diversity）和鲜明个性（individuality）。综上，我们希望能够将教材编出新意，并体现专业性、实用性、思想性、时代性、知识性、学术性、趣味性、前沿性、创新性及独特性。

---

① 笔者事先不可能知道 2006 年教育部批准部分高校试办本科翻译专业（BTI）以及 2007 年开始设置翻译硕士专业学位。凭借口笔译实践"出身"的背景，笔者在 21 世纪初于浙江大学开创翻译（专业）的新天地。

② Nida, Eugene A. *Language, Culture, and Translating* [M]. Shanghai: Shanghai Foreign Language Education Press, 1993: 1.

鉴于处于学科/专业培育阶段的新编教材、教材建设（以及教学大纲、方法和手段、师资队伍建设、教学评估和管理）还有待深入探索、试错实践，本系列教材也有待在使用中不断提高、完善。我们真诚欢迎广大师生、专业人士、同业同行以及关心（浙江大学）翻译学科建设的所有人士不吝批评指正，帮助我们更上一层楼。

※　　　　　　※　　　　　　※

毋庸置疑，习近平总书记关于加强与改善国际传播工作，展示真实、立体、全面的中国的指示，国家多部委有关《翻译人才队伍建设规划（2021—2025）》的发文，以及习近平总书记针对外语院校及教师培养"三有"（有家国情怀，有全球视野，有专业本领）人才的回信，乃是我们编写"新世纪翻译本科 R&D 系列教材"的指导思想和行动准则，我们要将中国学术话语、大众话语、个人话语和国际话语等主动、自觉地用于编书实践之中。党的二十大报告指出，要"深化教育领域综合改革，加强教材建设和管理"，"统筹职业教育、高等教育、继续教育协同创新，推进职普融通、产教融合、科教融汇，优化职业教育类型定位"。①翻译学科/专业是服务于国家战略和社会需求的，翻译人才是国家战略人才。本系列教材的编写正是按照党的二十大报告的精神去努力的。翻译实践之职业特性鲜明，因此，融合高等教育和职业教育等要素也正是教材编写的重要方向——做到"职普融通、产教融合、科教融汇"，优化翻译专业的高教定位和职教定位。

"三化"不是树干，而是树根。"三化"是我们编好本系列教材的根基，也是学好翻译、教好翻译的大愿之行。根深才能叶茂。我们要有"三化"这一"深根"的理念和"叶茂"的理想，同时要有实现"三化"之方法，将其落到实处，以满足社会需求、人民需求、行业需求、国家需求、幸福生活的需求。

万丈高楼平地起。我们要重视本科，以本（科）为本；重视实践，以练为本；重视转换，以（文）本为本；重视通才，目标专才。

我们的教材和教师要引导、引领学生知行合一，我们的社会实践和社会服务要促使、培养学生译思并举，我们的"三化"观、"需求"观、成才观要使学生懂得天道酬勤，学道酬苦，业道酬精。

十五年前，我们的口号是：There is more to do in Translation Studies.

十五年后，我们的口号是：There is more to do in translation and communication.

总主编　谨识

2022 年初夏初稿

2024 年末定稿

新世纪翻译学 R&D 系列著作分册书目

---

① 习近平. 高举中国特色社会主义伟大旗帜　为全面建设社会主义现代化国家而团结奋斗——在中国共产党第二十次全国代表大会上的报告. 人民日报, 2022-10-26(01). http://paper.people.com.cn/rmrb/html/2022-10/26/nw.D110000renmrb_20221026_3-01.htm.

工具书缩略语表（本书）

《辞海》——《辞海（缩印本）》第 6 版，上海辞书出版社，2010.

《规范》——《现代汉语规范词典》第 3 版，外语教学与研究出版社，2014.

《现汉》——《现代汉语词典》第 7 版，商务印书馆，2016.

CCED——*Collins COBUILD English Dictionary*, Collinsdictionary.com, HarperCollins Publishers Limited & Shanghai Foreign Language Education Press, 2000.

CamD——*Cambridge Dictionary* (online), Cambridge University Press.

LDCE——*Longman Dictionary of Contemporary English*, The Commercial Press & Longman, 1998.

MWALED——*Merriam-Webster's Advanced Learner's English Dictionary*, Encyclopedia of China Publishing House, 2010.

MWCD——*Merriam-Webster Collegiate Dictionary* (11th ed.), 21st Printing Quad Graphics Versailles, KY, 2018.

NOD——*New Oxford Dictionary*, Oxford University Press, 1998.

NOAD——*New Oxford American Dictionary* (online), Oxford University Press, 2010.

OALD——*Oxford Advanced Learner's English-Chinese Dictionary* (6th ed.), The Commercial Press & Oxford University Press, 2004.

OLD——*Oxford Learner's Dictionaries (American English)* (online), Oxford University Press.

RHWD——*Random House Webster's Dictionary of American English*, Random House, Inc.1997.

前　言

（首部服务于 **BTI & BA** 学位论文写作与答辩的专业指南）

迄今，BTI 教学点高校已有三百几十家。BTI 毕业生加上英语专业中撰写翻译方向毕业论文的 BA 生的数量非常可观。2006/2007 年以来，高校翻译专业虽然发展较快，但除了缺乏翻译专业化、职业化的师资外，还缺专门指导 BTI & BA 学位论文写作与答辩的翻译专业教科书。希望这本《翻译专业本科毕业论文写作与答辩教程》能为我们的师生"排忧解难"。

虽然此教程是首部单独服务于 BTI & BA 生的专业指南，但其实 2015/2016 年浙江大学出版社业已出版了全国首部服务于四类翻译生（BTI & BA 生+ MTI & MA 生）的《翻译论文写作与答辩指南》（陈刚，2015a）——有志于攻读 MTI 或 MA 的 BTI & BA 生同样很有必要阅读此书。

每年，大量翻译专业、英语专业本科生必须或主动选择翻译（学）作为他们撰写毕业论文的方向。他们需要按照国内外学术规范用英文撰写自己的毕业论文。如何撰写学位论文，如何进行学位论文答辩，是摆在这些准毕业生面前的头等大事。

据笔者所知，有涉及本科英语专业毕业论文写作指南的书籍——书中会包含文学、语言学、翻译（学）、英语教学、跨文化交际等多种主题，但迄今尚未有一部以翻译（学）为单一主题的毕业/学位论文写作与答辩的专业指导性教程问世。考虑到上述诸多因素，笔者特地利用自己担任杭州第 19 届亚运会及亚残会译审专家工作的"空窗期"，熬夜加班加点，将"新世纪翻译本科 R&D 系列教材"中的这部教材作为首部分册赶写完成，以便早日与读者见面。

在设计、构思及编著本书的过程中，笔者根据本科生的特点、自己指导论文写作的经验、学生初学毕业论文撰写的"正道"，依据学术论文写作的要求和规律，按照较高的学术标准，努力做到"求真""务实"。

所谓"求真"，就是向学生传输写作"真实"和答辩"真实"，即客观真实和反映学术规范、规则、规律、惯例之真实。所谓"务实"，就是有引领性的实践，具体从细节（detail）、基准（benchmark）、高度（altitude）、远见（farsight）、先见（foresight）五个方面着手。"细节"决定高下与成败，"基准"是成功之起点，"高度"体现态度和标准，"远见"反映抱负和视野，"先见"将再现自我实现。

为确保做到并做好上述"五大要求"，笔者提出一个理念和两项公式。

●一个理念是："要快得先慢"（you have to go slow to go fast）。孔子曰，"欲速则不达"（more haste, less speed）。当代有 slow science（慢科学），基于这样的理念："... science should be a slow, steady, methodical process[①]" "scientists should not be expected to provide 'quick fixes' to society's problems"。慢科学支持 curiosity-driven scientific research（好奇心驱动的科学研究）。当代商务法则也有 "slowly but surely"（慢且稳）的理念。因此，只要认真细读本书，相信你定会获得"道"（真知灼见）与"术"（规则条例）。

● **两项公式是：**

公式①   ┃Know-how┃ > ┃Know-what + Know-why┃

公式②   ┃Ability + Application + Methodology┃ ⇨ ┃Innovation┃

公式①告诉我们，know-how 的要求高于、难度大于 know-what + know-why。因为学生最终是要拿出一篇合格的毕业论文的，所以他/她必须具备 know-how 的能力。当然，know-how 也不是学生先天就具有的，它建立在学生的 input（输入）+ law（法则/规律）的基础之上。要获取理论知识、专业知识、百科知识、AI 知识，就需要输入；要掌握学习、研究、写论文的规律，就需要懂得并运用逻辑（logic）、推理（reason）及原理（principle），这就是所谓的 "know-what + know-why"。在此基础上，我们才可能慢慢学习、获得并掌握 know-how。由此推理，当你的 ┃Know-how┃ < ┃Know-what + Know-why┃ 时，你的论文就只能写得"平平"（从"基准"视角出发），因为你的动手能力即实践能力较弱，你运用（理论）知识的能力不强；而当你的 ┃Know-how┃ = ┃Know-what + Know-why┃ 时，你的论文也很难写得"出神入化"。

公式②告诉我们，innovation（创新）要满足三个要件：能力 + 实施（[能]力）+ 方法论。首先，ability 意为 "the fact of having the skill, power, or other qualities needed in order to do something"（LDCE 第 2 页），即指或强调你具备了"能力"这个事实。其次，application 意为 "effort made to work hard in order to complete something successfully"（MWALED 第 67 页），即指你能为成功完成任务而辛勤工作。再次，methodology 一词二义：一是术语，意为 "the set of methods used for study or action in a particular subject, as in science or education"（LDCE 第 950 页）；二是 "a set of methods, rules, or ideas that are important in a science or art: a particular procedure of or set of procedures"（MWALED 第 1025 页）。当三个要件都能够较好地或高程度地满足后，创新才有可能发生。没有（科研）能力，论文创新的基本事实或素质就不存在；缺乏勤奋、努力加决心，就无法实施、实践、实验自己的科研思想；不懂得基本的方法论，就不可能知道何为创新、如何创新、如何突破。因此，要创新，这三者缺一不可。

前言第一段我们提及，每年都有不少本科生需要撰写翻译类的毕业论文。如果说，20 世纪八九十年代的学生和老师的（毕业）论文存在一些不足实属正常，那为什么 21 世纪已经走过了 20 多年，我们（一流专业）的本科生的毕业论文质量怎么还不见得有新的、大幅度的提高，或有所提高呢？我们这么多硕士、博士研究生充实了高校英语、翻译教师队伍，为什么本科生毕业论文的品质却没有提高呢？根据笔者 21 世纪的有限观

---

① 全书的下画线，如无特别说明，均由本书作者所加。

察，由于扩招，相当多英语/翻译方向本科生的毕业论文品质堪忧，无法公开展示以证明各个高校培养的学生是高质量的——起码是合格的。这里就明显地存在师生们尚不符合公式①提出的三个基本要求（know-what、know-why、know-how）。排除学生、教师的理念和责任心以及学校的管理能力等方面的诸多不足（这些问题不是本书所能解决的），师生们（系统）缺乏完整、全面撰写（翻译类）毕业论文的知识、技能和理念等无疑是重要原因。因此，笔者下了大决心，一定要写出一部专业性尽可能强的毕业论文写作指南，专门服务于 BTI & BA 生，并抛砖引玉，给学界填补空白。

"打铁还须自身硬。"如果没有学好翻译的基本课程（包括理论课程、知识课程和通用实践课程等）以及特殊领域的专业翻译课程，学生自身就"缺料"（"学术之料"），"学术之躯"远非"膀阔腰圆"，写出的论文自然也就缺乏学术养分。有学术积累的学生，"身强力壮"，开夜车①下笔如有神；缺乏学术积累的学生，白天写作"打瞌睡"，即使开夜车也无话可写，写了也是言之无物，甚至出现"剽窃"等学术失范现象，虽然本科毕业论文属于习作性论文。

尽管如此，那些"下笔千言"的好学生，其论文依然不符合学术规范。就"舶来品"学术论文而言，其撰写是有章可循的——有国际学术标准和规范，有各高校依据国际标准而"因地制宜"的标准等。不会撰写学位论文的本科生相当多，这是情理之中的，因为本科生乃学术生涯中首次撰写如此长度的学位论文。

自翻译专业应运而生以来，撰写 BTI 学位论文和 BA 学位论文的本科生人数在不断增长。虽然以（相对）重学术研究能力的 BA 生撰写的学术学位论文与（应）重实践应用/研究能力的 BTI 生撰写的专业学位论文之间存在诸多不同，需要在书中一一加以阐述，但这两类本科生都需要掌握必要的研究方法论。BA 生要具备较强的研究能力，所以理应更强于掌握研究方法；BTI 生要写学位论文，要有较强的逻辑思辨能力，即归纳能力、分析判断能力、演绎能力。因此，学习、了解并且掌握翻译研究的常用方法，不仅需要，更是必要。

虽然对本科生撰写论文的要求似乎不必"过高"，然而不少"985/双一流高校"撰写翻译主题学位论文的 BTI & BA 生，都具备不低的翻译理论水平和（研究）方法水平，这点从本书所举的案例中可见一斑。他们中少数学生的学位论文已经接近甚至达到了MTI/MA 学位论文的水平。

有鉴于此，笔者策划、设计的这部指南，既具有教科书的功能，又提供具有研究特色的资料，注重两大写作特色：

其一，"二合一"的框架。紧紧抓住 BA 和 BTI②两种毕业论文撰写之主题，并由此展开，详略是否得当，全基于笔者在 21 世纪前 15—22 年的观察、鉴别与判断。

其二，英文的"可见度"高。较多篇幅直接使用英文（包括引用英文原文，篇、章标题均使用英汉双语），目的是训练、帮助学生尽快具备英文撰写（翻译类）学术论文的

---

① 开夜车赶写学位论文是学生的家常便饭。
② 中国外语教育史上，先有 BA，再有 BTI。

能力。考虑到学生最终是用英文撰写论文，书中有意识地增加了英文的"可见度"。除了笔者授课笔记是全英文的，还要求教师和学生有意识地多使用英文，以培养英语语感和正确、规范、地道的学术论文写作方法。

因此，希望本书能够成为 the <u>one-stop resource</u> for BTI & BA students who want to know <u>how to research</u>, <u>how to reference</u>, <u>and ultimately how to write</u> an <u>undergraduate-level degree thesis</u>。

本着直接指导"两类生"开展基于实践的研究，同时使"两类生"加深对理论及研究方法的理解和应用的目的，笔者挑选了一些学生的学位论文作为案例分析和写作的样本。需要说明的是，笔者选择的案例，主要是基于便于论文写作分析与展示、仅为案例分析与研究提供一些方法这两点，并不意味着笔者全部认同所选论文中的观点，也不意味着这些论文是最佳选择，读者完全可以使用自己更为偏爱的论文作为案例来分析与研究，授课教师更可以选择适合本校学生水平的案例进行教学与研究。

本书分为 3 篇 10 章。内容之丰富，用于 32 课时的教学绰绰有余。任课教师可以根据情况自行增减书中内容，给学生布置每章的全部或部分开放性的【焦点问题探讨】或【研究与实践思考题】。**由于篇幅所限，书中部分内容将通过二维码呈现。**

"导引篇"仅含 1 章，重点介绍翻译（专业毕业）论文的 ABC，其中强调作者的综合人文素养，它对论文选题、设计及动笔等的作用非常重要。

"务实篇"包括 9 章：

第 2 章，直接进入开局——从总体框架出发谈论文写作如何起步。

第 3 章，在"入门"后，学生需要对论文进行开题——如何设计、撰写开题报告以及开题报告如何答辩。

第 4 章，开题报告撰写过程中，最大的难度是如何撰写文献综述。文献综述也是学位论文的重要组成部分——没有文献综述，就没有论文之研讨。提醒学生特别关注，两种/类论文对文献综述的要求有不同的侧重。

第 5 章，理论框架同样是开题报告和学位论文的重要组成部分。缺乏必要的理论基础和支撑，论文势必缺乏"底气"和"耐力"，质量也不会高，甚至不合格。BTI 论文如此，BA 论文更是如此。

第 6 章，重点转移至如何将理论与实践有机地结合。对此，两种/类论文的具体要求是不同的。而如何结合算是符合某一种论文的（最低）要求，即"基准"怎么定，此章有具体、详细的案例分析。

第 7 章，论文总是带有研究性质的，好的研究体现了好的方法（论）。是撰写纯理论的研究论文，还是撰写基于实践的研究论文，采取哪种研究方法，进行哪个领域的理论/实践研究，等等——要了解各种研究方法及研究方法论，此章是重头戏。

第 8 章，撰写论文，难免要引用他人的文献（包括 AI 文献）。如何规范引用，是有国际标准、国家标准及学界、行业、各校标准的。遵循这些学术规范，责无旁贷。这也是向剽窃说"不"的必读内容。

第 9 章，涉及"礼"与"法"。撰写论文，要对导师以及帮助过你的人"感恩""致谢"；学生自己独立完成的论文，应归为学生的"独创性作品"，应受到法律（如版权法）的保护。这些都需要做出书面的"公开声明"。由于培养你的母校有权保留并向国家有关部门或机构送交论文的复印件及其他版本，有权将自己毕业生的论文作为图书馆的纸质、电子文献资料，等等，因此学生还必须在论文使用授权声明书上签字。

第 10 章，开题报告答辩管的是学生的论文是否可以"开题"/"开写"，本章管的是学生的论文答辩是否可以通过，从而得以毕业、获得学位，是本书论及的两大话题（论文写作+论文答辩）之一，是学生不可不读的一章。

"手册篇"，看似"副片"，实为"正片"也，内容包括学术规范与操作、拒绝剽窃、论文撰写的经验之谈、论文案例以及口译研究建议。其重要性，不言而喻。

书最后的"参考文献"具备了有关信息备查、索引、索取之功用。

本书作者在此郑重告知，"我国拟立学位法：利用人工智能代写学位论文等行为或被撤销学位证书"[①]。

由于作者水平有限，"二合一"之类书籍似无先例可循，书中一定存在着诸多缺点、疏漏和不足，敬请读者批评指正，以便作者与时俱进，不断加以修正、提高、完善。

笔者自担任"新世纪翻译本科 R&D 系列教材"总主编以及本册作者以来，一直受到浙江大学本科生院、外国语学院以及浙江大学出版社的大力支持，同时从复旦大学、上海外国语大学匿名外审专家的辛勤工作、宝贵意见和建议中受益良多，感谢本院党政领导的政治和业务把关，感谢另一总主编、同事卢巧丹的全力配合、协助，感谢责编的全程专业把关、技术支持、鼎力相助。学校对我们这个全国一流翻译专业的建设给予了无私的资助，笔者再次致以衷心感谢！对本书引用过的论文之学生作者（已在相关页做了脚注），在此再次致以深深的谢意！

有了你们，本书将会成为指南。

有了你们，本书将会尽显精彩。

有了你们，本书将会赢得读者。

有了你们，本书将会彰显风采！

陈　刚

2024 年暑假修改于杭城翠微湖畔

---

① 参见 http://www.npc.gov.cn/c2/c30834/202308/t20230828_431187.html。

目 录

导引篇（First Things First）

务实篇（On the Way to Completion）

导 引 篇◆◆

First Things First

　　作为服务于教育部本科一流翻译专业，同时亦服务于本科英语专业（翻译方向）学位论文写作与答辩的专业指南，本书的任务和目标是从"双一流高校"的高度，从专业、学术、实用的角度帮助即将本科毕业的学生靠自己的实力，写出一篇合格的、优质的、干干净净的论文，并顺利通过论文答辩，最后获得光荣的、象征本人专业学术水准的毕业证书和学位证书。

　　2020 年 12 月 24 日，教育部印发了《本科毕业论文（设计）抽检办法（试行）》，自 2021 年 1 月 1 日起施行。这是为加强和改进教育督导评估监测，做好本科毕业论文（设计）（以下简称本科毕业论文）抽检工作，保证本科人才培养基本质量而制定的办法。当然，学术规范和学术道德也是高校思政建设的重要内容，不容小觑。

　　中国古代有"论说文"一说。根据刘勰的观点，论说文有的偏重学术，如柳宗元的《天说》，有的更讲究技巧，如韩愈的《师说》，其实并无大异。

　　虽然中国古代说理辨析的论说文与我们现当代的论文有诸多相似之处，但论文这个概念毕竟是"舶来品"，中国学生用母语（即汉语）写论文都觉得颇难，更何况使用非母语（即外语，如英语）写一篇一两万字的论文。写论文不仅是很多人生平第一次（first-time experience），而且也可能是最后一次（last-time experience/ultimate experience），可见本书的意义非凡。

　　作为帮助学生读懂全书的"导引篇"，必须把"引导"和"带领"作为首要任务，而且要让来自不同类型大学的翻译类毕业生一同受益，因此，"专业性""学术性""实用性"是写好全书的指导方针和政策：

　　●就"专业性"而言，本书指导学生如何最终写出合格的、优质的（翻译）本科毕业论文（how to write an undergraduate thesis）；

　　●就"学术性"而言，本书将教会学生如何从国际标准的学术角度，结合中国人的写作特点，写出自己独具理论价值/应用价值的学位论文（produce his/her own thesis of theoretical value or practical value）；

●就"实用性"而言，本书向学生提供"一站式服务"（the one-stop resource）。

顾名思义，本书的中心成分是 a practical guide (from first idea to finished product)，或类似 a coaching guide。我们的开篇是"导引篇"——First Things First，亦为重中之重。

读懂全书当从"导引篇"开始，首先是引导学生从以下几个关键词入手——这些关键词将建构成一个创新、成功的导引流程[①]：

$$\boxed{\text{Know-how}} > \boxed{\text{Know-what} + \text{Know-why}}$$

$$\boxed{\text{Ability} + \text{Application} + \text{Methodology}} \Rightarrow \boxed{\text{Innovation}}$$

最后，学生被"导引"成功，则是此开篇之成功，更是本书之成功。

---

① 导引流程中的英文，希望学生独立查证，了解其内涵。

第1章　翻译论文 ABC[①]

The ABC of Translation Theses

◎学习目标◎

　　BTI & BA 生要撰写翻译主题的毕业/学位论文，必须先对论文的基本常识和应知应会有一个大致了解，对相关理念有一个正确认知，为论文撰写打下一个初步基础，尤其要关注毕业论文写作（设计）工作五大环节之首的选题环节等。通过本章学习，学生将能够：

- 了解书名的实际含义；
- 了解有关论文的不同概念及表达；
- 了解有关论文撰写的理念问题；
- 了解毕业论文撰写的大致准备工作；
- 了解人文素养、选题要义、设计思路等；
- 了解自己可能选择的论文形式。

1.1　书名解读

　　本书书名《翻译专业本科毕业论文写作与答辩教程》具有丰富的内涵，其实际含义及其产生的解读难点是我们必须先搞明白的。

1.1.1　"论文"描述

　　此处仅限于书名本身的解读，概念详述将专设一节。由于（本科）毕业论文这一概念起源于西方近代大学，因此毕业论文本身就是一个舶来品。"论文"和本书书名所指的（毕业）"论文"的英文解读或描述见表 1-1。

表 1-1　论文、毕业论文、学位论文英汉对照表

序号	英文名称	汉语释义	备注
1	paper; essay; article; academic/ research/scientific paper	论文；学术文章	通常在学术杂志上发表，或者在学术演讲或会议上宣读；一般篇幅较短
2	(graduation) thesis	毕业论文	本科毕业论文；研究生毕业/学位论文

---

① "翻译论文"是本书使用的一个简单表达，指以翻译实践和/或研究为主题的毕业论文或学位论文。

（续表）

序号	英文名称	汉语释义	备注
3	thesis/dissertation	硕士/博士论文	两个英文名称均可用来指硕士研究生（学位）论文和博士研究生（学位）论文（英语）；前者用于学士、硕士学位论文较多（英/美语），后者用于硕士、博士较多（美语）
4	(degree) thesis; dissertation	学位论文	用于学士、硕士、博士的学术学位和专业学位论文；用于硕士/博士论文
5	undergraduate thesis	本科生（毕业）论文	用于本科类综合性大学
6	postgraduate thesis/dissertation	研究生（毕业）论文	用于硕士、博士
7	doctoral thesis/dissertation; PhD thesis/dissertation; professional doctorate thesis	博士论文	任何种类博士论文；（一般文科）学术学位博士论文（不含神学博士论文 Th.D. thesis）；专业学位博士论文
8	BA (degree) thesis	文学学士(学位)论文	用于学术学位（academic degree）
9	BTI (degree) thesis	翻译学士(学位)论文	用于专业学位（professional degree）
10	MA (degree) thesis	文学硕士(学位)论文	用于学术学位
11	MTI (degree) thesis	翻译硕士(学位)论文	用于专业学位
12	DTI degree thesis	翻译博士(学位)论文	用于专业学位

本书要讨论的"论文"主要关乎中国大陆本科翻译/英语专业中的以下两种/类涉及翻译（研究）的毕业论文：

①翻译专业本科毕业论文——BTI thesis；

②英语专业本科毕业论文（翻译方向、笔译方向、口译方向）——BA thesis (in translation/interpreting)。

1.1.2　"写作"难题

在西方大学，毕业论文是大学职能由人才培养向科学研究拓展的必然产物，因此，写（毕业/学位）论文（thesis writing）自然应该遵循西方大学的专业学术规范。有关这些规范，完全需要一本乃至数本书来加以说明。

由于我们的大学生不太习惯按照西方大学的规范来写论文，而且大学之间、地区之间的翻译教育水平和质量管理存在着不少差异，因此学界对是否需要撰写本科毕业论文（仍然）存在着争议。有关写作难题主要可以概括为四个方面（包括如何做变通解决）：

其一，涉及本科生自身。换言之，涉及从学生身上暴露出来的问题。例如，各个专业都存在着不少毕业生糊弄毕业论文的现象（特指态度不认真、不按照规定和规范写作、不同程度的剽窃等），写出来的东西不仅没有多少意义及价值（自己独立完成的规范论文，其本身就具意义和价值），而且属于学术失范、违（反版权）法行为。如果是普遍现象，写毕业论文岂不是对谁都没有好处，还不如取消算了。再如，对本科生来说，撰写翻译专业的毕业论文，挑战会更大，要求会更高。起码，毕业生必须或原则上应具备用外语（本书仅指英语，除非另有所示）进行学术写作的能力。全国有一千多所大学设置了本科英语专业，三百几十所大学设置了本科翻译专业。前者有部分（假设 1/5 至 1/3）学生选择撰写翻译（学）方向的毕业论文（另有文学、语言学等方向），后者则是全部学生必须选择翻译（学）作为论文写作的主题。如此多的本科毕业生，个个都能用比较准确或可接受的（非母语）英文写出一篇万儿八千词的论文吗？

事实上，自 1977 年恢复高考以来，能用 acceptable English 写出英语专业本科毕业论文的本科生并非占绝大多数，更何况论文还要遵循学术规范。如果用英文来撰写翻译（学）主题的毕业论文，那难度自然是有增无减。

因此，不少英语毕业论文被认为是 rubbish。加上疏于对毕业论文写作的管理，"无知就无畏"（针对不少本科类大学英语专业学生）——抄袭现象严重；还有的改用汉语撰写毕业论文；更有甚者，一些自费生、议价生、全日制本科生等花钱买论文，进而"买文凭"。

面对这样一种局面，无怪乎有相当多的人士提出（英语专业）本科毕业论文还不如不写，或者不写也罢。

其二，涉及指导教师自身。这个问题比较敏感，一般人都予以回避，但它却是一直以来造成英语/翻译类本科生毕业论文水平不高甚至低下的主要原因。因为从学生身上暴露出来的问题，根子却在教师身上。换言之，（称职的）翻译师资不够，甚至奇缺。

必须指出的是，本科生撰写翻译论文的主题丰富多彩，我们的笔译师资中自己在文学翻译和应用翻译（或非文学翻译）的实践方面合格（符合标准及要求）的较少（如文学翻译涉及散文、小说、诗歌、戏剧、传记、对联、歌曲译配、影视文学等多种体裁及其亚体裁，很少有教师做过有关的翻译实践，还有英到中、中到英两个方向及其足量的实践；再如应用翻译涉及专门领域，如新闻、旅游、法律、商务、会展、科技、广告、导游、联络、会议等领域英汉双向的口笔译实践）。我们很难给学生规定一个（狭窄的）范围，说本校翻译专业只指导某几个领域/方向的笔译，超出这些主题范围的口笔译论文恕不指导。翻译论文指导的挑战性还来自教师对（常用）口笔译理论的基本掌握、对翻译研究的持续进行及与时俱进。

由此可见，**就专业角度而言，指导翻译论文的挑战具有"多元性""实践性""专业性""理论性""专题性"**。这"<u>五个性</u>"——我们的翻译论文指导教师个体和团体是"难以应付/解决""刚能应付/解决""基本能应付/解决""能够应付/解决"，还是"完全能应付/解决"——是衡量学生毕业论文水平高低的尺度。这"五个性"的尺度，也完全可以用来最终判断某翻译学院、外语学院、翻译系、外语系等是否具备专业"资格"和专业"资质"来设立（高水平）翻译专业或笔译方向/口译方向。

其三，涉及毕业论文评分。教学过程固然重要，但教学结果更能说明问题。论文写作的难题还不可避免地影响到最后给毕业论文评分这个问题。生源的问题，师资的问题，势必造成毕业论文的质量问题，而且这些问题非常普遍。与西方发达国家比，我国的本科教育不易实行"淘汰制"，所以很少听到英语专业和翻译专业的本科生不能毕业或难以毕业。换言之，英语/翻译类本科生毕不了业的学生非常少。也就是说，我们的英语/翻译类本科生几乎都能毕业。这从侧面表明，即便毕业论文写得不怎么样，也照样毕业。

这从反面告诉我们抓毕业论文质量的必要性、重要性和紧迫性，尽管我们面临的困难重重，面对的挑战艰巨。本书就是要努力解决英语/翻译类毕业论文的质量问题。

其四，涉及变通与改良。既然我们有相当数量的本科生无法按照规定和规范撰写好毕业论文，我们的师资力量尚难以满足需求，我们的高校管理还有待加大力度改革及改善，那么我们在坚定走"一流专业"道路的同时，不妨实行变通的政策、办法，作为一项长期的、固定的政策和规定。有关要点描述如下：

①把翻译/英语本科培养方案的总学分分为：本科学历部分学分+学士学位部分学分。

②完成学历部分学分的学生可获本科毕业证书，予以毕业。

③设置毕业论文的资格要求，即设置"门槛"，若跨过"门槛"，该学生可以申请撰写学士学位论文。如某知名外国语大学规定，按教学计划要求，所有语言/翻译类专业学生三下、四上的专业必修课平均成绩达到 75 分及以上者，有资格撰写学士论文。[①]

④通过论文答辩者，授予学士学位证书；无法通过者，则不授予学士学位证书。

1.1.3   "答辩"话题

这里涉及毕业论文"开题报告答辩"和"毕业论文答辩"（thesis defense、thesis oral defense、oral defense）两层含义。二者都有比较程式化的规定、做法、方法，还有学生须知的如何撰写答辩陈述词、注意事项、答辩技巧、存在的问题等。

1.1.4   "指南"含义

这里的"指南"（guide、guideline、guidance、tips、how-to、know-how）是指对本科翻译专业和英语专业毕业"论文撰写"和"论文答辩"这两项工作的手把手实践性指南——从最初的思想萌芽到最终产品的完成并获得质检通过。基于对"指南"的上述分项解读，其内涵可以解读为：

How to Prepare BTI & BA Translation Theses & Defense:
A Practical Guide from First Idea to Finished Product

考虑到整套系列教材有篇幅要求，于是将副标题改成 A Basic Coursebook，即

How to Prepare BTI & BA Translation Theses & Defense:
A Basic Coursebook

1.2   毕业论文概念解读

1.2.1   概念解读（定义）

从定义出发，<u>毕业论文</u>指"高等学校教学计划的组成部分。本科以上学生在毕业前总结性的独立作业。有些高等专科学校也采用。目的在于培养学生运用在校期间所学课

---

① 参照《北京外国语大学英语学院本科毕业论文写作与指导手册》。

程，解决专业领域内某一理论或实际问题的能力，并使他们获得独立进行科学研究的训练。完成毕业论文是获取学历证书的必要条件之一"；而<u>毕业设计</u>，指"高等学校技术科学专业本科生在毕业前总结性的独立作业。要求学生综合运用专业理论和技术，做出解决实际问题的设计。相当于高等学校其他专业本科生的毕业论文"（《辞海》第 111 页）。

本书讨论的毕业论文（graduation thesis），亦称学位论文（degree thesis），主要指翻译专业本科毕业论文（或翻译与口译学士学位[Bachelor of Translation and Interpreting]论文，简称 BTI[学士学位]论文）和英语专业本科毕业论文（或文学学士[Bachelor of Arts]学位论文[翻译方向]，简称 BA[学士学位]论文）。

上述两种论文包括的毕业设计，不是本书讨论的重点。

1.2.2　概念解读（本体）

从本体出发，毕业论文之"毕业"乃就学业或学位而言，"论文"则就文体或写作而言。毕业论文要遵照学术论文的规范要求来写，属于议论文中的学术论文，其学术内涵（即论点、论据、论证"三要素"）应与学术论文无异。它不仅是本科生在完成专业学习任务之后的标志性学术成果，也是对学习成绩和探索能力的综合性总结和检阅，还是从事科研的初步尝试。大学生须知，毕业论文绝不是拉长了的"心得体会"。

毕业论文（thesis/dissertation）虽属学术论文中的一种，但与专家学者撰写的学术论文（paper/essay/article）相比，又有自己的特点：

其一，指导性。毕业论文一定是在导师（supervisor/adviser/mentor）指导下独立完成的科学研究成果。

其二，习作性[①]。毕业论文的写作是对所学专业基础知识的运用和深化，是独立进行的科研活动，是分析和解决某一理论问题或实际问题、把知识转化为能力的实际训练。其主要目的是培养毕业生综合运用所学知识解决实际问题的能力，为将来作为专业人员写出内容更为深刻、更有创意的学术论文做好准备。可见，毕业论文实际上是一种习作性的学术论文。

其三，层次性。硕士/博士研究生毕业论文或学位论文的水平和要求未必比（学术期刊上发表的）学术论文低，但一般的本科生毕业论文的水平和要求则比学术论文低。就学术价值而言（不包括低水平重复之类的论文等），专业人员的学术论文一般反映某专业领域最新或较新的学术成果，对学科发展、科学事业的发展起推动作用。本科生的毕业论文由于受各种条件的限制，学校或学术机构对论文学术质量方面的要求相对较低。就本科生而言，作为初学者，他们缺乏综合积累、写作经验和科研能力，而论文又必须在规定的有限时间内完成（特殊情况除外），因此，他们是难以写出具有较高学术价值的论文来的。每位本科生都能按照"国（家）标（准）"（或"教指委的标准"）完成毕业论文应是我们翻译专业/英语专业本科生教育改革的最大成果（之一）了。

其四，特殊性。翻译专业学位的论文强调毕业生的专业翻译能力（professional

---

① 其内容具有很强的实践性，但特指（学术论文的）"练习写作"。另一具体解释见"1.2.3　概念解读（意义）"。

translation competence/professional interpreting competence），它的重要组成部分是学生自己对一篇按照规定撰写的具有相当长度的源语文本（source text/ST；source language/SL speech/dialogue）进行独立的信息（内容+形式，包括语言、文化、技术、符号等）之转换，使之成为译语/目的语文本（target text/TT），亦称为 long translation（长篇翻译）。笔译完后，学生要对 TT 或翻译过程（translation/translating process）进行评述/译评，这种论文写作方法叫 translation with commentary 或 annotated translation，可以使用的理论、技巧可谓多维度的，涉及语言学、跨文化交流、行为学、认知心理、意识形态、技巧综合运用、归化及异化、目的论、文本类型、话语分析等。

学生选择做口译论文，即 do a recorded interpretation，要对 recorded interpretation/interpreting 做分析、研究、评述，可以涉及整个口译过程（the whole interpreting process），包括理解（understanding/comprehension）、记忆（memorizing）、信息处理（解码+编码/decoding + encoding）、表达（delivery）等；亦可涉及口译中的某一重要环节，如笔记技巧（note-taking techniques）、口译技能（interpreting skills）、质量评估（quality assessment）、认知研究（cognitive studies）、语言学研究（linguistic studies）、译员培训（interpreter training）研究等。

这类专业学位论文写作（方法）与传统学术论文写作有着诸多的不同，它不是纯学术研究性质的论文（conceptual/theoretical research），而是（接近/倾向于）实证研究（empirical research），但包含着理论研究或阐释研究（中的诸多成分）——这就是专业学位论文写作之特殊性。

尽管如此，不同层次的论文（毕业论文或供发表、宣读的学术论文），只要是属于人文社会科学领域的，一般应具有三大特点：学术性/理论性、科学性、创造性。前两个特点是必不可少的。

①学术性/理论性（academic/theoretical）。即要求作者"谈学术"，包括论文要有理论框架/路径（theoretical framework/approach）和研究方法论（research methodology），要符合论述逻辑（logic）和学术规范（normative，如写作规范、杜绝剽窃等）。具体地说，在立论上不应带有个人偏见，不得主观臆造，须从客观实际出发，通过学术论证得出既是专业/学术的又是符合实际的结论。即便是讨论翻译实践这种艺术性质的活动，作者也应尽可能客观、科学、逻辑，摆事实讲道理——一句话，以学术为本。

②科学性（scientific）。即要求作者论述具备"科学性"。学术论文这类议论文，与一般非学术性议论文不同，不能只是材料的简单罗列或最多做一些简单的分析（如只将 TT1 和 TT2 一放，仅做一两句简单概括），而应对足量的翻译案例（sufficient translation cases）等事实、材料进行分析、探讨、研究，将感性认识上升到理性认识。一般来说，学术论文具有论证特性，或具有论辩色彩。论文的内容必须符合唯物论、辩证法。换言之，符合"实事求是"（fact-finding）、"有的放矢"（goal-oriented/to-the-point）、"既分析又综合"（analytic & synthetic）的科学研究方法。

③创造性（creative）。即要求作者具有"创新意识"（innovative），论文尽可能具有"原创性"（original）。科学研究是对新知识的探求，创造性是科学研究的生命。学术论文的创

造性在于作者要有自己独到的见解，能提出新的观点、新的理论。翻译理论可以创新，可以推陈出新；翻译实践更应该是创新的（creative translation）——这是翻译的最高境界。

可见，论文一般应具备上述"三大特性"，好的论文更应该或必须具备创造性。这是因为"科学可看作'人类的真正有积累性和进步性的唯一活动'"（萨尔顿语）。"科学方法的另一特点是，<u>科学总要发展，并有新的发现</u>，这或许也影响到人们的价值观。<u>科学方法主要是发现新现象、制定新理论的一种手段，因此在不断地扩大人类知识的体系；</u>只要科学方法应用得上，旧的科学理论就必然会不断地被新的理论所推翻。关于这一点，美国的科学史权威萨尔顿说过：'<u>科学总是革命的和非正统的</u>；这是它的本性；只有科学在睡大觉才不如此'。"（详见梅森，1977：第 48 章"科学和历史"）

1.2.3　概念解读（意义）

从意义出发，毕业论文涉及个人的学业、事业、人生的诸多重要环节和节点，还涉及国家改革开放及全球化的发展。

（1）撰写毕业论文，是本科生培养方案中学分最高的最为重要的教学环节。毕业论文之优劣，是决定学生毕业时可否被授予学位的重要依据，甚至是唯一依据。

（2）撰写毕业论文，既是高校人才培养的重要体现，又是衡量办学质量和办学效益的重要评价内容。因此，毕业论文是考查学生综合能力、评估学生学业成绩的一个重要方式，也是检验学生在校学习成果的重要措施。

（3）毕业论文是大学生完成学业的标志性作业，它不仅是学生毕业和学位资格认证的重要依据或唯一依据，也是结束大学学习生活走向社会的桥梁。

（4）不少用人单位对毕业论文的质量非常重视，因为毕业论文可反映出该毕业生学业的综合水平，反映出该生所在学校教育水平之高低，更反映出该校综合实力的强弱。因此，不应存在任何轻视毕业论文的想法。

（5）毕业生走向社会，参与社会工作，不管其性质是否为研究型，他/她都要适合新的工作岗位，并发挥一般作用或重要作用，撰写毕业论文这样一种综合训练对一位新的工作者是有百利而无一弊的。大学生的各种知识和能力在撰写毕业论文时受到了一次全面考核，涉及"七大性"：

——系统性（系统地掌握专业知识）；

——全面性（全面地熟悉各类知识）；

——运用性（有效地运用专业知识及百科知识）；

——逻辑性（逻辑思维能力）；

——习作性（练习性、草稿性和实验性三项功能）；

——开拓性（探索、开拓新的知识领域，同时开拓个人自己的勇气、耐力、信心、信念等）；

——创新性（培养科研创新意识，乃至真正实现创新）。

需要特别指出的一个"老生常谈"是：实践证明，撰写毕业论文对提高专业/学术/技术写作能力的帮助相当之大。试想，学生生平第一次几乎用全英文（非母语）撰写一万单词左右的本科毕业论文/学士学位论文，有语言要求，有翻译要求，有内容要求，有思想要求，有逻辑要求，有学术（规范）要求等，谈何容易啊！学生在撰写毕业论文过程中所培养出来的"七大性"，在工作上会发挥不可低估的作用（如全球化召唤"开拓创新型"人才），不仅使工作单位受益，使个人自己受益，同时也使国家受益。

（6）翻译使全球化成为可能，可以毫不夸张地说，没有翻译，就没有全球化。全球化的快速发展急需各行各业尤其是特殊领域的复合型高级专业口笔译人才。目前，中国最多可称为"翻译大国"，离"翻译强国"的地位可谓任重道远。外语专业早已从单科的"经院式"人才培养转向宽口径、应用性、复合型人才的培养模式。外（国）语（言文学）不仅仅是一种学科/专业（强调"人文性""学科性"），更多地表现为一种发挥巨大功能的交流工具（强调"工具性"及"专业交流"，包含"人文性""学科性"等）。外语专业的毕业生原则上都被要求直接用所学的外语撰写毕业论文。同理，全国一流翻译专业的毕业生也应用所学的第一外语撰写毕业论文，尽管有些学校仅要求用汉语撰写翻译专业毕业论文。

我们强调并且坚持培养学生的译写功底。学生应以高标准严格要求自己，提高自己的译写能力，这是翻译专业毕业生必须达到的目标（之一），也是经济全球化、文化全球化/多元化发展的迫切需求。对个人而言，用非母语作为目标语（target language/TL）撰写毕业论文，是学生提高 TL 运用能力和建构合理 TL 语篇能力的良机；对国家而言，培养更多的翻译专业学生娴熟运用非母语之目标语宣传中国的软实力、巧实力，讲好中国故事，参与共建"一带一路"，实现中国梦，构建人类命运共同体，可谓长期的战略计划和目标。

1.2.4　概念解读（类型）

从类型看，（翻译类）毕业论文一般归属于人文社会科学这一大类，从理工科视角探索、研究翻译的不在此书讨论。根据内容性质和学科研究方法（research methodology），毕业论文分为理论性论文（theoretical research）、实验性论文（empirical research）、描述性论文（descriptive research）和毕业设计性论文（graduation design）。一般认为，后三种论文（设计）主要是理工科大学生选择的论文形式，第一种则为文科大学生所采用。然而，翻译类毕业论文可以包括上述四种形式。

根据本书着重讨论的翻译专业学士学位/毕业论文，根据 BTI（翻译方向）侧重口笔译实践和实战能力、注重翻译实战独立操作和练习等特性，毕业论文应反映有关学位的专业性和专门化（professional/specialized）、应用性（practical/pragmatic/applied）、职业性（professional/ occupational/trade-specific）、技术性（technical）、翻译原创性（original）；根据 BA 等学术学位侧重理论性、学术性、通用性（普适性）、借用性（借用他人理论和/或译文研究）等特点，BTI 论文和 BA 论文又可细分为常用的和可选用的 15 种（见表1-2）。

表1-2　翻译专业毕业论文/学位论文形式简介

序号	论文形式		适用范围
1	翻译及翻译评述（translation with commentary）		BTI/BA
	备注要求	①"翻译"指 long translation，主要涉及实用文本和技术性问题，或非文学类文本，包括音乐、舞蹈、美术等。②有关翻译必须由学生自己独立完成，ST 没有现成的 TT（作为参考）。③翻译评述可以运用他人的理论、技巧，也可以使用自己独特/独创的翻译策略、方法等。④较为常见的论文形式。⑤有些学校把这种论文形式作为 BA 论文的可选择范围。⑥可以采用机助翻译（CAT）。⑦BTI 论文和 BA 论文可以采取同一种论文形式。	
2	实践研究论文（practice-based research; translation-based/interpreting-based research）		BTI/BA
	备注要求	①"实践"指 translation/interpreting，对 BTI 生来说，应是自己的 translation/interpreting；对 BA 生来说，可以借用他人的 translation。②对（理论）研究的要求更高、更全面、更有竞争力。③"翻译"指 long translation（包括某书中的一章或该章的部分内容），主要涉及实用型文本和技术性文本，或非文学类文本，包括音乐、舞蹈、美术、宗教等。④有关翻译必须由 BTI 生自己独立完成，ST 原则上没有现成的 TT（作为参考），一般不期待本科生的复译品质大大高于原译；BA 生可以借用现成的 TT。⑤可以进行"重译"（重译本要基本超越原译水准）。⑥翻译评述可以运用他人的理论、技巧，也可以使用自己独特/独创的翻译策略、方法等，强调理论的较高水准的运用。⑦可以采用机器/机助翻译（MT/CAT）和/或数据库研究等。	
3	理论性研究论文（theoretical/conceptual research）		BA/BTI
	备注要求	①可以由 BA/BTI 生自己选择，但原则上不鼓励 BA/BTI 生撰写。②运用纯粹的抽象理论为研究对象，研究方法是严密的理论推导和数学运算，有的也涉及现成译文、口笔译实验与观测，用以验证论点的正确性。③以对译本/口译录音（文本/过程）的研究、调查、考察所得观测资料以及有关文献资料为研究对象，研究方法是对有关资料进行分析、综合、概括、抽象，通过归纳、演绎、类比，提出某种新的理论观点和新的学术见解。	
4	论辩型论文/议论性论文（argumentative thesis）		BA/BTI
	备注要求	①一事一议，采取案例分析法，适用于 BA 生。②若是立论性的毕业论文，要求从正面阐述论证自己的翻译观点和主张，做到论点鲜明、论据充分、论证严密、以理和事实服人（可以他人或自己的译文作为事实依据）。③若是驳论性毕业论文，要求通过反驳别人的翻译论点来树立自己的翻译论点和主张，论点、论据、论证这"三要素"缺一不可。④若是 BTI 生选择③这一论文形式，可以将自己的 retranslation 与原译（the original translation）做一对比分析、评论，说明自己的重译有哪些优点、原译存在哪些不足等。	
5	描述型论文（descriptive research）		BA/BTI
	备注要求	①对 BA/BTI 生一般不太合适。②对某一翻译问题(理论的或实践的)或现象加以分析、描述及说明，"论"的篇幅较小，重点是描述和说明，理论性较强。③在描述研究的基础上可以有一定的结论，但不一定也不必在理论和实践层面提出解决问题的方法或方案。	

（续表）

序号	论文形式		适用范围
6	宏观研究论文（macroscopic research）		BA/BTI
	备注要求	①对 BA/BTI 生一般不太合适。②着眼于所涉翻译问题观念、功能等层面的问题。③少量涉及微观层面的翻译问题，但都是为了论证宏观层面的问题而进行。	
7	微观研究论文（microscopic research）		BTI/BA
	备注要求	①微观研究适合这两种学位论文，而且占比相当之大。②可以谈及宏观层面的问题，但着重讨论局部性的、经验性的翻译问题。③着眼操作层面、语言结构、具体可见（即形而下）的翻译问题或现象。	
8	专题型论文（subject thesis; subject/problem-based research; subject/problem-oriented research; project; monograph; disquisition）		BTI/BA
	备注要求	①又称专题研究论文，或专题/问题/导向论文，适合这两种学位论文。②针对翻译行业/译界/翻译学科建设中的一些现实问题（如培训、价格、职业道德、翻译伦理、专业/行政/行业管理等），运用所学到的专业知识（理论和方法）展开探讨、研究，提出新的见解、观点和方法，并加以科学论证。③针对翻译实践或理论中的某个专题（subject）、热点话题（hot topic）、要点（worthy point）、问题/难题（problem），提出自己的对策或解决问题的方法（solution）；或者在分析前人实践/研究成果的基础上，以直接论述的形式发表见解，从正面或反面提出自己的观点等。	
9	综述型论文（survey/review/overview）		BA/BTI
	备注要求	①主要适合 BA 学位论文，不提倡 BTI 生撰写。②在归纳、总结前人或今人对翻译学科/专业中某一学术问题/实践问题已有研究/实践成果的基础之上，加以介绍、评论或译介，由此发表自己的见解（翻译观）。	
10	综合型论文（comprehensive research）		BA/BTI
	备注要求	①更适合 BA 学位论文。②一种将综述型和论辩型两种形式有机结合起来写成的论文。③BTI 生可以对出版译文（一种以上为佳）进行对比分析、研究，或者对某一特殊领域（specialized domain/area）的重点问题（如术语翻译的发展）做一综述，然后提出自己的译文、观点以及值得继续研究、探讨的实践问题和理论问题。	
11	翻译项目（translation project）		BTI/BA
	备注要求	①适合 BTI 学位论文，（建议）BA 生也可以做。②对 ST 进行独立翻译，并根据自己的 TT 就翻译问题写出研究报告。③字数要求：BTI 论文——笔译部分的 ST>8000 汉字（C-E），TT>10000 汉字（E-C）（有的学校定为 8000 汉字）+研究报告或评论部分>3000 英文单词+其他论文/项目必要组成部分的字数。	
12	翻译实验报告（translation experiment report）		BTI（/BA）
	备注要求	①适合 BTI 学位论文，（建议）BA 生也可以做。②就笔译任务/环节或口译的某个/某些环节展开实验，并就实验结果进行分析，写出不少于 5000 words/characters 的实验报告[作为完整的毕业论文（实验报告+其他部分）的总词/字数应不少于 10000 words/characters（因口笔译涉及双语）]。	

（续表）

序号		论文形式	适用范围
13		笔译/口译实践报告（translation practice report/task-based translation report/task-based interpreting report）	BTI/BA
	备注要求	①适合 BTI 学位论文，（建议）BA 生也可以做。②根据任务描述、口笔译/任务过程、译例/案例分析、口笔译/任务总结进行详尽描述；从案例分析中选取有代表性的一定数量的译例，然后从理论视角、口笔译策略、ST/TT 特征、方法/技巧、翻译问题/错误[①]等方面展开讨论、分析、译评；最后在口笔译任务总结部分陈述具有一般意义的启示和结论，陈述应是理论性的和方法性/技巧性的。	
14		翻译重要岗位实习报告（internship report of key positions）：①翻译项目经理实习报告（project manager internship report）；②项目翻译实习报告（project translator internship report）；③审校实习报告（reviser internship report）；④（通用）翻译实习报告（translation internship report）	BTI
	备注要求	①翻译项目经理实习报告：围绕项目控制的关键点（如人员、成本、质量、周期、工具的应用等）对项目做总结评价和各阶段实施情况的总结，涉及项目中背景介绍、计划、实施评估、技术应用总结、团队合作评估等具体分项。若是实战项目，应增加用户满意度调查等。②项目翻译实习报告：围绕翻译任务背景介绍、需求分析、时间管理、工具使用、翻译质量控制等方面展开，着重总结翻译过程中遇到的问题、所采取的措施以及获取的经验。③审校实习报告：围绕翻译任务的质量标准等要求（以合同、协议或 translation brief 中规定的为准）、时间管理、工具使用、质量控制过程、质量评估等内容展开，根据审校实习过程写出观察到的问题和切身体会，并提出改进建议，应重点结合实用理论、翻译策略及方法、文本规范、编辑业务指南等元素。④（通用）翻译实习报告：一般指无专业领域、无具体或固定岗位的翻译实习，忙闲不均，工作量不确定，有稿就译，无稿"打杂"，口译也做，此时实习报告应谨防流于心得体会类；有时也会碰上很有挑战性的翻译任务，具有专业/学术价值。	
15		翻译调研报告（translation research report）	BTI/BA
	备注要求	①围绕任务描述（调研目的、调研对象、调研方式等）、任务过程（受试的选择、调研的组织、调研数据的收集等）、调研结果分析、调研的结论与建议等展开。②报告应有新意，强调典型和个性相结合，避免重复，防止"流水账"。	

　　上述 15 种论文形式，只要确保品质，都是值得采用的。根据目前中国大陆的翻译生态环境，我们建议采取如表 1-3 所示的 8 种（类）形式。

---

① "翻译问题/错误"概念源自 Christiane Nord 的术语 translation problems/errors (Nord, 2001)。

表 1-3　翻译毕业论文/学位论文形式推荐

现序号/ 原序号	论文形式	适用范围	说明
(1)/1	翻译及翻译评述	BTI/BA	①最为常用。②字数根据"国标"/"教指委"或各校自己的标准制定。③建议总字数①：8000（ST/TT）+3000（评述）+其他。
(2)/2	实践研究论文	BTI/BA	有关要求同上。更强调理论性、学术性、应用性、创新性。
(3)/4/7/8	论辩型论文/议论性论文；微观研究论文；专题型论文	BTI/BA	①有关要求见"表 1-2　翻译毕业论文/学位论文形式简介"相关部分。②字数要求——本科生论文：10000 words。
(4)/10	综合型论文	BA/BTI	有关要求同上。BTI 生可以不主动选择此论文形式。
(5)/11	翻译项目	BTI/BA	有关要求见"表 1-2　翻译毕业论文/学位论文形式简介"相关部分。
(6)/12	翻译实验报告	BTI/BA	有关要求同上。此外，口译学生应提供口译语篇的录音文件（一套）。
(7)/13	笔译/口译实践报告	BTI/BA	有关要求同上。
(8)/14-③	翻译重要岗位实习报告之③审校实习报告	BTI	有关要求见"表 1-2　翻译毕业论文/学位论文形式简介"相关部分。

表 1-3 推荐的论文形式，均强调"翻译以实践为本""翻译的本体研究""基于翻译实践的研究"等翻译核心理念和思想。

随着翻译生态环境的不断改善，我们可以自由选择更多种类的毕业/学位论文形式。根据过去十几年 BA/BTI 毕业论文写作情况，就论文层次、高度、质量等要素而言，就"985 高校""双一流建设高校"对学生的要求而言（校本规定，如要求有文献综述、外文翻译等；多重准备，如国内外读研、跨专业读研、高校任教、从事研究等），建议尽量选择表 1-3 中的前 4 项；如果选择后 4 项，务必重视理论元素，并要做到言之有物，避免理论和实践脱节的"两张皮"倾向/现象。简言之，目标远大，不负韶华，自我挑战，从高要求。

1.3　毕业论文写作准备

1.3.1　理念先行

谈论文写作的准备，必先涉及理念问题。仅从步骤上谈，并不是一件高深莫测的事情，我们在本章只是先点到为止，详细谈论、具体指南将在后九章逐步展开。

---

① 所列字/词数均为"底线"字/词数（characters/words）。下同。

Research Paper Smart 一书的作者指出：

Of a good beginning, cometh a good end.

John Heywood

Perhaps the most difficult part of any project is getting started. The broader the range of topics in front of you, the more difficult it is to begin. The starting point, however, is one of the most critical points of your research project. Embarking down the path of research on a topic that offers little or no information will be among the most frustrating tasks you can imagine. A good topic is like a good book—always satisfying and challenging.（Buffa, 1997: 10）

　　显然，下画线部分清楚地告诉我们撰写（好）论文的最为浅显也最为深刻的一个道理：**选题最难**。正所谓"善终先善始""万事开头难"。"题好文一半"（直译：好的题目犹如一部好的书），既令人满意，也富于挑战。选题范围越宽，题目就越难选。你的选题"无料"，那是多么使人产生挫败感啊！

　　如何才能选好题呢？除了操作层面的程序、步骤需要一一交代——我们权且称之为"治标"，最为重要的，即能"治本"的，应是论文作者的综合素养。文科生、文科导师、拿文科学位的翻译本科毕业生（暂不涉及科技翻译的 BTI）的综合素养可以说是"人文素养"，或称不分家的"文史哲知识"。当然，这个"文史哲"包含了百科知识，强调"杂学"暨"博学"。

　　谈及翻译，抛开译界/学界不言自明的翻译能力（translation competence/the competence of translators）的内涵不论，我们总觉得自己的知识面（range of knowledge）太窄，我们的常识（general knowledge/common sense）太缺，我们的专业知识（subject knowledge）太少，我们的思辨能力（critical thinking ability）太弱，我们的直觉（hunch）太差，如此等等。的确，好的译者，这些都不缺或不太缺；反之，你什么都缺。在正式步入撰写（毕业）论文之前，以下"八大方面"可比喻为写出优质论文的专业"入门"——其专业"门槛"不低，但也不高，总之"抬脚"入内是需要花点气力的，还需要日积月累，集腋成裘。

1.3.2　八面着手

　　本小节涉及撰写毕业论文的八大重要方面，包括：1. 人文素养；2. 何为研究；3. 合格研究的原则；4. 选题要义；5. 设计思路；6. 实验与观察；7. 资料搜集与处理；8. 提纲与动笔。详细内容，请扫描二维码【拓展阅读】。

◎焦点问题探讨◎

1.　什么是论文？论文大致分为几种？

2.　书名的含义主要包括哪些内容？

3. 根据你自己的理念和学习积累，如何解读论文和书名？

4. 如何从"定义""本体""意义""类型"的视角解读毕业论文的概念？

5. 应该如何准备撰写毕业论文？

6. 撰写（毕业）论文，为什么要理念先行？

7. 所谓"八面着手"中，为什么把"人文素养"放在第一位？

8. 何为研究？请详述你自己的观点。

9. "合格研究"意味着什么？

10. 你对如何撰写本科毕业论文有一个入（学术之）门的概念吗？请具体谈谈。

务 实 篇◆◆

On the Way to Completion

    顾名思义，所谓"务实篇"（on the way to <u>completion</u>[①]）的英文解读是"竣工篇""完成篇"，乃至"成功篇"——这是结果导向的解读。若直译，则是"在成功之路上"——这是过程导向的解读。撰写论文、参加答辩、获得学位、顺利毕业，既要强调过程，也要或更要强调结果。如果学生、导师比较 philosophical，更为看重过程，享受过程，也算是一种 satisfactory completion（圆满完成）。这当然是一种精神享受，但难道不也是另一种形式的"务实"吗？——着实是一种真真正正的享受（real enjoyment）啊！

    所谓"务实"，我们要从细节（detail）、基准（benchmark）、高度（altitude）、远见（farsight）、先见（foresight）五个方面着手。

    其一，细节。"God is in the <u>detail</u>"（细节之处见真章）之深层含义是：凡做事，均应认真、彻底，注重细节。换言之，细节最为重要。就写毕业论文而言，说细节决定高下，细节决定成败，毫不夸张。

    其二，基准。其本意指"测量时的起算标准"（《现汉》第 604 页）。而 benchmark 除了与汉语中的"基准"同义之外，还指"something which can be used as a standard by which other things are judged or measured"（LDCE 第 117 页）。论文的整体质量是否符合毕业标准，经答辩能否获得通过并获得学位，都要有一个标准，即基准。作为论文的组成部分或个体部分之（文后）"参考文献"是否符合最低的著录规则要求，"题目""摘要""关键词""文献综述""理论框架"等是否符合格式要求和写作规范，也都有一个最低标准（minimum standard），即基准。

    其三，高度。之所以借用英文 altitude，一来它可以指"a high level (as of quality or feeling)"（MWCD 第 34 页），二来它用于"Attitude is altitude"来表达"态度即

---

① 作为其动词形式的 complete 意指"to make whole or perfect"（OALD 第 335 页）。

高度"这样一个当今社会特别看重的要素——态度决定一切。学生对撰写论文抱什么态度、导师对指导学生抱什么态度，的确是一个具有高度或需要用高标准、严要求来衡量的问题。著名励志演讲家、残疾人尼克·武伊契奇（Nick Vujicic）①说得好："Nothing is impossible. Achievements profit from our approach, and most of approaches derive from our attitudes."

其四，远见。读本科、读研（硕博），不能过于功利，只看见眼前的利益。我们要提倡、鼓励学生应有远见（farsight/farsighted）：Being farsighted means being "able to see the future effects of present actions"（LDCE 第 537 页）——直译指能够预见眼下的行动能在将来产生效果，即中国人说的"目光远大""有先见之明""有远见"。很多政治家、科学家、社会学家、作家、未来学家等都具有远见卓识。我们写论文，不能就事论事，为写论文而写论文，为毕业而写论文，这样是写不出好论文来的。相反，如果注重"细节"，把握"基准"，攀登"高度"，你就会自然而然地具有远见，就会主动地、自觉地为圆满完成自己的学业而追求卓越。

其五，先见。上述四个方面的要求，相信学生们还是容易做到的，这第五个方面的要求的确是高了。先见，即 foresight，指 "the ability to predict what is likely to happen and to use this to prepare for the future"（OALD 第 684 页）。有时候，我们有 foresight 的反义词 hindsight（后见之明；事后聪明）已经不错了。其实，对"双一流大学"或 2017 年以前被称为"985 工程"大学、"211 工程"大学的本科生，我们完全可以因人而异：对所有的本科生，应实行"有教无类"②的原则，即每位毕业生都应该撰写学位论文；对本科生中的优质生，不妨试行/实行"因材施教"的原则，培养他们具备"先见"。我们多次发现，一些优秀本科生已经具备撰写硕士研究生学位论文的能力和潜力，他们的论文就是明证。

笔者正是从观念/理念和"道"的高度，而非单纯从"术"的角度来主张、强调何为"On the Way to Completion"（务实篇）。无论如何，写毕业论文的过程就是 on the way to completion，认真阅读"务实篇"就是 on the right track（following a course that will lead to success③）。

---

① 1982 年生于澳大利亚墨尔本，天生没有四肢，但勇于面对身体残障，创造了生命的奇迹。
② 注意这是一种成语活用。"因材施教"亦同。
③ 见 MWALED 第 1745 页。

第 2 章　如何动手（总体准备）

How to Get Started (General-oriented)

◎学习目标◎

从第 2 章起，我们进入翻译类毕业论文总体准备阶段，即如何开始、如何动手，有关知识性介绍和操作指南是本章的重点。通过本章学习，学生将：

- ●熟悉论文的结构（中英文版）；
- ●熟悉论文的封面设计（中英文版）；
- ●掌握论文题目的写法（中英双语）；
- ●熟悉论文声明的写法（中英双语）；
- ●熟悉论文致谢的写法（中英双语）；
- ●掌握论文摘要的写法（中英双语）；
- ●（初步并逐步）了解并熟悉论文目录纲要的写法（中英双语）。

2.1　论文的总体实施

一篇翻译类本科毕业论文，与其他所有文科生的毕业论文一样，有一个总体一致的基本结构、写作规范和格式要求（论文的字体和字号要求，纸张打印格式，封面、前置部分、主体部分等格式要求，本书不做介绍，均以各校实际规定为准）。

为加强 BTI & BA（翻译方向）毕业论文（设计）规范化管理，不断提高毕业论文（设计）质量，我们既要见树木（中观层面），也要见森林（宏观层面）。所谓森林是指主要环节，即 BTI/BA 学位或毕业论文中的选题、开题、论文（设计）实施、中期检查、论文答辩等五大环节（其中，选题、开题环节，详见第 3 章；中期检查和论文答辩环节，详见第 10 章；论文实施[含撰写前、中、后等问题]，详见全书）。所谓树木涉及上述五个环节中的每个中观层面。每棵树的树干、树枝、树叶等则涉及微观层面，包括论文撰写过程中涉及哪些迷你微观（微微观）的具体问题。我们不妨先从论文结构出发做一了解、探寻。

在以下表格中，主要的元素或组成部分是必备的（*），只有少数元素是备选的。从"总体准备"思路出发，我们先通过表格给读者一个总览（general picture）（表 2-1、表 2-2），然后再按照顺序，就论文开始部分——（1）—（3）和（15）—（19）项目进行必要的详略介绍。

表 2-1　论文结构(中文版)

序号	论文结构（适用于翻译类专业学位/学术学位①）
	开始部分
（1）	封面*
（2）	扉页*
（3）	论文标题*
（4）	学位申请人*
（5）	导师姓名及职称*
（6）	学科/专业名称*
（7）	专业/方向名称*
（8）	学校/学院/系所名称*
（9）	论文提交日期*
（10）	论文作者签名*——论文评审页
（11）	指导教师签名*——论文评审页
（12）	论文评阅人 1、2、3——论文评审页
（13）	答辩委员会主席；委员 1、2——论文评审页②
（14）	答辩日期——论文评审页
（15）	声明（"学位论文独/原创性声明"与"学位论文版权使用授权声明"，或合并为"本科生毕业论文承诺书"）*
（16）	致谢*
（17）	汉语摘要（含关键词）*
（18）	英文摘要（含关键词）*
（19）	目录* ①表目录；②图目录
	●正文部分 I　研究部分（BTI 学位论文） ①章节结构；②章节标题 ●正文部分（BA/BTI 学位论文） ①章节结构；②章节标题
（20）	绪论*
（21）	本论之文献综述*
（22）	本论之研究方法*
（23）	本论之分析研讨*
（24）	结论*

① 从论文设计、撰写规范出发，BTI 学位相当于本科专业学位论文（参照 MTI[专业]学位论文），而 BA（翻译方向）学位则相当于本科学术学位论文（参照 MA[学术]学位论文）。

② "论文评审页"基本要素包括学生信息、论文信息、答辩委员会签字等。

（续表）

序号	论文结构（适用于翻译类专业学位/学术学位）
	结尾部分
（25）	参考文献*
（26）	附录
	正文部分 II 实践部分（BTI 学位论文）
（27）	项目/课题翻译（源语文本+译语文本）*/口译音视频设备（MP3/4/5/6、U 盘、VCD 等）*
（28）	项目/课题翻译参考文献*/口译音视频资料背景说明*
（29）	项目/课题翻译尾注
（30）	论文作者简历（专业学位/学术学位申请人）

【注】①BTI 学位论文的正文部分包括"研究部分"和"实践部分"，二者之赋分占比可大致控制在三七开，即 30% vs. 70%。换言之，"实践部分"之重要性占比七成。②第（27）（28）项为 BTI 学位论文的必要组成部分。

表 2-2 论文结构(英文版)

Serial No.	The Structure of a Thesis (component-oriented) （for BTI/BA degree theses in T & I studies）
	The beginning part/The preliminaries/Front matter
（1）	Cover design/Title page*
（2）	Title page*
（3）	The title of the thesis*
（4）	The applicant*
（5）	The name of the supervisor + Professional title*
（6）	Discipline/Major/Specialty*
（7）	Major/Specialty/Concentration*
（8）	Department/Institute/School/University*
（9）	The date of submission*
（10）	The author's signature (page)*—Approval sheet
（11）	The supervisor's signature (page)*—Approval sheet
（12）	Thesis reviewer 1/2/3—Approval sheet
（13）	Committee chair; Committee member 1/2—Approval sheet
（14）	The date of oral defense—Approval sheet[①]
（15）	Declaration of originality and copyright declaration[②], or combined into the undergraduate thesis commitment*
（16）	Acknowledgements*

① The approval sheet 包括 student information、thesis information、committee signatures 等基本要素。

② 亦可为 copyright page。

（续表）

Serial No.	The Structure of a Thesis (component-oriented) （for BTI/BA degree theses in T & I studies）
(17)	Abstract in Chinese (keywords included)*
(18)	Abstract in English (keywords included) *
(19)	Table of contents/Contents* ①List of tables; ②List of figures ●**The body part I/Research part** (for BTI degree thesis)/**The text** ①Organization of chapters①; ②Chapter titles and headings ●**The body part** (for BA/BTI degree thesis)/**The text** ①Organization of chapters; ②Chapter titles and headings
(20)	Introduction*
(21)	Literature review*
(22)	Methodology/Method(s) of the investigation*
(23)	Results and interpretation +discussion *
(24)	Conclusion(s)*
	The ending part/Reference materials/Back matter/End matter
(25)	Bibliography/List of works cited & Consulted/References*
(26)	Appendices
	The body part II/Practice part (for BTI degree thesis)
(27)	Translation project/task (ST +TT)* or Audiotaped/Videotaped interpretation*
(28)	References*/Background notes of recorded interpretation*
(29)	Endnotes (footnotes)
(30)	Bio-data of the author (of the BTI/BA degree thesis)

　　［NB］　①The main body of a BTI thesis consists of a research section and a practice section, and the proportion of the marks assigned to each of them can be roughly controlled at 30∶70, namely, 30% vs. 70%. In other words, the importance of the practice section is 70%. ②Items (27) and (28) constitute a necessary part of the BTI thesis.

2.2　封面设计

　　论文封面，在学位论文结构中，可以称为标题页（title page②）/书名页，所以论文封面设计（cover design）也就是论文标题页设计。"表 2-1　论文结构（中文版）""表 2-2 论文结构（英文版）"有关封面的介绍是一种比较完整的结构介绍，每所学校的学位论文

① 亦为 dissertation chapters/chapters of a thesis/thesis chapters。
② 就书这类出版物而言（论文等除外），title page 意为扉页，与封面的意义不同。

封面会有所不同，但总体上大同小异，一般都有"涉密论文""公开论文"等字样及"校徽"等，举例如表 2-3。

表 2-3 翻译专业学士学位论文封面设计

涉密论文 □   公开论文 □

浙 江 大 学

本 科 生 毕 业 论 文（设计）

外文题目：_____

中文题目：_____

姓名与学号   _____

指导教师   _____

年级与专业   _____

所在学院   _____

提交日期   _____ 年 ___ 月 ___ 日

还有一种是全英文的 title page（表 2-4）。

表 2-4　翻译专业学士学位论文英文标题页设计

Title of the Thesis

XXXXXXXXXXXXXXXXXXXXXXXXXXXXXX

By
SO-AND-SO

A Thesis Submitted to
the School of International Studies
of Zhejiang University
in Partial Fulfillment of the Requirements
for the Degree of Bachelor of Translation and Interpreting

Supervised by
SO-AND-SO

May 202×

此外，再提供一种简易的全英文毕业/课题设计的封面版式（参考顾曰国，2004: 100），笔者做了部分改动（表 2-5）。

表 2-5　BTI 学士学位论文英文标题页设计

Project Title
　　Note-Taking Efficiency Tested for Better Conference Interpreting

Investigator
SO-AND-SO

Supervised by Dr. SO-AND-SO
Department of Translation & Interpreting

In partial fulfillment of the requirements for
the Degree of BTI
May 202×

2.2　题目写法

　　论文题目的写法看似简单，其实不然，经常是学生论文完成了，题目还无法确定。我们已在"1.3.2 之 **4. 选题要义**"中提出了四点：①做熟悉的研究；②做小不做大；③做文献研究；④分选题与标题。以下，我们接着详述"④分选题与标题"。

　　（1）搞清"三 T"之含义。这"三 T"指 thesis、topic 和 title。

　　1）搞清"论题"与"话题"。"论题"即 thesis，与英文中的"论文"是同一个词，在此指"a <u>statement</u> or an <u>opinion</u> <u>that is discussed in a logical way and presented with evidence in order to prove that it is true</u>"（OALD），等于"命题"或"论点"。而"话题"即 topic，在此指"a <u>subject</u> <u>that you talk</u>, <u>write</u>, or learn about"（OALD），等于"主题"。

　　2）搞清"选题"与"标题"。从内涵看，既可选题≠标题，又可选题=标题。我们从英文词汇层面辨析便一清二楚。<u>subject/topic/title</u> <u>selected</u> 都可译为"选题"，但其中之一则可译为所选择的 title，可见该"选题"便等于"标题"或"题目"（title = the name of a book, poem, painting, piece of music, etc.）。

　　3）搞清"三 T"的英文诠释。由于毕业论文需要用英文撰写，因此很有必要让学生通过英文的诠释来辨析"三 T"之关键差异：

　　①The thesis is not just your topic, but what you're saying about your topic.

　　②While you're writing your paper, your thesis is a "working thesis," one that can still be changed.

　　③As you continue to write, read, and think about your thesis, see if your thesis still represents your opinion.

　　④When you set your topic, you would still have to work hard on the title of your paper.

　　⑤Your title could not be set until after the completion of your paper.

　　⑥Your title could also be set without much difficulty since the title you've given best suits your paper.

　　（2）题目写法原则。此原则是"topic/thesis"先行，"title"后定。

　　1）搞清研究方向及论文形式。换言之，脚踏实地，回归自我。BTI 比较适合选择翻译实践+评述这类目的在于解决具体翻译问题的主题（subject）论文，即以选择 translation with commentary 为宜；BA（翻译学方向）更适合选择基于翻译实践的应用理论研究，即以选择 practice-based research 为佳。

　　2）选择源语文本及研究方法。换言之，锁定专题，自行微调。比如，BTI 必须先确定翻译方向——E-C 还是 C-E，再确定源语文本（ST）非文学翻译（即应用翻译）主题——旅游笔译或导译①，还是新闻编译或全译，然后根据自己的翻译实践确定是着眼于"翻译技巧"研究，还是"翻译策略及方法"研究。

---

① 旅游翻译/导译中涉及山水文学翻译主题，在此暂不包括此主题。

3）选妥源语文本的"三要诀"。换言之，兴趣驱动，自知之明。其一，强烈兴趣；其二，资料充足；其三，量力而行——特指你是否具备必要的 background（专业/学术背景）和 expertise（内行/专家水准）。比如，若某 BTI 生不会跳舞，则最好避免选择舞蹈类的 ST 来翻译。从深层次看，这"三要诀"实质上反映了论文选题的"可行性""科学性""创造性"三原则。后两个原则我们已经在第一章比较具体地论述过了。

4）先大后小，小题大做。例如，假设某 BTI 生喜欢舞蹈，那么"舞蹈"便是选题（选择 ST 主题）的一个 broad category，你只需要将其范围缩小（narrow down），直至合适你为止。例如：

● **Subject:** source texts concerning dance（涉及"舞蹈"专题/主题的各种 ST）

● **Limited subject:** source texts concerning modern dance（涉及"现代舞蹈"专题/主题的各种 ST）

● **Less difficult ST:** a textbook (I/O monograph) concerning modern dance（涉及"现代舞蹈"专题/主题的一本教科书，而非学术专著）

● **Initial topic:** on flexible use of major techniques in translating the dance textbook into Chinese（讨论灵活运用几种主要的翻译技巧来翻译该教科书——算作假设）

● **Tentative topic:** on professional Chinese translation of English dance terminologies in the textbook（译完整本教科书或其中的章节后——新的认识）

● **Working title:** On Professional Chinese Translation of English Dance Terminologies: A Case Study of the Modern Dance Textbook（暂定或几乎是确定的论文题目——有待确定）

再如，BA 生偏爱诗歌的翻译研究，那么"诗歌翻译研究"便是选题（选择 ST 和 TT 以及相关理论为主题）的一个大范围，你只需要将其缩小到符合你的研究兴趣、能力水平即可。例如：

● **Subject:** poetry translation research（涉及"诗歌翻译"+"理论研究"专题/主题）

● **Limited subject:** C-E translation in the Song lyrics and translation theories（涉及"宋词英译及多种翻译理论"专题/主题）

● **Further limited subject:** on English translations of Song poet Su Dongpo's poems within the framework of dynamic equivalence（涉及动态对等理论框架下的"宋朝诗人苏东坡诗词一个以上英译本的"专题/主题研究）

● **Tentative topic:** a comparative study on the translations of Su Dongpo's lyrics by Xu Yuanzhong[①] and Xu Zhongjie—Translating from the perspective of dynamic equivalence（从动态对等视角比较研究许渊冲和徐忠杰的两个苏词翻译版本）

● **Finalized title:** A Comparative Study on the Translations of Su Dongpo's Lyrics by Xu Yuanzhong and Xu Zhongjie from the Perspective of Dynamic Equivalence（最后提交论文时的题目）

5）题目撰写注意事项：

①编制、检索要求。题目应能概括论文的特定内容，有助于选定关键词，符合编制

---

① 翻译家许渊冲（1921—2021）将自己的全名拼写为 Xu Yuanzhong，简称为 XYZ。

题录、索引和检索的有关原则。

②英语结构要求。英文题名以短语为主要形式，尤以名词短语最常见（冠词可酌情省略）；一般不用陈述句类的完整句①。

③同一篇毕业论文的英文题名与中文题名内容上应一致，形式可以灵活。

6）中英文标题举例：

①内容直截了当（straightforward）：

> 论 *Tourism in China* 翻译项目目标语风格、体例的统一问题

②使用日期、冒号（date & colon）：

> **English Translators and Outbound Travel Guidebooks:**
> **Xi'an, 2002—2012**

③使用副标题（subtitle）：

> 中国古典戏剧台本唱词翻译的对比研究
> ——以《牡丹亭》的两个英译本为例

④使用大字标题（headline）：

> 目的论适合文学翻译：赏菊诗重译与研究
> （**c.f. The Crisis in American Journalism: The Good News and the Bad News**②）

⑤标题学术化（academic）：

> **On Slang Translation of Chinese *Kung Fu* Fiction**
> —A Case Study of *The Deer & the Cauldron* from the Perspective of *Skopostheorie*

⑥标题有创意（creative）：

> 全球化视角下看奈达功能对等理论指导科技文本汉译的积极作用③

⑦中英文内容/形式对等：

英文题目	中文题目
A Functionalist Analysis of the Translation of Western Economic Classics —A Case Study of Two Chinese Versions of North's *Structure and Change in Economic History*	从功能翻译理论视角评析经济学著作的翻译 ——诺斯《经济史的结构与变迁》的两个中译本对比研究

⑧节约篇幅，不必"谦逊"：

Original Title	**Suggested Modifications**
A Tentative Study of Nominalization in C-E Translation of Scientific Text	Nominalization in Chinese-English Translation of Scientific Text
The Study of the Learning Mode of Chinese Students in Foreign Language Learning	The Foreign Learning Mode of Chinese Students

---

① 理由是：论文题目主要起标示作用，而陈述句容易使题目具有判断式的语义，且不够精练和醒目。少数情况（评述性、综述性和驳斥性）下可以用疑问句做题目，因为疑问句有探讨性语气，相对客观、公允。

② 该论文题目引自美国哥伦比亚大学新闻学院教授 Michael Schudson。

③ 该论文获"浙江大学 2012 届百篇特优本科毕业设计（论文）奖"。

Devlin's advice	I have not changed my mind about one thing: Students <u>should not waste precious space in a title</u> by including phrases such as "a preliminary research project on…" or "a tentative study into…". Such titles are often preferred by students because they sound modest and unassuming. <u>While readers understand and appreciate a writer's desire to be a little bit self-effacing, a good title needs to be more direct than that.</u> To illustrate what I mean I have listed two titles suggested by post- graduate students at Tsinghua together with my suggested changes.

（参考 Devlin, 2004: 23）

7）题目验证标准：

①简洁、明确、具体、概括的标准。或者 **ABC 原则**（accuracy + brevity + clarity）。

②专业性、学术性、创新性的标准。

③中英文字数标准——建议中文主标题不超过 20 个字，英文主标题不超过 20 个词；如果主标题较长或有副标题，应作为 subtitle 处理。

就**纯英文论文**而言，国外（科技）期刊一般对题名字数有所限制。例如美国一些重要学术期刊有规定，题名不超过 2 行，每行不超过 42 个印刷符号和空格；还有一些要求题名不超过 14 个词。又如英国有的学术期刊要求题名不超过 12 个词。虽未必严格执行，但这些规定可供我们参考。总的原则是：题名应确切、简练、醒目，在能准确反映论文特定内容的前提下，题名词数越少越好。

④结构标准。题名结构，中英文均以短语为主要形式，特别是名词短语（noun phrase），要围绕短语中的中心词（head/head noun）展开。

⑤冠词标准。如今题名中的冠词使用有简化的趋势，凡可用可不用的冠词均可不用。

⑥大小写标准。题名字母的大小写有如表 2-6 所示的三种格式。

表 2-6　论文英文题名中的大小写

格式	题名举例	备注
(a) 字母全部大写	A LINGUISTIC APPROACH TO 4-CHARACTER IDIOM TRANSLATION IN MAO'S WORKS	该格式出现频率不高
(b) 首单词之首字母大写	A linguistic approach to 4-character idiom translation in Mao's works	其余字母均小写；该格式有增多的趋势
(c) 每个实词的首字母大写	A Linguistic Approach to 4-character Idiom Translation in Mao's Works	该格式用得最多；3 个或 4 个字母以下的冠词、连词、介词全部小写

⑦缩略语标准。已得到整个学界/业界/科技界公认的缩略词语，才可用于题名中，否则不要轻易使用。

⑧可持续发展的标准——

●已做先期研究，对主题（topic）有一清晰认识；

●对研究资料来源（reference sources）很了解；

●已有一个给力的论题（strong thesis statement）；

●有一个初步的写作大纲（a preliminary outline）；

●有用于论文写作的参考文献（a working bibliography）；

●已经认真阅读了基本的有关资料，并做了详细的笔记（notes）。

8）总体原则：宁小勿大，宁专勿泛，宁新勿陈，宁深勿浅，宁安勿躁。

2.4　声明写法

所谓"论文声明"包含两项内容，一是"学位论文独创性声明"，二是"学位论文版权声明"或"学位论文版权使用授权书"。一般而言，本科生毕业论文/学士学位论文内均须在正文前附上"独创声明"和"版权声明"/"版权使用授权书"，分别独立成页。现在浙江大学采用"本科生毕业论文（设计）承诺书"的形式。

具体写法，详见"第 9 章　如何致谢与声明（知法守礼）"。

2.5　致谢写法

这部分可以放在论文的"开始部分"，也可以放在"结尾部分"。笔者以为，放在"开始部分"会显得对人更为礼貌，对导师更为尊重。

该部分主要简述自己做毕业论文的感受和体会，并应对指导教师和协助完成论文的有关人员（包括自己的亲朋好友）表示谢意。

具体写法，详见"第 9 章　如何致谢与声明（知法守礼）"。

2.6　摘要写法

1.　文科论文摘要概念①

美国国家标准学会（American National Standards Institute/ANSI）给"摘要"下的定义是：An abstract is an abbreviated, accurate representation of the contents of a document, preferably prepared by its author(s) for publication with it.

（1）人文学科类论文摘要需要完成下列三项任务：

①to briefly summarize the topic and ideas of the thesis statement；

②to highlight the most important parts of the paper that support the thesis statement；

③to give the conclusion。

（2）社会科学类论文摘要有所不同。根据《美国心理协会写作手册》（*Publication Manual of the American Psychological Association*），实证研究报告（report of an empirical study）的摘要应描写以下内容：

①the problem under investigation, in one sentence if possible；

②the participants or subjects, specifying pertinent characteristics, such as number, type, age, sex, genus, and species；

① 有关摘要内容编写参考从丛、李咏燕（2003: 331-333），所引内容仅作为指导性参考，并非固定不变。

③the experimental method, including the apparatus, data-gathering, complete test names, and complete generic names and the dosage and routes of administration of any drugs (particularly if the drugs are novel or important to the study);

④the findings, including statistical significance levels; and

⑤the conclusions and the implications or applications。

（3）如果是个案研究，有关摘要应描写以下三点：

①the subject and relevant characteristics of the individual or organization presented;

②the nature of or solution to a problem illustrated by the case example;

③the questions raised for additional research or theory。

2. 翻译类毕业论文摘要概念

"浙江大学本科生毕业论文（设计）编写规则"规定："中文摘要的字数一般为300—600字，英文摘要实词在300个左右。英文摘要应与中文摘要内容相对应。摘要最后另起一行，列出3—8个关键词。关键词应体现论文特色，具有语义性，在论文中有明确的出处，并应尽量采用《汉语主题词表》或各专业主题词表提供的规范词。"

根据外语学院翻译学科专业的特点，可以规定（待译成英文的）中文摘要300字左右（从实际出发，若是先写中文摘要，将其译成英文，一般的规律是英文词数占中文字数的**60%左右**，除非遇到较多的中国文化内涵深厚的表达法），关键词5个左右。翻译类毕业论文的摘要，是对论文研究内容的高度概括，应包括对翻译研究问题及研究目的的描述、对使用的方法和研究过程的简要介绍、对研究结论的简要概括等内容。摘要应具有独立性、自明性/自含性、完整性。换言之，摘要应聚焦于对研究对象、研究问题、研究方法、研究结论的论述，尤其是研究结论、研究背景，需简洁精练，尽量三言两语概括清楚，不要使用太多文字。

这种对摘要的要求，同时适合学术学位论文和专业学位论文。它可以有两种写法：描写型和信息型。

（1）描写型摘要——A descriptive abstract, <u>now somewhat out of favor</u>, simply describes what a thesis/paper is about and what methods are used. It does not include the results or conclusions.（参照 Devlin, 2004: 5）

（2）信息型摘要——An informative abstract summarizes the key information contained in a larger document and will typically include these elements:

●identifying information (the name of the document, the writer and the writer's institution);

●the <u>thesis statement</u>; and

●the key information.

Most of the abstract will be devoted to <u>summarizing the important findings, conclusions</u> and recommendations.

Abstracts may be written for many purposes including summarizing research findings, presenting the results of a survey in brief, summarizing an article or thesis, or even a chapter in a thesis.（参照 Devlin, 2004: 5）

需要补充或重复指出的是：

①The abstract should include <u>a brief but precise statement of the problem or issue, a description of the research method and design, the major findings and their significance, and the conclusions</u>. The abstract should contain the most important words referring to method and content of the thesis: these facilitate access to the abstract by computer search and enable a reader to decide whether to read the entire thesis.（参照 Slade, 2000: 38-39）

②The abstract is a summary of your study. It should be coherent by itself. It provides information concerning the following aspects; <u>the purpose of the study, the research questions to be addressed, the subject involved, the instruments used to collect the data, the procedures for collecting and analyzing the data</u>, the <u>findings and the conclusions</u>.

In the Chinese context, you are also expected to <u>write an abstract in Chinese</u>. No doubt, the content of the abstract in Chinese should be the same as that in English. However, <u>a literary translation of the English version is definitely unsatisfactory</u>.（参照文秋芳, 2004: 254-255）

3. 摘要写/译具体要求

（1）字/词数要求（word limit）

尽管"权威性"的论文指南有不同的说法，但我们在此将信息型摘要字数的上限和下限列出，仅供参考：

①本科（翻译类）毕业论文的中文摘要一般不宜超过 200 汉字，英文摘要不宜超过 120 个单词[①]（或实词）；字数下限为 100 汉字/60 words。若整篇论文总字数在两万以上，说明内容丰富，那么摘要字数可以放宽到 500 汉字——这需要导师或作者自行具体判断。

②用于宣读、交流或发表的（翻译类）论文（paper）的中文摘要一般不宜超过 150 汉字，英文摘要不宜超过 90 个单词（或实词）；字数下限为 90 汉字/54 words。

【注】有的论文写作指南说摘要字数不要超过论文字数的 5%。这似乎有些不太合理。比如某校本科毕业论文字数，下限为 6000 汉字，但有学生写了 10000 汉字，难道二者的摘要字数之间的差距是 200 个汉字吗？其实，在主题不变的情况下，信息型论文摘要值得作为"要旨"或"精髓"写在前头，其字数 300 足矣，因为本科论文一般没有这么多属于创意、创新的实质内容（essence/essential content）供"展示"（此处不涉及例外）。

（2）具体内容

①研究目的和重要性或要解决的问题（purpose; significance; what I wanted to do?）；

②研究内容/问题（subject/question[s]）或完成了哪些工作（what did you do?）；

③研究过程（procedures）；

④研究方法（method[s]）或解决问题的方法及过程（how you did it）；

⑤研究结果/结论（results/findings/conclusions）；

⑥研究创新/独到之处（what's new [and original] in your thesis?）；

⑦关键词（keywords）。

[①] 若是将中文摘要译成英文，根据此类文本的比例，应为 120 words（200×60%）左右，上下浮动 5%。

（3）具体内容解析

中英文摘要的写作/写译并没有整齐划一、一成不变的格式，但论文摘要是对论文的简短陈述（summary of your research/study），应具有**短小、精悍、完整**"三大特点"，并具有**独立性、逻辑性和自含性**"三大特性"；其功能应是使读者不读论文原文就知全文。它一般在论文全文完成之后形成，也可以事先写一个草稿（draft）。论文摘要由**目的、方法、结果和结论**四大部分组成，可以独立使用，也可以引用，还可以用于翻译应用推广。简言之，论文摘要可供读者确定有无必要阅读原论文全文，或提供给文摘第二次文献采用。从原则上讲，中文摘要编写的注意事项都适用于英文摘要，但英文译写有其自己的表达方式、语言习惯，在将 ST（中文摘要）转换成 TT（英文摘要）时应特别注意。

①研究目的。主要说明作者撰写此论文的目的，或此论文主要解决的问题。虽然中文和英文的 discourse pattern（大）不相同，但论文写作本身就是"舶来品"，故写作手法（包括 discourse pattern 的运用）应基本/原则上保持一致。因此，一篇好的中/英文摘要，一开头就应该把此论文的目的或要解决的（主要）问题非常明确地交代清楚。换言之，要做到言简意赅，不谈或尽量少谈背景知识；避免在摘要的第一句（重复）使用论文的题目或题目的一部分。

②研究方法。主要说明作者的研究过程及所用的方法（或研究方法论），应包括所运用的翻译/文学/语言学等理论或理论视角（theory/theoretical approach）、收集数据的手段/工具（instruments）等。在摘要中，过程与方法的阐述起着承前启后的作用。开头交代了要解决的问题（research questions/problem[s]；what I wanted to do）之后，接着要回答的自然就是如何解决问题（how I did it），而且，最后的结果和结论也往往与研究过程及方法是密切相关的。大多数学生在阐述过程与方法时，最突出也最常见的问题是泛泛而谈或空洞无物，只有定性的描述，使读者（包括评审专家）很难清楚地了解论文中解决问题的过程和方法。

③结果+④结论。这两部分即指"What results did I get?"和"What conclusions can I draw?"。结果和结论部分代表着文章的主要成就和贡献。论文有没有价值，值不值得读者阅读，或论文（及其答辩）是否可获通过并使答辩者获得相应的学位，主要取决于你在论文中所获得的结果和所得出的结论。因此，在写作结果和结论部分时，一般都要尽量结合论文研究类别——conceptual/theoretical study 或 empirical study（Williams & Chesterman, 2004: 58）等来加以说明，使结论部分言之有物，言之有据。只有这样，论文的结论才有说服力。如有可能，在结尾部分还可以将论文的结果和他人最新的研究结果进行比较，以突出论文的主要贡献和创新、独到之处——以此回答"What is new and original in this thesis?"。

⑤关键词。关键词要根据论文（及摘要）中的主题词（subject terms/words）并且在论文中出现率最高或较高的词当中选择。关键词一般为 3—5 个，或 6—8 个，总之不宜超过 10 个。关键词之间用分号隔开（也有使用逗号的）。

（4）具体注意事项

①只谈新的信息。

②既简练又有"料"。

③尽量用短句。

④描述作者的研究工作一般用过去时态。

⑤在陈述由这些工作所得出的结论时应使用现在时态。

⑥一般应使用主动语态。

⑦少用现在完成时、过去完成时，进行时态和其他复合时态。

⑧避免用阿拉伯数字作首词。

4. 双语摘要案例①

【案例1】本科生毕业论文摘要（样例一）

中文题目	试论金融翻译学习的一种综合模式
英文题目	On an Integrated Model for Learning Financial Translation
中文摘要	翻译学习者在翻译这项社会实践中获得统一的自我认同感很重要。论文作者以金融翻译为例，在吸收了 Cliff Schimmels 博士的教育思想的基础上，提出一个集"四型"（研究型、融合型、社群型、人文型）学习于一体的翻译自学模式。本文的主要研究方法是叙述研究，案例源自与翻译初学者和职业译者的访谈。研究表明，"四型"自学模式的指导思想和操作方法亦适用于不同领域和层次的翻译教学。
英文摘要	It is important for translation learners to acquire a unified self-identity in translation as social practice. To achieve this, the author of the thesis adapts Cliff Schimmels's education framework into a RICH Learning Model for financial translation—Research-based Integrated Community Humanistic Learning. The author adopts narrative inquiry as the main research method, interviewing translation learners and professional translators about their learning and working experiences, which are presented in cases. The research shows that the guidelines and operations for this learning model are also applicable to translator training in different domains at different levels.
关键词	金融翻译；"四型"（研究型、融合型、社群型、人文型）学习模式；学习自主性；翻译教学
Keywords	financial translation; RICH (Research-based Integrated Community Humanistic) learning Model; learner autonomy; translator training

【案例1解析】

①毕业论文规格：（翻译类）BA 学位论文（即研究翻译的本科毕业论文）。

②英中摘要词/字数之比：93 words/155 个汉字=60%——非常理想的数字比例。

③摘要与题目的关联度：很强——重建关联度。

④关键词：4 个——符合要求。

⑤摘要结构剖析：

---

① 以下所引四个案例中，案例1、案例2、案例4均选自笔者指导的浙江大学 BA 生和 BTI 生，案例3选自西安外国语大学高级翻译学院 BTI 学位论文（其作者是笔者指导的保送浙江大学的 MTI 生）。另外，本书直接选自学生论文的案例文本存在各种错误与不足，一般不做修改，特此说明。

●研究目的——通过运用"四型"翻译学习模式，帮助（金融）翻译学习者通过翻译这项社会实践获得统一的自我认同感。

●研究问题——"四型"学习模式是否适用于金融翻译学习者以及其他领域和层次的翻译教学（/翻译自学者）。

●研究方法——叙述研究+访谈。

●研究结果——可行。

●研究结论——该项学习模式还适用于不同领域和层次的翻译教学。

●创新/独到之处——"四型"综合模式原为体现 Cliff Schimmels 博士的教育思想的一种教育模式，现在可以运用于金融等多领域多层次的翻译实践。

【案例2】本科生毕业论文摘要（样例二）

中文题目	英汉歌曲翻译的功能主义途径
英文题目	A Functionalist Approach to English-Chinese Song Translation
中文摘要	在中国译界罕有学者研究歌曲。尽管近年来更多的学者开始关注这一被遗忘的领域，并在英汉歌曲翻译的实践经验研究方面做出了许多努力，然而，从翻译理论角度进行的研究则为数甚少。本文试图以功能主义翻译理论为基础，并以一首 2008 年北京奥运歌曲 *Forever Friends* 为例，对其英汉译配整个过程进行了详尽研究，证明歌曲译配可分为原文分析与配乐改译两大步骤，并提出一系列指导原则和具体方法，以期在学术和实践两方面对全面理解歌曲译配、有效指导歌曲译配实践有所帮助。
英文摘要	Few scholars have studied song translation in Chinese translation circles. While in recent years more scholars have begun to devote their efforts to English-Chinese song translation research from a practical perspective, theoretical researches have still been rather limited. This thesis is an attempt to apply a functionalist approach to an exhaustive study of the entire English-Chinese translating process of the 2008 Beijing Olympic song *Forever Friends*, proving that song translation should follow two main steps, namely, the source-text (words) analysis and adaptation to music. On the basis of her own practice, this Author[①] proposes some guiding principles and specific methods for song translation, which would be of both academic and practical use to how to understand song translation comprehensively and guide it effectively.
关键词	英汉歌曲译配；功能主义途径；步骤；原则；方法；原文（歌词）分析；译配
Keywords	English-Chinese song translation; functionalist approach; procedures; principles; methods; source-text (words) analysis; adaptation

【案例2解析】

①毕业论文规格：（翻译类）BA 学位论文（即研究翻译的本科毕业论文）。

②英中摘要词/字数之比：124 words/197 个汉字≈63%——相当理想的数字比例。

---

① 注意该词可大写，表明是专有名词，亦常见于西方国家的论文中。例如，"Copyright is owned by the <u>Author</u> of the thesis…The thesis may not be reproduced elsewhere without the permission of the <u>Author</u>."（选自梅西大学某国际项目之学位论文）。

③摘要与题目的关联度：很强——重建关联度。

④关键词：7 个——符合要求。

⑤摘要结构剖析：

●研究目的——试图通过运用德国功能主义对歌曲译配进行基于案例的理论研究，以期证明歌曲译配可分为原文分析与配乐改译两大步骤。

●研究问题——2008 年北京奥运歌曲 *Forever Friends* 英汉译配全过程。

●研究方法——案例研究，即以自己译配 *Forever Friends* 为研究案例。

●研究结果——可行。

●研究结论——通过案例研究提出一系列指导原则和具体方法，将在学术和实践两方面对全面理解歌曲译配、有效指导歌曲译配实践有所帮助。

●创新/独到之处——迄今，该主题/案例研究在本科生毕业论文中罕见，因为既懂歌曲译配，又有翻译理论基础，且作者本人又是（准）专业歌手的本科生很少。

【案例 3】本科生毕业论文摘要（样例三）

中文题目	简明英语写作原则在英译宣传册《走向世界的"和平"牌紫阳富硒茶》中的应用
英文题目	Applying Plain English Principles to C-E Brochure Translation—A Case Study Based on Translating *Heping Ziyang Se-enriched Tea Seeking Fame Around the World*
中文摘要	本文是基于《走向世界的"和平"牌紫阳富硒茶》的英译实践而撰写的一篇翻译实践报告。原文以宣传手册的形式，分别从"得天独厚的资源""闻名遐迩的品牌""科学严格的加工""诚信灵活的经营"四方面介绍了紫阳和平茶厂及该厂著名产品紫阳富硒茶。本报告主要分析作者在翻译实践过程中的一个重要问题，即简明英语写作原则在英译宣传手册中的应用。在翻译实践报告中，作者结合英语宣传手册简洁易懂的语言特点，研究了"篇章布局合理""言简意赅""使用主动语态和人称代词 you"三种简明英语写作原则在提高译文质量方面的作用，以期为今后翻译类似文本提供一定的借鉴。
英文摘要	This thesis is a practice report based on the Author's C-E translation of *Heping Ziyang Se-enriched Green Tea Seeking Fame Around the World*, a brochure describing and promoting the Ziyang Heping Tea Factory and its famous product Ziyang Se-enriched Green Tea in the four parts of "Blessed Resources", "Renowned Brand", "Scientific and Rigorous Processing", and "Honest and Flexible Management". Taking into consideration the language features of English brochures—plain, concise and understandable, the Author discusses the application of plain English principles to brochure translation, and specifically, the effect of employing three plain English principles of "logical textual organization", "being economical and comprehensible", and "the use of active voice and second person (*you*)" in improving translation quality. It is thus hoped that the reflection report may shed some light on the translation of a similar text type like brochures in the future.
关键词	简明英语；宣传手册；写作与翻译
Keywords	plain English; brochure; English writing and translation

【案例 3 解析】

①毕业论文规格：（翻译类）BTI 学位论文——实践报告（翻译本科专业毕业论文）。

②英中摘要词/字数之比：140 words/238 个汉字≈59%——相当理想的数字比例。

③摘要与题目的关联度：很强——重建关联度。

④关键词：3 个——符合要求。

⑤摘要结构剖析：

●研究目的——分析作者在翻译实践过程中的一项重要问题，即简明英语写作原则在英译宣传手册中的应用。

●研究问题——研究简明英语写作原则是否可以应用于宣传手册的汉译英。

●研究方法——案例研究，即以作者本人亲自翻译的宣传手册为研究案例。

●研究结果——可行。

●研究结论——英语宣传手册简洁易懂的语言特点以及"篇章布局合理""言简意赅""使用主动语态和人称代词'you'"等三种简明英语写作原则在提高译文质量方面可以发挥重要作用，即完全可行。这一结论能为今后类似文本的翻译实践提供有益的借鉴。

●创新/独到之处——源语文本（ST）原载 2006 年 5 月 9 日《安康日报》，题目是《走向世界的"和平"牌紫阳富硒茶》，没有现成的英译文，完全是学生自己的首译，不论译文质量高低，均为学生自己的 the original translation 和 the original research。这也是 BTI 教学和论文写作应该提倡的做法。

【案例 4】本科生毕业论文摘要（样例四）

中文题目	现代舞术语翻译方法与原则初探 ——以 *A Primer for Choreographers* 为例
英文题目	Translation Principles & Methods of Modern Dance Terminology: A Case Study of *A Primer for Choreographers*
中文摘要	迄今对舞蹈术语的英译汉研究非常有限，比较典型的案例属现代舞术语的翻译及其研究。作为首次翻译英文版现代舞教科书的论文作者，希望通过翻译实践总结出有关此类翻译的原则和方法，并希望准确规范的术语翻译便于中外舞者进行高效高质的交流，深化对外来舞蹈艺术的理解。针对舞蹈术语之丰富性、科学性和系统性，翻译应针对不同的类别采用不同的方法。据此，作者总结出：（1）针对编舞元素、动作描述、身体结构、流派名称、抽象概念和外来语等，采用简洁、抽象、明确的 TL 词汇；（2）针对身体训练等词汇，采用音译+释义+直译；（3）针对编舞创作等词汇，采用直译+简化+具体化；（4）针对约定俗成的词汇，则沿用之；（5）针对全新概念等词汇，采用释义。
英文摘要	Limited English-Chinese translation and research of dance terminology have been carried out so far. Modern dance terminological translation and its research make a typical case. This Author who first translated *A Primer for Choreographers* into Chinese attempts to summarize translation principles and methods of the said text type through her own practice with a view to facilitating communication among Chinese and foreign dancers in correct and standard

	translated terms and deepening the understanding of foreign dance arts.
	Dance terminology is characterized by being rich, scientific and systematic, which requires different translation methods for different dances. Therefore, the Author summarizes four principles and methods: (1) to choose concise, abstract and clear TL terms for those for choreographic elements, act description, body structure, names of schools, abstract concepts, and foreign words and expressions; (2) to choose transliteration + paraphrase + literal translation for terms for body training; (3) to choose literary translation, simplification, and specification for choreographic terms; (4) to follow established dance terms; and (5) to choose paraphrase for brand-new concepts.
关键词	术语翻译；现代舞术语；原则与方法；思维方式
Keywords	terminological translation; modern dance terminology (MDT); principle and methods; thinking mode

【案例 4 解析】

①毕业论文规格：（翻译类）BTI 学位论文开题报告之摘要。

②英中摘要词/字数之比：168 words/267 个汉字≈63%——相当理想的数字比例。

③摘要与题目的关联度：很强——重建关联度。

④关键词：4 个——符合要求。

⑤摘要结构剖析：

●研究目的——通过自己翻译《现代舞入门》（*A Primer for Choreographers*）及舞蹈术语，推动中外舞者之间高效高质的交流，深化对外来舞蹈艺术的理解。

●研究问题——共五个：其一，如何翻译编舞元素、动作描述、身体结构、流派名称、抽象概念和外来语等；其二，如何翻译身体训练类词汇；其三，如何翻译编舞创作类词汇；其四，如何翻译约定俗成的词汇；其五，如何翻译全新概念等词汇。

●研究方法——案例研究，即以自己翻译的《现代舞入门》或其中某一章为案例。

●研究结果——（预估）可行，有待论证。

●研究结论——初步认定，对研究问题总结出五种翻译方法：其一，采用简洁、抽象、明确的 TL 词汇；其二，采用音译+释义+直译；其三，采用直译+简化+具体化；其四，沿用；其五，采用释义。

●创新/独到之处——作为舞者的作者首译英文版现代舞教科书，获得了不少独特、新鲜的翻译心得体会，为同行提供了舞蹈术语的翻译原则和方法等。

5. 摘要撰写小结

根据中西学界有经验的作者与学者对撰写论文摘要的要求、标准及建议，特将摘要撰写做如下小结。

（1）摘要内容

An abstract should briefly:

●(Re-)establish the topic of the research project.

●Give the research problem and/or main objective of the project (this usually comes first).

● Indicate the methodology used.

● Present the main findings.

● Present the main conclusions.

（2）大致长度

The abstract may run from a paragraph to half a page in length.（参考 Buffa, 1997: 74）

（3）何时撰写

笔者建议动笔撰写论文之前应大致草拟或试写一个摘要（tentative abstract）。之后，在撰写、修改论文的过程中，可以不断地对摘要初稿进行调整、加工、修正，最后定稿。换言之，摘要是在论文完稿后写就的。

（4）句型模式

表 2-7 所示的句型，无论对直接用英文撰写摘要者，还是对用中文撰写摘要后译成英文者，均有所帮助。

表 2-7　本科生毕业论文摘要句型（举例）

This thesis	aims to…/ presents an analysis of … A comparison between X and X is made. It concludes that…
In this thesis	…is treated./ … are defined./ … are derived. It is shown that…
This thesis	investigates the relationship between three different views of… We show that…/ We argue that…/ We also discuss…/ We find that…
This thesis	examines data from an ongoing project which analyze…/ The data are…/ We analyze…/ Also, we analyze…/ Our data show that…
The purpose of this thesis	is to examine… The thesis is divided into five parts concerning the five aspects of… respectively. Part I (Chapter I) covers… Part II (Chapter II) describes… Part III (Chapter III) introduces… Part IV (Chapter IV) considers… Part V (Chapter V) establishes… The thesis shows that…/ Results are obtained concerning…/ Recommendations of… are provided.

（从丛、李咏燕, 2003: 333；引用者做了少量的文字调整）

2.7　目录纲要写法

1. 目录概念

毕业论文的目录（contents/table of contents）应列出所有以下元素，构成论文中主要段落的简表（短篇论文不必列目录）。为帮助学生使用地道的英文，特引用原版专著中的有关段落："In a thesis…the table of contents precedes all the sections it lists. The table of contents should list all elements of the preliminaries—the chapter (part or section) titles, the main headings and subheadings in the text, and the reference materials. The beginning page number for each section is indicated along the right-hand margin. The numbering of chapters and the wording, capitalization, and punctuation of titles and headings should be exactly the same as they are in the text."（Slade, 2000: 41）

中国学者在专著中指出："<u>The table of contents lists the headings of the beginning, body and ending part of a thesis.</u> The beginning part is marked by Roman numbers while the remaining parts are sequenced by Arabic numbers. <u>For the body of a thesis, the subheadings of each chapter are listed.</u> They are intended to show their different levels. It is not common to put all levels of subheadings in the table of contents. <u>Three levels</u>[①] are usually demonstrated."（文秋芳，2004: 256）

有些毕业论文还包含"表目录"（list of tables）和"图目录"（list of figures），通常紧跟于论文目录之后。

需要特别加以解释的是，the reference materials 指 back matter 或 end matter，包括 appendix/appendixes、glossary、endnotes、bibliography/works cited/works consulted/references、index 等。

2.　纲要概念

（1）中西概念

"纲要"（outline）即"大纲""提纲"，是构成"目录"的一个重要或主要部分。在"3. 案例解析"中，我们会把二者融合起来讲解。"大纲"指"（著作、讲稿、计划等）系统排列的内容要点"（《现汉》第 240 页）；"提纲"指"（写作、发言、学习、研究、讨论等）内容的要点"（《现汉》第 1285 页）。

（2）编制方法

1）两种编制法。根据 Slade（2000: 21），要 outline the thesis/paper，有两种编写法——"大纲导向法"和"边写边改法"："Some researchers <u>begin with a tentative, or working, outline that guides the choice of research materials;</u> others <u>let the outline grow from their research and writing.</u> If you develop an outline in advance, it should remain open to change as you read and take notes. <u>Formulating and revising an outline throughout the processes of researching and writing can help you give your paper a logical and meaningful structure.</u> After you have written a draft of your paper, check it against an existing outline or attempt to make an outline from the draft. <u>Creating a final outline involves making decisions about the thesis statement, the principles of organization, the type of outline, and the format of the outline.</u>"

2）论题导向法。Slade（2000: 21）指出："<u>The answer to the question with which you began your research, or the substantial hypothetical statement, will eventually become the thesis statement,</u> or <u>controlling idea, for the paper.</u> <u>As your outline evolves and your research leads you in new directions, your thesis statement may change,</u> and you should frequently consider revising it as your work progresses. You might even find that you have completely reversed your conclusions in the process of doing research." "<u>Your final thesis statement should cover all the points made in the paper.</u> <u>It need not enumerate each point,</u> but you should not disconcert your reader by straying into an area of inquiry not suggested by the thesis statement."

---

① 意为"三级标题"（three-level heading/format/model/organization/structure）。中英文论文都有一级（one-level）标题、二级（two-level）标题和三级（three-level）标题等。

3）结构导向法。Slade（2000: 22）指出："The organization of a paper often develops naturally in the course of research and during the writing of early drafts. Nevertheless, it is often instructive to try out various principles or patterns of organization with your material or can lead you to new insights."

为方便大家从概念上了解所谓的"结构导向法"，我们既原汁原味地把 Slade 推荐的 5 种常用原则以表格（本书作者制表）的形式呈现出来，也把中国大学生容易明白的概念加以分类概述，双向地介绍给学生读者，详见表 2-8、表 2-9。这样既与国际"接轨"，又帮助学生编制好英文版的论文纲要。

表 2-8　毕业论文大纲编制常用原则

5 Principles	Contents	Notes
Chronology	● Explain each of the steps in a sequentially ordered process ● Often appropriate for a paper describing a series of historical, political, or sociological processes or events	● These five principles are among the most useful principles for restructuring a research paper.
Comparison and Contrast	● Present the similarities and/or differences between two or more persons, places, or things ● A logical development entailing discussion of the same qualities of both subjects ● Appropriate when a subject can best be understood by distinguishing it from others in its class	● These patterns of development are often used in combination. ● They can be applied to individual paragraphs as well as to an entire paper.
Spatial Pattern	● Develop the physical layout or geographical dimensions of a topic ● Be able to guide the reader through a topic that includes several locations	● Your outline will develop naturally from the principle of organization you select. ● A paper involving comparison and contrast or cause and effect will usually have two major divisions.
Cause & Effect	● Present the events or forces that produced certain results, speculate about how things might have turned out if conditions had been different ● Report controlled experimentation to determine the factors important to a particular outcome ● Difficult to determine, particularly in the social sciences ● Valid work that should either control for or take into account as many factors as possible	● A paper organized chronologically, spatially, or analytically may have a number of major divisions. ● After you have identified the large segments of the paper, you can fill in the points to be made in each part.
Analysis	● The process of dividing a subject into its parts and classifying them, given that some subjects can best be understood by an examination of their component parts ● A research paper on the responsibilities of a hospital administrators that might proceed by grouping the duties by types and discussing each type	

（表格内容选自 Slade, 2000: 22-23）

表 2-9　毕业论文大纲编制三大模式

大纲编制 三大模式	大纲内容	备注
总分式	●绪论 ●本论 ●结论	①绪论应提出中心论点（thesis statement）； ②本论应分别提出论点之一、二、三，展示论据之一、二、三，然后进行论证； ③言简意赅，一语中的，具说服力。
推进式	●提出问题 ●叙述现象 ●分析原因 ●找出问题 ●解决问题	①拟定论文题目，提出研究问题和中心论点； ②围绕中心论点或研究问题列出已经掌握的材料与形成的观点； ③根据自选原则（如因果关系原则、逻辑关系原则等），按照一定的大纲形式，对这些观点和材料进行合理编排； ④对英文大纲的逻辑性、连贯性及整体性做出全面审视，剔除与
成分式	●绪论 ●研究方法 ●调查与观察之结果 ●分析与论证 ●结论	主题（thesis/subject）无关的材料，增加论证过程中必不可少的观点； ⑤始终记住编制论文大纲是一个不断完善的过程——故在英文中这个大纲/纲要/提纲被称为 a working outline 或 a tentative outline。

4）英文纲要写法分类。编制、撰写英文纲要/大纲，要求风格正规（formal）、语言表达前后一致（consistent）。通常，用英文撰写的论文纲要有两大分类：topic outline（主题词纲要）和 sentence outline（主题句纲要）。

根据 Slade（2000: 23），"[the] entries in a topic outline are words, phrases, or clauses; that is, they are not complete sentences. The entries should be parallel; they all should take the same grammatical form. If you use a noun phrase for one entry, you should continue using noun phrases consistently. You have to rework some of your entries to make them parallel, but paying attention to grammatical form often contributes to clear and logical thinking." "The entries in a sentence outline are complete sentences. The process of writing a research paper involves writing sentences from the topics in the topic outline, in effect producing a sentence outline. A sentence outline, therefore, serves as a beginning for the paper and as a test of a logic of the outline."

3. 案例解析

【案例 1】三级标题目录/大纲（部分样例）①

TABLE OF CONTENTS

Page

---

① 参考 "An example of part of a table of contents"（文秋芳，2004: 256）。

【案例 1 解析】

这是"三级标题"的论文目录。用英文表达，即：

The three-level format divides the body or text of the thesis into

①The first level (within the text);

②The second level (within the text);

③The third level (within the text).

【案例 2】二级标题目录/大纲（部分样例）[①]

---

① 参考"An example using PART and CHAPTER together"（文秋芳，2004: 258；引用者对部分大小写做了修改）。

Chapter Three　The quantitative design

Chapter Four　The qualitative design

PART III　RESULTS AND DISCUSSION

Chapter Five…

Chapter Six…

Part IV　CONCLUSION

【案例 2 解析】

这是"二级标题"的论文目录。用英文表达，即：

The two-level format divides the body or text of the thesis into

- The Part, the first level (within the text);
- The Chapter, the second level (within the text).

【案例 3】四级标题目录/大纲（部分样例）

Table of Contents

…

4　Translation Techniques

    4.1　Amplification/Annotation

        4.1.1　Application to Main Types of Nouns

            4.1.1.1　Personal Names

            4.1.1.2　Scenic Spot Names

            4.1.1.3　Geographical Names

            4.1.1.4　Time

        4.1.2　Transliteration/Literal Translation with Amplification/Annotation

            4.1.2.1　Transliteration with Amplification/Annotation

            4.1.2.2　Literal Translation with Amplification/Annotation

        4.1.3　Summary

    4.2　Analogy

        4.2.1　Analogy in Translation

        4.2.2　Problems in Presenting Analogy

        4.2.3　Case Analysis

            4.2.3.1　Case of Tang Xianzu

            4.2.3.2　Case of Wuzhen

…

【案例 3 解析】

这是"四级标题"的论文目录，主题涉及旅游参观点 CSI（文化专有项）的翻译及其研究。

【案例 4】五级标题目录/大纲（部分样例）

【案例 4 解析】

这是"五级标题"的论文目录，主题涉及魔幻小说《魔戒》的翻译与根据功能主义翻译理论进行的大陆版译文与台湾版译文之对比研究。

【案例 5】BA 毕业论文目录/大纲（样例）

【案例 5 解析】

　　这是比较完整的 BA 毕业论文目录，主题涉及小说《色·戒》的翻译与目的论指导下的翻译风格研究。

【案例 6】BTI 毕业论文目录/大纲（样例）

Terminological Translation of *A Primer for Choreographers*:
A Preliminary Study

Acknowledgements

Abstract in Chinese

Abstract in English

Part I　Translation-based Research

1　Introduction

    1.1　The Rationale of Translation and Its Research

    1.2　Terminological Translation and Research Problems

    1.3　Research Methodology and Data Collection

2　Literature Review

    2.1　The First Chinese Translation of *A Primer for Choreographers*

        2.1.1　A General Survey of Terminological Translation

        2.1.2　A Detailed Description of Specific Techniques of Terminological Translation

        2.1.3　A Detailed Description of Terminology Translation of Modern Dance in China

    2.2　A Brief History of Modern Dance and Its Legacy

        2.2.1　Early Modern Period

        2.2.2　Central Modern Period

        2.2.3　Late Modern Period

        2.2.3　Contemporary Dance

3　Case Study of Terminological Translation in *A Primer for Choreographers*

    3.1　Geometry Terms

    3.2　Musical Terms

    3.3　Descriptive Terms

    3.4　Borrowed Terms

4　Translation Principles and Methods

    4.1　Domestication vs. Foreignization

    4.2　Applicable Methods/Techniques

        4.2.1　Transliteration

        4.2.2　Simplification

        4.2.3　Paraphrase

        4.2.4　Substitution

5　Conclusions

    5.1　New Findings

    5.2　Major Conclusions

Part II Translation of *A Primer for Choreographers*

Working Bibliography

【案例 6 解析】

　　这是比较完整的 BTI 毕业论文（开题报告）目录，主题涉及现代舞教科书 *A Primer for Choreographers* 首次汉译及其研究，重点放在现代舞术语的翻译与研究上。请读者注意目录中的 "<u>Working</u> Bibliography"，最终定稿后，应将 "Working" 删去。

◎研究与实践思考题◎

1. 将本章介绍的"论文封面设计"要求与读者自己所在学校的有关要求做一对比分析、研究。就这些要求的异同写一篇内容归纳综述（在完成任务过程中，可以参考本书其他有关章节。下同）。

2. 将本章介绍的"论文题目写法"与读者自己所在学校的有关要求做一对比分析、研究。就这些要求的异同写一篇内容归纳综述。

3. 将本章介绍的"论文声明写法"与读者自己所在学校的有关要求做一对比分析、研究。就这些要求的异同写一篇内容归纳综述。

4. 将本章介绍的"论文致谢写法"与读者自己所在学校的有关要求做一对比分析、研究。就这些要求的异同写一篇内容归纳综述。

5. 将本章介绍的"论文摘要写法"与读者自己所在学校的有关要求做一对比分析、研究。就这些要求的异同写一篇内容归纳综述。

6. 将本章介绍的"目录纲要写法"与读者自己所在学校的有关要求做一对比分析、研究。就这些要求的异同写一篇内容归纳综述。

7. 在参考本章的基础之上，自己独立完成有关上述论文写作的前六项要求的 preliminaries，内容不要重复。

8. 参考学生自己所在学校的有关要求，自己独立完成有关上述论文写作的前六项要求的 preliminaries，内容要保持完全一致。

9. 厘清论文结构前 19 个项目的中英文概念意义。

10. 你认为有更为先进、更为简便的方法可用作论文前六项写作/翻译的要求吗？

第3章　如何设计（开题准备）

How to Propose a Thesis (Proposal-oriented)

◎学习目标◎

　　开题报告乃是毕业论文（设计）工作五大环节之第二环节，为毕业论文撰写的关键一环。它是开题者对论文（即研究课题）的文字说明材料。开题者把自己的开题报告内容向答辩委员会进行陈述，然后由委员会对报告进行评议，确定是否通过。只有开题报告答辩通过者，才能进入论文撰写的后续环节。本章将帮助学生：

- ●了解、熟悉开题报告的概念；
- ●了解、熟悉开题报告的结构；
- ●了解、熟悉开题报告各组成部分及其写法；
- ●通过案例分析重点学会如何撰写论文绪论；
- ●通过案例分析熟悉开题报告的整体写法；
- ●通过案例分析了解、熟悉论文文献翻译；
- ●了解、熟悉 BTI 和 BA 开题报告的不同要点；
- ●了解、熟悉开题报告答辩的有关知识、程序和管理。

3.1　论文正文写法

3.1.1　论文开题难

　　（1）客观存在。万事开头难。撰写毕业论文的真正之难，起于论文开题报告的设计、策划及撰写。开题报告写不好，论文本身也就难以写好，往往后来会写不下去，直至返工，结果是费时、费脑、费神、费力，还费钱。（绝）大多数学生都觉得论文最难写，于是造成抄袭、剽窃等不端行为，网上论文工厂（online paper mill）应运而生，败坏了学术风气，破坏了道德风尚。

　　的确，本科生在正式动笔撰写论文之前，都要求先写出开题报告，以便指导教师根据学生的文献综述（a review of literature/literature review）和对所选论题的认识（thesis statement），确定其可行性（feasibility）。

　　（2）前提条件。启动开题环节是有前提条件的。首先，导师要有足够的时间指导学生，定期与学生进行交流、讨论，为学生答疑，检查学生的工作进度和质量；其次，下达任务书，对文献综述和开题报告提出具体要求，推荐参考文献，审定学生拟定的课题研究方案，审阅学生文献综述、外文翻译、开题报告、毕业论文（设计）及相关附件。作为论文和开题报告写作主体的学生，其职责是按任务书要求，完成毕业论文（设计）工作；根据导师要求，定期向导师汇报毕业论文（设计）工作。需要特别强调的是，毕业论文（设计）还涉及安全问题。对毕业论文（设计）内容中涉及的有关技术资料，学生负有保密责任，未经许可不能擅自对外交流或转让（尽管 BTI/BA 生这类情况极为罕见）。

3.1.2　开题要求多[①]

（1）选题要求。本科生毕业论文（设计）选题要求包括：①遵守国家法律法规和方针政策；②符合专业培养目标要求，鼓励学科间交叉；③提倡毕业论文（设计）与科研训练、学科竞赛、创业计划及校内外"产学研"合作教育等实践项目相结合；④教师与学生采取双向选择的方式确定，保证学生一人一题。

（2）管理要求。院（系）内部本学科专业的毕业论文（设计）管理和跨专业选择课题的管理，长期以来有一套与时俱进的制度和方法。在新形势下，出现了跨院（系）、校外毕业论文（设计）管理等问题。跨院（系）毕业论文（设计）是指学生在校内选择并完成非其所在院（系）教师申报的课题或自拟题目由校内非其所在院（系）教师指导。校外毕业论文（设计）是指学生选择并完成非校内教师申报的课题或自拟题目由校外单位教师指导，包括校外境内毕业论文（设计）、境外毕业论文（设计）。就这方面的管理，学校有具体规定及要求（以下以浙江大学为例）：

①在选题前，由学生本人提出申请，填写《浙江大学本科生申请赴外单位进行毕业论文审批表》，提供证明材料，院（系）审批备案；

②采用双导师制，在过程管理上采取以学生所在院（系）指导教师为主、以外单位指导教师为辅的合作管理方式；

③参加校内院（系）统一组织安排的开题及毕业论文（设计）答辩；

④论文（设计）实施过程中出现的其他问题，由院（系）和外单位协商解决，如有必要，签订相关协议。

3.2　开题报告写法

3.2.1　开题报告概念

据 Brian Devlin，开题报告（proposal/proposal outline/initial proposal/thesis proposal/proposal for the thesis）是 "a brief sketch, perhaps two or three pages long, of the research a student proposes to do. The fuller or more elaborated version of a proposal will generally include these elements: the applicant's identity and contact details, a descriptive title, summary of the intended work (including the problem to be investigated), a critical synopsis of the literature, a

---

① 参考"浙江大学本发〔2018〕3号"文件。

timetable (including the sequence of work), some discussion about the goal of the project, an itemized list of requirements… and a budget… The term 'research proposal'…includes thesis proposals and proposals for research grants, although it isn't much concerned with the latter" （Devlin, 2004: 5-6）。

换言之，开题报告是毕业生将自己初步选定的题目之内容、思路等（研究问题或/和翻译项目），以书面的形式首先向自己的导师汇报，（通过后）再向论文答辩委员会（defense committee）做一汇报（书面、PPT/PDF/Word 形式等）及简要说明。

针对 BTI/BA 生做进一步阐释，开题报告是我们将收集的文献资料（BTI 生还包括 ST）进行整合后撰写的论文论证以及研究方法规划。这份报告不仅需要详细地写出论文中的 **research questions**（指的是在翻译实践和/或研究中存在但却没有研究、没有研究明白或者没有得到[彻底]解决的问题，能够从中发现新观点、新问题、新知识）和/或 **translation problems to be tackled**（需要攻克/有待解决的翻译难题），还需要将研究问题的论据和解决翻译难题的方法、思路写明白，并对研究背景、研究价值（如创新点）、解题背景、解题价值、前期准备以及目前的进展进行简述。因此，开题报告不仅可以帮助学生明确选题的主要思想、研究范围和/或解题方法，同时（通过答辩）还有助于论文写作水平和 TT 质量的提高。

首次撰写毕业论文的学生需要明白的关键点是：所有的研究都是从提出问题开始的。在思考、撰写论文过程中，要谨防下列常见问题发生：①不清楚到底想写什么问题，无法收集相关的参考文献；②没有搞明白研究问题之所在，对问题背景和研究价值十分模糊；③有的问题太大，一篇本科论文无法完成；④有的问题太难，大大超出学生本身的研究能力；⑤有的问题太小或过于简略，难以做有价值的论述；⑥有的问题的提出，缺乏论点与论据之间的逻辑联系；如此等等。这些问题最后均可能导致返工重写，甚至不得不放弃有关选题。

综上，写（好）毕业论文，先要写（好）开题报告，而开题报告需要经过答辩程序。答辩程序是在学生初步确定选题的基础上进行的，有两大目的：

（1）通过开题报告，学生能将所选课题的[①]
- 概况/内容框架
- 源语文本（原则上尚无译语文本，复译/改译另议）
- 研究现状/翻译现状
- 意义/理据
- 研究问题/难点
- 翻译或口译问题/难点
- 实践创新点
- 理论创新点
- 论文结构

---

① 下列项目根据毕业生的学位性质（BTI/BA 或专业学位/学术学位）来做出选择，有些项目是共有的。

●主要引证材料

●参考文献

等做一总体思路的勾画，学生对选题/项目的前因后果、来龙去脉进行有序的组合、清理，为最终撰写毕业/学位论文做好充分的准备。

（2）通过开题报告，学生能听取答辩委员会专家们及其他有关人士的宝贵意见，并在此基础上重新理顺论文思路，使论文得到必要的修改，以免走弯路。

对于科研经验缺乏的本科生而言，一个好的开题报告或研究方案，可以保证整个研究工作有条不紊地进行。换言之，开题报告水平的高低，是一篇毕业论文质量与水平的重要反映。与此同时，有一个合理可行的方案，可以使学生避免迈出第一步后不知如何迈开第二步的尴尬情况。

3.2.2　开题报告结构

开题报告有固定的格式，各校大同小异。它未必为表格形式，但与按照规定填表有相似之处。这样的形式，即把要报告的每一项内容转换成相应的小标题或栏目，既避免了遗漏，又便于评审者一目了然，把握要点。

1. 开题报告封面

（1）BTI 学位论文开题报告封面（英文）

Zhejiang University

School of International Studies

Proposal for BTI Thesis

Title_____

_____

Full name_____

Student No._____

Subject area_____

Research orientation_____

Primary supervisor_____

Secondary supervisor_____

Date for submission_____

（2）BA 学位论文开题报告封面（英文）

Zhejiang University

School of International Studies

Proposal for BA Thesis

Title_____

_____

Full name_____

Student No._____

Subject area_____

Research orientation_____

Supervisor_____

Date for submission_____

【注】各大学的开题报告的封面设计主要包含了上述基本内容。BTI 学位论文封面的设计中，含有"primary supervisor"和"secondary supervisor"（即"第一导师"和"第二导师"，亦为"supervisor"和"assistant supervisor"）两项，主要有两层意思。第一，根据目前中国大学翻译导师队伍的现状，我们提倡毕业/学位论文指导"双导师制"（dual-supervisor system）。第二，翻译专业学位论文的指导教师原则上需要一名在校导师、一名行业导师，于是自然形成双导师制；谁为主，谁为辅，可以依情形而定。这主要是因为有些学生论文的主题是行业翻译。

2. 开题报告基本组成部分

（1）BA 学位论文开题报告组成部分（英文）

1. **Working Title**

2. **Abstract and Keywords (bilingual)**

3. **Introduction**

  (1) Rationale and Significance of the Research

  (2) Research Questions

  (3) Research Methodology and Data Collection

  (4) Outline of the Thesis

[e.g.] 1 / Part I / Chapter I

    1.1

        1.1.1

        1.1.2

    1.2

        1.2.1

        1.2.2

    …

4. Literature Review

5. Theoretical Framework

6. Date Interpretation/Processing (e.g. illustrative cases)

7. Tentative Conclusions (including major findings, significance, limitations, suggestions for future research, etc.)

8. Working Bibliography (as per MLA bibliography format, GB/T 7714—2015, and Chinese academic journals like *Chinese Translators Journal*, etc.)

9. Research Schedule

Dates	Progress	Remarks

（2）BTI 学位论文开题报告组成部分（英文）

No.	Structure
1	**Working Title**
2	**Abstract and Keywords (bilingual)**
3	**Part I　Practice-based Research**
4	**1.1　Introduction** (1) Rationale and Significance of the Proposal (2) The Source Text (3) Translation Problems (4) Research Questions (5) Translation & Research Methods (6) Data Collection **1.2　Outline of the Proposed Thesis** **1.3　Literature Review**

	(1) About the Source Text
	(2) About the Target Text(s)
	(3) About Related Researches
	1.4　Theoretical Framework (if any)
	1.5　Illustrated Typical Cases (representative parts of the translation & research)
	1.6　Tentative Conclusions (including major findings, significance, limitations, suggestions for future translation and research, etc.)
	1.7　Working Bibliography (as per MLA bibliography format, GB/T 7714—2015, and Chinese academic journals like *Chinese Translators Journal*, etc.)

5	**Part II　Translation Project / Translation Task / Translation Practice** (in full/in parts)	
	The Source Text	The Target Text
	(1)	(1)
	(2)	(2)
	(3)	(3)
	…	…

6	**Translation & Research Schedule**		
	Dates	**Progress**	**Remarks**

3.2.3　开题报告组成部分写法

1. 题　目

论文题目应用中英文撰写，中文在前，英文在后。其目的是让指导教师、论文开题报告答辩委员会及其他相关观众、读者等明白毕业论文的大致范围和方向，即论题（thesis: a statement that someone wants to discuss or prove; a statement or an opinion that is discussed in a logical way and presented with evidence in order to prove that it is true［分别参见 MWALED 第 1705 页和 OALD 第 1832 页］）。当问及你的论题为何时，作为准毕业论文答辩者，你该如何答复呢？

You may be called upon to present a thesis statement. <u>The thesis statement is just that—a statement. It is not a question. You can, however, use a question to form a thesis statement. All you need to do is to answer it.</u> For example, if your preliminary research has led you to wonder: "Was Mozart poisoned by his rival, Salieri?" All you need to do to turn this into a thesis statement is <u>to answer the question the way you *suspect* your research will go</u>. For example, your thesis statement may be that:

"Mozart was not poisoned by Salieri, but rather died of a plague, a common affliction of the time."

or

"Mozart was poisoned by his jealous rival, Salieri, in one of the great murders of the day."

You may want to present a statement that has some background information in it, explaining just a line or two about your thesis, for example:

"Mozart was one of the great composers of all time. Despite the great amount we know about his life, his death has always been shrouded in mystery. It is my intention to show that Mozart was in fact poisoned by his jealous rival, Salieri, in one of the great unpunished murders of all time."

You don't need to know ahead of time what the answer will be. It is, however, appropriate to do some research before you pose your thesis. You don't want a situation in which you have no answer. You want to be certain that there is enough scholarly work on the subject for you to draw some sort of conclusion. Although it is possible to reach a conclusion that one can't tell how Mozart died, obviously it is preferable, and more satisfying to either prove or disprove your thesis.

Most professors will want your thesis statement before you get too far along in a project so that they may help you if your scope is too broad or your topic is too unfocused. You may also modify your thesis statement as you proceed. You may find that your thesis is a little off and further clarification is necessary. Perhaps you discover that it wasn't Salieri, but another composer of the time who was most suspected in Mozart's mysterious death.

A good thesis statement will give direction to your research. It is a goal you set out to attain, and prevents you from becoming diverted. （Buffa, 2003: 65-67）

【题目例析一（BA 论文）】

中文题目	论儿童文学翻译中的"儿童本位"翻译观 ——《彼得·潘》四汉译本对比研究
英文题目	On the Child-oriented Views on Translation of Children's Literature —A Comparative Study of Four Chinese translations of *Peter Pan*

　　上述中英文题目清楚地说明有关毕业论文的大致范围和方向，即论题的范围和方向。其一，范围是围绕《彼得·潘》的四个汉译本进行对比研究。其二，方向是遵循"儿童本位"翻译观，以此指导相关的对比研究。

【题目例析二（BTI 论文）】

中文题目	天津博物馆近代历史展馆英译的功能对等翻译策略研究
英文题目	On the Translating Strategies of the Modern History Exhibition in Tianjin Museum: A Functional Equivalence Approach

上述中英文题目也清楚地说明有关毕业论文的大致范围和方向。就范围而言，论文将研究天津博物馆近代历史展馆的英译本。就方向而言，论文将运用功能对等路径对翻译策略进行研究。[①]

2. 摘　要

作为开题报告内容之一的毕业论文摘要，应用汉英双语分别撰写，汉语在前，英语在后。既然"A good thesis statement will give direction to your research. It is a goal you set out to attain, and prevents you from becoming diverted."（Buffa, 2003: 67），于是，"The abstract is a brief summary of your paper. It should state the goals and the results of your research."（Buffa, 2003: 74）

【摘要例析一（BA 论文）】

中文摘要	本文以《彼得·潘》四个汉译本为研究基础，旨在讨论儿童文学的英汉翻译。笔者认为，不少英文儿童文学的汉译本可谓不懂"童心"，而好的儿童文学翻译则是"儿童本位"翻译，其前提是对儿童读者的全面认识。另外，儿童文学读者的特殊性决定了儿童文学翻译不同于其他翻译实践。儿童的阅读习惯、阅读兴趣和阅读能力是儿童文学译者必须考虑的因素。笔者试图通过对《彼得·潘》几个汉译本的比较研究，从实践中总结出儿童文学翻译之规范/标准，涉及词汇层、主题层和文化层等的诸多转换。
英文摘要	This thesis aims to discuss some aspects of the E-C translation of children's literature based on the example study of four Chinese versions of *Peter Pan*. The author maintains that quite a few Chinese translations of English literature for children are a failure to understand children's hearts and innocence, while good translation of children's literature is child-oriented translation, which firstly involves a comprehensive understanding of the intended child reader. Furthermore, due to its particularity of the intended readers, translation of children's literature differs from other translation practice in general. Its translators are required to have an implied reader image in their minds all the time, producing the target text in accordance with the reading habit, interest and ability of the target children. Through the case study of the E-C translations of *Peter Pan,* the author attempts to summarize the translation norms of children's literature from the practical transfers at lexical, thematic and cultural levels.

摘要应点明选题的研究目的。上述摘要指出，该文以《彼得·潘》四个汉译本为研究基础，旨在讨论儿童文学的英汉翻译；试图通过对《彼得·潘》汉译本的比较研究，探讨、总结儿童文学翻译中儿童化的遣词造句和跨文化因素处理的一般规律。

上述摘要虽然文字不多（亦可扩展），但却回答了下列重要问题，也是毕业论文需要讨论、解决的问题：

①研究的主题、范围——儿童文学翻译（以《彼得·潘》四个汉译本为对比材料）。

②研究的背景——不少英文儿童文学的汉译本可谓不懂"童心"。

③研究的目的——通过对《彼得·潘》四个汉译本的比较研究，试图从实践中总结

---

① 题目例析一选自浙江大学 BA 生开题报告，题目例析二选自南开大学 BTI 生开题报告（该生保送浙江大学读 MTI，导师是本书作者）。

出儿童文学翻译之规范/标准，涉及词汇层、主题层和文化层等的诸多转换。

④研究的方法——四个译语文本对比研究。

⑤有哪些主要研究发现或观点——从翻译实践中总结出儿童文学翻译在词汇层、主题层和文化层等诸多方面之规范/标准。

⑥研究带来的启示——不少英文儿童文学的汉译本可谓不懂"童心"，而好的儿童文学翻译则应是"儿童本位"翻译（儿童的阅读习惯、阅读兴趣和阅读能力是儿童文学译者必须考虑的因素）。另外，儿童文学读者的特殊性决定了儿童文学翻译不同于其他翻译实践。

【摘要例析二（BTI 论文）】

中文摘要	天津博物馆作为天津市的主要旅游景点之一，值得推介。它通过大量珍贵文物、文献和照片向中外游客们展现了一个真实、完整的天津。它记载历史，传承文化，为世人进行历史研究奠定了可靠基础，散发出其独特的魅力。 为向游客更好地传播天津的历史文化，也为更好地推进国际化，天津博物馆提供了双语文本供游客阅读。本文应用尤金·奈达的功能对等理论来分析天津博物馆现代历史馆的文本翻译。 论文旨在通过运用功能对等理论分析天津博物馆的翻译文本，进一步探讨译文的上升空间，为传播天津的历史文化做出些许贡献。 译本对比研究的结论是：翻译标准应定为——其一，译文是否在整体上契合目标语及其文化；其二，译文是否契合目标语受众；其三，译文是否契合特殊信息之语境。 与此同时，研究还给我们带来一些新"发现"：天津博物馆的大多数译文令人满意，少量翻译问题瑕不掩瑜；对翻译专业学生，值得学习、欣赏的译文部分多于需要批评指正的。作者会将一些不妥的译文告知博物馆管理层。
英文摘要	As one of the major scenic spots in Tianjin, Tianjin Museum is worth promoting. It demonstrates an intact and true Tianjin for visitors both at home and abroad by showing a large number of cultural treasures, written materials and pictures. With a record of history to disseminate culture, Tianjin Museum lays a good foundation for people interested in research, which manifests its special glamour. Tianjin Museum furnishes the visitors with bilingual texts not only for their better understanding of Tianjin culture and history but for faster convergence into globalization. This thesis analyzes the translation texts of the Modern History Exhibition in Tianjin Museum from the perspective of Eugene Nida's functional equivalence. The thesis aims to improve the translation texts after applying Nida's theory to practice and make a contribution to transmitting the history and culture of Tianjin. The research results show that the translation criteria should be established by judging whether the translation fits into the receptor language and culture as a whole, into the receptor-language audience, and into the context of the particular message. At the same time, the research has also brought about some "new findings": Most of the translation is satisfactory except for some errors. More is to be appreciated and learned for us translation majors than to be criticized. This author will convey inappropriate translation to the museum management.

上述摘要点明，论文旨在通过收集、整理天津博物馆向中外游客提供的双语文本，应用尤金·奈达的功能对等理论来分析天津博物馆现代历史馆的文本翻译：

①研究的主题、范围——天津博物馆解说词英译研究。

②研究的背景——天津博物馆作为天津市的主要旅游景点之一，值得推介。它通过大量珍贵文物、文献和照片向中外游客们展现了一个真实、完整的天津。

③研究的目的——旨在通过运用功能对等理论分析天津博物馆的翻译文本，进一步探讨其上升空间，为传播天津的历史文化做出些许贡献。

④研究的方法——源语文本和译语文本的对比研究。

⑤有哪些主要研究发现或观点——翻译标准应定为：其一，译文是否在整体上契合目标语及其文化；其二，译文是否契合目标语受众；其三，译文是否契合特殊信息之语境。

⑥研究所带来的启示——研究还给我们带来一些新"发现"：天津博物馆的大多数译文令人满意，少量翻译问题瑕不掩瑜；对翻译专业学生，值得学习、欣赏的译文部分多于需要批评指正的。作者会将一些不妥的译文告知博物馆管理层。

3. 绪 论

"绪论"亦称"引言"或"导言"（introduction），为论文或开题报告的开始部分（beginnings）。它有如下几个要点值得牢记：

（1）定基调（to set the tone for your whole thesis）。作者应将论题（thesis）或写作目的、准备如何解决研究问题（research questions）等做一交代，让读过绪论的都能对论文内容有比较清楚的了解。

（2）明目的（clear purpose）。即把研究的意图和过程做一清晰的陈述（to give a clear statement of intent and process）。

（3）语精练（concise language）。强调言简意赅，篇幅不必太长，短的可以一至两页。

（4）正式体（formal style）。语言风格应正式，因为撰写的是专业/学术论文，而且最先正式阅读论文开题报告的是导师及其他专家。

（5）礼谦逊。尽管专家们见多识广，智力过人，但未必对你研究的课题都十分清楚。应以平等礼貌的文字勾勒出你的研究纲要，杜绝/避免无意识中流露出"居高临下"的写作态度和话语（to clearly outline your research without talking down to the reader）。

（6）选代词。有不少导师和专家不喜欢毕业论文中（过度）使用第一人称"I"，如果你的导师亦如此，甚至"顽固不化"（dead-set against I），或者出于安全考虑，建议选用第三人称，如"this/the thesis will show""the Author of this/the thesis""this Author/author""the purpose of this thesis is to address…""while online translation papers have many brilliant insights, it is this Author's intention to prove…"等。

（7）正观点（a positive view of the topic itself）。根据 Buffa（2003: 80）："Don't ever start off by apologizing for your topic, research or ideas. If you don't feel good about what you are writing, you will end up with a less than satisfactory paper. Don't say something 'Though there was not much information on this topic…' or 'While the assertions I will make may sound foolish…' You don't want your reader to start off by looking for flaws in your writing.

If your topic wasn't a good one, or the information was scarce, you should have moved to a different topic."

（8）知结构。绪论通常由三部分组成：研究概述、研究需要和论文结构；或者，研究理据及意义、研究问题/翻译难题、研究纲要。

①研究概述（a general description of your research/translation project）/研究理据及意义（the rationale and significance of the study/the thesis rationale and significance）。开篇句型有：

●固定型：The research was/will be undertaken to find out…

●固定型：This government translation project was assigned to complete…and to study…

●灵活型：Translation studies and globalization studies have expanded enormously in the 21st century. And when it comes to C-E news trans-editing, it is actually referring to both studies. This Author has adopted her intern experience in the local branch of Xinhua News Agency as a case study, which increased her translation ability and sense of globalization. This valuable working experience enabled the Author to realize what kind of expertise news translators or news editors should have and how news agencies function during the process of news speed trans-editing…

●灵活性：The Chinese-English agreement translation project concerning the Insigma Group Sino-foreign Fund Project is contributive to the successful signing of the said agreement between the Insigma Group and the foreign party, which marks the new development of this international enterprise. In addition to the implications of the agreement translation practice, the related practice-based research on agreement/contract translation is a worthwhile trial to a Translation Major like this Author[①] of the thesis. The Author's acceptance of the said translation project is due to her ambitious plan to become a professional translator in the domains of law, finance, media and tourism. Therefore, it is professionally sound to choose legal texts like contracts or agreements for translation as an essential part of the BTI degree thesis/project.

②研究需要（the need for the research）/研究问题（research questions）/翻译难题（translation problems）。有关要点及文字表述有：

●to explain why the research is worth undertaking;

●to offer some background information about the topic/subject;

●to explain in terms of theoretical as well as practical value;

●to confirm or disconfirm a theory/hypothesis;

●to modify an existing theory;

●to clarify a controversial issue;

●to tackle translation problems;

---

① 该绪论部分原出自浙江大学 MTI 论文（作者本科就读于武汉大学），本书作者暨其导师将其用作 BTI 论文讲解。

●to discuss translation for practical purposes；

●to conduct a comparative study of translations for theoretical importance；

●to develop a new model for specialized translation like menu/sign translation；

●to enrich our understanding of a translation phenomenon；

●to provide a practical solution to TCM translation problems；

…

③论文结构（the [overall] structure of the thesis）/研究纲要（the [brief] outline of the study/thesis）。开题报告中提供的毕业论文结构或研究纲要，一般不必很详尽（如可详尽，当然更好），但起码应有"二级目录"，最好是"三级目录"。根据文秋芳（2004: 264）：

"When describing the overall organization of the thesis, the chapter headings should be covered. If 'Part' is the first-order heading and 'Chapter', the second-order, the description should cover both Parts and Chapters. In some cases, the Introduction chapter also includes the definitions of key terms, delimitations, and assumptions of the study… In my opinion, the conceptual definitions of key variables are better included in the Literature Review chapter since they must be developed based on others' definitions; the operational definitions are better placed in the Methodology chapter where the instrument is introduced… Although the Introduction is the first chapter in the manuscript, it is written when the other chapters have been finalized. The reason is obvious. The research questions which were developed in your proposal may have been modified in one way or another almost until you finish writing up the chapter of Results and Discussion."

4. 文献综述

通常单独成章。详见第 4 章。

5. 理论框架

通常单独成章，但在 BA 论文中，亦可包括在第 1 章（参看 3.3）。详见第 5 章。

6. 典型译例

通常单独成章。详见第 6 章。

7. 初步结论

通常单独成章。详见第 7 章（即 7.8）。

8. 参考文献

对参考文献的规定，因校而异。比如，浙江大学（外国语学院）规定，外语学科本科生参考文献数量不少于 10 篇/部，其中 5 篇/部是英文，5 篇/部是中文。参考文献类别包括学术论文、学术专著、教科书、词典及其他参考文献。

这部分内容应单列。详见第 8 章。

9. 文献翻译

"文献翻译"（literature translation/academic literature translation/translation of academic literature）是（浙江大学）BA 和 BTI 学位论文撰写整体要求的一部分。浙江大学本科"**毕业论文（设计）文献综述和开题报告考核**"的成绩比例是：

成绩比例	文献综述（占 10%）	开题报告（占 15%）	外文翻译（占 5%）
分　值			

这一要求通常在某些重点大学实施，即将数千字/词（如 2000）的汉语/英语的学术文章（论文或专著中的有关内容）译成目标语。主要要求如下：

①原则上，提倡英译汉，汉译英对本科生来说要求过高。

②源语文本（ST）原则上应为需做综述的文献专著、论文或教材中的足量字词数的章节或段落。

③源语文本不应有现成译文，学生翻译前需经导师（或导师组）认可。

④源语文本字词数为 2000—2500（以汉字计数）。

⑤按照规定或一定的格式提交文献翻译。

由于"文献翻译"这一要求目前尚不普遍，我们不在此做详述。有关的两个案例，请参看本章的"**研究与实践思考题**"。

3.3　开题报告例析

3.3.1　BA 论文开题报告例析

1．BA 论文开题报告主要项目讨论清单

A List of Major Items for Discussion[①]

Working Title

摘　要

Abstract

I　Introduction

　　1.1　Research Significance

　　1.2　Research Questions and Methods

　　1.3　Theoretical Framework

　　1.4　Outline of the Thesis

II　Literature Review

…

III　Data Collection

…

IV　Representative Case Studies

…

V　Conclusion

…

Working Bibliography

---

① 该清单仅用于本书开题报告部分，实际操作可以省略，各校会有所差异。

2. 开题报告例析一（BA 论文）

BA Thesis Proposal

Working Title

试析全球化视角下功能对等在中国科技翻译中的作用

On Applying Functional Equivalence to Chinese Technical Translation

in the Context of Globalization

中文摘要

为求客观精确，科技语篇向来使用的是贴近字面的译法，但这常常会在实践中导致中文食洋不化。在全球化进程中，各种科技语篇涌入中国，导致大量西式中文出现在报纸、杂志和网络上，甚至进入日常语言交流领域。本论文讨论了西式中文的现象/译例，尝试分析奈达功能对等在科技翻译中的应用，看其能否在不影响译文准确性的前提下，利于翻出更为自然的译文。本文通过将源语科技文本区分为"技术部分"和"非技术部分"两类，进而试图证明功能对等理论不仅适用于科技翻译，而且能够保持汉语的灵性和意合特征。

关键词：功能对等；科技翻译；西式中文；形合；意合

Abstract

In order to be objective and accurate, Chinese translators have long maintained the literal translation method when doing technical translation (E-C), which is often misleading in practice. With the impact of globalization, technical texts from overseas have constantly been introduced into China in large quantities. As a result of the literal translation of technical texts, "westernized Chinese" appears both in newspapers and magazines and on the Internet, even becoming available in daily verbal communication. This thesis discusses the phenomena/cases of westernized Chinese and explores how Eugene Nida's functional equivalence can help produce more natural technical translation in Chinese without sacrificing accuracy. Furthermore, by dividing source texts/ materials into the "technical part" and "non-technical part", it attempts to prove that functional equivalence is both applicable to Chinese technical translation and beneficial in preserving the paratactic features of the Chinese language.

Keywords: functional equivalence; technical translation; westernized Chinese; hypotaxis; parataxis

I Introduction

1.1 Research Significance

The ever-deepening globalization has made the world smaller. High-technology has led us onto a new stage where we are closely connected to each other and inevitably facing an information explosion. As we try hard to stand firm in the trend, any discussion about cultural issues today cannot go without mentioning the topic of globalization. From a cultural perspective, information explosion and globalization have brought us not only opportunities but also challenges. What people worry about the most is how to maintain our cultural identity in the context of globalization.

Actually, the relation between globalization and translation could be a subtle one. Translation greatly pushes globalization forward, while globalization plays a crucial role in the development of translation. There is adequate evidence to show that the new version of westernized Chinese is reappearing in the 21st century.

The significance of this research lies in the following points.

Firstly, in the past, Chinese translation studies experienced two major trends of westernization, which could be described as "Westernization 1.0" during the May 4th Movement (1919), and "Westernization 2.0" during the 1980s. Both movements focus on humane aspects like literature, politics, etc. In the past 20 years, high-tech development has produced a huge need for specialized translation in the areas of technology, business, law, finance, and so on, among which technical translation makes up at least 75% of a professional translator's daily work (陈刚, 2011: 590). So it is important to study technical translation in the context of globalization, and how it relates to what we call "Westernization 3.0" of the Chinese language.

Secondly, Nida's translation theory, mainly his functional equivalence, has experienced a big "rise and fall" in Chinese translation circles since its introduction into China's Mainland in the 1980s. A typical case can be reflected from the age in which "people don't discuss translation without quoting Nida" to that in which "people don't discuss translation without criticizing Nida". However, few discussions have been carried out concerning technical translation (E-C). Presumably, it is agreed that literal translation was and still is the most proper method in technical translation. Although some scholars stand for the applicability of functional equivalence in technical translation, they have expressed their views in a "by the way" manner on many occasions. In this context, therefore, this thesis will address the special issue concerning the preservation of natural/idiomatic Chinese language in technical translation from the perspective of functional equivalence, which is rare research so far.

Thirdly, a reasonable approach is applied to the non-technical part of the original technical text (source text/ST), which is a new approach. By examining the nature of the source text, this thesis divides the ST into the "technical part" and "non-technical part", which call for different translation strategies/methods. "Standardized translation" is good for the technical part, whereas functional equivalence is highly recommended for the translation of the non-technical part.

1.2 Research Questions and Methods

In this thesis, the author is going to discuss

(1) the necessity of functional equivalence in technical translation from English into Chinese in the context of globalization;

(2) the applicability of functional equivalence in technical translation.

The research methods to be applied include selected case studies and comparative case studies.

1.3 Theoretical Framework

Under the guidance of functional equivalence, the thesis aims at exploring the nature of technical translation and the problems it faces in the context of globalization. As Nida puts it, "translating means communicating, and this process depends on what is received by persons hearing or reading a translation. What is important is the extent to which receptors correctly understand and appreciate the translated text", accordingly, "it is essential that functional equivalence be stated primarily in terms of a comparison of the way in which the original receptors understood and appreciated the text and the way in which receptors of the translated text understand and appreciate the translated text." In order to achieve this goal, Nida gives up the concept of the form of words and suggests the use of "kernel sentence" to deliver the meaning. Thus, the structure of language is totally deconstructed. Also, in order to better recognize and discuss matters of equivalence, Nida introduces the concept of "isomorphs", matters of likeness. For example, the numbers 2-4-8 and 16-32-64 may be said to be isomorphic since each successive number is the double of the preceding one. So it doesn't matter whether the translated 16-32-64 is different from the original 2-4-8, as long as the mathematical formulas are representations of what they refer to, which means functional equivalence is achieved. And then Nida goes on to establish some principles for producing functional equivalence. Realizing that there are too many different types of situations in technical translation, the thesis adopts a translation strategy that classifies the source text into the "technical part" and the "non-technical part". Finally, as Nida adds, "what is needed are not elaborate formulas or theories, but translators with unusual sensitivity to the resources of language, the importance of culture, and the art of translating."

1.4　Outline of the Thesis

1　Introduction

    1.1　Research Significance

    1.2　Research Questions and Methods

    1.3　Theoretical Framework

    1.4　Outline of the Thesis

2　Literature Review

    2.1　Studies on Nida's Theory

        2.1.1　Development of Functional Equivalence

        2.1.2　Framework of Functional Equivalence

        2.1.3　Criticisms of Functional Equivalence

    2.2　Studies on Technical Translation

3　The Need for Functional Equivalence in Technical Translation

    3.1　The Irresistible Trend of "Westernized Chinese 3.0" Calls for Attention

        3.1.1　Technical Translation Has Been a Big Driver to "Westernized Chinese" in the Context of Globalization

        3.1.2　Technical Translators Should Play Their Due Role in the Process of Chinese Westernization

    3.2　Functional Equivalence Is Needed in Creating Authentic Chinese in Technical Translation

        3.2.1　"Translating Means Translating Meaning" Also Applies to Technical Translation

        3.2.2　Technical Translators Could Still Be Free and Should Aim at the Upper Rigging

4　On Applying Functional Equivalence to Technical Translation

    4.1　Translating Standards for Technical Texts

4.2   Translating Strategies for Technical Texts

4.3   Technical Translators' Striving Direction in the Context of Globalization

5   Conclusion

Working Bibliography

II   Literature Review

…

III   Data Collection

…

IV   Representative Case Studies

…

V   Conclusion

…

Working Bibliography

(1)   Bassnett, Susan. *Translation Studies* [M]. Shanghai: Shanghai Foreign Language Education Press, 2004.

(2)   Ma, Huijuan. *A Study on Nida's Translation Theory* [M]. Beijing: Foreign Language Teaching and Research Press, 2003.

(3)   Newmark, Peter. *A Textbook of Translation* [M]. Shanghai: Shanghai Foreign Language Education Press, 2001.

(4)   Nida, Eugene A. *Language and Culture*: *Contexts in Translating* [M]. Shanghai: Shanghai Foreign Language Education Press, 2001.

(5)   Nida, Eugene A. *Toward a Science of Translating* [M]. Shanghai: Shanghai Foreign Language Education Press, 2004.

(6)   Nida, Eugene A. & Charles R. Taber. *The Theory and Practice of Translation* [M]. Shanghai: Shanghai Foreign Language Education Press, 2004.

(7)   陈刚. 翻译学入门[M]. 杭州：浙江大学出版社，2011.

(8)   范祥涛. 研究生科技语篇英汉翻译教程[M]. 苏州：苏州大学出版社，2011.

(9)   方梦之，等. 科技翻译教程[M]. 上海：上海外语教育出版社，2008.

(10) 郭建中. 科普与科幻翻译——理论、技巧与实践[M]. 北京：中国对外翻译出版公司，2004.

(11) 霍金. 时间简史[M]. 许明贤，吴忠超，译. 长沙：湖南科学技术出版社，1998.

(12) 钱寿初. 中文科技语言文字的西化问题[J]. 编辑学报，1996(4).

(13) 谭载喜. 奈达和他的翻译理论[J]. 上海外国语学院学报，1989(5).

(14) 王佐良. 新时期的翻译观[J]. 中国翻译，1987(5).

(15) 叶子南. 高级英汉翻译理论与实践 [M]. 北京：清华大学出版社，2001.

(16) 叶子南. 论西化翻译[J]. 中国翻译，1991(2).

(17) 余光中. 怎样改进英式中文——论中文的常态与变态[J]. 明报月刊，1987(10).

（1）论文题目

①双语撰写。汉语在前，英语在后。

②论题目的。要让导师和评审委员会及其他读者/听众等明了有关论题，即毕业论文的大致范围和方向。

③题目简明。上述所给论文题目不仅简洁明了，而且具有视野和高度：《试析全球化视角下功能对等在中国科技翻译中的作用》（"On Applying Functional Equivalence to Chinese Technical Translation in the Context of Globalization"）。

④题目字数。原则符合要求（英汉字词数之比：60%）。

⑤暂定题目。即 working title，其中 working 意为"used as a basis for work, discussion, etc., but likely to be changed or improved in the future"（OALD 第 2036 页），如 working theory/hypothesis/agreement 等。

（2）选题的研究目的

通过将源语科技文本区分为"技术部分"和"非技术部分"两类，论文试图证明功能对等理论不仅适用于科技翻译，而且能够保持汉语的灵性和意合特征（见"摘要"）。

（3）选题研究的动机及意义

为求客观精确，科技语篇向来使用的是贴近字面的译法，但这常常会在实践中导致中文食洋不化。在全球化进程中，各种科技语篇涌入中国，导致大量西式中文出现在报纸、杂志和网络上，甚至进入日常语言交流领域。本论文讨论了西式中文的现象/译例，尝试分析奈达的功能对等在科技翻译中的应用，看其能否在不影响译文准确性的前提下，利于翻出更为自然的译文（见"摘要"）。

从细处出发，上述段落还（可/应）说明以下几个重要问题：

①选题的根据/背景；

②选题的突破/价值（理论视角）；

③选题的突破/价值（实践角度）。

据此，我们不难发现，在全球化进程中，西方科技文章不断进入中国，因翻译质量不高，西式中文译文频繁见于国内的报纸、杂志和网络上，甚至进入日常语言交流之中。论文（作者）试图运用世界著名翻译学者奈达的"功能对等"理论，分析英文科技文本的汉译，看看能否在不影响译文准确性的前提下改变汉译中的西化现象，最终利于产出更为自然的译文。如果真的有效，那就具有了实践意义上的"选题价值"——是理论联系实际的一个较好的案例（参考"摘要"并做扩展解读）。

④英文阐释选段：

Actually, the relation between globalization and translation could be a subtle one. …

The significance of this research lies in the following points.

Firstly, …

Secondly, …

Thirdly, … "Standardized translation" is good for the technical part, whereas functional equivalence is highly recommended for the translation of the non-technical part.（应引用部分

共 387 words，详见本部分案例之"1.1　Research Significance"第 2—5 段）

（4）研究问题和研究方法

①the necessity of functional equivalence in technical translation from English into Chinese in the context of globalization；

②the applicability of functional equivalence in technical translation；

③selected case studies and comparative case studies。

（5）理论框架

这部分在 BA 论文中并非必不可少，但从高要求出发，我们鼓励有能力的学生不妨一试。如果要求撰写"当前国内外对该论题的大体研究"，则是对所研究课题的宏观了解及把握；如果要求撰写"理论框架"，则是微观综述。这部分可以写成当前研究的理论综述，也可以写成研究方法的基础介绍，也可以是二者的结合。

详细地说，你要把研究放在一个清晰的理论框架下来探讨，这就是所谓的概念化过程（conceptualization）。基于已有的、成熟的（established）相关研究，我们往往对自己所提出的研究问题（research questions)可以有某些假设（hypotheses）。实证研究检验的是假设。这里的关键是，预期的假设不是你的凭空猜想，而是根据有关理论和他人的研究可以"分析"或"推断"出来的，即需要有某种理据（theoretical grounding），你要阐述的是你做这种分析或推断的逻辑。这种分析不能仅仅根据你的想当然或者常识/直觉/一般知识（common sense/intuition/general knowledge）来判断。

不少学生以为在论文中单独介绍一下某个理论，就是有理论框架了，其实不然。任何理论框架的应用，关键是应用这一理论背后的推断逻辑（即对两个或多个现象之间具有某种关系的理性陈述）。为此，需要把理论涉及的主要方面放到你自己的研究情景（context）下进行具体化应用，包括概念定义、操作定义（conceptualization and operationalization）。

以下是选自学生论文开题报告中的"理论框架"部分：

Under the guidance of functional equivalence, … Finally, as Nida adds, "what is needed are not elaborate formulas or theories, but translators with unusual sensitivity to the resources of language, the importance of culture, and the art of translating."（应引用部分共 295 words，详见本部分案例之"1.3　Theoretical Framework"）

（6）论文撰写大纲

1　Introduction

　　1.1　Research Significance

　　1.2　Research Questions and Methods

　　1.3　Theoretical Framework

　　1.4　Outline of the Thesis

2　Literature Review

　　2.1　Studies on Nida's Theory

　　　　2.1.1　Development of Functional Equivalence

　　这个论文大纲/纲要属于比较成熟、完整的一类。详细之处，是"三级"目录。具体来看，

　　①"引言"一章，包含常见的三个组成部分：Research Significance、Research Questions and Methods（、Theoretical Framework）和 Outline of the Thesis。

　　②"文献综述"一章，包括该论文应该涉及的两大类文献：其一，关于奈达功能对等理论的研究现状（发展、框架、批评）；其二，关于科技翻译的研究现状。"文献综述"原则上该如何撰写，我们还将在第 4 章中做详细讨论。

　　③"科技翻译对功能对等理论的需要"一章，有关视角比较独特：

3　The Need for Functional Equivalence in Technical Translation

3.1　The Irresistible Trend of "Westernized Chinese 3.0" Calls for Attention

　　3.1.1　Technical Translation Has Been a Big Driver to "Westernized Chinese" in the Context of Globalization

　　3.1.2　Technical Translators Should Play Their Due Role in the Process of Chinese Westernization

3.2　Functional Equivalence Is Needed in Creating Authentic Chinese in Technical Translation

　　3.2.1　"Translating Means Translating Meaning" Also Applies to Technical Translation

　　3.2.2　Technical Translators Could Still Be Free and Should Aim at the Upper Rigging

　　④"试析功能对等在科技翻译中的作用"一章是论文/论题的重点内容，讨论了科技文本翻译的标准、策略以及科技翻译工作者在全球化背景下应努力的方向：

4   On Applying Functional Equivalence to Technical Translation

4.1   Translating Standards for Technical Texts

4.2   Translating Strategies for Technical Texts

4.3   Technical Translators' Striving Direction in the Context of Globalization

⑤"结论"一章应表明：通过对研究问题的分析论证，其结果如何？有何指导意义？有哪些方面需要继续研究？还存在什么不足之处？

⑥"参考文献"部分，即 working bibliography。由于 working 意指"you can use it at a basic level"（OALD 第 2036 页），因此各院校系所对论文写作的参考文献有一个底线要求。比如浙江大学对外语类本科毕业论文的参考文献数量要求是 10 篇/部中英文论文/著作（含专著、教材等）。其实多数学生最后的（working）bibliography 都（远远）超过底线要求。

（7）文献综述

本书主要讨论的文献综述局限于本科层次两种学位论文之文献综述。

顾名思义，"文献综述"（review of the literature）首先是对（论文研究问题/翻译实践问题）学术观点和理论方法的整理。其次，文献综述是评论性的（review 意指"评论"），因此要求论文作者带着本人批判的思维（critical thinking）或眼光来归纳和评论有关文献，而不仅仅是对相关领域、有关话题的学术研究、翻译实践的"甲乙丙丁戊"式的罗列或堆砌。评论的主线，要按照研究问题展开，换言之，别的学者/译者是如何看待和解决你提出的问题的？他们研究问题的理论/途径/策略/原则（theory/approach/strategy/principle）和解决问题的方式方法（solution/method/way/how-how）存在哪些值得吸收的地方，是否存在什么缺陷？综述要尽可能全面、完整、客观、公正，评论要做到既"典型"（typical）又"具体"（specific），避免"片面"（one or two sources only）、"偏见"（biased picture）、"无点评"（uncritical of the sources used）的做法。详见第 4 章。

（8）数据收集

①数据概念。

这里讨论的"数据"特指英文的 data。根据 RHWD（专为二语学习者编纂的 an ESL dictionary），data 指"individual facts, statistics, or items of information"；"a body or collection of facts; information"。

所谓数据，就是数值，也就是我们通过观察、实验或计算得出的结果。数据有很多种，最简单的就是数字。数据也可以是文字、图像、声音等。数据可以用于科学研究、设计、查证等。

②数据驱动研究。

考虑到 BA/BTI 生不可能达到（纯）理论研究的程度（theoretical sophistication/theory-driven research/pure translation studies），我们应该多多鼓励学生进行数据驱动研究（data-driven research）和应用理论研究（applied translation studies）。换言之，毕业生应从现有的理论（existing theory）或分析框架（analytic framework）出发进行数据驱动研究，通

过收集（自己的）数据来验证有关理论或分析框架是否可行。

从这个意义出发，我们毕业生进行研究的原创性和创造性（originality + creativity）表现在立足于学生自己的数据收集（data collection）、理论/框架对数据的运用（application of the theory or framework to your data）和亲历的研究过程（the research process you go through）。这种/类研究往往会取得意想不到的结果，甚至会"推翻""颠覆"原有的理论/框架。

③数据简单分类。

数据根据来源（origin）可以简单地分为可追溯性数据（retrospective data/intuitive data）和非追溯性数据（non-retrospective data/eyewitness data）两类。

④数据收集方式。

根据数据收集的不同方式/方法，数据收集方式/方法（manner of data collection）可基本分为 6 种：

i.　记录（note-making）；

ii.　采访（interview）；

iii. 日志（journal-keeping）；

iv. 问卷（questionnaire）；

v.　录音（audio-taping）；

vi. 录像（video-taping）。

⑤数据造假/操控。

收集到的数据未必一定是自然、真实的。信息、数据造假现象（manipulation of data）也是不少见的。根据顾曰国（2004: 163）：

"In terms of manipulation, there are

(a) naturally occurring data, that is, no interference;

(b) experimental data, that is, participants are put in a special circumstance for their performance;

(c) solicited data, e.g. participants' response is framed by the questions put to them."

⑥数据收集原则。

i.　真实原则（authenticity principle）；

ii.　自然原则（naturalness principle）；

iii.最大值背景信息原则（maximum background principle）；

iv. 最低限度信息操控原则（minimum manipulation principle）。

（参照顾曰国, 2002: 164-165）

数据收集后，接着是进行数据解读（data interpretation），即研究者要理解、解读出有关数据的意义。

这样，就为开题报告和论文撰写的可行性增加了"砝码"。于是我们自然过渡到了"代表性案例研究"。

（9）代表性案例研究①

例如，如何论证论文作者在开题报告中提出的一个论点：

论点之一	3.2.1　**"Translating means translating meaning" also applies to technical translation**
论证过程	After Mr. Yu Guangzhong wrote his article named "How to Correct Westernized Chinese—on the General and Metamorphic State of the Chinese Language", in which he discreetly classified westernized Chinese by syntactic character, from nouns, conjunctions, prepositions, adverbs, adjectives, to verbs, his argument was further revised by Qian Shouchu, who switched the focus onto the realm of technology discourse and reclassified westernized Chinese concerning technical translation into six categories (钱寿初, 1996). According to Qian, the problems concerning technical translation can be categorized as the following six points: Noun plague Pseudo-jargon Confusion concerning prepositions and conjunctions Adverbs and adjectives putting on airs Overuse of passive voice Halfhearted attempts at betterness To illustrate the problems, we can draw some examples from the translation of the book *A Brief History of Time*, which we believe enjoys a large readership in China and thus has a great influence on Chinese readers. **1. Noun plague** Unlike the Chinese language, technical English tends to use more abstract nouns as subjects, hence the weakening of the usage of verbs. Such a phenomenon is called nominalization. But in the Chinese language, subjects are more likely to be concrete nouns or people. And there are many simple, short Chinese verbs to replace those big, abstract nouns. For instance, a sentence like "The major problem in fabrication is the control of contamination and foreign materials" should be translated as "制造过程中的主要问题是如何控制污染和杂质". If translators don't pay attention, there could be some awkwardness. Here are some other examples. [Case I] [ST1] We go about our daily lives understanding almost nothing of the world (郭建中, 2004: 52) [TT1] 我们在几乎对世界毫无了解的情形下<u>进行日常生活</u>。 [Analysis] Here the word "进行" is a typical disappointing word that should not appear too frequently in the Chinese language. And the following is another case of stiff westernized

Chinese.

[Case II]

[ST2] The use of satellites makes it possible to observe the universe much better. (ibid: 71)

[TT2] 使用卫星，<u>使得</u>更好地观察宇宙成为可能。

…

（10）结论

以下是引自上述论文作者开题报告结论中的部分文字，集中于"结论"本身：

After careful analyses, we come to the conclusion that apart from the literal translation method, which is said to be the main method in technical translation, Nida's functional equivalence, which holds the view that "translating means translating meaning", is also applicable to technical translation and beneficial in preserving the paratactic features and uniqueness of the Chinese language in the context of globalization.

（11）参考文献（暂定）

参考文献一般是英文文献在前，中文文献在后，以英文字母顺序排列。具体规范参照、遵循 MLA bibliography format（国际标准）、GB/T 7714—2015（国内标准）以及 GB/T 7713.2—2022（国内标准）等。就国际标准而言，虽然也可以参考 APA 格式，但 APA 一般用于社会科学，而人文学科通常采纳 MLA 格式等。国内标准既参照了国际标准，也根据国内的具体情况采取并规定了更有利于学术规范化的做法。

以下是引自上述论文作者开题报告中的 working bibliography，共 17 项，其中包括英文专著（Susan Bassnett、Peter Newmark 和 Eugene Nida 等）、中文专著（如陈刚、郭建中等）、中文教材（如范祥涛、方梦之等）、中文论文（如钱寿初、谭载喜、叶子南、余光中等）、译著（如霍金《时间简史》的汉译本）等。

Working Bibliography

Bassnett, Susan. *Translation Studies* (3rd ed.) [M]. Shanghai: Shanghai Foreign Language Education Press, 2004.

Ma, Huijuan. *A Study on Nida's Translation Theory* [M]. Beijing: Foreign Language Teaching and Research Press, 2003.

Newmark, Peter. *A Textbook of Translation* [M]. Shanghai: Shanghai Foreign Language Education Press, 2001.

Nida, Eugene *A. Language and Culture: Contexts in Translating* [M]. Shanghai: Shanghai Foreign Language Education Press, 2001.

Nida, Eugene A. *Toward a Science of Translating* [M]. Shanghai: Shanghai Foreign Language Education Press, 2004.

Nida, Eugene A. & Charles R. Taber. *The Theory and Practice of Translation* [M]. Shanghai: Shanghai Foreign Language Education Press, 2004.

陈刚. 翻译学入门[M]. 杭州：浙江大学出版社，2011.

范祥涛. 研究生科技语篇英汉翻译教程[M]. 苏州：苏州大学出版社，2011.

方梦之，等. 科技翻译教程[M]. 上海：上海外语教育出版社，2008.

郭建中. 科普与科幻翻译——理论、技巧与实践[M]. 北京：中国对外翻译出版公司，2004.

霍金. 时间简史[M]. 许明贤，吴忠超，译. 长沙：湖南科学技术出版社，1998.

钱寿初. 中文科技语言文字的西化问题[J]. 编辑学报，1996(4).

谭载喜. 奈达和他的翻译理论[J]. 上海外国语学院学报，1989(5).

王佐良. 新时期的翻译观[J]. 中国翻译，1987(5).

叶子南. 高级英汉翻译理论与实践[M]. 北京：清华大学出版社，2001.

叶子南. 论西化翻译[J]. 中国翻译，1991(2).

余光中. 怎样改进英式中文——论中文的常态与变态[J]. 明报月刊，1987(10).

更为详细的讨论，参看第 8 章。

3.3.2　BTI 论文开题报告例析

1．BTI 论文开题报告主要项目讨论清单

A List of Major Items for Discussion①

Working Title

摘　要

Abstract

1　Introduction

…

2　Outline of the Thesis

…

3　Theoretical Foundation

…

4　Typical Case Illustrations

…

5　Conclusion

…

Working Bibliography

2．开题报告例析二（BTI 论文）

BTI Thesis Proposal

Working Title

简明英语写作原则在英译宣传册

《走向世界的"和平"牌紫阳富硒茶》中的应用

Applying Plain English Principles to C-E Brochure Translation

---

① 该清单仅用于本书开题报告部分，实际操作可以省略，各校会有所差异。

—A Case Study Based on Translating

Heping Ziyang Se-enriched Tea Seeking Fame Around the World

中文摘要

本文是基于《走向世界的"和平"牌紫阳富硒茶》的英译实践而撰写的一篇翻译实践报告。原文以宣传手册的形式，分别从"得天独厚的资源""闻名遐迩的品牌""科学严格的加工""诚信灵活的经营"四方面介绍了紫阳和平茶厂及该厂著名产品紫阳富硒茶。本报告主要分析作者在翻译实践过程中的一个重要问题，即简明英语写作原则在英译宣传手册中的应用。在翻译实践报告中，作者结合英语宣传手册简洁易懂的语言特点，研究了"篇章布局合理""言简意赅""使用主动语态和人称代词 you"三种简明英语写作原则在提高译文质量方面的作用，以期为今后翻译类似文本提供一定的借鉴。

关键词：简明英语；宣传手册；写作与翻译

Abstract

（详见 **2.6**　摘要写法）

1　Introduction

This thesis is based on the author's C-E translation practice of *Heping Ziyang Se-enriched Tea Seeking Fame Around the World*, which will be published on the official website of Heping Tea Company to introduce its product Ziyang Se-enriched Tea to foreigners. Starting from the fame of the Company and Tea, the source text presents the blessed natural environment in Ziyang County, the superior quality of Ziyang Se-enriched Tea, scientific tea processing steps and the honest management of the Company.

China boasts the longest history of producing tea and this traditional drink is not only favored by Chinese people but also fascinates numerous foreign drinkers. More streamlined and simplified Chinese import and export procedures have allowed an increasing number of small-and-middle-sized enterprises like Heping Tea Company to sell their products to overseas clients. Against this background, the author received the translation project from the Heping Tea Company to translate its Chinese brochure into English.

In the course of translation, the author encountered some difficulties arising from the two aspects. In the first place, the source text is not logically organized, if translated into English literally, it will confuse target readers who depend heavily on clear logic for comprehension. In the second place, there are some repetitions, which are either Chinese cohesive devices or just errors made by the brochure writer. In English, however, repeated information should be avoided. If the Chinese rhetoric expressions and sentence structures in the source text were translated word-for-word into English, translationese would occur, making the target text awkward, foggy and over-long for target readers to understand.

Considering these translation difficulties and the plain, clear and easy-to-understand language style of brochures, the author applies the plain English principles to her translation. This thesis will give a brief account of plain English principles and then focus on the application of three principles, namely, be logically arranged and clearly organized, be concise and to the point, and use active voice and personal pronouns like "you".

2　Outline of the Thesis

3　Theoretical Foundation

3.1　Plain English

（1）论文题目

①双语撰写。符合要求。

②论题目的。将"简明英语写作原则"运用于宣传册《走向世界的"和平"牌紫阳富硒茶》之英译，即为 BTI 生毕业论文的大致范围和方向，是为汉译实践而撰写的一篇翻译实践报告。

③题目简明。符合要求，一目了然，且非常实际。

④题目字数。原则符合要求。考虑到中文题目"偏长"（因宣传册名称本身较长），故英文正题后增加了副标题（subtitle）——A Case Study Based on Translating *Heping Ziyang Se-enriched Tea Seeking Fame Around the World*。

（2）选题的研究目的

该论文是一份翻译实践报告，主要分析论文作者在翻译实践过程中的一个重要问题——简明英语写作原则在英译宣传手册中的应用。在翻译实践报告中，作者结合英语宣传手册简洁易懂的语言特点，研究了"篇章布局合理""言简意赅"和"使用主动语态和人称代词 you"三种简明英语写作原则在提高译文质量方面的作用，以期为今后翻译类似文本提供一定的借鉴。

（3）翻译实践报告介绍概述

①第一个自然段，开宗明义：This thesis is based on the author's C-E translation practice of *Heping Ziyang Se-enriched Tea Seeking Fame Around the World*, which will be published on the official website of Heping Tea Company to introduce its product Ziyang Se-enriched Tea to foreigners. …

②第二个自然段，简述了作者接受这个翻译任务的背景：越来越多的中小茶叶公司要走向世界，需要做自我推介，因此，"the author received the translation project from the Heping Tea Company to translate its Chinese brochure into English"。

③第三个自然段，作者特别提及自己在翻译过程中碰到的诸多问题，如源语文本的逻辑问题、表达问题、句子结构问题以及信息处理问题等。

④第四个自然段，作者针对翻译过程中的问题，提出试图解决问题的方法："Considering

these translation difficulties and the plain, clear and easy-to-understand language style of brochures, the author applies the plain English principles to her translation."具体地说，是"三大原则"，即"the application of three principles, namely, be logically arranged and clearly organized, be concise and to the point, and use active voice and personal pronouns like 'you'"。[①]

（4）理论基础

作为毕业论文之 BTI 生翻译实践报告，对必不可少的"理论基础"环节或其翻译理据的支撑/合理性，进行了简明、到位的介绍和阐释：

3　**Theoretical Foundation**
3.1　Plain English
3.1.1　The History of the Plain English Campaign
3.1.2　The Definitions of Plain English
3.1.3　The Principles of Plain English
3.2　Brochure
3.2.1　Definition of Brochure
3.2.2　Types of Brochures
3.2.3　Designing the Brochure
3.3　The Relations Between Writing and Translation

（5）典型案例举证

这一部分不可或缺，其意义在于，不少本科生对自己的翻译实践（翻译项目、翻译报告、翻译任务等）是否典型、正确、可取、可行尚未形成成熟的观点/看法，需要将自己的"典型案例"或有代表性的案例列举出来，让导师和答辩委员会分析、判断。

就上述论文（即翻译实践报告）而言，作者通过分门别类，从三个方面的举证/典型案例来证明自己这篇实践报告的合理性和可行性（下述英文由本书作者修改提供）：

英文表达	举证说明
Specifically, the author has put the following three major plain English principles into use when translating this brochure.	论文作者从三大简明英语原则用于翻译推介词的三个主要方面进行论证。
第一原则	第一方面（举例）
Logical arrangement and clear organization	[Case 1] [ST1] … [TT1] …
第二原则	第二方面（举例）
Conciseness and pointedness	[Case 2] [ST2] … [TT2-1] … [TT2-2] …

---

① 这里引用的英文（出自学生真实文稿）有需要改进的空间。

第三原则	第三方面（举例）
The use of active voice and personal pronouns like "you"	[Case 3]
	[ST3] …
	[TT3-1] …
	[TT3-2]

（6）结论

作者在对翻译实践报告做一概述后，得出以下结论：

"From the analysis of the application of plain English principles to the C-E brochure translation practice, the author concludes that these principles and strategies are effective in creating a plain English language style of brochure to achieve its purpose of informing and appealing to readers. The author thus recommends that translators doing brochure translation adopt plain English principles in their translation to improve translation quality."

（7）参考文献（暂定）

详见前述"（11）参考文献（暂定）"。

3.3.3　BA 与 BTI 论文开题报告要点比较

通常，BA 论文及开题报告和 BTI 论文及开题报告在 15 个方面存在异同点（表 3-1）。

表 3-1　BA 和 BTI 论文及开题报告之异同点

项目	BA 论文及开题报告要点	BTI 论文及开题报告要点
题目	①更显学术（研究）型 ②可以是应用研究型	①更显专业（应用）型 ②可以是专业和学术相结合
摘要	①按照研究型论文章法撰写 ②按照实践研究的套路撰写	①开门见山——发现问题，解决问题 ②开宗明义——目的为何，结论为何
关键词	①呼应论文题目，紧扣中心思想 ②论题要点节点，主题高频标签	①论题突出实践，理论技巧并行 ②分清口译笔译，讲明应用意义
目录	①结构纲要多层次 ②三级四级均可以	①结构纲要层次简明 ②三级目录基本足矣
绪论	①详尽较长层次多 ②背景理据重意义	①简明扼要背景清 ②专业行业相结合
数据收集	①数据收集必不可少 ②讲清来源分析处理	①数据收集必不可少 ②讲清来源分析处理
研究问题	①理论实证均可 ②主观客观结合	①强调具体问题 ②紧密联系实际
方法论	①强调学科研究方法 ②明确具体研究方法	①强调翻译实践方法 ②技巧方法理论任选

（续表）

项目	BA 论文及开题报告要点	BTI 论文及开题报告要点
文献综述	①较为全面完整典型 ②10 篇/部文献为底线	①突出论题抓重点 ②围绕重点写综述
理论框架	①鼓励运用适用理论 ②设定框架研讨问题	①可有可无建议尝试 ②原则方法必不可少
典型例证	①初步讨论，典型例证 ②论证论题，以获通过	①初步讨论，典型案例 ②实践论证，以保通过
结论	①结论清晰，给人启示 ②论文价值，最终体现	①结论清晰，给人启示 ②论文价值，最终体现
参考文献	①论文专著，应有尽有 ②研究特色，充分体现	①论文专著，原著译著 ②实践研究，特色尽显
翻译实践	①不设规定，但可尝试 ②有闲有能，不妨一试	①不可或缺，占比大头 ②提倡 E-C，鼓励 C-E
总字数	①两千开题+两千文献概述+两千译文 ②两千开题+两千译文亦可接受	①两千开题+一万译文（评述后补） ②两千开题+足量译文（译文及评述后补）

3.4　开题报告答辩①

3.4.1　概念简述

1．开题答辩

该答辩由"开题报告"（proposal/thesis proposal/research proposal/proposal for the thesis）和"答辩"（oral proposal defense/proposal defense）两部分组成，目的是检查论文是否具备了应有的思路性、方向性、可行性等问题。

2．开题意义

通过学生（BA/BTI candidate）的答辩，其导师和答辩委员会会确定论文写作（含学术论文、翻译项目及研究、翻译实践报告、口译实证研究等）的基本逻辑/基本原理是否可行、学生是否可以开始论文初稿的撰写等。它实际体现了毕业生对学位论文或项目设计的初期规划阶段的成果，也是对毕业论文进行全面审核的一种形式，或称为"先期验收"（advance check/check in advance）。

3．开题管理

开题报告答辩实则是一种现代化的科学管理手段。开题报告是毕业生（即开题者）对毕业论文（亦是科研课题、翻译工程/项目等）的一种文字说明材料，是一种新的应用写作文体，这种文字体裁是随着现代科学研究活动计划性的增强和科研选题程序化管理

---

① 请结合参见"10.1.1　开题报告答辩概念"。

的需要应运而生的。当然，本科毕业论文开题报告的陈述与答辩，（远）没有一些重要科研课题或项目的汇报、答辩那样严格、严谨、严密。

4. 开题程序

开题报告是毕业论文答辩委员会对学生答辩资格审查的依据材料之一，因此，答辩涉及答辩申请、认可及批复、答辩时间及地点、答辩委员会组成、秘书安排等基本步骤、流程问题。

3.4.2 程序与管理

1. 开题修改

导师须对学生的开题报告（假设导师已经进行了论文撰写的必要指导）进行先期把关，修改是必不可少的环节。当导师确认开题报告的质量"达标"了，学生才能提出开题报告的答辩申请。

2. 答辩申请

管理这一环节的严格做法之一是学生填写书面申请（如表 3-2、表 3-3 所示）[①]。

表 3-2　申请 BA 学位论文开题报告答辩评审表

学生姓名	年级	研究方向	导师姓名	职称	填表日期
论文题目（中文）					
英文题目（英文）					
阅读文献情况及文献翻译[②]情况					
开题报告全文及内容提要	（1）报告文本（全文另附）。 （2）内容提要如下：				
导师对开题报告的评语	 导师签字：				

[①] 所推荐的表格仅供管理参考之用，属于一种高度理想状态。各校都有自行操作的简化表格设计。

[②] 有些学校 BA 毕业论文开题报告的组成部分中没有"文献翻译"这一项内容。

	姓名	专业、职称	导师类别	院/系/所
答辩委员会成员及意见				

答辩委员会主席签字：

开题报告答辩日期：

表 3-3　申请 BTI 学位论文开题报告答辩评审表

学生姓名	年级	研究方向	校导师姓名	职称	填表日期

论文题目（中文）	
英文题目（英文）	
翻译实践部分情况介绍	
开题报告全文及内容提要	（1）报告文本（全文另附）。 （2）内容提要如下：
导师对开题报告的评语	

学校导师签字：

实践导师签字：

	姓名	专业、职称	导师类别	院/系/所
答辩委员会 成员及意见				
	答辩委员会主席签字： 开题报告答辩日期：			

3．浙江大学做法

浙江大学对全校本科生采取"整齐划一"的做法，即本科生毕业论文（设计）的组成部分包括"文献综述和开题报告"。具体见表3-4、表3-5、表3-6。

表3-4　毕业论文（设计）题目（专页之一）

一、题目：

二、指导教师对文献综述和开题报告的具体要求：

指导教师（签名）＿＿＿＿＿＿＿＿

年　　月　　日

表3-5　指导教师对文献综述和开题报告具体要求

目　录

指导教师对文献综述和开题报告具体要求

一、文献综述

　1　背景介绍

　2　国内外研究现状

　　2.1　研究方向及进展

　　2.2　存在问题

　3　研究展望

　4　参考文献

二、开题报告

　1　问题提出的背景

　　1.1　背景介绍

　　1.2　本研究的意义和目的

　2　论文的主要内容和技术路线

> 　　2.1　主要研究内容
>
> 　　2.2　技术路线
>
> 　　2.3　可行性分析
>
> 　3　研究计划进度安排及预期目标
>
> 　　3.1　进度安排
>
> 　　3.2　预期目标
>
> 　4　参考文献
>
> 三、外文翻译
>
> 四、外文原文

表 3-6　毕业论文（设计）文献综述和开题报告考核

对文献综述、外文翻译和开题报告评语及成绩评定：			
成绩比例	文献综述 占（10%）	开题报告 占（15%）	外文翻译 占（5%）
分　值			
开题报告答辩小组负责人（签名）＿＿＿＿＿ 　　　　　　　　　　　　　　　　　年　　月　　日			

4. 答辩流程

（1）学生陈述。由毕业论文开题报告申请人陈述 5—20 分钟。建议使用 PPT 或 Word/PDF 等文件形式对开题报告加以展示，并向答辩委员会（事先）提供书面开题报告。这样，图文并茂，音像结合，有利于整个进程高效率进行。完整的陈述部分包括以下 10 项内容：

①论文题目；

②研究目的（含在摘要中）；

③创新点/实用价值/理论价值等（含在摘要中）；

④研究问题和研究方法（可含在摘要中或另作话题）；

⑤文献综述和理论框架（开题报告的组成部分）；

⑥论文纲要（三级目录）；

⑦典型案例论证（实践的或理论的，或二者相结合的）；

⑧初步结论及/或存在的不足；

⑨进度安排；

⑩其他未尽事宜。

（2）专家点评。学生完成陈述之后，由答辩委员会委员点评，时间长短因人而异，有话则长，无话则短，完全看评委的点评。学生应认真听取开题答辩评委的意见，随时记录好答辩委员会的问题和意见，并言简意赅地回答评委的问题。

（3）答辩结果。答辩通过的学生需认真按计划完成之后的各阶段工作。答辩未通过的同学，会后应尽快与自己的导师协商并及时做出修改，待时间、条件成熟后，申请开始第二次开题报告的答辩。通常，只要导师认真对待开题报告，其专业/学术水平和判断能力原则上都会确保学生通过答辩。在论文开题报告答辩通过之前，学生不能进入毕业论文正式撰写阶段或毕业设计阶段。

（4）答辩成绩。答辩委员会评出成绩，答辩秘书填好开题答辩记录。答辩成绩一般分为合格与不合格两种。未通过开题答辩者，不得进入毕业论文撰写阶段；未通过开题答辩，擅自进行毕业论文撰写者，毕业论文成绩视为无效。

5. 延期答辩

（1）学生出于各种原因延期参加开题报告的答辩，实属正常现象。

（2）延期答辩者需要办理申请延期答辩的手续。

（3）从严格管理的角度出发，有关程序之一是延期答辩者须填写"延期答辩申请表"（见表3-7）。该申请表适用于三种类型延期答辩者：

①延期开题报告答辩者；

②延期预答辩者；

③延期毕业/学位论文答辩者。

表 3-7　延期答辩申请表

姓名		学号		班级		导师姓名	
已修学分	必修课						
	选修课						
①开题报告答辩时间		①　　（ √ / × ）					
②预答辩时间		②　　（ √ / × ）					
③毕业论文答辩时间		③　　（ √ / × ）					
正常毕业答辩时间							
延期答辩理由							
预期答辩时间							
本人签字				导师签字			
主管领导签字				备案存档时间			

　　综上所述，本科生毕业论文的开题报告是用文字体现的论文总构想，因而篇幅不必太长，但要把计划研究的课题、如何研究、如何实践、理论适用等主要问题写清楚。开题报告可以是文本形式的，也可以是表格形式的，或者二者相结合的。

　　采用表格形式（起码包括表格形式），是把要报告的每一项主要内容转换成相应的栏目，这样做，既避免遗漏，又便于评审者一目了然，把握要点。

　　为确保"完美"，本书推荐表格形式与文本形式相结合的方法。

◎研究与实践思考题◎

1.　根据本章关于 theoretical framework 的介绍，独立分析以下这篇 BTI 毕业论文中有关该主题的内容。

章节标题	**2　The theoretical foundation**[①]
具体阐释段落	**2.1　Plain English** **2.1.1　The history of the Plain English Campaign** 　　In 1979, the Plain English Campaign was launched in the United Kingdom, advocating for the application of plain English in all public information, such as forms, leaflets, contracts, agreements and official documents. The Campaign soon gained governmental support and the British government officially adopted the plain English policy in 1982. 　　Besides the United Kingdom, other English-speaking countries like the United States, Australia, and Canada also carried out plain English policies for the most simple, clear and easy-to-understand expressions. Moreover, plain English, originally adopted only by governments, has spread to other public fields, and law, health and business, and many fields have made their own guidelines for document writing. (张煜，康宁，于巧峰 & 车云宁, 2012) **2.1.2　The definitions of plain English** 　　The British organization Plain English Campaign's definition of plain English is "we define plain English as writing that the intended audience can read, understand and act upon the first time they read it. Plain English takes into account design and layout as well as language." (http://www.plainenglish.co.uk/files/howto.pdf) 　　The definition given by the Plain Language Action and Information Network (PLAIN) in the United States is: 　　　　Plain language (also called Plain English) is communication your audience can understand the first time they read or hear it. Language that is plain to one set of readers may not be plain to others. Written material is in plain language if your audience can: find

---

① 本书提供真实文稿，文中错误与不足在所难免。下同。

what they need; understand what they find; and use what they find to meet their needs.

(http://www.plainlanguage.gov/howto/guidelines/FederalPLGuidelines/index.cfm)

Robert Eagleson, a formal linguistics professor at the University of Sydney defined plain English as:

Clear and straight-forward expression, using only as many words as are necessary. It is a language that avoids obscurity, inflated vocabulary and convoluted sentence construction. It is not baby talk, nor is it a simplified version of the English language. Writers of plain English let their audience concentrate on the message instead of being distracted by complicated language. They make sure that their audience understands the message easily (as cited by 张煜 et al., 2012, pp. 20-21).

Although these definitions depict plain English in different ways, the essence is the same, that is to "use simple, concise and easy-to-understand English in (writing) documents."

2.1.3　The principles of plain English

According to the guide: *How to Write in Plain English* on the website of Plain English Campaign (2014), the main ways to make writing clearer are:

- Keep your sentences short
- Prefer active verbs
- Use "you" and "we"
- Use words that are appropriate for the reader
- Don't be afraid to give instructions
- Avoid nominalization
- Use lists where appropriate

In the United States, the Plain Language Action and Information Network (PLAIN) (2014), a group of federal employees from many different agencies and specialties who support the use of clear communication in government writing, also put forward many writing techniques. Among the most common are:

- Logical organization with the reader in mind
- "You" and other pronouns
- Active voice
- Short sentences
- Common, everyday words
- Easy-to-read design features

The European Commission launched the Fight the Fog Campaign in 1998 and released a booklet *Fight the Fog: Write Clearly* (Wagner, 1998) for all its writers and translators of English to help them write clearly and make sure the message ends up in the readers' mind:

- Put the reader first
- Concrete, not abstract
- Active verbs, not passive

- Making sense—managing stress
- KISS: keep it short and simple
- False friends and other pitfalls

Twelve years after the Fight the Fog Campaign, the European Commission started the Clear Writing Campaign in 2010. Unlike the former one masterminded only by English translators, the new campaign is wider-based, with a steering group from several Commission departments: the all-important Secretariat General, the Legal Service, DG Communication, DG Human Resources (training) and DG translation. Its booklet (European Commission & Directorate-General for Translation, 2010) offers and illustrates 10 top tips for clear writing:

- Think before you write
- Focus on the reader—be direct and interesting
- Get your document into shape
- KISS: keep it short and simple
- Make sense—structure your sentences
- Cut out excess nouns—verb forms are livelier
- Be concrete, not abstract
- Prefer active verbs to passive—and name the agent
- Beware of false friends, jargon and abbreviations
- Revise and check

In the book *Theory and Practice of Non-literary Translation*, Chinese scholar Li Changshuan (李长栓, 2004) concluded several plain English guides and booklets (including the above first three) into thirteen basic principles:

- Be logically organized and clearly arranged
- Be concise and to the point
- Introduce new information on the basis of the old information. Present every action in a logical order, and put the most important information at the end of a sentence if necessary
- Use short sentences
- Use active voice

Sentences in the active voice are shorter and clearer, while in the passive voice longer and vaguer. When we write, the active voice should almost take up 90% of a text. But you can still employ passive voice in some sentences when it is necessary, such as to stress the receiver of the action, to put new or surprising information at the end, or to evade responsibility.

- Avoid nominalization

Verbs, not nouns, are preferred in English. Many nouns ending in "-ion" are simply verbs in disguise, but they make the sentence obscure. Turn them into corresponding verbs to make the sentence clearer.

●Use words that are appropriate for the reader

In plain English, complicated, abstract, Latin, foreign and archaic words or jargon that are not familiar to the audience should be avoided. Don't use a phrase if a word can do.

●Prevent vagueness and ambiguity by putting modifiers in the right places and avoid a series of noun attributes and prepositional phrases

●Try personal pronouns

●Avoid an implied sexual bias

●Use positive language

Use negative sentences as less as possible, especially double negatives, which take more time to comprehend. Simply turn them into positive ones.

●Keep an appropriate visual design

●Name the agents of each action and put the actions in the order in which they occur.

2.2　Brochure

2.2.1　Definition of brochure

Brochures are printed publications that promote the products and services offered by a business or that promote the image of a business or an organization by providing general or specific technical information important to a target audience. The goal of a brochure is to inform or to persuade or both. (Alfred, Brusaw, & Oliu, 2007, p. 54)

2.2.2　Types of brochures

The two major types of brochures are sales brochures and informational brochures. Sales brochures are created specifically to sell a company's products and services. Informational brochures are created to inform and educate the reader as well as to promote goodwill and raise the profile of an organization. (Alfred et al., 2007, pp. 54-55)

2.2.3　Designing the brochure

Before you begin to write, determine the specific purpose of the brochure: To provide information about a service? To sell a product? To educate readers about a public health issue? You must also identify your target audience (general readers). Experts? Potential or existing clients? Understanding your purpose, audience, and context is essential to creating content and design that will be both rhetorically appropriate and persuasive to your target audience. (Alfred et al., 2007, p. 55)

2.3　The relations between writing and translation

Translation is a form of writing. The only difference between the two is their references. The reference of writing is either direct experience or indirect experience while that of translation is always indirect experience. Direct experience plays a supporting role in the comprehension of source text. Therefore, it is commonly recognized that the principles of writing should also be followed in translation. (李长栓, 2004, pp. 13 & 158)

2.　根据本章关于 theoretical framework 的介绍，独立分析以下这篇 BA 毕业论文中有关该主题的内容。

1　Introduction	

1.1　Significance of This Study

…

1.2　Research Questions

…

1.3　Theoretical Framework

　　This study is influenced by two basic concepts: purpose and choice, which exist in the text-production process as well as the translational activities. In this study, literary stylistics will be employed to provide a theoretical foundation for the analysis. Shen Dan's distinction between linguistic form and fictional facts, coupled with their mutual influence, is regarded as the basic model of argumentation (Shen, 1995: 19). Leech and Short's checklist for analysis provides practical guidance when the theories are applied to analyzing the selected text at four levels, namely, the lexical categories, the grammatical categories, figures of speech, and cohesion and context (Leech & Short, 2007: 61-64).

　　To evaluate the translation of fictional style, the *Skopostheorie* and its three rules will serve as the yardsticks with reference to the context. The fictional styles of four levels are measured against the *Skopos*, and deficiencies, if any, will be exposed and discussed.

1.4　Research Methodology and Data Collection

…

3.　有些学校的英语专业把"文献翻译"作为 BA 学位论文开题报告的一部分，有些学校则没有。在此，特提供有关文献（ST）的出处（出于篇幅原因，ST & TT 省略），仅供参考。

BA 学位论文·文献翻译[①]	
SL excerpts from	Williams, J & A. Chesterman, *The Map—A Beginner's Guide to Doing Research in Translation Studies*. Shanghai: Shanghai Foreign Language Education Press, 2004.
Mode of translation	Full translation
The source text	
Source Text Analysis	
…	
Comparison of Translations and Their Source Texts	
…	
Translation with Commentary	
…	
Translation Quality Assessment	
…	

---

① 本书提供真实译稿（选自浙江大学英语专业本科生毕业论文），文中错误与不足在所难免。

Technical Texts

…

The Place of Technology in Translator Training

…

Terminology and Glossaries

…

The target text

源文本分析

……

译文和源文本的比较

……

加注翻译

……

翻译质量评估

……

科技文本

……

科技在翻译培训中的地位

……

术语和索引

……

4. 特提供 BTI 生选择按照 BA 学位论文写作要求而独立进行的文献翻译，仅供参考。

Literature Translation	
SL excerpts from	Dollerup, Cay. *Basics of Translation Studies*. Shanghai: Shanghai Foreign Language Education Press, 2007: 97-104.
Mode of translation	Full translation
The source text	
Internalised linguistic features	
Alliteration, wordplay, puns …	
Jokes, cartoons …	
Poetry, songs …	
Strategy and modes …	

Language pairs	
…	
Translator competence	
…	
Geographical differences	
…	
Cultural differences	
…	
The Target Text	
内化的语言特征	
头韵，俏皮话，双关语	
……	
笑话，漫画	
……	
诗歌，歌曲	
……	
策略与方式	
……	
语言对	
……	
译者的能力	
……	
地理差异	
……	
文化差异	
……	

5.　根据本章关于 thesis proposal 的介绍，独立分析以下这篇 BA 毕业论文开题报告（主要部分）。

Proposal for BA Thesis

By ×××[①]

Working Title:

Slang Translation of Chinese _Kung Fu_ Fiction

—**A Case Study of _The Deer and the Cauldron_ from the perspective of _Skopostheorie_**

中文标题：

目的论视角下中国武侠小说中俚语的翻译研究

——以《鹿鼎记》为例

---

① 选自浙江大学英语专业本科生毕业论文开题报告的真实文稿，文中错误与不足在所难免。

摘　要

陈刚（2006）和吴丛明（2011）的研究都强调了跨文化翻译的重要性，并研究了在武侠小说《鹿鼎记》英译过程中所偏重的翻译策略（归化和杂合化）。本文正是从中受此启迪，运用目的论的相关理论，以案例分析的方法研究此小说中的俚语在汉英翻译过程中所使用的处理方法。作者认为，综观《鹿鼎记》的翻译，目的论在其许多俚语翻译过程中，被证明是颇为有效的。在具体翻译过程中，需要考虑如何确定特定的翻译技巧，诸如直译、意译和省略等，这就取决于译者所要达到的目的。

关键字：俚语翻译；武侠小说；目的论；可读性；《鹿鼎记》；翻译技巧

Abstract

The writing of this thesis gains inspiration from Chen Gang (2006) and Wu Congming (2011) who have laid special emphasis on cross-cultural translation and its preferred strategies (*domestication* and *hybridization*) in translating the *kung fu* fiction *The Deer and the Cauldron* into English. By applying the *Skopostheorie* (about *readability* in this case) to the Chinese-English translation of slang to be dealt with in the thesis, this Author deems it highly useful in the specific rendering of many slang(y) expressions in the said fiction, concerning how decisions would be made in choosing such specific translation techniques as literary translation, free translation and omission.

Keywords: slang translation; Chinese *kung fu* fiction; the *Skopostheorie*; readability; *The Deer and the Cauldron*; (some) translation techniques

Outline of the Proposal

1　Introduction

A noticeable phenomenon is that Chinese culture, especially literature, has attracted a large proportion of Western people's attention, which can be to some extent, traced from Mo Yan's winning the Nobel Prize in literature. A considerable number of translators are devoted to translating the masterpieces of Chinese literature, both at home and abroad. Featuring rich Chinese characteristics and no corresponding genre that can be found in other cultures, the Chinese *kung fu* fiction seems not witness prosperity in the translation industry. In accordance with Xiao (2011), he extended that the published English versions of Chinese *kung fu* fiction were characterized by a small amount, supposed to be resulted from the wide cultural gap between different cultures (pp. 43-45). It is a prerequisite that in cross-cultural communication, the acceptability and favor rank the first for the purpose of stimulating the readership of a certain text in another language, and especially in an absolutely different culture. It is the ground that the *Skopostheorie* leans against. This theory, established by Hans Vermeer, lays emphasis on translation as an activity with an aim or purpose, and on the intended audience of the translation. Within the framework, the concept of the translation itself is highlighted, and it posits all translating is acting and that all acting is oriented (Andrew, 1998). It is supposed that the functional approach has a great affinity with *Skopos* theory, while the function of translation is dependent on the knowledge, expectations, values and norms of the target readers (Kussmaul, 1995). Evidently, a person nurtured within a place is bound to be greatly influenced by the local environment and culture, which can be perceived by his speeches, or rather, words. When it comes to the Chinese *kung fu* fiction, where a considerable number of slang and dialects are supposed to appear, it is of no doubt burdens the translators to deliver the cultural information that contained to the target readers. Nevertheless, Jin Yong's last masterpiece *The Deer and the Cauldron*, whose English version was given by John Minford, has enjoyed a great readership in western countries. Vermeer's *Skopos* theory (2000) treats translation as a form of action. *Skopostheorie* is expected to equip the translators with a framework for exploring significant aspects of translation without losing sight of their inter-relatedness. Thereinafter, a case study of the translation of the slang and dialects within will be analyzed for the purpose of providing *Skopos* framework with empirical data.

1.1　Rationale and Its Significance

The studies of slang translation have developed increasingly, as the employment of slang has witnessed huge prosperity in our daily conversations, in TV series, in literature works, etc. On the other hand, research on the translation of the Chinese *kung fu* fiction has been conducted by a lot of scholars. But the case is that although scholars have comprehensively probed Chinese *kung fu* fiction, it still remains a blank among the present research. There are two reasons that explain the significance of this thesis. Firstly, in the studies of slang translation, relatively few have focused on the C-E translation, let alone those in Chinese *kung fu* fiction. As a matter of fact, the majority of the research efforts are paid to the E-C slang translation, most of which appear in TV series and movies. This thesis, has tried to investigate the C-E translation techniques that were applied in slang translation in *The Deer and the Cauldron*, which is regarded as a milestone in Chinese *kung fu* fiction. Secondly, the *Skopostheorie* has been proved to be very useful in applied texts, but few of the studies have put an eye on its application in literature works. This thesis has aimed at probing the slang translation in *The Deer and the Cauldron* from the perspective of *Skopostheorie*, and finding out the relationship between the translation techniques and their *Skopos*.

1.2　Research Questions

In order to probe the slang translation in *The Deer and the Cauldron*, three questions serve as the thread for the thesis. First and foremost is what translation techniques are preferred in translating the slang contained in *The Deer and the Cauldron*. The next is what impacts the translation techniques have on the translated version of the slang. The last one is what the relationship is between the translation techniques and their *Skopos*.

1.3　Research Methodology and Data Collection

The study is intended to investigate what strategies are preferred in the process when translating the slang contained in the Chinese *Kung fu* fiction. A case study of *The Deer and the Cauldron* was conducted so as to probe the relationship between the translation techniques and their *Skopos*. Slang that appears from Chapter 1 to Chapter 20 was selected as the subject, which in further declaration acts as proof that the translation techniques chosen were in line with the translator's purpose/ *Skopos*.

1.4　Outline of the Thesis

Chapter1　Introduction

    1.1　Rationale and Significance of the Study

    1.2　Research Questions

    1.3　Research Methods and Data Collection

Chapter 2　Literature Review and Theoretical Framework

    2.1　About Slang

    2.2　About the *Skopostheorie*

    2.3　About Minford's Version of *The Deer and the Cauldron*

Chapter 3　Case Studies of Slang Translation

    3.1　The Translation Techniques used in *The Deer and the Cauldron*

        3.1.1　Literal Translation

        3.1.2　Free Translation

        3.1.3　Omission

    3.2　The Translating Techniques and Their *Skopos*

Chapter 4　Conclusion

Bibliography

2　Literature Review and Theoretical Framework

2.1　About Slang

In accordance with the *Collins COBUILD Advanced Learner's English-Chinese Dictionary*, *Slang* "consists of words, expressions, and meanings that are informal and are used by people who know each other very well or who have the same interests".

Yao (姚玲, 2005) posted that slang had enjoyed huge popularity in our daily lives, in literature works, in newspapers as well as in TV series and movies. The author also pointed out that as a style of language, slang is born to be interwoven with culture. As a matter of fact, the slang translation is expected to explain the culture contained in the ST (Source Text) in a way that was understandable for the TL (Target Language) readers. A fact that cannot be ignored is that translation, as a bridge of two or more languages, is aimed at representing the ideas and thoughts of ST in another language. None of the slang is an exception. Slang, largely coming from the subculture group, contributes a lot to the expression and delivery of subculture within a certain social group.

Lu (卢艳春, 2005) examined slang's pragmatic function and its translation approaches through the case study of *Water Margin*'s English version. It is supposed that the novel originates from daily life and illustrates its culture. The *Water Margin*, known as the Chinese vernacular novel, contained a great deal of daily conversations, in which slang takes a considerable proportion. She pointed out that the pragmatic function varies when slang is employed in different contexts, and that four main approaches are used in *Water Margin*'s slang translation, i.e. literal translation, free translation, the combination of literal and free translation, and omission. According to Lu, Sidney Shapiro's version of *Water Margin*, has achieved the goal of "pragmatic equivalence", which was put forward by an English translation theorist, Leo Hickey. In Hickey's theory, the perlocutionary acts hit the priority in the translating process. As a result, the TT is required to be equivalent to ST both in pragmatic function and pragmatic meaning so as to make the target readers get a similar understanding to the ST readers.

Gao (高俊雪, 2010) also put an eye on the slang translation in the *Water Margin*, especially on three expressions. In translating "撮鸟", Shapiro respectively used "the bird", "knave", "wretch", "scurvy knave", and "scoundrel" in the TT in order to serve different cultural images and contexts. When comes to "泼贼", Shapiro adopted such a version as "filthy rogue", "dirty robber" and "filthy wretch". In terms of "奸贼", "treacherous thief" and "treacherous knave" were chosen. It seems that though to translate the same Chinese expression, different alternatives are available under different circumstances.

A noticeable fact is that so far, though researching efforts have been paid to the slang translation, most of the current researches focus on the E-C translation. Among the C-E translation studies, those on slang translation in literature works take a small proportion, let alone the Chinese *kung fu* fiction.

2.2 About *Skopostheorie*

Research on translation theories has long and increasingly been recognized in translation studies. Stipulated by different guidelines, translators may produce various versions given the same source text.

Hans J. Vermeer has done pioneering work in shedding light on translating and interpreting, especially for the establishment of the *Skopostheorie*, which has been considered the center of the functional school of translation studies. Andrew (1998) has made an evaluation of Vermeer's *Skopostheorie* of translation. In the review, he thought highly of Vermeer's fundamental efforts in overcoming the difficulty of relating loyalty to the text-producer's or sender's intention, as the *Skopos* provides a higher standpoint allowing the translator to disregard the source text if necessary. He criticized that Vermeer's book is not readable, with abstract expressions, frequent digressions, and conceptual specifications. The author has also extended only when the theory can be grounded in empirical data, it can bring us new knowledge about translation, and that only in relation to actual culture-specific translation activity, including the ethical dimension, that a theory generate testable empirical hypotheses.

His point has been backed by Peter, Flynn (2004), who conducted an ethnographic study of literary translators in the Netherlands and Belgium. The findings were based on a qualitative data analysis of in-depth interviews with twelve translators of Irish poetry. However, the research focused more on translators, which may lead to a relatively subjective result. Furthermore, the research conducted attached the main focus on the translation of Irish poetry, making further exploration of other literature styles possible.

The *Skopostheorie*, being taken as a particular type of general functional theory, is well established on the ground of translation studies, and is duly referred to in all textbooks. As is pointed out by Kussmaul: "the fundamental approach has a great affinity with the *Skopostheorie*" (1995, p. 149). He also extended that the function of translation relies greatly on the knowledge, expectations, values and norms of the target-text recipients, and that in order to satisfy the *Skopos*, it is acceptable to modify, or even change the source text. A retrospective assessment was made by Schäffner (1997). According to the scholar, it is not the source text or the source-text recipients that matter; instead, during the process of translation, it is the prospective function or *Skopos* that defines the target text.

Nord (2005) has proposed her basic principles of functional translations:

The translation purpose determines the choice of translation method and strategy (principle of functionality).

The acceptability of translation purposes is limited by the translator's responsibility with regard to her/his partners in the cooperative activity of translation (principle of loyalty).

The translation purpose is defined by the translation brief, which (implicitly or explicitly) describes the situation for which the target text is needed.

The most important factor of this target situation defined by the translation brief is the function or hierarchy of functions expected to be achieved by the target text.

…

The function (or hierarchy of functions) intended for, and/or achieved by, the target text may be different from that or those intended for, and/or achieved by, the source text, as long as it is not contradictory to, or incompatible with, the source-text author's communicative intention(s). (pp. 142-143)

Fendos (2010) has extended that translation has developed into an era when the target-oriented approaches are placed more emphasis on. He put forward that:

The history of translation in the West reveals that theoretical discourse on translation has moved back and forth between source and target. In contemporary Translation Studies the pendulum is clearly swinging in the direction of the target. *Skopostheorie*, for example, describes translation as a purposeful action leading to a new situation or object. (p. 50)

Domestically, Zhang (张锦兰, 2004) emphasized that the *Skopostheorie* was regarded as the most important in the functional school of translation studies. And based on the theory, the researcher postulated a translator is always stipulated by a certain purpose or aim, so as to achieve the setting goal. It held that determined by the intended purpose of the target text, the translation approaches went against the conventional translation criteria, not seeming to conform to the source text and adapting to the receptors' cultural environment. It indicates that in cross-cultural communication, the mutual-interaction relies on true understanding and comprehension.

As a central theory of Functional School in translation studies, the *Skopostheorie* has been considered to be an integrated crystal, to which a lot of scholars' efforts amount. Li (李永秀, 2012) has made an introductory retrospect of the relevant scholars' theoretical contributions, i.e. Katharina Reiss, Vermeer, Holz-Manttari, and Christiane Nord, and further reaffirmed the importance as well as the practicality of *Skopostheorie*. In his study, two concrete cases were introduced for the expression of the theory's practical application. And within the study, the explicit purpose of a certain text is laid great importance, as it helps the translator to decide the translating strategies in the translating process.

It is assumed that during the translation process, a *Skopos* will serve as the thread, either for the recipients' acceptance or for the transmission of the cultural images. In line with a certain goal, a variety of strategies and approaches will be adopted to achieve the established purpose, or rather, the *Skopos*. Scholars have argued for the different strategies of foreignization and domestication, which lays emphasis respectively on the source text and the target reader. However, this problem seems to be solved by the emergency of the *Skopostheorie*. It just plays as a mediator, combining both of the approaches so as to make them act as its servants.

2.3 About Minford's Version of *The Deer and the Cauldron*

Though the theoretical literature matters, it is of importance to get the knowledge of the relevant empirical research, which may help to inform the recent research as well as provide the relevant data for further comparisons.

When comes to the current situation of translating the fiction of such a genre, Xiao (肖强, 2011) put forward that so far, though having achieved great success among Asian countries, the Chinese *kung fu* fiction is characterized by a small amount of English versions in paperback. Furthermore, the record of such translations in China's Mainland remained blank, while the solutions were supposed not yet been found owing to the wide cultural gap between the two absolutely different cultural backgrounds. It was estimated that the difference in politics, economics and culture between China's Mainland, Hong Kong, and Taiwan led to the differences in the translation and study of such kind of work. It should be admitted that the researcher's exploration to some extent, had arrested some scholars' attention, and promoted the development of the translation in such a genre. But merely a general landscape was presented in this paper, and case studies were exclusive, leaving us space for further investigation.

Chen's (陈刚, 2006) primary study of the samples selected from the English translation of Mr. Luis Cha's *The Deer and the Cauldron* showcased that the strategy of domesticating translation is considered to serve as the preferred approach in cross-cultural communication. An overall comparison has been made between the original text and John Minford's English version, and it demonstrates that the strategy of domestication was prominently applied in the translation of captions for each chapter, proper names, and the title of the book, as well as the images filled with culture meanings. A convincing conclusion was reached that the function and purpose of translation, the translators' view on translation, and the acceptability of cultural differences played a crucial role in the decision-making process. It is the work that inspires the current study, as it navigated a direction for further analysis, and offered a new eye to bind the specific translation strategies with the macro culture and macro society. Nevertheless, due to the limitation of length, the scholar seemingly did not pay more attention to the translation of detailed slang, which is also distinct in cultural recognition.

Cultural influence has long been the spotlight since the translating activity began. Wu (吴丛明, 2011) has noticed that the language serves as a carrier of the culture, which is manifested by the "cultural images". It is of no doubt that the transformation of the cultural image between two languages within different cultures is bound to cause a great deal of difficulties. Assuming that the approach of hybridization was adopted in John Minford's translation, the paper has analyzed the strategies and approaches in the delivery of cultural images by exploring from three dimensions, that is, the nicknames of characters, martial moves, and the terms of factions.

It seems that the translation strategies or approaches have been taken more seriously in translation studies. Wu (吴玉光, 2011) carried out a study on the English version of Mr. Louis Cha's *kung fu* fiction in the view of domestication and foreignization, and argued that the former strategy ought to be preferred to be introduced to English-speaking readers. It was illustrated that the translations should be in line with English linguistics and culture in order to increase its readership among the target readers. In the study, the author selectively made a comparison of the frequency of domestication and foreignization strategies in translating the names of places, names of characters, and martial styles, from which a conclusion has derived that in the translating process, the approach of domestication was preferred as the ultimate purpose of the English translation is to promote the *kung fu* fiction' readership in western countries. It is also the case that the study has neglected the analysis of the translation of the slang contained. What is more, it is the frequency of the adopted strategies that the research cared for, while the guiding theory of the translator was not taken into consideration.

Fortunately, the blank has to some degree, been made up for by some scholars. Zhao (赵路也, 2012) has pointed out that translation is considered to bear the responsibility in cross-cultural interaction. And since *kung fu* fiction is of particularly Chinese characteristics, it is of importance to fully deliver the relevant culture-loaned information to the target recipients so as to achieve the expected purpose. In this paper, the author initiated an investigation of some translation cases of Trinket's (the hero of *The Deer and the Cauldron*) discourses, and tried to develop an explanation in terms of the expression and delivery of cultural information. Nevertheless, the idea, that is, the theoretical framework that directs the translation progress seemed to be concealed.

Some researchers have tried to make the translation practices adhere to the theories. An increasing number of studies on the translation practice at home have been carried out from the perspective of *Skopostheorie*, as it gradually satisfies the needs of the target recipients and the initiators. Wu (2011) has investigated the translation of Trinket's (the hero in *The Deer and the Cauldron*) discourses in light of the functional school of translation studies. Nurtured in a brothel, the hero's speeches were bound to flow with vulgar slang. The researcher has analyzed some specific cases on John Minford's English translation of Trinket's slang, and found that the three primary rules contained in the *Skopostheorie*, i.e. *Skopos* rule, coherence rule, and fidelity rule, made the target text acceptable in the recipients' culture. The paper appreciated that the functionalism translation theory provides a macro-framework in the process of translating Jin Yong's martial arts fiction *The Deer and the Cauldron*, and makes it live up to the expectation of the mainstream in international cultural communication.

Tang (汤琳琳, 2013) has also conducted a study on the strategies for translating names and nicknames in martial arts fiction from the *Skopostheorie*. She has noticed that though the translation industry witnessed great prosperity, the development in translation of *kung fu* fiction seems to encounter a considerable amount of difficulties, such as the translation of names, nicknames of the characters, and the names of all sorts of movie types in martial arts. A noticeable fact was that few relevant fiction so far have been translated and published, let alone almost the Chinese translators were exclusive among those authors. In the paper, the author therefore analyzed the translation of names and nicknames of the characters in Mr. Louis Cha's *kung fu* fiction in the guide of the *Skopostheorie,* and postulated that the strategies of domestication and foreignization that were employed in the translating process were target-reader oriented, and was determined by the *Skopos* of the recipients' acceptance.

Recently, a review of the translation of *kung fu* fiction in light of the *Skopostheorie* was published, in which a case study on the *Fox Volant of the Snowy Mountain* was implemented, and thus a brief illustration is that literary translation is preferred demonstrating the genre itself, while free translation for presenting the original author's story-telling talent (吴雅莉, 2013). The paper has been a proponent for the *Skopostheorie*, as it presents a brand-new point for translation studies, both practically and theoretically.

3　Theoretical Framework

Generally, the *Skopostheorie* will be applied as the framework for the current research. It is anticipated that in the process of creating the English version of *The Deer and the Cauldron*, the translator was oriented by the acceptability of the target recipients. Given the hypothesis, the slang and dialects of the characters in the text are to be analyzed from the perspective of *Skopostheorie*.

4　Tentative Conclusions

With the acceleration of cross-cultural communication, translators are supposed to bear more responsibilities, serving as the inter-medium between people who share different cultures. It is anticipated that in order to satisfy the needs of the target-text recipients or the initiators, the *Skopos* theory is greatly applied in the translating process. It is assumed that this is also a guideline for translating the slang and dialects in Chinese Martial Arts fiction. This study, inspired by the *Skopos* theory, was developed to analyze the strategies that have been adopted when translating *The Deer and the Cauldron*, and thus provide the theoretical framework with vivid instances. It should be acknowledged that this research is exploratory, and there will be problems with the statistical model. One major drawback of the study is its inaccuracy, as the classification of the adopted strategies is subjective, which may interfere with the effectiveness of the results. Indeed, this study represents just a small step in this field and more studies are in need for more convincing and effective data.

Working Bibliography

[1] Chesterman, A. Hans J. Vermeer. A *Skopos* Theory of Translation: (Some Arguments For and Against) [J]. *Target*, 1998, 10(1): 155-159.

[2] Nord, C. *Translating as a Purposeful Activity: Functionalist Approaches Explained* (Translation Theories Explained) [M]. Shanghai: Shanghai Foreign Language Education Press, 2005.

[3] Schäffner C. *Skopos* theory. In: *Routledge Encyclopedia of Translation Studies* [Z]. London & New York: Routledge, 1998: 235-238.

[4] Fendos, P. G., Jr. Culture, Looking Back, and Translation of the *Book of Changes* [J]. *Translation Quarterly*, 2010, 57: 50-85.

[5] Kussmaul, P. *Training the Translator* [M]. Amsterdam & Philadelphia John Benjamins, 1995.

[6] Flynn, P. *Skopos* theory: An ethnographic enquiry [J]. *Perspectives*, 2004, 12(4): 270-285.

[7] 陈刚. 归化翻译与文化认同——《鹿鼎记》英译样本研究[J]. 外语与外语教学, 2007(12): 43-47.

[8] 高俊雪. 浅析《水浒传》粗俗俚语的翻译[J]. 文学界（理论版）, 2010(2): 53-54.

[9] 李永秀. *Skopos*: The Central Theory of Functional Approach [J]. 海外英语, 2012, 24: 73.

[10] 卢艳春. 语用学与翻译——《水浒传》中粗俗俚语的翻译之管见[J]. 内蒙古农业大学学报（社会科学版）, 2008(3): 132-135.

[11] 汤琳琳. 从目的论看武侠小说中人名和绰号的翻译策略[J]. 甘肃联合大学学报（社会科学版）, 2011, 27(5): 103-106.

[12] 肖强. 中国武侠小说英译及其研究现状[J]. 内江师范学院学报, 2011, 26(3): 43-45.

[13] 吴雅莉. 目的论观照下武侠小说的英译——以《雪山飞狐》英译本为例[J]. 鸡西大学学报（综合版）, 2013, 13(11): 59-62.

[14] 吴丛明. 从《鹿鼎记》英译本看武侠文化意象的传递[J]. 巢湖学院学报, 2011(4): 75-79.

[15] 吴玉光. 从功能翻译理论看《鹿鼎记》英译本中韦小宝语言的翻译[J]. 长沙铁道学院学报（社会科学版）, 2011(3): 138-140.

[16] 姚玲. 英汉俚语翻译中的文化"传真"[J]. 乌鲁木齐成人教育学院学报, 2005, 13(1): 61-63.

[17] 张锦兰. 目的论与翻译方法[J]. 中国科技翻译, 2004, 17(1): 35-37+13.

[18] 赵路也. 闵福德《鹿鼎记》英译本韦小宝中误用语的翻译和跨文化信息的传递[J]. 湖北函授大学学报, 2012, 25(11): 111+122.

Research schedule

Date	Progress	Remarks
20××/月/日—月/日	确定导师、课题调研、确定研究范围、资料查阅、确定选题、完成译文、文献综述及开题报告，并进行开题答辩	导师认可
20××/月/日—20××/月/日	撰写初稿，并及时向导师进行进度反馈	导师认可
20××/月/日	上交初稿，请指导老师给予指导	导师认可
20××/月/日—月/日	完成二稿、三稿	导师认可
20××/月/日	上交定稿给本科生科（包括：目录中英文内容提要、论文定稿、译文及原稿、文献综述、开题报告、论文中文摘要等）	导师认可

6. 根据本章关于 thesis proposal 的介绍，在线上/线下寻找符合自己兴趣的 BTI 生毕业论文开题报告（不少于一篇），并对这些开题报告进行独立分析。

7. 根据本章关于 thesis proposal 的介绍，请在线上/线下寻找符合自己兴趣的 BA 生毕业论文开题报告（不少于一篇），并对这些开题报告进行独立分析。

8. 试着独立撰写一篇开题报告（BTI/BA）。

9. 可自发或有组织地举行一个学生开题报告讨论会或师生开题报告讨论会。

10. 请本专业专家做一场针对性强的毕业论文开题报告讲座。

第4章　如何发展（文献综述）

How to Develop (Literature-oriented)

◎学习目标◎

文献综述是论文写作、学术研究的重要环节，也是本科生初涉毕业论文写作的一项学术技能。本章所涉文献综述相对简单，不是作为学术论文的综述，而是特指在确定选题后作为本科毕业/学士学位论文组成部分的（文献）综述，即某一（较小的）研究领域文献的梳理、批评和总结。做好了文献综述工作，相当于完成了论文写作的一半。本章将帮助学生：

- 熟悉文献综述的概念；
- 学会文献综述的写法；
- 了解文献的基本概念；
- 了解文献收集的常用方法；
- 了解翻译常用数据库网站；
- 了解如何查找综述所需的文献；
- 熟悉 BTI/BA 本科生层级文献综述分类；
- 熟悉并学会 BA 论文文献综述案例分析；
- 熟悉并学会 BTI 论文文献综述案例分析。

4.1　文献综述概念

4.1.1　流程解读

就毕业论文撰写的主要流程而言，文献综述这一阶段或环节是"如何发展"的重要阶段，可谓一实质性环节。Buffa 指出："As you get past the beginning, into the meat of the paper, it is necessary to present the facts for your case. You need to prove that you have completed the research part of the research paper and that you've comprehended what you've read and its relevance to your subject."（1997: 82）可见，"如何发展"（how to keep it going）就是要做文献准备，做文献综述。

4.1.2　定义解读

（1）专家解读：A literature review is a written argument that promotes a thesis position by building a case from credible evidence based on precious research. It provides the context

<u>and the background about the current knowledge of the topic</u> and lays out a <u>logical case to</u> <u>defense the thesis position taken</u>.[①]

从画线部分解读，综述的文献要可靠、真实可信，学术含金量要高（如最好选择出自权威杂志、著名出版社、专家学者的文献）；要做有价值的、有关联度的研究；要提出逻辑性强的观点、立场，并提出论据加以论证。

根据文秋芳（2004: 258），"[an] <u>introduction is followed by a literature review</u> in which <u>the relevant existing literature is reviewed to indicate what has already been done and what</u> <u>problems remain to be solved</u>. Equipped with the knowledge of this chapter, the reader can visualize the research context where the link between the proposed study and the previous ones is displayed and its potential contribution to the existing literature is demonstrated"。

从画线部分不难读出，在毕业论文的"绪论"之后，应该"轮到"文献综述。在这一部分，要综述现有的、相关的文献，搞清楚哪些地方已经研究过了，哪些地方还存在什么问题，需要加以解决，你自己现有的研究和以前的研究有什么差异，有什么联系，从而努力为新的研究做出贡献。

换个视角说，文献综述在论文的开题报告中扮演着很重要的角色，因此，学生需要对已有的、相关的代表性成果及观点做出科学的、客观的分析评价（基于自己所参考的文献，即 working bibliography/references list），表述出能进一步探讨或突破的地方（包括口笔译实践），具体阐明本选题相对于已有研究之独到的应用价值、学术价值和社会意义，尤其是在应用/学术价值及社会意义等方面需要重点描述。作为本科毕业/学位论文组成部分的文献综述是对一个研究/实践问题的研究成果或进展进行相对全面的描述（需要叙述、分析、评论），务必避免文献综述与研究问题之间没有联系，或逻辑关系不强等内在问题。

（2）一般解读：文献综述（literature review/review of the literature）简称综述（review 或 survey/overview），是针对某一领域、某一专业或某一方面的课题、问题或研究专题搜集大量相关资料，通过分析、阅读、整理，提炼当前课题、问题或研究专题的最新进展、学术见解或建议，做出综合性介绍和阐述的一种学术论文。

文献综述是一种不同于毕业论文的文体。它不仅要求作者从概念上将其与"背景描述"（background description）区分开来，而且要求作者既要对所查阅资料的主要观点进行综合整理、陈述，还要根据自己的理解和认识，对综合整理后的文献进行比较专门的、全面的、深入的、系统的论述和相应的评价，而不只是相关领域学术研究的"堆砌"。

要写好一篇高质量的文献综述，起码从图 4-1 中可见一斑。

（3）特殊解读：本书讨论的文献综述，专指 BTI 生、BA 生（翻译方向）等学习阶段撰写的毕业论文中的一个重要组成部分。在此语境下的文献综述不会很复杂，篇幅也不会太长，它受限于本科生撰写学位论文所要求阅读文献篇/部数的底线。换言之，本科生撰写翻译论文，一般规定的 10 篇/部参考文献是下限，总字数下限是数百英文单词（若

---

① 引自美国专家 Prof. Lawrence A. Machi。

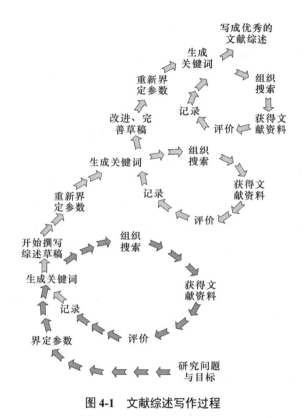

图 4-1　文献综述写作过程

作为论文正文中的一部分）/2000 英文单词（若作为开题报告中的一部分）。①因此，文献综述或文献概述是基于这 10 篇/部撰写的。换言之，在此范围内，文献综述是作者对所选课题以往同类研究成果（即 10 篇/部）的综合阐述与分析批评，不一定包括所有的资料，但一定要尽可能在上述范围内做到使你的文献**具有代表性、较为全面、学术性强、与时俱进**。文献综述应反映作者所选研究课题的下列要素：

● 选题动机目的；
● 相关研究情况；
● 何种研究方法；
● 解决了什么问题；
● 还留下什么问题；
● 本研究有何新意。

总体而论，综述不是开列清单，而是整理课题研究的逻辑进展，进而引入自己的研究与突破。好的文献综述，不但可以为下一步的学位论文写作奠定一个坚实的理论基础和实践论证，而且能表明撰写学位论文文献综述的作者对既有研究文献的归纳分析和梳理整合的综合能力，从而有助于提高对学位论文水平的总体评价。学位论文中不包含文献综述是不可想象的。

---

① 这个"规定"并非全国一个标准。

4.2　文献综述写法

4.2.1　综述过程

1. 文献综述过程

文献综述过程通常分为六个步骤，从表 4-1 中便可一目了然。

表 4-1　文献综述过程

文献综述过程（**the literature review process**）[①]	
步骤一（step 1）	选择论题（to select a topic）
步骤二（step 2）	查找文献（to search the literature）
步骤三（step 3）	展开论证（to develop the argument）
步骤四（step 4）	文献研究（to survey the literature）
步骤五（step 5）	文献批评（to critique the literature）
步骤六（step 6）	综述撰写（to write the literature）

2. 文献收集

确定选题后，收集文献便显得很关键。表 4-1 中，唯有步骤二（to search the literature）属于"工具运用"性质的问题。此处，to search the literature 可译成检索文献、查找文献、查阅文献等。

为方便学生收集文献，同时对文献的概念有一具体了解，我们有必要首先提供有关文献资料收集的常用方法，其次对文献概念进行举例阐释，这样更有利于学生做文献收集和文献综述。

其一，时常利用有关的检索工具，收集文献资料。

表 4-2 所示是本书作者特别推荐的译界/学界常用文献数据库（本校生所具有的免费上"内部网"之特权除外）。

表 4-2　翻译常用数据库网站

序号	中文指引	英文指引
1	中国知网	https://www.cnki.net/
2	科学引文索引数据库	Web of Science
3	谷歌学术搜索	Google Scholar
4	科研学术文献导航	Sci-Hub
5	施普林格旗下数据库	SpringerLink
6	中国特色话语对外翻译标准化术语库	http://210.72.20.108/index/index.jsp
7	中国思想文化术语	https://www.chinesethought.cn/

[①] 根据 Lawrence A. Machi 教授的观点列表。

（续表）

序号	中文指引	英文指引
8	中国核心词汇	https://www.cnkeywords.net/index
9	联合国术语库	https://unterm.un.org/UNTERM/portal/welcome
10	术语在线	https://www.termonline.cn/
11	中国规范术语	http://shuyu.cnki.net/index.aspx
12	语料库	http://yulk.org/
13	BCC 汉语语料库	http://bcc.blcu.edu.cn/
14	英国国家语料库	http://www.natcorp.ox.ac.uk/
15	美国当代英语语料库	https://www.english-corpora.org/coca/
16	英文写作学习网站	https://www.linggle.com/
17	英文重要索引语料库	https://lextutor.ca/conc/eng/
18	英国学术口语语料库	https://warwick.ac.uk/fac/soc/al-archive-deleted/research/base
19	英语语料库大全	https://www.english-corpora.org/
20	英语句子搜索网站	https://ludwig.guru/
21	中国特色大国外交话语	http://cdd.cascorpus.com/
22	智能化多语种教学与科研平台	https://instcorpus.com/

其二，善于利用原始文献和三次文献。

例如，从原始文献引注中找三次文献（即文献之文献）。三次文献包括综述、述评、百科全书、年鉴、手册、地方志、教科书、各类人名词典、各类地名词典、各类人名翻译词典、各类地名翻译词典等。再如，你阅读并引用从英文译成中文的论文、专著、教材，这些引文属于三次文献。从严谨的学术角度出发，最好找出原文献，因为翻译会造成某些错误，或使你"莫名其妙"。

总之，不管是电子文献，还是纸质文献，文献类型要全面，既要有期刊论文，也要有著作、译作、报纸文章、会议演讲等。

虽然要求 BTI/BA 生毕业论文参考、引用的文献数相对有限，仅仅不低于 10 篇/部，但实际情况往往是，学生收集到的有用文献是 15—20 篇/部，多的超过 40 篇/部，个别达到五六十篇/部。有鉴于此，我们需要对文献的概念有一个具体的了解。

其三，正确使用概念对文献进行基本分类。

所谓文献，指的是有历史价值或参考价值的图书资料。用作学术研究的文献，通常分为代表性/种子文献（seminal document/work/paper/article/data）与次要文献（secondary document/work/paper/article/data）。以下几点是需要特别了解的。

（1）代表性文献的有关释义。

①CCED 对 seminal 的释义：Seminal is used to describe things such as books, works, events, and experiences that have a great influence in a particular field.

②Academic Research Guide 对 seminal work 的释义：Seminal works, sometimes called pivotal or landmark studies, are articles that initially presented an idea of great importance or influence within a particular discipline.

③如何鉴别 seminal article：Seminal articles are referred to time and time again in the research, so you are likely to see these sources frequently cited in other journal articles, books, dissertations, etc. Identifying seminal articles relies heavily on your own thoroughness in the examination and synthesis of the scholarly literature. Typically, there will not be any explicit labels placed on articles, identifying them as seminal. Rather, you will begin to see the same authors or articles cited frequently. Keep in mind that seminal studies may have been published quite some time ago, so it is best to not limit your search results by date.（引自 Academic Research Guide, https://resources.nu.edu/researchprocess/seminalworks）

④国内的比喻释义：代表性文献展示相关研究领域大致的发展方向和脉络，仿佛人体的骨骼。

（2）次要文献的有关释义。

①国内的比喻释义：次要文献则是对重要文献（如代表性/种子文献）提出的问题进行更多视角、更多方向、更多层次的挖掘和补充，它们仿佛人体的血肉。在代表性文献的基础上，那些不那么经典的、重要的文献能帮助我们把综述类文章写得更加全面、充实，因此，不应低估次要文献的综述价值。

②William H. Hannon Library 的释义（含一次/原始、二次、三次文献内容）见表 4-3。

表 4-3　一次、二次、三次文献说明

Item	Primary	Secondary	Tertiary
Definition	Event being researched, created or experienced concurrently with the event being researched	Works that analyze, assess, or interpret a historical event, an era, or a phenomenon. Generally uses primary sources	Sources that identify, locate, and synthesize primary and secondary sources
Character-istics	First hand observations, contemporary accounts of the event. Viewpoint of the time	Interpretation of information, usually written well after an event. Offers reviews or critiques	Reference works, collections of lists of primary and secondary sources, finding tools for sources
Examples	Interviews, news footage, data sets, original research, speeches, diaries, letters, creative works, photographs	Research studies, literary criticism, book reviews, biographies, textbooks	Encyclopedias, bibliographies, dictionaries, manuals, textbooks, fact books

（Courtesy William H. Hannon Library）

其四，灵活使用检索工具和/或求助导师查找相关文献。

查找代表性文献的最为便利的、有效的途径，当然是请教导师或其他翻译教师、专家等。虽然翻译（学）方面的文献浩如烟海，导师或其他翻译学者的藏书汗牛充栋，同时我们鼓励学生 brain possible topics，但有时学生经过头脑风暴出来的主题并非导师（最为）擅长的研究领域或较为熟悉的行业领域，于是无法提供主要文献阅读清单或建议作为 long translation 的源语文本（STs）。若遇到这种情况，我们建议采用下面一些方法：

（1）确定最新研究选题，比如你想了解什么翻译（研究）话题较新、较热、较合适。

①（通过知网等）查找最近 2（—5）年发表在国内翻译类、外语类学术杂志上的涉"译"文章。

②发现比较新和/或热的理论研究话题有"国家翻译实践""知识翻译学""生态翻译学"等（仅举三例）。

③只要稍加/仔细分析，你就不难发现任东升、杨枫、胡庚申三位教授的论文或著作正是代表性文献，而其他围绕"种子"文献展开讨论的文献则是次要文献，而且数量不是很大。由于上述三位教授提出的理论正有待发展，因此 BA/BTI 生选择上述三个话题之一，都是可行的，也正好作为一次富有专业新鲜感的文献综述之学术训练，而且其难度（对"双一流高校的"的本科生而言）不是太大，尤其是知识翻译学这个话题。

（2）确定实践翻译主题，比如选择难易适中、理论联系实际的行业翻译。

①经过反复比较，认识到不是任何行业/专业或涉外实践/行业的口笔译材料都适合绝大部分本科生的。

②除非你是其他人文社科专业的 BA 生或其他非文科专业的理工农医等专业的学生（选择翻译为第二专业/学位或辅修），一般不建议选择诸如哲学、化学、医学、管理学、航空航天等专业的文献作为翻译课题/项目（long translation）。

③BTI 生最好选择难易适当的实用口笔译 ST 作为源语文本。因此，涉外旅游翻译或/和导译便是首选（涉外）行业翻译之一。比如，你不选择该行业的（会议）同传或交传，但可以选择景点（视译）同传、（参观点、购物点、医院等地的）陪同口译、涉及山水文学主题的导译等。再如，你可以选择众多笔译主题，包括公共服务领域（或语言景观/language landscape/linguistic landscape）翻译、菜单翻译、会展旅游翻译、"一带一路"旅游资料翻译等。

④（通过互联网搜索关键词"陈刚旅游翻译"或"陈刚导译"/"陈刚旅游导译"/"陈刚英语导译"等）搜索到笔者的代表性文献，如《旅游翻译与涉外导游》、《旅游英语导译教程》、《旅游英汉互译教程》（2.0 版/1.0 版）、《旅游翻译》等。

⑤通过笔者上述 primary publications（原始文献出版物；原始研究成果的一次出版物；主要出版物）①中的参考文献，便能找到这些出版物作者以及其他专家、学者的相关的重要文献和次要文献。

综上，BTI/BA 生不论选择翻译及述评主题，还是选择应用翻译研究主题，都可以（很）轻松地找到综述文献、理论框架，以及指导翻译实践的其他 strategy、principle、approach、methods、techniques 等。

（3）确定国家领导人著作或近年党代会报告、政府工作报告的翻译实践研究主题，

---

① 译文参考《简明英汉编辑出版词典》和必应词典。

比如选择《习近平谈治国理政》英文版或《习近平外交演讲集》等。

①经过导师的解释、说明，以及学生本人的反复思考，认识到《习近平谈治国理政》（四卷）和十九大、二十大报告，2022 年、2023 年总理政府工作报告的翻译难度之高，篇幅之长，对本科生挑战很大。

②《习近平外交演讲集》的两卷英文版，收录了习近平主席 2013 年 3 月至 2021 年 11 月在国际场合的演讲、讲话、致辞、发言等 136 篇。该书对于国内外读者深刻理解习近平外交思想的丰富内涵，深入了解构建人类命运共同体重要理念、习近平新时代中国特色大国外交伟大实践以及中国之路、中国之治、中国之理等，具有十分重要的意义。考虑到书中不少文本篇幅较短，翻译总体难度不如《习近平谈治国理政》，还是很适合专业水准较高的 BTI/BA 生作为毕业论文主题的。

③由于《习近平外交演讲集》（英文版）刚于 2022 年 7 月中旬出版，学生（不看官方译本）自己独立翻译其中难易程度较为适合的一篇及以上文章是完全可行的。有关理论框架、翻译原则、策略、方法等，可以由学生自己确定（因为有关翻译理论课程是必修的）。此外，学生还可以参考译者、专家、学者翻译或研究《习近平谈治国理政》（英文版）的论文、教科书等。这些代表性文献和次要文献很容易从数据库中找到。

文献收集的总原则是：代表性文献不能缺，次要文献要（相对）全面。

4.2.2　综述分类

文献综述根据本科生的研究目的（research purpose）或等级（BA level 或 BTI level），可分为以下两种：

（1）基本文献综述（the basic L/R）。即对有关研究课题的现有知识/翻译实践的现有水准进行总结和评价，以陈述现有知识的状况或现有译文的水平。

（2）高级文献综述（the advanced L/R）。即在选择研究论题/一种及以上译文之后，对相关文献（含译文）进行回顾、评述，确立研究论题，再提出进一步的研究/译文，从而建立一个研究项目，其性质可以是 pure translation studies 或 applied translation studies/practice-based translation research/practice-based interpreting research/product-oriented research/process-oriented research。

BA/BTI 生既可选择 practice-based translation/interpreting research、product-oriented research、process-oriented research，亦可选择 applied translation studies（最好得到导师认可）。

4.3　文献综述例析

4.3.1　BA 论文文献综述例析

1.　论文题目

A Functionalist Approach to English-Chinese Song Translation
—A Case Study of the 2008 Beijing Olympic Song

2. 参考文献

1. →Allvin, Raynold L. *Basic Musicianship* [M]. California: Wadsworth Inc., 1985.

2. √Calvocoressi, M-D. The Practice of Song-Translation [J]. *Music and Letters,* 1921, 2 (4): 314-322.

3. √Drinker, Henry S. On Translating Vocal Texts [J]. *Musical Quarterly,* 1950, 36 (2): 255-240.

4. →Kalisch, Alfred. The Tribulations of a Translator [J]. *Proceedings of the Musical Association,* 1914/1915, 41: 145-161.

5. Kamien, Roger. *Music: An Appreciation* [M]. 5th ed. New York: McGraw-Hill, Inc., 1992.

6. √M., W. Book-Review: *The Schubert-Mayrhofer Songs* [J]. *Music and Letters,* 1955, 36: 180-181.

7. →Nord, Christiane. *Translation as a Purposeful Activity: Functionalist Approaches Explained* [M]. Shanghai: Shanghai Foreign Language Education Press, 2001.

8. →Orr, C. W. The Problem of Translation [J]. *Music and Letters,* 1941, 22: 318-332.

9. √Peyder, Herbert F. Some Observations on Translation [J]. *Musical Quarterly,* 1922, 8: 353-371.

10. Spaeth, Sigmund. Translating to Music [J]. *Musical Quarterly,* 1915, 1: 291-298.

11. Strangways, A. H. Fox. Song-Translation [J]. *Music and Letters,* 1921, 2 (3): 211-224.

12. Strangways, A. H. Fox. Translation of Songs [J]. *Proceedings of the Musical Association,* 1922/1923, 49: 79-99.

13. →Shuttleworth, M. and Moira Cowie. *Dictionary of Translation Studies* [Z]. Shanghai: Shanghai Foreign Language Education Press, 2004.

14. √陈梦莉. 小议英文歌曲的汉译[J]. 三明高等专科学校学报, 2001, 18(1): 55-58.

15. √高延. 英文歌词翻译法之我见[J]. 锦州师范学院学报（哲学社会科学版）, 1998(1): 109-113.

16. √胡凤华. 评薛范著《歌曲翻译探索与实践》[J]. 中国科技翻译, 2007, 20(1): 56-58.

17. √李程. 歌词的英汉翻译[J]. 中国翻译, 2002, 23(2): 31-34.

18. √廖志阳. 外语歌曲翻译的标准和方法[J]. 艺海, 2007(1): 65-66.

19. √穆乐. 翻译实践中的功能主义主流与歌词翻译[J]. 运城学院学报, 2005, 23(1): 103-104.

20. √钱仁康. 谈歌词的翻译[J]. 上海音乐学院学报, 1999(4):54-58.

21. →孙慧双. 歌剧翻译与研究[M]. 武汉：湖北教育出版社, 1999.

22. √王浩, 温伟鸽. 浅谈英语流行歌曲的翻译[J]. 襄樊职业技术学院学报, 2006, 5(3): 114-116.

23. √王和玉. 从语篇分析角度看 Edelweiss 歌词的翻译[J]. 湖南城市学院学报, 2007, 28(4):85-87.

24. 王建国. 戴着"紧箍咒"的翻译艺术——《歌曲翻译探索与实践》评介[J]. 外语研究, 2006(4): 78-79.

25. √吴艾玲. 莱斯的翻译类型学与文本类型翻译在中国[J]. 南京理工大学学报（社会科学版）, 2005, 58(5): 58-62.

26. √薛范. 歌曲翻译探索与实践[M]. 武汉：湖北教育出版社, 2002.

27. 张锦兰. 目的论与翻译方法[J]. 中国科技翻译, 2004, 17(1): 35-37; 13.

28. →张美芳. 功能加忠诚——评介克里斯汀·诺德的功能翻译理论[J]. 外国语, 2005(1): 60-65.

29. √张志强. 英文歌词的翻译[J]. 河南师范大学学报（哲学社会科学版）, 1997, 24(2): 85-88.

30. →朱光潜. 诗论[M]. 上海：上海古籍出版社, 2001.

31. →朱志瑜. 类型与策略：功能主义的翻译类型学[J]. 中国翻译, 2004, 25(3): 3-9.

3. 文献综述

Literature Review[①]

Generally speaking, songs have attracted fewer translators compared with other text types, and even fewer in-depth or systematic studies have been conducted on song translation both at home and abroad.

I　In Western Countries

In Western countries, most of the related studies were about translating classical songs or operas within Indo-European languages, e.g. from German or French to English. According to several major journal databases online, the study on song translation dates back to 1915, when two articles sketchily discussing the topic came out. With an invaluable paper published in 1921 and an enlightening speech given in the next year, Strangways, the founder of *Music and Letter*, had aroused spirited discussions on the neglected art of song translation in 1920s (Calvocoressi, 1921; Peyder, 1922), and thus had contributed a lot to the initial study of the field. Later, Orr (1941) raised several problems in the translation of vocal music. E. G. Porter distinguished two kinds of song translation, the cribs and the re-creative transcription, in his translated song-book *The Schubert-Mayrhofer Song* (M. W., 1955). Drinker (1950) argued that an adequate English text for a vocal work should possess six requisites in *The Musical Quarterly*. However, little information after 1950s is available from online journal databases.

Although these papers had involved various aspects of song translation, such as the significance and difficulties of song translation, reasons why song translation developed slowly, and general principles and specific methods of song translation, it is important to note that they were all published on musicological journals and viewed the topic in the light of music studies, while no school of systematic translation theory has ever concerned the translation of songs—both shed light on the fact that song translation has not got its due attention in the circle of translation theory studies.

II　In China

Because of historical and political reasons, the translation of Russian songs has been prosperous from the 1950s through the early 1960s in China (Xue Fan, 2002), yet song translators in that period seldom conducted studies on the topic. Few translators had engaged in translating songs later, and the studies of song translation didn't emerge until the 1990s (Wu Ailing, 2005). Up to now, only about 30 papers related to the topic (most of which about the translation from English to Chinese) can be found in the Database of Chinese Journals (Hu Fenghua, 2007). Moreover, the terms addressing the topic never coincide in all the papers and part of the reason lies in that no scholar has ever given the activity of translating songs an explicit definition.

Among the researchers, Xue Fan, the distinguished translator of foreign songs (most of which are Russian), has made the greatest contribution for his publication of the first and sole monograph on song translation in China (2002), in which he has explored the topic systematically, summed up a series of song translation rules after carefully reviewing his own translating experience, and summarized the course of song

---

① 作者是浙江大学英语专业本科生。本书提供真实文稿，文中错误与不足在所难免。

translation in China. Other researchers have probed into the topic in terms of translating difficulties (Qian Renkang, 1999; Wang Hao & Wen Weige, 2006), translating standards (Liao Zhiyang, 2007), or specific translating methods (Zhang Zhiqiang, 1997; Gao Yan, 1998; Chen Mengli, 2001; Li Cheng, 2002).

All the efforts the above-mentioned researchers have made are from the perspective of translation practice rather than translation theory. Consequently, it is pleasant to find that a few scholars start to see the topic from translation theoretical approaches in recent years. Mu Yue (2005) tries to induce functionalism into the translation of song lyrics, though her discussion is not cogent enough. Another innovative study is Wang Heyu's attempt of comparing different Chinese versions of the song *Edelweiss* on the theoretical basis of discourse analysis in 2007.

On the whole, although the study of song translation got off to a late start in China, researchers of translation studies have become increasingly interested in the field. Nevertheless, in-depth studies on song translation still remain to be conducted, especially those from translation-theoretical approaches, and a number of aspects deserve to be further explored, for instance, standardizing and defining the term addressing the activity of translating songs, and systematically summarizing a whole system of procedures, principles and methods guiding the practice of song translation.

4.　综述例析

1）文献总量。上述所列全部有关文献共 31 项，大大超过本科生 BA 论文参考文献下限 10 篇/部。

2）文献引用。①就品质而言，所引文献，基本包括了重要书目，如首屈一指的薛范、专家钱仁康等；就德国功能派而言，引用诺德（Nord）是再合适不过的了。在歌曲译配方面，作者特别关注"小人物"的研究，所谓的译界"大咖"罕有涉及，而且着眼点很准。②就引用本身而言，31 项文献中，只有 2 项属于 works cited（参考文献/书目）。在其他 29 项 works consulted（引用文献/书目）中，打上"√"符号的文献有 16 项——出现在 Literature Review 部分；打上"→"符号的文献有 9 项——出现在 Research Background 和 Theoretical Framework 部分。其实，可以说有 25（16+9）项用于广义的"文献综述"中。因为"功能主义"是该论文采用的翻译理论，我们完全可以把二者合在一起，标题仍为"文献综述"，其中增加一节关于德国目的论/功能派的翻译理论文献综述。

3）综述分类。属于基本文献综述+高级文献综述级别。作为该文作者的导师，笔者综观全文并回顾当年答辩过程，并考虑截至当时之因素，很少有本科生能运用功能主义理论来指导歌曲译配的，可谓走出了一条新路。

4）综述过程。参照文献综述过程的六个步骤，作者完全达到了要求：

①选择论题——恰当、切题。

②查找文献——查找到的文献数目远超下限。

③展开论证——根据搜集到的文献，用功能主义理论指导歌曲译配算是"闯新路"。

④文献研究——通过文献研究、归类，整理出有足够说服力的 supporting evidence。

⑤文献批评——通过对歌曲译配的历史和正反两方面的情况进行学术批评，坚定了作者的论题：以功能主义翻译理论的系统应用为基础，并以北京奥运歌曲 *Forever Friends*

为例，对其英汉翻译过程进行详尽研究；试图说明歌曲翻译可分为原文分析与配乐改译两大步骤，并提出一系列指导原则和具体方法，以期在学术和实践两方面对全面理解歌曲翻译、有效指导翻译实践有所帮助。

⑥综述撰写——在前面五个步骤完成的基础上，作者顺利并高质量地去完成了最后一个步骤的任务。

⑦综述总评——文献综述（及理论框架）做得不错，确保了整篇论文有所创新，最后获得了优秀的成绩。

4.3.2　BTI 论文文献综述例析

1. 论文题目

On the Function-Oriented Translating Strategies of Modern History Exhibition in Tianjin Museum

2. 参考文献

1. √Nida, Eugene Albert and Charles Russell Taber. *The Theory and Practice of Translation* [M]. Leiden: E. J. Brill, 1969.

2. √Nida, Eugene Albert. *Language, Culture, and Translating* [M]. Shanghai: Shanghai Foreign Language Education Press, 1993.

3. √Nida, Eugene Albert. *Toward a Science of Translating* [M]. Leiden: E. J. Brill, 1964.

---

(1) Connor, Ulla. *Contrastive Rhetoric: Cross-cultural Aspects of Second Language Writing*. Shanghai: Shanghai Foreign Language Education Press, 2001.

(2) Grinder, Alison L., and E. Sue McCoy. *The Good Guide: A Sourcebook for Interpreters, Docents, and Tour Guides*. Florida: Ironwood Press, 1985.

(3) Li, Fang. *Translation Theories and Film Translating in China*. Salt Lake City: Academic Press Corporation, 2010.

(4) Mote, Frederick W. *Imperial China: 900—1800*. Harvard: Harvard University Press, 2003.

(5) Newmark, Peter. *Approaches to Translation*. Shanghai: Shanghai Foreign Language Education Press, 2001.

(6) ---. *A Textbook of Translation*. New York: Prentice-Hall International, 1988.

(7) √Nida, Eugene Albert, and Charles Russell Taber. *The Theory and Practice of Translation*. Leiden: E. J. Brill, 1969.

(8) √Nida, Eugene Albert. *Language, Culture, and Translating*. Shanghai: Shanghai Foreign Language Education Press, 1993.

(9) √---. *Toward a Science of Translating*. Leiden: E. J. Brill, 1964.

(10) Paine, Sarah CM. *The Sino-Japanese War of 1894—1895: Perceptions, Power, and Primacy*. New York: Cambridge University Press, 2005.

(11) Lum, Yansheng Ma, and Raymond Mun Kong Lum. *Sun Yat-sen in Hawaii: Activities and Supporters*.

Hawaii: University of Hawaii Press, 1999.

(12) Surhone, Lambert M., Miriam T. Timpledon, and Susan F. Marseken, eds. *Yamen*. Germany: VDM Publishing, 2010.

(13) Tianjin Municipal Bureau of Statistics. *Tianjin Statistical Yearbook 2004*. Beijing: China Statistics Press, 2004.

(14) *Cultural-China*. Web. 23 March 2013. <http://kaleidoscope.cultural-china.com>

(15) *Zs.gov*. 15 Oct. 2005. Web. 7 April 2013. <http://www.zs.gov.cn>

(16) 郭建中. 文化与翻译. 北京：中国对外翻译出版公司, 2000.

(17) 钱歌川. 英文疑难详解续篇. 香港：中外出版社, 1976.

(18) 王秉钦. 文化翻译学. 天津：南开大学出版社, 2007.

(19) 吴光华. 汉英综合大辞典. 大连：大连理工大学出版社, 2004.

(20) 朱蓉蓉, 王玉贵. 中国近现代史纲要. 苏州：苏州大学出版社, 2013.

3. 文献综述

Literature Review[①]

The American linguist, Eugene A. Nida, born on November 11, 1914, is a devoted translator and linguist.

He is prolific with his achievements unfolding in many areas. He is an expert in research in the Bible and a pioneer in Bible translation. He also stands out as a linguist.

Apart from putting forward many translation theories, he had been engaged in translation practices for a long time and made noticeable contributions. From structuralism to transformational generative grammar, from communicative function to modern semiology, Nida had instantly applied various theories to translation practice.

I Definition and Development of Functional Equivalence

Among all Nida's translation theories, the most notable and influential one was his dynamic equivalence, or functional equivalence. The former emerged in Nida's *Toward a Science of Translating* (1964) and was renamed to the latter in his work *The Theory and Practice of Translation* (1969).

In 1964, Nida's *Toward a Science of Translating* came out, in which he coined the concepts of formal equivalence and dynamic equivalence. "Formal equivalence focuses attention on the message itself, in both form and content", "in which the translator attempts to reproduce as literally and meaningfully as possible the form and content of the original" (159). However, Nida argued that languages differ so much in grammar, style and content that a formal equivalence is rare, as he wrote: "since no two languages are identical, either in the meanings given to corresponding symbols or in the ways in which such symbols are arranged in phrases and sentences, it stands to reason that there can be no absolute correspondence between languages. Hence there can be no fully exact translations" (156). On the other hand, dynamic equivalence aims at the naturalness of translation. It "is and therefore to be defined in terms of the degree to which the receptors of

---

① 该综述属于BTI论文中的文献综述，此处提供真实文稿，文中错误与不足在所难免。论文作者是南开大学翻译系本科生，保送浙江大学读研，导师为本书作者。

the message in the receptor language respond to is in substantially the same manner as the receptors in the source language" (Nida and Taber 24). That is to say, when translating, the translator should seek from the target language other expressions bearing the same performance with that of the source language. This argument, to some degree, dilutes the constant dispute over literal translation and liberal translation. It puts the receptors' response on its priority and focuses on the actual results in practice.

In his later work *Language, Culture and Translation*, Nida further expounded functional equivalence. In his opinion, there is a minimal level and maximum level of translation effectiveness, the former referring to "the readers of translated text should be able to comprehend it to the point that they can conceive of how the original readers of the text must have understood and appreciated it" (118) and the latter stating "the reader of a translated text should be able to understand and appreciate it in essentially the same manner as the original readers did" (118). Then anything below minimal level cannot be considered as functional equivalence and the maximum level is an ideal translation which a translator is always expected to achieve but can hardly reach.

A basic example of functional equivalence is when people describe something "as white as snow", snow does exist in this language system. But if translated to some place where people have never seen snow and rule this word out of their vocabulary, say, a tribe in Middle Africa, the translation could be more flexible by simply saying "very white". This is an example of dynamic equivalence at word level which is the fundamental unit in functional equivalence. There are even more complicated cases concerning grammar level, semantic level, text level and style level.

II Principles Governing Functional Equivalence

In his *Toward a Science of Translating*, Nida described dynamic translation as "the closest natural equivalent to the source-language message" (166), in which the essence is closest, natural and equivalent. Since these standards are a little bit abstract and cannot be employed as a criterion to measure the quality of a translation work, he further puts forward several requirements for dynamic equivalence. For a readable rendering, the foremost is to achieve naturalness. Naturalness means that when a bilingual reads the translation work, he would agree "Yeah! That is how we put it". A translation work can never be considered natural unless it conforms to the receptor language and culture as a whole, the receptor-language audience and the context of the particular message.

A. The Receptor Language and Culture as a Whole

In Nida's opinion, meaning is more significant than form and formal translation may impair communication between different cultures. Whether a rendering fits the receptor language and culture is not easy to notice. When a translation work obeys such a rule, readers probably do not take care, since the naturalness distracts their attention. A good translation work requires the naturalness of language on various levels: word classes, grammatical categories, semantic classes, discourse types and cultural contexts. Chinglish, which apparently carries the aura of the original work, is the reverse side of the principle. However, the removal of all origin trace is impossible (especially in translating terms identifying cultural specialties), since there are many cultural elements that cannot be naturalized.

In summary, the translation should be acceptable in terms of (i) lexicon; (ii) grammar; and (iii) culture.

B. The Target Audience

In this sense, the audience's responses are emphasized rather than texts. Before Nida, arguments on the quality of translation were mainly around source texts and target texts. Nida shifted the attention to how the target audience reacts to translation work. To what extent the target audience can understand and appreciate the target texts in the same way as the source audience do determines to what degree the translator achieves functional equivalence. One point to mention is that the experience and the decoding ability of the audience should be taken into account.

In a nutshell, this requirement focuses on how the target audience reacts to the translation.

C. The Context of the Particular Message

There are many details in the context of the particular message, like intonation and sentence rhythm. How does the translator deal with slang and vulgarism? How to avoid anachronisms? Apart from proper message of separate words, readability of the translation is also affected by how to arrange these words and how to select the style. A successful translation should also involve the right emotional tone to deliver the author's opinion objectively, and the proper characterization of individuals to better depict their features concerning social status, educational background, dialects, etc.

To sum up, several factors worth mentioning here includes: (i) figures of speech; (ii) style; and (iii) the author's point of view.

4. 综述例析

1）文献总量。参考文献总数 21 项，上述所列全部有关文献共 3 项。由于毕业论文的实际性质不同，就综述一种理论或 theoretical approach（指功能对等）而言，作者选择了奈达的有关 3 部著作，符合要求。总体来说，参考文献数量大大超过 BTI 生论文参考文献下限 10 篇/部。

2）文献引用。综述介绍奈达功能对等理论的 3 部专著，作者全部运用，综述总字数约 1100。

3）综述分类。属于基本文献综述级别，因为论文本身不存在理论创新和实践创新的地方。

4）综述过程。参照文献综述过程的六个步骤，作者完全达到了要求：

①选择论题——恰当、切题。

②查找文献——查找到的文献数目完全够用。

③展开论证——根据搜集到的文献，用功能对等理论来指导博物馆介绍词的翻译，完全站得住脚。

④文献研究——奈达自己是该理论的提出者，所以通过对其文献的研究、归类，整理出来的综述材料有说服力。

⑤文献批评——文献整理、批评得好。作者运用功能对等理论对天津博物馆的翻译实例进行了有效的分析，旨在通过运用功能对等理论分析天津博物馆的翻译文本，进一

步探讨其上升空间，为传播天津历史文化做出贡献。

　　⑥综述撰写——在前面五个步骤完成的基础上，作者顺利地、高质量地完成了最后一个步骤的任务。

　　⑦综述总评——文献综述做得不错，确保了较高水平地完成整篇论文，作者论文答辩成绩为优。

◎研究与实践思考题◎

1. 如何准确解读 BA/BTI 毕业论文中的文献综述？你有自己初步或比较成熟的观点吗？

2. 如何分别撰写 BA/BTI 学位论文中的文献综述？请不同专业（方向）、不同层级的学生用英文独立完成一篇文献综述。

3. 文献综述过程一般可以分几步走？书中的观点你赞同吗？你有自己的观点吗？开展一次（课堂）专题讨论会（全班或分组）。

4. 文献综述分类合理吗？有必要吗？选若干篇"上""中""下"水平的文献综述，分别做一书面评述，或开一次小型课外研讨会。

5. 独立重评本章"BA 论文文献综述例析"。

6. 独立重评本章"BTI 论文文献综述例析"。

7. 建议本书任课教师或翻译专业/方向课程负责人在大一（其他任何主题类型的）翻译课中，给学生开书单，提前布置有关文献阅读的任务。

8. 了解文献概念并熟悉查找文献的各种方法。

9. 了解、熟悉本章推荐的翻译常用数据库网站。

10. 撰写翻译常用数据库简介（言简意赅即可）。

第 5 章 如何理论（理论框架）

How to Theorize (Framework-oriented)

◎学习目标◎

理论思考，是新时代（重点高校）本科生不可或缺的能力，对有志攻读硕博学位的本科生来说尤为重要。将毕业/学位论文中的理论框架单独成章，有助于学生拓展理论思维，更是将论文内容推向纵深的重要和必要环节，同时也对本科生首次正式与理论"打交道"形成思维挑战、学术挑战、能力挑战、机遇挑战。理论框架与文献综述之间存在着互动、互文、互补、互证、互助、互利之关系。学会文献综述有利于理论框架的撰写，反之亦然。本章将帮助学生：

● 对理论框架及其在论文中的作用有一正确的认知；

● 多视角了解理论框架的多元诠释和解读；

● 较为全面地了解翻译理论框架的诠释和解读；

● 通过案例学习，了解、熟悉并掌握 BA 论文中理论框架的具体写法；

● 通过案例学习，了解、熟悉并掌握 BTI 论文中理论框架的具体写法。

5.1 理论框架认知

所谓"认知"，就是通过思维活动认识、了解。

我们在第 4 章指出，"就毕业论文撰写的主要流程而言，文献综述这一阶段或环节是'如何发展'的重要阶段"，那么本章可谓"进一步如何发展或展开"（how to keep it going further）的重要阶段。

本章标题比较通俗，意指在论文中如何说理、如何与别人理论（theorize）。用学术语言来表达，总该有一个或若干个依据或理据。换言之，你依据的标准、尺度是什么？有边界吗？有界限吗？如何在一个框架范围内说理——这就是本章要讨论的"理论框架"。

5.1.1 理论框架认知解读

（1）理论框架与文献综述的直接关系

毕业论文中的文献综述是 how to keep it going，而理论框架则是 how to keep it going further。在撰写毕业论文的过程中，我们不自觉地会发现：理论框架的（部分）内容是（可以）包含在文献综述里的。那么，通过综述，我们怎样来构建分析、研究等要运用的理论框架呢？

　　——纵向分析的（沿着时间轴将理论的起源、发展、成熟及未来归类整理）；

　　——横向分析的（对有关理论在国内外的研究现状做分析、归纳与整理）；

　　——从大到小的（从研究对象理论的外延到内涵，层层分剥至研究的领域和方向）。

　　一般而言，我们常用的理论框架是纵向分析与横向分析的结合，而从大到小更多的是在理论综述阶段运用。根据 Williams 和 Chesterman（2004: 91-92）："The literature review is a kind of meta-analysis, in which you select and critically review the most relevant existing research from the perspective of your own research topic. You do this in order to justify the theoretical framework, concepts and methods that you have decided to use, and to establish the background to your particular problem or research question. This literature review sets the scene for your contribution, and highlights the gap that your work aims to fill."

　　（2）理论框架概念解读

　　不少学生以为，只要在论文中或研究计划书中单独介绍一下某个理论，就是有理论框架了，其实不然。任何理论框架的应用，关键是应用这一理论背后的 logic（逻辑）与 reasoning（推理）。为此，你需要把理论涉及的主要方面放到你的研究情景（context）下进行具体化应用，包括概念定义、操作定义（conceptualization and operationalization）。以下，我们特引用国外对理论框架的种种解读[①]，帮助学生读者从多个视角来认知这个概念，并"各取所需"。这对本科生来说是一次很好的、难得的学术训练和思维训练。

　　【解读一】

　　The theoretical framework in a study works as a map for the research. After an initial reading of the literature, researchers often rewrite the original research question based upon the theoretical framework. It is during this stage that researchers develop hypotheses.[②]

　　【解读二】

　　A theoretical framework is the research from previous literature that defines a study's core theory and concepts. In social science research, previous research serves as the basis for future research. Social scientists use the theoretical framework to craft a logical argument for a need for their research.

　　【解读三】

　　The search for a theoretical framework narrows the research question and helps researchers create hypotheses. With the initial research question in mind, social scientists read all of the existing literature on the topic. While reading, researchers highlight different definitions of the same terms and the varying methodologies to find answers to key questions. Researchers develop a consistent definition for each concept and find the theories upon which their study seeks to build. The framework also reputes theories that oppose assumptions within the study. Critical analyses of the methodologies within the existing literature develop the methodology

---

[①] 较多篇幅地直接引用原文，是本书的一个特色，其目的是训练、帮助学生尽快具备撰写（翻译类）英文学术论文的能力。

[②] 参见 http://www.ask.com/world-view/theoretical-framework-5dc9afd72afb3440。

for a new study. <u>These separate elements create one theoretical framework.</u>①

【解读四】

The theoretical framework is supposed to <u>help the reader make logical sense of the relationships of the variables and factors</u> that <u>have been deemed relevant/important to the problem</u>. <u>It provides a definition of relationships between all the variables so the reader can understand the theorized relationships between them.</u>②

【解读五】

<u>A theoretical framework is a collection of interrelated concepts, like a theory</u> but <u>not necessarily so well worked-out</u>. A theoretical framework <u>guides your research, determining what things you will measure, and what statistical relationships you will look for.</u>

【解读六】

Theoretical frameworks are <u>obviously critical</u> in deductive, theory-testing sorts of studies. In those kinds of studies, <u>the theoretical framework must be very specific and well-thought out</u>.

【解读七】

Surprisingly, <u>theoretical frameworks are also important in exploratory studies, where you really don't know much about what is going on, and are trying to learn more.</u> There are two reasons why theoretical frameworks are important here. First, <u>no matter how little you think you know about a topic, and how unbiased you think you are, it is impossible for a human being not to have preconceived notions, even if they are of a very general nature.</u> For example, some people fundamentally believe that people are basically lazy and untrustworthy, and you have kept your wits about you to avoid being conned. These fundamental beliefs about human nature affect how you look things when doing personnel research.

【解读八】

In this sense, <u>you are always being guided by a theoretical framework</u>, but you don't know it. Not knowing what your real framework is can be a problem. <u>The framework tends to guide what you notice in an organization, and what you don't notice.</u> In other words, you don't even notice things that don't fit your framework! We can never completely get around this problem, but <u>we can reduce the problem considerably by simply making our implicit framework explicit. Once it is explicit, we can deliberately consider other frameworks, and try to see the organizational situation through different lenses.</u>③

【解读九】

●<u>Theoretical Frameworks Arise from Disagreement</u>

Ideally, this might be a shared understanding of the film and agreement on its merits.

---

① 【解读二】【解读三】均据 The University of Southern California's Library Guide 或 Research Guides at USC（https://libguides.usc.edu/writingguide/theoreticalframework）。

② 参见 http://www.answers.com/Q/What_is_the_role_of_theoretical_framework_in_research。

③ 【解读五】—【解读八】均参见 http://www.analytictech.com/mb313/elements.htm。

More realistically, each of you may have a better understanding of the film and of each other's evaluation process. To do this, you need to establish a theoretical framework for the discussion.

● A Theoretical Framework Provides Limits and Boundaries

You might begin by discussing the first scene, in which Michael Keaton is seated with his back to the viewer. As the scene develops, the camera draws back and we see that Keaton is in a dressing room seated in yoga's lotus position but hovering several feet above the floor. You find this fascinating; your friend thinks it's a cheap trick that violates common sense.

To make any progress, you need to frame the discussion in film theory. Often this requires introducing many questions, some as general as "What makes a film good or bad?" and others as specific as "Is the filmmaker limited to showing only what we normally experience?" As you ask these questions and discuss them, you are beginning to build a theoretical framework that allows you to analyze the film in ways you agree to allow. The theoretical framework provides boundaries for your discussion and limits it to topics within those bounds.

● Connecting the Framework to Other Theories and Views

At some point, you and your friend may begin to see that you bring different assumptions to your view of the film. By making these assumptions explicit, you allow them to be critically evaluated. You may also discover that you and your friend are asking questions that have been answered many times. By connecting to existing knowledge and earlier film theories, each of you begins to make your arguments more meaningful.

A film theory that emphasizes the value of social realities may evaluate "Birdman" less positively than a theory that emphasizes art as a form of free play. The theoretical framework used to evaluate the film gives both of you ways of understanding and evaluating the assumptions underlying your divergent critiques.

● Working with Framed Conclusions

Articulating your assumptions about the film and then comparing your assumptions with other film theories allows you to understand the limits of your generalizations. As scholar Richard Swanson observes in a 2007 article for the "Human Resource Development Review," the theoretical framework provides a structure that holds or supports the theory, allowing you to understand its assumptions and limits. This in turn allows you to come to meaningful conclusions about that theory. Once the theory has been qualified or confirmed, it can then be applied to further instances—in the "Birdman" example, perhaps of future films by the same director or of other films with magical elements. At that point, the theory can be examined again in the light of this new information and consequently refined further.

(by Patrick Gleeson, "What is the meaning of theoretical framework"[1])

---

[1] 参见 https://www.theclassroom.com/meaning-theoretical-framework-6382450.html。

【解读十】

●<u>The framework for scientific research</u> is that <u>it should report all observations as honestly and accurately as possible</u>, <u>it should be published so that other scientists can find out about it</u>, <u>it should be reproducible so that it can be confirmed</u>, <u>it should be assessed by means of mathematical and logical reasoning</u>.

●In science or in any other area where <u>research and analysis often begin with a question</u>, <u>answering that question requires mapping the context of the question and describing the conditions that determine the validity of proposed answers</u>—in other words, <u>the theoretical framework that leads to an answer</u>. Students unfamiliar with the concept may incorrectly assume that a theoretical framework is something unprovable—"a mere theory"—as opposed to something concrete and real. <u>By definition</u>, <u>a theoretical framework allows researchers to test the theory and describe the results</u>.

（by Patrick Gleeson, "What is the meaning of theoretical framework"）

5.1.2　翻译理论框架解读

毕业论文中的理论框架和研究种类密切相关。科学研究/学术研究主要分为两大类：概念/理论研究（conceptual/theoretical research）和实证研究（empirical research）。搞清楚"理论框架"与"概念研究"的关系，对读懂本章、写好论文中的"理论框架"部分意义重大。

根据 Williams 和 Chesterman（2004: 58-60），我们把上述两种研究的来龙去脉简单地讲明白，从二者之区分具有历史传统讲起（了解这点也是学生读者的必备能力）：

<u>The distinction goes back to the traditional debate between hermeneutics and positivism</u>: hermeneutics (<u>the science of interpretation</u>) has often been thought of as <u>the basic research method of the humanistic disciplines</u> (philosophy, literary theory, aesthetics…), whereas <u>positivist methods based on empirical observation and experiment have characterized the hard sciences</u>. At its simplest, <u>the distinction is between a focus more on ideas and a focus more on data</u>.

Conceptual research <u>aims to define and clarify concepts, to interpret or reinterpret ideas, to relate concepts into larger systems, to introduce new concepts or metaphors or frameworks</u> <u>that allow a better understanding of the object of research</u>.

Empirical research, on the other hand, <u>seeks new data, new information derived from the observation of data and from experimental work</u>; <u>it seeks evidence which supports or disconfirms hypotheses, or generates new ones</u>.

<u>Both approaches are necessary, in Translation Studies as in other fields</u>. The differences between the two have perhaps been exaggerated by scholars taking one side or another… You cannot observe anything without some kind of preliminary theory (concept) what you are observing; even what you take to be a fact or piece of data depends on your initial theoretical assumptions about what would constitute a relevant fact in the first place; an any hypothesis

must be formulate in terms of concepts of some kind. On the other hand, concepts that have no link to empirical data are not much use to science (however interesting they might appear).

Conceptual research (*conceptual analysis*) often takes the form of an <u>argument</u>…

Conceptual arguments need to show that they are in some way <u>more convincing than alternative or proceeding analyses of the concept in question</u>…

<u>One reason why conceptual analysis is important is that concepts drive action</u>; <u>what you think</u> (e.g. <u>your concept of translation</u>) <u>influences</u> <u>what you do</u> (e.g. <u>how you translate</u>). But conceptual analysis is also an integral part of empirical research, too. It involves processes like the following:

- <u>defining key terms</u> (X is defined here as Y)
- <u>comparing definitions/interpretations by different scholars</u>
- <u>explicating and interpreting the overall</u> <u>theoretical framework</u>…(e.g. 'translation is seen here as a kind of creative performance'…)
- <u>setting up classification systems</u> (concept X understood as consisting of categories ABC)
- <u>defining the categories use in the analysis</u>
- <u>deciding what to do with borderline cases</u>, i.e. how to interpret category boundaries…
- <u>interpreting the results of an analysis</u>
- <u>considering the implications of an argument</u>
- <u>coming up with new ideas that might lead to new research methods and results</u>

上述引文清晰地、多层次地阐释了"理论框架"及与之关系密切的诸多重要概念，如"概念/理论研究""实证研究"以及它们的重要性、必要性；再如二者研究的目的及主要内容、它们之间的辩证逻辑关系、概念研究具体包含哪些内容等等。

简而言之，理论框架是概念研究中的一项重要内容，在论文中需要加以阐明——"explicating and interpreting the overall theoretical framework… (e.g. 'translation is seen here as kind of creative performance'…)"。

一般而言，翻译学属于人文社科，有关研究更多地采用"概念"研究——阐释研究法，其目的包括定义概念、阐释概念、解读思想，同时要将概念与更大的体系相连接，并引进新概念——包括"（理论）框架"，这样有助于对研究对象形成一个更好的认识（*Conceptual* research aims to define and clarify concepts, to interpret or reinterpret ideas, to relate concepts into larger systems, to introduce new concepts or metaphors or frameworks that allow a better understanding of the object of research）。

翻译论文中的理论框架与翻译研究课题和翻译实践/研究方法关系密切。相关的理论框架的构建，必须基于充分或有代表性地收集和较为系统地掌握该翻译研究领域或该翻译主题领域的有关成果。选择的理论不宜过多，比如，BA/BTI 论文，选择一个或两个就够了。运用理论是为了解释问题、解决问题，不是为了炫耀你会同时使用多种理论。一句话，以需求/需要为导向，即从论文提出的研究问题入手，根据解决问题的需求/需要来选择、确定使用一种还是多种理论，并由此探讨理论框架的形成。

5.2   理论框架案例

5.2.1   BA 论文中的理论框架

Theoretical Framework[①]
—A Functionalist Approach to Song Translation

Functionalism, focusing on the function of texts and translation, was put forward in the 1970s by what is now often referred to as the "German School" represented by Katharina Reiss, Hans J. Vermeer and Justa Holz-Mänttäri. Among them, Vermeer had played a major role in the development of the trend with his establishment of *Skopostheorie*, a Greek word meaning "a theory of purposeful action". Christiane Nord, another representative of the school, further developed the theory in the 1990s.

3.1   Defining song translation

3.1.1   Functionalist definition of translation

"[T]he main idea of *Skopostheorie* could be paraphrased as 'the translation purpose justifies the translation procedures'." (Nord, 2001: 124) The theory holds a dynamic concept of text meaning and function: "A text is made meaningful by its receiver and for its receiver", and "the viability of the translation purpose depends on the circumstances of the target culture, not on the source culture" (ibid.: 31). Accordingly, "the term *Skopos* usually refers to the purpose of the target text" (ibid.: 28), and "one of the most important factors determining the purpose of a translation is the addressee, who is the intended receiver or audience of the target text with their culture-specific world-knowledge, their expectations and their communicative needs" (ibid.: 12). Correspondingly, the source text in *Skopostheorie* is "dethroned" and regarded as an "offer of information", from which any receivers (including the translator) select the items they regard as useful (or adequate) to the desired purpose (ibid.: 25; 31).

Therefore, in Vermeer's terminology, to translate means "to produce a text in a target setting for a target purpose and target addressees in target circumstance" (ibid.: 12), which emphasizes the significance of *Skopos* and addressees; and "a translation is thus a new offer of information in the target culture about some information offered in the source culture and language" (ibid.: 26), which means that a "translator cannot offer the same amount and kind of information as the source-text producer" (ibid.: 35). It can then be concluded that the functionalist definition of translation emphasizes three primary factors: *Skopos*, addressees, and a new offer of information.

3.1.2   Functionalist definition of song translation

As is defined in the *Longman Dictionary of English Language and Culture (English-Chinese)*, a "song" is "usually a short piece of music with words for singing", which indicates two inseparable elements of a song (music and words) and the basic function of it (for singers to sing). However, singing is a way of

---

① 选自浙江大学英语专业本科生毕业论文真实文稿，文中错误与不足在所难免。

communication involving not only singers but also listeners, which can be both regarded as **addressees** in the translating activity. As far as the "expectations and communicative needs" of addressees are concerned, a translated version cannot be claimed as adequate if it is either awkward for singers to sing or difficult for listeners to comprehend within a few minutes (since a song is often short).

Furthermore, a song text is rather expressive than informative (王和玉, 2007: 86). According to Reiss's translation text typology, a song text belongs to audio-medial text type, because it is accompanied by music, a medium other than language (朱志渝, 2004: 8; 吴艾玲, 2005: 60), and the audio effect of a target text far outweighs anything else. Accordingly, a song translator has done all that can be required of him to realize the *Skopos* of song translation once he has produced "**a new offer of information**" with the spirit or substantial meaning of the original reserved and a tolerably good audio effect.

Being concluded from the above functionalist approach, **song translation** can be defined as an interlingual activity of producing a target song-text which reproduces the substantial meaning of the source text and could be set to the original music so as to be singable for target singers and intelligible for target listeners with both of them enjoying its audio effect.

3.2　Function-plus-loyalty approach

3.2.1　Function—the *Skopos* rule

In the framework of *Skopostheorie*, the top ranking rule for any translation is the *Skopos* rule, which could be easily interpreted as "the end justifies the means", that is, a translational action is determined by its *Skopos*—usually the communicative purposes aimed at by the target text in the target situation (Nord, 2001: 28-29).

The definition of song translation obviously indicates the *Skopos* rule guiding the process of song translation: translate in a way to enable the target song text to reproduce the substantial meaning of the source text, be singable for target singers and intelligible for target listeners with both of them enjoying its audio effect.

3.2.2　The coherence rule and the fidelity rule

Under the prime principle of *Skopos*, Vermeer put forward other two rules: the coherence rule and the fidelity rule. "The coherence rule" specifies that the target text should conform to the standard of "intra-textual coherence" to make sure that it is sufficiently coherent with (or make sense in) the receivers' situation so that they are able to understand it. A further principle, "the fidelity rule", refers to the principle that a kind of "inter-textual coherence" or "fidelity" should exist between the translation and the corresponding source text, while the form it takes depends both on the translator's interpretation of the source text and on the translation *Skopos* (ibid.: 32). What's more, the fidelity rule is considered subordinate to the intra-textual coherence rule, and both are subordinate to the *Skopos* rule (ibid.).

In the practice of song translation, the coherence role requires that the target text should at least likely to be meaningful to and acceptable by target-culture singers and listeners; while according to the fidelity rule, the target text should then at least reserve the spirit of the original lyrics and be set by the original music. Once the two requirements cannot coexist, the later usually has to be sacrificed for the former so as to meet the translation *Skopos*.

3.2.3 Loyalty—the loyalty principle

In the 1990s, Nord added one more general rule called "the loyalty principle" to the functionalist theory with translating being viewed as an interpersonal interaction, and thus proposed a function-plus-loyalty approach. "Function" refers to the factors that make a target text work in the intended way in the target situation; while "loyalty" is an interpersonal category referring to the responsibility translators have toward their partners of both the source and the target side (including the source-text producer, target-text receivers, etc.) in translational interaction. (Nord, 2001: 125-128).

For instance, song translators have to deal with their relationships with the target singers (target-text users), the target listeners (target-text receivers), and the original lyric writer and the composer (both are source-text producers). The original lyric writer and the composer have a right to demand respect for their individual intentions and expect a particular kind of relationship between their text and its translation, hence a song translator must duly respect their communicative intentions apart from paying attention to the expectations and communicative needs of the target singers and listeners.

The above four principles are intended to guide any type of translation, and song translation is not an exception. Thus song translators should regard the *Skopos* rule, the loyalty principle, the coherence rule and the fidelity rule as the guiding principles.

To be specific, the whole translating activity should aim at producing a target song-text reserving the substantial meaning of the original lyrics, singable for target singers and intelligible for target listeners with both of them enjoying its audio effect (the requirement of the *Skopos* rule). In order to achieve the *Skopos*, song translators have to, on the one hand, consider expectations and communicative needs of the target singers and listeners (the requirement of the loyalty principle) in the hope of helping the target text make sense in the communicative situation (the requirement of the coherence rule); and on the other hand, reserve the spirit of the original lyrics and ensure that the target text could match the original music (the requirement of the fidelity rule) to show their respect to the communicative intentions of the original lyric writer and the composer (the requirement of the loyalty principle).

3.3 The role of source-text analysis

The target-text purpose has the priority in *Skopostheorie* while the source text suffers a "dethronement", yet the latter is still relevant in that it "provides the offer of information that forms the starting point for the offer of information formulated in the target text" (Nord, 2001: 62). Actually, analysis of the source text is essential for guiding the translation process to realize the function of the target text as well as helping the translator to be loyal to the source-text producer (张美芳, 2005: 64). Hence Nord designed a "translation-oriented model of text analysis in translation" to identify the function-relevant elements in both the existing source text and the prospective target text, including the "analysis of extra-textual and intra-textual aspects of the communicative action" (Nord, 2001: 14).

In order to locate the problems that will arise in the translation process and thus devise a holistic strategy for their solution, translators have to adopt the model of source-text analysis as the initial step of translating a song. In a source song-text, it is four "function-relevant elements", namely, textual translation problems, poetic features, musical features and communicative intention (the former two are intra-textual and the latter two extra-textual), which provide a whole "offer of information", and thus they should be analyzed comprehensively.

3.3.1　Intra-textual aspects in a source song-text

There are two kinds of intra-textual aspects in a source song-text: textual translation problems and poetic features.

A source text of any text type (including song texts) often contains some translation problems that can be categorized as pragmatic, cultural, linguistic, and text-specific (which are specifically bound to one particular source text and their solutions cannot be generalized or applied to similar cases) (Nord, 2001: 65-67). All of the four categories are directly related to the text (i.e. song lyrics) itself rather than being inferred from the relationship between words and music, they are hence referred to as "textual translation problems" in the present paper. Such problems had better be identified in advance so as to facilitate the later translation activity.

Regardless of the music, the words of a song always constitute a poem. In order to fully grasp the substantial meaning of the song, appreciate the aesthetic beauty of the lyrics, keep the final version as faithful to the original as possible and show his/her loyalty to the original lyric writer, a translator had better regard the song lyrics as a poem and carefully analyze its poetic features such as its structure, contents, artistic conception, rhythm, rhyme, wording, rhetorical devices, tone and theme.

3.3.2　Extra-textual aspects in a source song-text

The extra-textual aspects of song text can be subdivided into two categories: musical features and communicative intentions.

Words and music are two inseparable parts of a song. It is the words of a song that are translated; the music is relatively stable, yet not irrelevant at all. In fact, the prospective target text will be confined by the music and will have to meet its requirements. For this reason, a translator must beforehand be quite familiar with the musical features of the song (including such basic musical elements as musical form, rhythm, melody distinctiveness, musical mood and color, and sometimes even its performing arrangement) by consulting the background information about the characteristics of its composer, studying its music score and listening to its record, analyze the way in which the music matches the words (both coordinating with its form and reflecting its spirit), and thus further indicate the problems to be solved and try hard to be loyal to the composer while translating.

As is mentioned in **Section 3.1.2**, singing is a way of communication. The creation of both words and music of a song as well as their fitness to each other is to carry out its communicative intentions (i.e. the original producing intentions) of the lyric writer, the composer, and the initiator. A translator can infer the communicative intentions by analyzing the song or find them directly with the help of relevant literature. Then s/he should compare the source-text functions with the translation *Skopos*, which would help him/her design translation strategies that will lead to a target text both demonstrating his/her loyalty to the original producers and meeting the requirements of the translation purposes.

3.4 Adaptation

Each target text in *Skopostheorie* is "a new offer of information" which is, more or less, different from what the source text offers. "The comparison between the source-text and the target-text profiles shows very clearly what source-text information or linguistic elements can be kept invariant and what **has to be adjusted to** the requirements of the translation purpose" (Nord, 2001: 64; the words highlighted by this Author), which presupposes that adaptation is needed in the translation process. Actually, Nord views adaptation as a relative quantity reflecting a translation's *skopos*. According to her, any one translation will be characterized by the relative proportion (or percentage) of adaptation which it contains (Shuttleworth and Cowie, 2004: 4).

3.4.1 Genre conventions and adaptation

A conception closely related to the need for adaptation is "genre conventions", which means that texts of a certain type acquire their own conventional forms due to the standardization of communication practices. Genre conventions are mostly culture-specific, and play an important role in functional translation. A translator has to be familiar with both the conventions that the target text is to abide by, for the purpose of making it acceptable as representative of a target-culture genre, and those of the genre to which the source text belongs, so as to evaluate the linguistic features of the source text in terms of conventionality or originality. Moreover, "[a] comparison between the conventional features of the source text and the genre conventions implied by the translation purpose may highlight the need for adaptations in the translation process" (Nord, 2001: 53-54).

3.4.2 Genre conventions of English and Chinese song lyrics

Like many other text types, song lyrics in different cultures have their own conventional forms as well. A comparison between the genre conventions of English song-texts and those of Chinese song-texts is made in the following three main aspects: rhythm, rhyme, and tone.

3.4.2.1 Rhythm

Both language and music have rhythm. It is generally believed by songwriters that the rhythm of song lyrics should coordinate with that of music. But songwriters from China and English speaking countries have different ways for observing the rule due to differences between the two languages.

First, the ways for English lyrics and Chinese lyrics to match a certain piece of music in terms of pauses are different. In music, notes of different durations constitute different rhythm patterns, which make the melody sound as if there are minute pauses between musical phrases or within one phrase①. In language, the rhythmic units of English poetry and Chinese poetry are different. Since the syllables of English words are fixed to be either stressed or unstressed, the rhythm of English poetry is based on the regular and constant recurrence of "foot" which contains one stressed syllable and one or more weaker ones. Whereas the rhythm of Chinese poetry largely depends on *dou* (or *dun*), or *caesura*, a term borrowed from French

---

① A phrase is a musical idea, generally associated with a segment of a melody. (see Allvin, 1985: 126, 176)

poetry to refer to the slight pause in reading, marking the completeness of semantic meaning, which often divides two Chinese phrases (薛范, 2002: 117).

Second, a composer always tries to set stressed syllables on musical strong beats or relatively strong beats (ibid.: 79) to make the language rhythm closely fit to the musical rhythm, which is relatively easier to achieve in Chinese songs than in English songs. Though the first character of a Chinese phrase is usually felt emphasized rather than the rest ones, the distinction between stressed and unstressed syllables in the Chinese language is generally not as regular and sharp as in the English language. Therefore, most Chinese characters (except function words and softly-and-quickly-read classifiers) can be set on accented beats during composing, especially the first character of a phrase (ibid.: 127-135).

3.4.2.2　Rhyme

The prime function of rhyme in poetry is to make various sounds join together and form a complete tune (朱光潜, 2001: 165). So is it in song lyrics and they are always rhymed verses. End-rhyme is the most frequently used rhyme in both English and Chinese song lyrics (薛范, 2002: 80). But the distinction is that end-rhymes in English song lyrics can be changed quite frequently, while the rhyming norms of Chinese song lyrics are much more rigid.

The rhythm of English song lyrics is distinct enough in that the stressed syllable and unstressed one(s) in each foot are almost invariant and in sharp contrast, so there is no need for drawing support from rhymes; however, the rhythm of Chinese song lyrics relying on caesuras is relatively weaker and thus has to turn to the recurrence of rhymes for help (朱光潜, 2001: 164). Moreover, a song is often quite short and a song frequently changing rhymes sounds to a Chinese ear as though it had no rhyme at all. Accordingly, rhyme is a factor of crucial importance to the composition of Chinese song lyrics, and Chinese lyric writers insist that dense and unified rhymes are better than sparse and changeable ones and lay particular stress on rhyming in the hope of producing an integrated whole and meeting the Chinese aesthetic notion and audio requirement of songs (薛范, 2002: 87).

3.4.2.3　Tone

One of the great distinctions between the pronunciation of English and Chinese is that the latter is a typical "tone language", while the former is not.

There are four tones in modern standard Chinese pronunciation. The first is called *high and level tone*; the second *rising tone*; the third *falling-rising tone*; and the fourth *falling tone*. And it needs to add that there is the *neutral tone*, which is articulated softly and quickly. Phrases transcribed into the same Chinese phonetic letters yet of different tones often have different meanings. If the pitches of notes keep unchanged throughout a song, the melody would be static and boring. Similarly, the meaning of Chinese phrases can be hardly expressed accurately if there are no different tones in Chinese pronunciation (孙慧双, 1999: 239).

The tone of each Chinese character in a particular context is fixed, but they would possibly change under the influence of pitch change while being sung (ibid.: 240). Once the change of tones goes against that of pitches, the meaning of phrases may be ambiguous or mistaken (ibid.: 239). Consequently, while Chinese composers are setting a song to music and while Chinese lyric writers are writing words for a song, both of them have to pay much attention to the rising and falling of tones in addition to considering the rhythm and rhyme of song lyrics (薛范, 2002: 136).

The above comparison clearly indicates that the conventional features of English song-texts and Chinese song-texts differ considerably from each other, and adaptation in the translation process is essential for matching the music, producing a tolerably good audio effect and thus realizing the translation *Skopos*. Actually, more often than not, a song translator recreates the text rather than translating it word for word, as long as it conveys the spirit of the original lyrics. Hence, the wording and syntax of the two corresponding texts may not be identical in many places except for where of vital importance or essential emphasis. Therefore, after carefully analyzing the source text, a song translator should get down to the second step of song translation—make adaptation to music in three main aspects: rhythm, rhyme and tone.

3.5　Theoretical claims

The above introduction to functionalist translation theory and the systematic arguments of its correlation with song translation may prove that the functionalist approach could provide a theoretical groundwork for the topic that this study intends to explore as well as giving clue to the answers to the research questions put forward at the beginning of the paper. Several claims could be then established as follows:

(a) In terms of the principles of song translation, a song translator should keep the *Skopos* rule, the coherence rule, the fidelity rule and the loyalty principle in mind throughout the overall translation process.

(b) In terms of the procedures of song translation, it can be divided into two main steps: source-text analysis and adaptation to music.

(c) In terms of the methods of song translation, a song translator should carefully analyze the communicative intentions, textual translation-problems, poetic features and musical features of the source text before setting about to translate, and then skillfully make adaptation to music in rhythm, rhyme and tone.

【框架简析】

理论框架是这篇 BA 论文的第 3 章，涉及理论框架主题，即 "Theoretical Framework—A Functionalist Approach to Song Translation"，有关小标题如下：

3.1　Defining song translation

　　3.1.1　Functionalist definition of translation

　　3.1.2　Functionalist definition of song translation

3.2　Function-plus-loyalty approach

　　3.2.1　Function—the *Skopos* rule

　　3.2.2　The coherence rule and the fidelity rule

　　3.2.3　Loyalty—the loyalty principle

3.3　The role of source-text Analysis

　　3.3.1　Intra-textual aspects in a source song-text

　　3.3.2　Extra-textual aspects in a source song-text

3.4　Adaptation

3.4.1	Genre conventions and adaptation
3.4.2	Genre conventions of English and Chinese song lyrics
	3.4.2.1　Rhythm
	3.4.2.2　Rhyme
	3.4.2.3　Tone
3.5　Theoretical claims	

从小标题不难看出：

①框架全面。围绕"歌曲译配""目的""功能""ST 分析的作用""译配""理论主张"有序展开。

②概念清晰。仅举与论文主题关系最密切的概念"歌曲译配"为例——**song translation** can be defined as an interlingual activity of producing a target song-text which reproduces the substantial meaning of the source text and could be set to the original music so as to be singable for target singers and intelligible for target listeners with both of them enjoying its audio effect。

③层次合理。分述层次细致到出现四至五级的目录，不仅说明作者解剖分析的能力，也说明作者比较专业（该学生是浙江大学文琴合唱团团员）。

④细分到位。3.1—3.5 都是需要、重要并值得进行理论框架设定的方面和节点。

⑤文字充足。总词数逾 3400 words，且言之有物。

⑥总评等级。作为 BA 学位论文，主观判分为 A。

5.2.2　BTI 论文中的理论框架

Theoretical Framework[①]

3.1　Theoretical Framework

3.1.1　Three Rules of Translation under the *Skopostheorie*

In 1971, Katharina Reiss, developed a new model of translation analysis with the relationship between the ST and the TT as its focus in her monograph *The Possibilities & Limitations of Translation Quality Assessment* (2000). Her work, though still under the influence of the equivalence theory, marked "the starting point of the scholarly analysis of translation in Germany" (Nord, 2001: 9). Later, this analysis evolved into the *Skpostheorie*, which forms the theoretical framework for this thesis.

The *Skopostheorie*, developed by Vermeer, stresses the interaction of translation and the pragmatic characteristics of translation. Vermeer states that "translation is activity form of translational action based on a source text, which may consist of verbal and/or non-verbal elements" (Nord, 2001: 11). He held the belief that the choice of the form of the target language should be decided by its function, namely the purpose which the context of target language requires to achieve.

By this principle, translators no longer focus on the ST and its function, but on the communicative purpose which the translated version aims to achieve in its context. This is because all translation has its

---

① 选自浙江大学提前通过 MTI 保研考试的本科生毕业论文的真实文稿，文中错误与不足在所难免。

targeted audience, and translation itself means to "produce a text in a target setting for a target purpose and target addressees in target circumstance" (Nord, 2001: 2).

Vermeer has developed three rules of translation under the *Skopostheorie*. Firstly, he believes that a translational action is determined by its *Skopos*, that is "the end justifies the means" (Reiss and Vermeer, 1984: 101). In other words, the purpose of the translation determines the way it is translated. He says:

> Each text is produced for a given purpose and should serve this purpose. The *Skopos* rule thus as follows: to translate/interpret/speak/write in a way that enables your text/translation to function in the situation in which it is used and with the people who want to use it and precisely in the way they want it to function. (Vermeer, 1989: 20, qtd. and trans. Nord, 2001: 29)

Nord simplified the essence of *Skopos* rule to "a translation action is determined by its *Skopos*" and "the end justifies the means" (Nord 2001: 29). When it comes to E-C tourism translation, the *Skopostheorie* means to translate the original English text in a way that enables the Chinese readers to get the exact information they want, and the guidebook to attract more travelers.

The second rule is the coherence rule. It can also be interpreted as "intratextual coherence". It stresses that target text "must be interpretable as coherent with the target text receiver's situation" (Nord, 2001: 32). That is to say the translated text should be acceptable and meaningful in a sense that it is coherent with the situation in which it is received. In other words, it should coherent with the language context. In the process of translating, translators should conform to the language features and styles in the TL and circumstances, and change the information offered in the SL to acceptable and accessible one in the TL to the target readers, taking their background knowledge into consideration. The third rule is the fidelity rule, also named "intertextual coherence" which emphasizes the relationship between the source text and the target text. The ruled of fidelity go hand in hand with the coherence rule. This rule stresses the coherence between the information received by ST readers, the interpretation the translator makes of this information and the information received by the TT readers. It enables the translator to achieve a "maximally faithful imitation of the source text" (Nord, 2001: 32).

3.1.2   A Functional Classification of Translation Errors

Seeing the translation errors as "a failure to carry out the instructions implied in the translation brief and as an inadequate solution to a translation problem" (Nord, 2001: 75), Christiane Nord divided translation errors into four groups: pragmatic translation error (PTE), cultural translation errors (CTE), linguistic translation errors (LTE) and text-specific translation errors (TTE) (ibid.: 75).

PTEs are attributed to translators' "inadequate solutions to pragmatic translation problems" (ibid.: 75). For instance, the translators' insufficient consideration of the TT readers can lead to the improper diction in translating. Although "PTEs are not very difficult to solve (once they have been identified as problems!)", their consequences can be serious (Nord, 2001: 76). The decision about the translation type is the first step of translating; it will guide every following step in the translation process (ibid.: 76).

CTEs are common errors because translation is just a switch between cultures. These errors are caused by "in adequate decision with regard to reproduction or adaptation of culture-specific conventions" (ibid.:

75). Usually, the sharper the differences between the two languages are, the more the cultural translations errors there will be. Cultural translation errors depend on whether the conventions need to be adapted to the target culture (ibid.).

LTEs focus on language structures. This refers to the "deviation from linguistic norms" which "lead to an inadequate interpretation of the referential function" (ibid.: 76). TTEs, "related to text-specific translation problems, can be evaluated from a functional or pragmatic point of view" (ibid.: 76).

【框架简析】

从论文第 3 章简单明了的二级目录可以明白：

3.1　Theoretical Framework

　　3.1.1　Three Rules of Translation under the *Skopostheorie*

　　3.1.2　A Functional Classification of Translation Errors

①框架简明。围绕论文主题 "A Case Study of English-Chinese Translation of Outbound Travel Guidebook: Error Analysis and Re-translation From the Perspective of *Skopostheorie*"（《目的论视角下出境游指南英译汉个案研究：问题分析与重译》）展开，主要涉及"目的论"的三项翻译规则与翻译错误的功能分类两大问题。

②概念清晰。紧紧围绕上述两大问题"搭框架"，没有拖泥带水的地方。

③层次合理。一两个层次即说明问题，没有牵强附会之处。

④细分到位。在合理细分的层面，搭建框架到位。

⑤文字充足。总词数逾 830 words，说明问题即可。

⑥总评等级。主观判分为 B 或 B⁺，给今后撰写 BTI 学位论文做好了必要的铺垫。

综上所述，不论是撰写 BA 学位论文，还是 BTI 学位论文，都应切记（翻译）理论框架/概念框架的三个特征：**逻辑性、指导性、简明性**。

◎研究与实践思考题◎

1. 如何准确解读 BA/BTI 毕业论文中的理论框架？你有自己初步或比较成熟的观点吗？

2. 如何分别撰写 BA/BTI 学位论文中的理论框架？请不同专业（方向）、不同层级的学生用英文独立完成一篇理论框架短文。

3. 根据本章的有关介绍以及你自己的理解，分析以下的"理论框架"。

The Translation Brief
3.1　*Skopos* Analysis

In order to translate CSIs properly, the author has to acquire a profound understanding towards the translation *Skopos*. According to the *Skopostheorie*, a translation brief should be notified as it "specified what kind of translation is needed" (Nord 2001: 30). In this case the author would like to outline the following aspects which contribute to determining the *Skopos* of the CSI translation.

3.1.1 Functions of Text Types of CSIs in Hong Kong

The so-called CSIs in Hong Kong collected by Tang Zhixiang (2009) total 68 in number. However, the 68 items do not actually refer to the CSIs defined according to the standards set in this thesis. For these items are defined and studied by a comparison of the culture in Hong Kong and that in Macao or China's Mainland. Furthermore, many of the 68 items originating from England are listed below:

官守议员: Official Member

全英赛: The All England Open Badminton Championships

栋笃笑: stand-up comedy

督爷: dude

太平绅士: Justice of the Peace, JP

Besides, items including "次文化(subculture)", "轻铁(light rail)", "便服日(casual day)", "新移民 (new immigrants)", "负资产(negative asset)", "官津学校(government-funded schools)" and "羁留中心 (detention centre)" are also common in present English culture. In addition, as "山顶(the Peak)" and "半山 区(mid-levels)" have been widely recognized as landmarks in Hong Kong, there is no need to revise these translations. Consequently, in this case these 14 items should be excluded from the group of CSIs in Hong Kong.

Considering the Author's living experience in Hong Kong, phrases "早茶", "糖水", and "鬼佬" can be regarded as CSIs. As a result, Hong Kong CSIs, numbering 57 in this case, are listed for discussion as follows:

百万行, 拍拖报, 平安米...and 鬼佬.①

The TT function should be in keeping with the ST function. Following the functions of the ST, Katharina Reiss grouped text types into 3 categories: the informative, the expressive, and the operative. "In informative texts the main function is to inform the reader about objects and phenomena in the real world." (Nord 2001: 37) The said function focuses on delivering objective messages to TL readers, for instance, instructions of a product, reports of a new medicine, and "the translator should attempt to give a correct and complete representation of the source text's content and should be guided, in terms of stylistic choices, by the dominant norms of the target language and culture" (ibid.: 38).

Expressive texts emphasize the expressiveness and aesthetic feelings, and literature is a particular example in this case. "The stylistic choices made by the author contribute to the meaning of the text, producing an aesthetic effect on the reader. This effect has to be taken into account in translation...the translator of an expressive text should attempt to produce an analogous stylistic effect. In this case, stylist choices in translation are naturally guided by those made in the source text."(ibid.: 38)

And operative texts, such as advertisements and slogans, pay attention to readers' feedbacks so that readers could respond to the received messages. "The translating of operative texts into operative texts

---

① 本书作者注：此处省略了论文原有的 55 项 CSIs。

should be guided by the overall aim of bringing about the same reaction in the audience, although this might involve changing the content and/or stylistic features of the original." (ibid.: 38) Usually a text has multiple functions, but is embedded with a focus.

In terms of three functions, the 57 CSIs in Hong Kong can be classified into 3 groups[①]:

(1) The informative: 外展, 东华三院, 劳役中心…and 哇啦哇啦.

(2) The expressive: 笼屋, 家乐径, 夹心阶层, 皇家工…and 灿妹.

(3) The operative: 地茂馆, 百万行, 拍拖报, 平安米…and 毅进计划.

3.2.2 Expected Addressees

The addressees should also be taken into consideration as "the receiver, or rather the addressee, is the main factor determining the target-text *Skopos*" (ibid.: 38). Before we start translating we have to bear our addressees in mind. According to Theodore Savory who wrote *The Art of Translation*, addressees can be divided into four groups with different levels of target language ability and personal interests (qtd. in 谭载喜 2004: 206). In this case, therefore, the Author takes as expected addressees English-speakers in Hong Kong who are learning local (Cantonese and/or Hong Kong) language and culture. As this group is lacking in knowledge about the local society, culture and language, footnotes, endnotes, and comments are necessary to make the translations clear and acceptable in the TL language and culture.

4. 根据本章的有关介绍以及你自己的理解，分析以下的"理论框架"。

Theoretical Framework

3.1 An Overview of Rewriting Theory

3.1.1 General Aspects of Rewriting Theory

Rewriting theory is one of the most important and effective theories in the study of the function of translation in the receiving culture. According to Theo Hermans, "Lefevere first took 'refraction' to mean 'the adaptation of a work of literature to a different audience, with the intention of influencing the way in which that audience reads the work'" (Hermans, 2004: 127). Later, the "first full presentation" of the notion of "rewriting" and its fundamental elements, according to Theo Hermans (ibid.: 126), occur in André Lefevere's "Why Waste Our Time on Rewrites", in which Lefevere "summed up his position and demonstrated its potential to guide research in *Translation, Rewriting and the Manipulation of Literary Fame*". Lefevere further developed the concept of "rewriting" in his remarkable work *Translation, Rewriting and the Manipulation of Literary Fame*, where he defined rewriting in an otherwise way, "…texts that rewrite the actual text in one way or another, such as plot summaries in literary histories or reference works, reviews in newspapers, magazines, or journals, some critical articles, performances on stage or screen, and, last but not least, translations" (Lefevere, 2004/2010: 6). Theo Hermans held that "Lefevere consciously differentiated his own systems concept from Even-Zohar's, and devised his own categories and terms. The most important of these are patronage, ideology, poetics and 'universe of discourse'" (Hermans, 2004: 125). He also analyzed Lefevere's theory about "literary system":

---

① 本书作者注：以下三组举例，分别省略 25 项、15 项、3 项。

Leaving the nature of the overarching social system for what it is, Lefevere concentrates on the literary subsystem. This literary system possesses a double control mechanism. One mechanism governs it largely from the outside, and secures the relations between literature and its environment. Here the keywords are patronage and ideology. The other keeps order within the literary system, and here the operative terms are poetics and a somewhat less well defined group referred to variously as "experts", "specialists", "professionals" and also "rewriters". (ibid.: 126)

3.1.2　Translation as Rewriting

In his *Translation in Systems: Descriptive and System-oriented Approaches Explained*, Theo Hermans says, "Rewriting includes such operations as translation, criticism, reviewing, summary, adaptation for children, anthologizing, making into a comic strip or TV film, and so on, in short any processing of a text whether in the same or another language or in another medium" (ibid.: 127). According to Lefevere,

> Translation is, of course, a rewriting of an original text. All rewritings, whatever their intention, reflect a certain ideology and a certain poetics and as such manipulate literature to function in a given society in a given way. Rewriting is manipulation, undertaken in the service of power and in its positive aspect can help in the evolution of a literature and a society. (Lefevere, 2004/2010: General editors' preface)

Lefevere held that "Translations are not made in a vacuum. Translators function in a given culture at a given time. The way they understand themselves and their culture is one of the factors that may influence the way in which they translate" (Lefevere, 2004: 14).

Among various concrete factors manipulating translation, Lefevere believed that:

> Two factors basically determine the image of a work of literature as projected by a translation. These two factors are, in order of importance, the translator's ideology (whether he/she willingly embraces it, or whether it is imposed on him/her as a constraint by some form of patronage) and the poetics dominant in the receiving literature at the time the translation is made. (Lefevere, 2004/2010: 41)

3.2　Three Key Factors in Rewriting Theory

3.2.1　Ideology

Originating from the Greek words "idea" and "logos", the term "ideology" was first coined by the French rationalist philosopher Antoine Destutt de Tracy in 1797 to refer to "the science of ideas". According to *COBUILD English-Chinese Dictionary*, an ideology is a belief or a set of beliefs, especially the political beliefs on which people, parties, or countries base their actions.

Since the cultural turn in Translation Studies in the late twentieth century, translation has been regarded as a kind of cultural and social product usually influenced by such elements as history, culture, ideology, and aesthetics in the target culture. Scholars in the field of language-related, cultural and Translation Studies then tend to define the concept of ideology beyond political sphere. Selden defined "ideology" as a system of representation (aesthetic, religious, judicial and others) which shapes the individual's mental picture of lived experience (Selden et al, 2004: 109). Earlier, ideology was understood by Lefevere as "the dominant concept of what society should (be allowed to) be" (Lefevere, 2004/2010: 14). He also referred approvingly to Fredric Jameson's concept of ideology: "Ideology would seem to be that grillwork of form, convention, and belief which orders our actions" (ibid.: 16). Later, Lefevere described ideology as "the conceptual grid that consists of opinions and attitudes deemed acceptable in a certain society at a certain time, and through which readers and translators approach texts" (Bassnett & Lefevere, 2001/2005: 48).

The Author of the thesis holds that ideology can be divided into social ideology and individual ideology. Alan Geyer believed that "Ideology is the picture of how society should be and how such a society is justified. It is an interconnected set of ideas and beliefs that articulate how the basic values of a group of people apply to the distribution of power in society" (Geyer, 1997: 54). As to individual ideology, "it refers to translator's personal character, education, working and life experience and aesthetic taste" (朱滕滕, 2009). And the translator is caught between his adherence to the ideology in the receiving culture and his faithfulness to the source text. The translator's ideology has a direct impact upon the translator's decision in the translation process, such as the selection of source texts, the evaluation of translation products, the formation of translation styles, and the choice of translation strategies.

3.2.2　Poetics

Mona Baker (1998: 167) considers "poetics of translation" as the inventory of genres, themes and literary devices that comprise any literary system. For Lefevere, poetics is "the dominant concept of what literature should (be allowed to) be" (Lefevere, 2004/2010: 14) in a given society. He also thinks of it as a code which makes literary communication possible. According to him,

> A poetics can be said to consist of two components: one is an inventory of literary devices, genres, motifs, prototypical characters and situations, and symbols; the other a concept of what the role of literature is, or should be, in the social system as a whole. The latter concept is influential in the selection themes that must be relevant to the social system if the work of literature is to be noticed at all. (ibid.: 26)

In Lefevere's opinion, "The functional component of a poetics is obviously closely tied to ideological influences from outside the sphere of the poetics as such, and generated by ideological forces in the environment of the literary system" (ibid.: 27). However, "The inventory component of the poetics of a literary system is not immediately subject to direct influence from the environment once the formative stage of the system is past. The functional component is more likely to undergo direct influence from outside the system. This influence tends to find its most obvious expression in the themes written about in various stages of the system" (ibid.: 33-34).

3.2.3　Patronage

Patronage can be understood to mean something like "the powers (persons, institutions) that can further or hinder the reading, writing and rewriting of literature" (ibid.: 15). According to Lefevere,

> Patronage can be exerted by persons, such as the Medici, Maecenas, or Louis XIV, and also by groups of persons, a religious body, a political party, a social class, a royal court, publishers, and,

last but not least, the media, both newspapers and magazines and larger television corporations. Patrons try to regulate the relationship between the literary system and the other systems, which, together, make up a society, a culture. (ibid.)

For Lefevere, patronage basically consists of three elements:

There is an ideological component, which acts as a constraint on the choice and development of both form and subject matter.

…

There is also an economic component: the patron sees to it that writers and rewriters are able to make a living, by giving them a pension or appointing them to some office.

…

Finally, there is also an element of status involved. Acceptance of patronage implies integration into a certain support group and its lifestyle. (ibid.: 16).

According to Lefevere, "Patronage can be differentiated or undifferentiated, or rather, literary systems can be controlled by a type of patronage that is either differentiated or undifferentiated in nature" (ibid.: 17).

5. 写好一篇"文献综述"和"理论框架"绝非易事，需要 input（输入）——不断的、大量的输入，根据自身的情况/特点把 close reading、critical reading、essential reading、extensive reading、intelligent reading、intensive reading、super-slow reading（按首字母顺序排列）等能力加以结合，培养自己的思辨能力、鉴赏能力、分析能力、综合能力、整合能力，一边 input，一边 output。建议学生读者，为写好一篇表明自己综合专业素质的毕业论文，早些做准备，做好准备，做足准备，平时多多积累，特别是在"文献综述"和"理论框架"方面多下些功夫，目标是"专业化"与"学术化"两不误。

第6章　如何整合（译论结合）

How to Integrate (Practice- & Theory-oriented)

◎学习目标◎

　　第 5 章讨论了如何学会理论思考，第 6 章则讨论如何整合理论与实践，即如何整合思考、整合研究。这为 BTI 生将"翻译+评述"作为毕业论文的首选类型/形式/模式打下良好基础。一名理想译者/译员应是实践和理论俱佳者。同理，一名希望成为能实践、会理论的职业口笔译的本科生，必须学会整合翻译实践和理论。通过本章学习，学生将：

- ●了解、熟悉何为译与论；
- ●对翻译技巧有一辩证、全面的认识；
- ●熟悉乃至掌握 296 种口笔译技巧、方法、策略、原则、途径和理论；
- ●通过案例学习，了解、熟悉并掌握 BA 论文中译论整合的具体写法；
- ●通过案例学习，了解、熟悉并掌握 BTI 论文中译论整合的具体写法。

6.1　译与论整合之解读

　　第一，"译"与"论"分别指"翻译实践"与"翻译理论"（及可用于翻译实践的相关理论）。"译"与"论"的整合，就是强调论文撰写时要注意理论与实践的整合——既指整合思考，也指整合研究。说得"要求"低一些，就是理论与实践的结合。此"结合"仅指一般的结合，但"整合"却指"having different parts <u>working together as a unit</u>"（MWALED 第 859 页）。可见，整合不是简单的结合或"组合"，乃至"凑合"，而是需要使两个及以上不同的部分作为一个整体或单位共同工作、共同发挥作用或功能。因此，本章的英文题目"How to Integrate (Practice- & Theory-oriented)"直译成汉语是：如何整合（以实践与理论为导向）。

　　第二，"译"的意思比较简单，而"论"就比较复杂。"论"，字面上指翻译及其相关理论。从应用视角出发，（应用）翻译理论可以包括翻译方法、策略、原则、技巧等。英国翻译学者彼得·纽马克（Peter Newmark）在"What translation theory is about"（Newmark, 2001a: 19）中指出：

- ●<u>Translation theory's main concern is to determine</u> <u>appropriate translation methods</u> for the widest possible range of texts or text-categories. Further, <u>it provides a</u> <u>framework of principles, restricted rules and hints</u> for translating texts and criticizing translations, a background for problem-solving.

●…the theory demonstrates the possible <u>translation procedures</u> and the <u>various arguments</u> <u>for and against</u> the use of one translation rather than another in a particular context. Note that <u>translation theory is concerned with</u> <u>choices and decisions</u>…

●…<u>translation theory attempts to</u> <u>give some insight into the relation between</u> thought, meaning and language; the universal, cultural an individual aspects of language and behaviour, <u>the understanding of cultures; the interpretation of texts that may be</u> <u>clarified and even</u> <u>supplemented by way of translation.</u>

●…<u>translation theory covers a wide range of pursuits, attempts always to be useful, to</u> <u>assist the individual translator both by stimulating him to write better and to suggest points of</u> <u>agreement on common translation problems. Assumptions and propositions about translation</u> <u>normally arise only from practice, and</u> <u>should not be offered without examples of originals and</u> <u>their translations.</u> As with much literature *á thèse*, the examples are often more interesting than the thesis itself.

　　第三，英汉互译实践与翻译技巧密切相关。翻译实践不是一味的实践或盲目的实践，需要并且提倡的是有理论指导的实践，因此，我们要"古为今用"，继承中国传统译论中的微观层面的翻译理论，其重点是翻译技巧——真正立足本土、适合中国翻译实践的理论。它之所以可以成为微观层面的翻译理论，是因为它可谓之"道"，同样也是"器"——笔者将其看作道器合一，二者可相互转换。"道"可以用来指导、思考，具有普适意义，而器可以用来解决具体的、特殊的问题，与单个的、独立的译者关系密切，甚至因人而异、因事而异，故具有较强的针对性和特殊性。对于熟悉"器"的译者，这个"器"就有规律可循，它可以上升为"道"（即"规律""道理"），具有普遍意义。其实，<u>翻译技巧</u>是一种翻译理念，一种翻译<u>思路</u>，一种翻译<u>视角</u>，一种翻译<u>方法</u>，一种翻译<u>对策</u>，一种翻译<u>途径</u>，一种翻译<u>策略</u>，乃至一种<u>实践总结的提升或升华</u>。<u>它既发挥指导翻译实践的作用，也起到解释翻译实践的作用（翻译理论之功能）。</u>

　　任何技巧，学好了，学活了，学透了，自然大有作为——这好比融会贯通，举一反三。历来就有无师自通者，但那是不多见的 genius，并非意味着翻译技巧无用。考察英美词典，不难发现，genius 就是包括了高超的技能：①MWCD: showing or suggesting great cleverness, <u>skill</u>, or originality: BRILLIANT。②CamD: to be especially <u>skilled</u> at a particular activity; very great and rare natural ability or <u>skill</u>, <u>especially in a particular area such as science</u> <u>or art</u>, or a person who has this。CamD 具体提到，genius 指特别在诸如科学或艺术这种特定领域天生具备罕见的 skill——口笔译就是一种艺术（art）；翻译学就是一种科学/学科（science）。有关 science 词条的另一定义及例证，MWCD 指出：a system or method reconciling practical ends with scientific laws//cooking is both a *science* and an *art*。

　　只要谈及翻译本体和翻译内部研究，翻译（过程）本身一定具有技巧这个不可否认的事实。事实上，做口笔译，谁不讲究方法和技巧？谁不讲求思路和对策？谁不秀自己的 know-how？一位拥有长期口笔译专/职业实践经验的教师和行业专家指出：

　　翻译技巧是翻译实践者经过长期的经验积累总结出的具体翻译方法，具有概括性、指导性和可操作性，能给翻译初学者指点迷津。然而，微观操作层面的技巧运用必须以宏观理论层面的指导为基础。各种翻译技巧的准确灵活运用，需要译者以分析诸如翻译目的、语篇类型、译文读者的认知环境和期待视野等多方面社会文化因素为前提，同时加强巩固自己的双语功底。

　　对翻译理论了解透彻，又能将翻译技巧纯熟、灵活地运用于翻译实践的译家，必定具有较强的翻译理论解释力。鉴于此，我们以为，"指导+操作层面"的具体翻译方法/技巧不能也不可能被翻译理论所替代或取消，而应该得到应有的重视。这不仅要体现在翻译教学中，也要体现在翻译实践中。考虑到翻译研究学科本身就来自翻译实践（practice-based; empirical），目前，翻译理论之所以难以有力地解释不少翻译现象，不是因为这些理论有多"纯"（pure），有多抽象（abstract），有多高贵（highborn），有多"阳春白雪"（highbrow），而是因为这些理论还远未完善，尤其是离开翻译技巧这一层面，翻译理论对翻译现象的解释就愈发显得"力不从心"。由此可见，（宏观）翻译理论（设为 A）与（具体）翻译实践或语言转换、运用能力的过程和/或结果（设为 C）之间有一个"缺环"（missing link），即微观翻译技巧（设为 B）。这 A、B、C 之间的关系可以有以下若干种：

　　● A ⇆ B ⇆ C;　　　　　　● A + B ⇆ C;　　　　　　● A ⇆ B + C。

　　在第一种关系中，A、B、C 既互动，又（相对）独立，乃理想状态。正因为 A、B、C 之间是互动的、辩证统一的，矛盾关系是相互转化的，故它们各自的"地位"在静止状态时不存在孰高孰低。如果要将 A、B、C 之间的关系比作金字塔，笔者以为 A、B、C 都有可能处在金字塔的最顶层。道理很简单，在特定条件下，它们之间的关系则变成动态了。当要将 ST 转换为 TT 的时候，C 构成主要矛盾，理应处在金字塔的顶层（见图 a），因为不会 C，谈何 B、A？但是 A、B 的基础夯得越实（即越处在底端），二者结合对 C 的解释力则越强，尤其是对 C 及以下水准的译作中位居金字塔顶峰的译作之解释力和描述力会更精彩。当要谈论 A（由 A' 和 A" 组成）时，如果是离 B、C（见图 b，处于底层）较远的 A'（纯理论），它当然高高在上（见图 b，处在第四层）；如果是离 B、C 较近的 A"（应用理论），那么 A" 则能较好地、较有效地作用于 B 和 C（见图 c，处在第一、二、三层）。当 B 成为矛盾的主要方面的时候，当 B 对 C 起决定性作用的时候，当 B 处在高屋建瓴的位置，就能对 C、A（或 A" 乃至 A'）起协调、衔接、解释、启示、建议、润滑等关键、微妙作用，就能名正言顺占据金字塔的高层直至顶层（见图 d）。（参考陈刚，2004: 173-176）

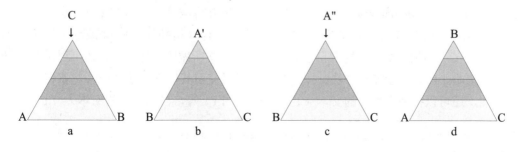

第四，根据长期的应用翻译和文学翻译的实践总结，笔者归纳、总结、（少量）自创了相对完整的（通用翻译实践中）**笔译技巧46种、口译/导译技巧30种**（部分与笔译技巧重叠，但具体处理方法不同）、**名词术语翻译方法40种、诗歌翻译常用策略/方法20种、对联翻译常用策略/方法14种、颜色词常用翻译法8种，以及长句翻译法/步骤18种、长句翻译复核/确认法6种、常用翻译理论/策略/原则/途径/方法等136种**（不包括专用新闻编译技巧，详见本系列教材之《新闻英汉编译教程》）。然而，<u>较好地或全面地运用这些技巧/方法之前提</u>有二：一是较好地或全面地理解源语文本；二是准确地、地道地使用目标语。当然，你的百科知识/杂学是应包含在对 ST 的解读和将其转换成起码是可接受的目标语文本（target text）的能力之中的。若能将这两种综合能力发挥到你个人的极致，那就是翻译的最佳状态和状况。若将这些所谓技巧比作"十八般武艺"，你是将其全部掌握好呢，还是仅掌握其中几招？回答不言而喻。详细内容，请通过二维码拓展阅读。

需要特别指出的是，上述"318+"种翻译技巧/方法等，应理解为是多种翻译思路、视角或路径等，不是用来死记硬背的，也无须作为口诀来记忆，而必须是通过长期不断的口笔译实践，通过"分类""跨界""综合""整合"等运用方法来加以逐步熟悉、了解、掌握。只要你掌握了，就像你掌握了"十八般武艺"那样，（几乎）完全可以融会贯通，运用自如，无须机械模仿，甚至可以将其"抛弃"。而需要补充说明的是，上述近 300 种翻译技巧/方法，并不都是用来作为实践之指南，有些主要是用来解释翻译现象、总结实践结果，并可根据实际翻译所发生的真实情况改变使用技巧或方法。

第五，结合"译"与"论"两大统一体，本章的主要意图是通过对纽马克关于翻译理论的定义、概念的解读，根据在中国进行英汉互译的这个特殊语境，就学生毕业论文中的有关章节做一介绍、分析，以帮助毕业生在（practice-based）论文撰写过程中更好地发挥研究潜力，特别是"译"与"论"的整合潜力和能力。

6.2　译论整合常用实践

BTI 生学习与研究的重点主要在（语言和翻译）实践上，同时根据学校/学科/专业/方向等对学业的要求，学习"不同专业课程要求的足量理论"（a sufficient amount of theory based on the teaching requirements of different subjects），做一些基于实践的（理论）研究，其重点在于指导翻译实践、解释翻译现象、评议 ST & TT 等。

因此，针对上述学习情况，我们推荐译与论相结合的一种普遍做法或常用实践——Translation with Commentary（翻译+评述/翻译兼评论/译与评），简称 TC（自创缩写）。

TC 中的"T"特指论文作者自己独立完成的翻译（指翻译过程和/或翻译结果，即译文[①]），"C"则指论文作者针对自己独立完成的译文所做的评述。该评述可以涉及翻译理论、策略、原则、途径、方法、技巧等，也可以使用其他学科的理论等。若将 T 的内涵扩展，还可以指他人翻译的文本（TT2、TT3、TT4 等，自己翻译的文本为 TT1），所

---

① Translation 既指 translation as a product（a translation），也指 translation as a process（the translating process）。

以 TC 还可以是 a theoretical comment on two translations，或 make a comparative study of TT1, TT2 and TT3 等。

TC 是一种内省式和回顾式研究（introspective and retrospective research）形式。根据 Williams 和 Chesterman（2004: 7-8），TC 中 commentary 的内容及价值包括：

● some discussion of the translation assignment；

● an analysis of aspects of the source text；

● a reasoned justification of the kinds of solutions you arrived at for particular kinds of translation problems；

● one value of such research that lies in the contribution that increased self-awareness can make to translation quality；

● helpful guidelines for your translation decisions in what you have read in Translation Studies；

● a classical example of a commentary where the translator describes in detail the various stages he went through during the translation of a poem。

6.3　论文案例分析研究

本节提供的案例及其分析涉及两种论文的两种论证方法：翻译理论与译例之整合分析、翻译技巧与译例之整合分析、翻译技巧与翻译理论之整合分析、专业/学术学位论文中的案例分析。

6.3.1　BA 论文案例分析研究

4. Case Studies:

Inadequate Translations and Adequate Translations[①]

4.1　Tourism Translation and the *Skopos* Rule

Among all the three rules of translation, the *Skopos* rule is of the most importance. The purpose of travel guidebooks is to appeal to visitors, stimulating their visiting interest and to provide information for their visit. To serve this purpose becomes the decisive factor to judge whether the translation conforms to the *Skopos* rule.

4.1.1　Cultural Translation Errors and the *Skopos* Rule

On grounds that New Zealand in the southern hemisphere is a country strongly influenced by the Great Britain, there is a huge cultural difference between New Zealand and China. The culture-loaded words and sentences constitute a barrier in the translating of the selected books. In the translating process, the translators have to decide whether the conventions need to be adapted to the target culture.

[Case 1.1.1]

ST: If you're really up for some super-human thrills, this is the highest skydiving in NZ, at 18,000 ft.

TT: 如果你真的已准备妥当并打算做一项超越人类极限的惊险运动，那么就来弗朗兹约瑟夫跳伞吧，

① 选自浙江大学英语专业本科毕业论文的真实文稿，文中错误与不足在所难免。

这里是在新西兰跳伞的最高点，<u>高 18000 英尺</u>。

[Case Analysis] The ST is cited from the introduction to activities in New Zealand. In the ST, the actual number of the height was quoted in order to emphasize the excitement of the skydiving. The word "ft (feet)" is a unit of length commonly used in English-speaking countries. However, Chinese tourists are not familiar with the actual length of "18000 英尺". Thus, the translators failed to achieve the writer's intention of emphasis. To fulfill the gap between two countries, the translators should have adopt another unit of length which the TT readers are familiar with, such as "米（m）" or "千米（km）" in that the TT readers can achieve the closest reading experience with the ST readers. In the revision (see Revision), apart from adapting the unit of length, the Author compared the height of skydiving to that of Shanghai Jin Mao Tower which many Chinese tourists know to ensure the translation achieve writers' expectation.

The Author revised the translation as follows:

[Revision] 如果你真的已准备妥当并打算做一项超越人类极限的惊险运动，那么就来弗朗兹约瑟夫跳伞吧，这里是在新西兰跳伞的最高点，<u>高约 5500 米（相当于 13 座上海金茂大厦）</u>。

To reproduce the culture-loaded words into acceptable and accessible ones in the TL is one of the ways to bridge the gap between the two different cultures. The other way is to retain the culture-loaded words to keep the exoticness. Whether to adapt the culture conventions is also decided by the *Skopos* of the translation.

[Case 1.1.2]

ST: …see main-street <u>marae</u> (meeting houses), join in a <u>hangi</u> (Maori feast) or catch a cultural performance with traditional Maori song, dance and usually a blood-curdling <u>haka</u> (war dance). And don't let us stop you from considering <u>tamoko</u>, tradition Maori tattooing (often applied to the face)

TT: 在主要商业街上看到毛利族聚会的房子，随时加入一场毛利族的盛宴，或者观看一场毛利族的文化演出——既有传统歌舞，也有令人震撼的战争舞蹈场面。当然不能忘了传统的毛利族文身——多半纹在脸上。

[Case Analysis] The Maori culture is an unavoidable part in the introduction to New Zealand. In the ST, the writer quoted words in Maori language and explained them in English with annotations. In this case, the readers caught a glimpse of the Maori language before they set foot in New Zealand and would not be at lost when they get acquainted with Maori language during their visit to these places. However, in the Chinese translated version, the translators just translated the Maori words. The function of quoting the original language has been ignored. Though the translator has emphasized the Maori culture by adding "毛利族的", after reading this part, the Chinese readers may take it for granted that the Maori people use English as well. And they will be confused at the sight of words in Maori Language during their visit. In the revision, the Author provides TT readers with the Maori words to emphasize the language difference between Maori and other regions in New Zealand. In which case, the TT readers can get prepared for the Maori language.

The Author revised the translation as follows:

[Revision] 在主要商业街上看到毛利族聚会的房子（毛利语：marae），随时加入一场毛利族的盛宴（毛利语：hangi），或者观看一场毛利族的文化演出——既有传统歌舞，也有令人震撼的战争舞蹈场面（毛利语：haka）。当然不能忘了传统的毛利族文身（毛利语：tamoko）——多半纹在脸上。

4.2　Tourism Translation and the Coherence Rule

The coherence rule stresses that the translated text should be acceptable and meaningful to TT readers. In other words, it should be coherent with the TT situation. In the process of translating, translators should take TT readers' background knowledge into consideration. They should adopt various translation techniques to conform to the TL features and styles, and reproduce the information acceptable and accessible in the TL culture. The commonly used translation techniques such as (1) Adopting the Established Popular Translated Names; (2) Amplification; (3) Domestication; (4) Information Restructuring; and (5) Shift of Perspective were adopted in the translating process of the said book.

4.2.1　Adopting the Established Popular Translated Name and the Coherence Rule

In travel guidebooks, there are many proper names, namely, those of towns and of tourist attractions. Some translation of proper names has been revised with the development of translation. During the translating process, translators should adopt the popular translated version confirmed by the authorities.

[Case 2.1.1]

ST: ...while the townships at either end—at Golden Bay and Karamea—will bring you back down to earth with the most laid-back of landings.

TT: 位于步道两头的<u>黄金海湾（Golden Bay）</u>和卡拉米亚（Karamea）都有小镇，在小镇上尽情地放松身心，它们将把你从壮美的高山步道上带回现实世界。

[Case Analysis] According to Wikipedia, Golden Bay was called Moordenaar's Bay, Massacre Bay and Coal Bay in its history. Then, in the late 1850s, with the discovery of gold in at Aorere, its name was changed to the current name of Golden Bay. Regardless of its meaning as a proper name, Golden Bay can be translated as "金色海岸". According to the search results online, there has not been a confirmed Chinese translation for "Golden Bay". In "google map", Golden Bay is translated as "戈尔登湾" (see Photo1). In Booking.com, Golden Bay is translated as "黄金海岸" (see Photo 2). In the revised version has included two emerging Chinese translations of "Golden Bay", and provided tourists with the English names in the original. Before the confirmation of one Chinese translation, the revised version can reduce the risk of misleading TT readers.

Photo 1

Photo 2

The Author revised the translation as follows:

[Revision] 位于步道两头的<u>黄金海湾（又名戈尔登湾，英文：Golden Bay）</u>和卡拉米亚（英文：Karamea）都有小镇，在小镇上尽情地放松身心，它们将把你从壮美的高山步道上带回现实世界。

4.2.2 Amplification and the Coherence Rule

Amplification is an important translation technique in translating tourism materials. It provided evidence for readers who were not familiar with the culture of the source text. Without ample amplification, specific cultures may lose their significance.

[Case 2.2.1]

ST: Kiwi food was once a bland echo of a British Sunday dinner.

TT: 早期的新西兰饮食单调，<u>主要以英式的烤肉为主</u>。

[Case Analysis] In Case 2.2.1, translating "British Sunday Dinner" requires strong cultural background knowledge. For people like Chinese who had no experience of living in Britain, it is hard to understand "British Sunday Dinner". If the translation went like this, "早期的新西兰饮食只是简单重复英式周日的晚餐", TT readers would be confused about the content of "英式周日晚餐". In the Chinese version, the translator replaced the phrase "British Sunday dinner" with "grill" which is the main dish in "British Sunday dinner". By adopting the translation technique of amplification, the translator fulfilled the culture gap between two countries where people can hardly share common background knowledge. Besides, in the translating of Case 2.2.1, translators also adopted the translation technique of Generalization.

[Case 2.2.2]

ST: Moby's mates

TT: <u>白鲸</u>莫比的朋友

[Case Analysis] In this case, the writer compared the whales to Moby's mates which is the main character in Moby Dick. This novel is more familiar to English readers than to Chinese readers. If the translator simply translated it as "莫比的朋友", the Chinese readers who did not read this novel before may be confused by this "Moby". To avoid the said conditions, translators added "白鲸" as a hint for readers but the Author believes that it is not enough for Chinese readers to understand the true story. It is suggested that the translator can provide an annotation or a note, stating that Moby came from the novel Moby Dick. Thus, the Author revised the translation as follows to provide brief introduction to the identity of Moby:

[Revision] 白鲸莫比（麦尔维尔小说《白鲸》的主要人物）的朋友

4.2.3　Domestication and the Coherence Rule

Tourism materials sometimes adopted popular sayings to make the text interesting and attractive. Because of the differences in cultures, TT readers have difficulties to understand the literal translation of these words. Sometimes, they can be misled by the literal translation. The translator should adapt the popular saying to one that share familiar meaning in the TL if possible.

[Case 2.3.1]

ST: The New 'Big Easy'

TT: 休闲天堂

[Case Analysis] This is a title for a chapter whose translation is supposed to be both short and informative. In the translation of the above case, the translators abandoned the SL structure and reproduced the meaning of the chapter title concerned.

"The New 'Big Easy'" contains a popular saying of "Big Easy". "Big Easy" is known as the nickname of the American city, New Orleans. The origin of the nickname is related to the relaxed atmosphere in New Orleans (concluded from the answers in wiseGEEK). The writer compared New Zealand to "The New 'Big Easy'" to emphasize that New Zealand is also a heaven of relaxation. However, for Chinese readers who rarely knows the meaning of "Big Easy", it is hard to understand the translation like "南半球的新奥尔良" or "新新奥尔良". the translator concluded the contents in this column with "休闲天堂". It showed ample orientation to the audience while keeping the original meaning of "Big Easy" which means paradise or place that makes people relaxed.

4.2.4　Information Restructuring and the Coherence Rule

Since the ST and the TT are targeted at readers with different cultural backgrounds, it is common and understandable that they have different expectations towards the content. What is important and interesting in the ST may make no sense in the TT. In the translating process, the translators should compare needs from different readers and reorganize the information to meet the requirements of the targeted readers.

[Case 2.4.1]

ST: Money—ATMs are widely available, especially in larger cities and towns. Credit cards accepted in most hotels and restaurants.

TT: 现金——自动柜员机随处可见，尤其是在较大的城市和城镇里。大多数的酒店与餐馆都接受信用卡——银联卡也能用。

[Case 2.4.2]

ST: Visas—Citizens of Australia, the UK and 56 other countries don't need visas for NZ (length-of stay allowances vary). See www.immigration.govt.nz.

TT: 签证——入境新西兰旅游的中国公民需要持有访问签证。入境要求：在离境日之前护照至少要有 3 个月的有效期，并且需要有效的入境签证。

[Case 2.4.3]

ST：Mobile Phones—European phones will work on NZ's network, but not most American or Japanese phones. Use global roaming or a local SIM card and prepaid account.

TT：手机——如果不想支付昂贵的国际漫游费，最明智的选择是在抵达新西兰之后买一张当地的通信公司 SIM 卡。

[Case Analysis] Strictly speaking, the TT is not translation of ST provided. In Case 2.4.1, the translators added "银联卡也能用" to the original text. This is a piece of information targeted at TT readers only. On the grounds that Union Pay is widely-used in China, whether Union Pay cards work or not is really crucial to Chinese visitors. Though the source text did not mention Union Pay cards, it is advisable to add this information.

In Case 2.4.2, it is about the visa applications to New Zealand. The Chinese version replaced the information with requirements for Chines visitors. Information in English version in this case is useless to Chinese readers. It would be redundant to provide the original information in Chinese.

The same went for the third case which was about the use of mobile phones for visitors in New Zealand. In translating travel guidebooks, it is important to take the receivers into consideration, especially when the two countries involved share little in common.

4.2.5　Shift of Perspective and the Coherence Rule

Each language has its own features. To conform to the coherence rule in translation, translators can alter the perspective and reproduce the meaning of ST. This is a common strategy adopted in Chinese-English and English-Chinese translation.

[Case 2.5.1]

ST: (1) Chances are these are the kind of images that drew you to New Zealand in the first place, and (2) these are exactly the kind of experiences that the Bay of Islands delivers so well.

TT: 这些美丽的明信片风景会在第一时间把你吸引到新西兰。而在岛屿湾，这些图片上的风景全部可以变成现实。

[Case Analysis] Clause (1) and clause (2) are sentences with inanimate subject. Inanimate Subject sentences are commonly used in English. If translated word by word into Chinese, it does not fit the conventions of the Chinese language. Thus, translators changed the subjects of two clauses to conform to Chinese way of expression. In this translation, translation techniques of Division and Reorganizing were also adopted.

4.3　Tourism Translation and the Fidelity Rule

The fidelity rule is also interpreted as the rule of "intertextual coherence" which emphasizes the relationship between the ST and the TT. It lays emphasis on the coherence between the information in the ST and the TT. Though the fidelity rule is subordinate to the two rules discussed above, it requires that the translator achieve a maximally faithful imitation of the source text.

4.3.1　Linguistic Translation Errors and the Fidelity Rule

Linguistic translation errors focus on language structures. It refers to the deviation from the linguistic norms. Though it is not commonly seen in publications, the Author still collects a few examples which should have been avoided. In the translating process, it is crucial to select a proper word in the TL with accurate comprehension of the meaning in the ST and the meaning of the word chosen. The variation of one word can alter the meaning of a phrase.

[Case 3.1.1]

ST: Need to Know

TT: 行前参考

[Case Analysis] "Need to Know" is the title for a column introducing important information for visitors preparation before they leave for New Zealand. In the first place, the translators worked to avoid pragmatic translation errors by adding the phrase "行前" to illustrate the function of the following content. However, the second phrase "参考" weakens the importance of this chapter. In the ST, the writer used the word "need to" instead of "for reference". As mentioned before, this chapter provides the readers with crucial information about pre-tour preparations for tourists in New Zealand, including the visa issues, the emergency numbers in New Zealand, the best season for travelling, the use of mobile phones and the conditions of the airports. In Chinese "参考" means something offered for reference which does not demand the readers to accept it. The content in this chapter is more than "reference".

The Author revised the translation as follows:

[Revision] 行前须知

"须" means "need to", which is an adequate equivalence of the diction used in the SL. The tone of emphasis in ST is retained.

[Case 3.1.2]

ST: The <u>ultimate</u> encounter is on a scenic flight, which often also provides grandstand views of Mt Cook, Westland forest and a seemingly endless ocean.

TT: 还可以乘坐观光飞机，在空中俯瞰库克山、韦斯特兰森林全貌以及好似无边无际的太平洋。

[Case Analysis] This is cited from the introduction to activities in Franz Josef & Fox Glaciers in chapter "20 Top Experience". Prior to the extracted part, the book illustrated several popular activities in the same region. The translated Chinese version ignored the word "ultimate" in the source text, which caused the loss of meaning. In English, "ultimate" means most extreme or important because it is either the original or final, or the best or worst. In the contents offered above, it means "the best". Scenic flight is recommended as the best activity in Franz Josef & Fox Glaciers. In Chinese translated version, "还有" meant "besides" or "what's more". The same level of importance was attached to scenic flight and other two activities mentioned before.

The Author revised the translation as follows:

[Revision] 若想领略最棒的风景，不妨乘坐观光飞机，在空中俯瞰库克山、韦斯特兰森林全貌以及好似无边无际的太平洋。

4.3.2　Pragmatic Translation Errors and the Fidelity Rule

Pragmatic translation errors are attributed to the translators' insufficient consideration of the TT readers. Although pragmatic translation errors are not very difficult to solve when they are identified, the consequences of them can be serious.

[Case 3.2.1]

ST: *Tramping in New Zealand*

101 Great Tramps

202 Great Walks: The Best Day Walks in New Zealand

Accessible Walks

Don't Forget Your Scroggin

TT: 《徒步新西兰》

《101 条徒步路线》

《202 条徒步路线：新西兰最佳单日徒步计划》

《简易徒步》

《带着斯可罗金去徒步》

[Case Analysis] The writers have recommended several books about tramping for readers. In the Chinese version, the translators translated the names of the books word by word followed by the English name. However, the translator ignored the fact that these books were all written in English. It was worth doubting whether these books have been translated into Chinese and whether these Chinese names correspond to the names used. According to my research on several online bookstores in China, most of these books do not have a Chinese version and for the only one that has, its translation dose not correspond to the names actually used. In translation, it is important to follow the pronunciation of the owners of the proper names. That is to say, the information in this part is misleading. The readers hardly can find the book they want by checking these names. In Jingdong.com, which is a cooperating website with Lonely Planet, *Tramping in New Zealand* is displayed as "新西兰漫游" (see Photo 3), and there is only English version available. And the other two books have no Chinese versions as well.

Photo 3

The solution is to borrow information from similar Chinese sources. There are a few popular websites concerning outbound tourism, where people shares experience(s). The translator can replace the books mentioned via website links with worth reading materials.

4.3.3　Text-specific Translation Errors and the Fidelity Rule

Text-specific translation errors are related to text-specific translation problems, such as corresponding translation problems. These problems can be evaluated from a functional or pragmatic point of view.

[Case 3.3.1]

ST: Auckland isn't your average metropolis. It's regularly rated one of the world's most livable cities, and while it's never going to challenge NYC or London in the excitement stakes, it's blessed with good beaches, flanked by wine regions and has a large enough population to support a thriving dining, drinking and live-music scene.

TT: 奥克兰是一座超乎想象的城市。它是世界上最宜居的城市之一，但是又不像纽约或伦敦那样充满刺激和冒险。奥克兰拥有美丽的海滩，四周布满葡萄酒庄，还有足以支撑其就餐、饮品和现场音乐等产业蓬勃发展的人口数量。

[Case Analysis] The paragraph above described Auckland by comparing it with New York and London. Judged separately, the translation of each clause is acceptable, if not satisfying. The problems were among the sentence relationships. The second sentence is a long and complex sentence with clauses and parallel structures. The Chinese version translated the meaning of each clause but confused the relationships between these clauses. The second sentence could be divided into two parts from the word "and". In the second part, the first clause [marked as clause (A)] served as the adverbial clauses for the following three clauses [marked as clause (a) (b) (c)]. The second clause can be divided as follows:

(1) It's regularly rated one of the world's most livable cities, (2) (A) and while it's never going to challenge NYC or London in the excitement stakes, (a) it's blessed with good beaches, (b) flanked by wine regions and (c) has a large enough population to support a thriving dining, drinking and live-music scene.

But the Chinese version has changed the inner logic among the sentences. In the translation, the translator combined the meaning of clause (1) and clause (2). And clause (2) served as the supporting evidence for clause (1), instead of the adverbial clauses for following three clauses. It's much clearer to see the logical relationship between sentences through back-translation. The Chinese version can be back-translated as followed:

It's regularly rated one of the world's most livable cities, but it's never going to challenge NYC or London in the excitement stakes. It's blessed with good beaches, flanked by wine regions and has a large enough population to support a thriving dining, drinking and live-music scene. (The "and while" has been changed to "but". And the last three clauses were separated.)

The Author revised the translation as follows:

[Revision] 奥克兰是一座与众不同的城市。奥克兰被评为是世界上最宜居的城市之一。虽然不像纽约或伦敦那样充满刺激和冒险，奥克兰拥有美丽的海滩，四周布满葡萄酒庄，还有足以支撑其就餐、饮品和现场音乐等产业蓬勃发展的人口数量。

【案例分析】

（1）作者在旅游翻译及其评述过程中，运用了德国功能主义翻译理论，涉及"三大原则"——"目的原则""连贯原则""忠实原则"。有关名词术语见下文中的画线部分

（下同）。

（2）作者通过找出文化翻译错误、语言翻译错误、语用翻译错误、文本特有的翻译错误，结合一些常用翻译技巧（如"约定俗成""增益""归化""信息重组""视角转换"等），对翻译案例进行分析。

（3）作者"译"与"论"之整合，从以下目录中可见一斑：

6.3.2　BTI 论文案例分析研究

3　Principles of Translating the Modern Dance Textbook[①]

3.2　Principles of Dance Textbook Translation

3.2.1　First Principle: Faithfulness

Although translation is inevitably a creative work based on original texts, faithfulness is still the very basic requirement in translation. For the three-character criteria of translation—faithfulness (信), expressiveness (达) and elegance (雅), faithfulness is always given top priority.

In translating *A Primer for Choreographers*, the translation of professional terms in choreography turns out to be the most important task calls for the principle of translating terminology, namely, faithfulness.

Different professions have their respective systems of terminology. In dance, different dance styles have their respective systems of expression, too. *A Primer for Choreographers* as an instructive textbook for beginning choreographers of contemporary dance reasonably has its particular system of terminology, as explained in the analysis of the linguistic features of the proposed source texts in 3.1.

The yardsticks for evaluating the quality of translation of terminology include:

①Clarity. The translated or TL term can reveal the SL meaning it implies and help recognize or understand it.

②Consistency. The expression of the same term should be fixed in case the inconsistency of terminology

---

① 选自浙江大学翻译专业 BTI 学位论文的真实文稿，文中错误与不足在所难免。

causes chaos in communication.

　　③Decency. The usage of the term obeys the regulations of the respective subject area, thus avoiding causing passive effects.

　　④Conciseness. The expression should be concise enough, like the use of abbreviation.

　　⑤Accuracy. The translation should be correct without missing any essential information.

　　⑥Domestication. The native or TL expression is preferred in adapting foreign terms. These yardsticks will serve as a helpful reference for the following analysis of the translation of *A Primer for Choreographers*.

　　(1) Key concepts in choreography

ST	TT
time	时、时间
space	空、空间
energy/effort	力、力效

　　(2) Variations in use of energy

quality	the characteristics of movement determined by the way energy is used (examples are swinging, percussive, suspend, sustained, and vibratory movement)	质感
intensity	presence of a greater or lesser degree of energy; relative level of energy concentration	力度
accent	a stress or emphasis on a specific beat or movement	重拍、强弱

　　(3) Formation

Terms used to describe two or more movements linked together:

(movement) phrase	舞句
(movement) combination	动作、组合、量
(movement) sequence	动作、组合、顺序、串、套
(movement) pattern	动作、组合

Terms used to describe the form of a dance, movements or body:

(dance/movement) shape	形、状
(dance/movement) form	形式（opposed to Contents; the shape, the sequence, the organization of the action）、结构
(body) posture	造型、姿势

　　(4) Time relationships: musical terms

ST	Definition	TT
rhythm	a structure of movement patterns in time	节奏、韵律
tempo	the pace or speed at which movement progresses; relatively slower or faster	速度、节拍
fugue	a musical form consisting of a theme repeated a fifth above or a fourth below its first statement	赋格曲形式

rondo	a musical form wherein a sequence of contrasting themes occur with an inevitable return to the first theme (for example, ABACADA)	回旋曲形式
canon	a musical term indicating a composition in which two or more parts recur, repeat, or interrelate with each other	卡农曲形式
sonata	a musical form using three or four contrasting rhythms and moods that are all related in tone and style	奏鸣曲形式
ABA form	in dance or in music, a represents one theme, B another; ABA being two contrasting themes followed by a repeat of the first	ABA 形式
cumulative rhythm	a pattern that progresses by adding units in sequence (for example, 1-2, 1-2-3, 1-2-3-4)	累加节奏形式
suite	a musical term describing an instrumental sequence made up of a series of forms appropriate to the dance, used in dance to indicate a sequence of related patterns or dances	组曲
accent	In music, accent refers to a stress or an emphasis on a musical event. Accents can be created by changes in loudness, by extreme pitches and by rhythmic placement.	重音
syncopation	a character of rhythm that occurs when accents occur in unexpected paces within an otherwise predictable or repetitive pattern	切分节奏形式
rubato	a flexible tempo; not strictly on the beat	弹性速度形式
theme	melodic subject of a musical composition	主题、主旋律
dynamics	the use of weight, space, flow and time to create different energetic statements	力度
legato	A word borrowed from musical language, but it is used in dance with the same meaning. It expresses a quality of movement in which flow doesn't stop, but the feeling is always continuous and fluent.	连奏形式
jam session	A **jam session** is a musical event, process, or activity where musicians play (i.e. "jam") by improvising without extensive preparation or predefined arrangements.	即兴

(5) Geometric terms: design and spatial relationships

range	the relative scope or extent of movement; technical range of movement is determined by body size and joint flexibility	动作、技巧幅度
diagonal lines of force	In the traditional box stage, the diagonal lines from upstage across to downstage on the other side. These lines gain force through the angles they form with each other and with the horizontal and vertical frame of the stage.	力的对角线
dimension	the apparent size of a movement, relative both to previous movement and to the stage space	动作幅度（长、宽、高）

level	an aspect of space dealing with height from the floor, ranging from a prone position to the greatest attitude of a leap; usually thought of in terms of horizontal planes	高度（抬腿、跳跃）
size	the physical magnitude of something (how big it is)	动作大小（长×宽）

Question and answer:	**问与答的形式：**
solo or group	独舞或群舞
initiate a movement	以一段动作开始
self or others respond by	自己或其他人作出回应
mirroring	镜像模仿
contrasting	形成对比
extending	拓展延伸
reversing	逆向运动
Relation to inanimate object:	**重新设定与他物之间的关系：**
move toward	向其移动
away	远离它
around	围绕它
over	越过它
under	位于其下
through	穿过它
from bottom to top	从下至上
as if it were not there	仿佛（它）并不存在
Relation to other dancers:	**同其他舞者之间的关系：**
move toward	向其移动
away	远离他
around	围绕他
over	越过他
under	位于其下
through	穿过他
with	与他随同
in opposition	与他反方向运动
in contrast	与他形成反差
as if they were not there	假设其他人并不存在

(6) Schools of philosophy or methodologies		
surrealism	an artistic flight from commonplace reality, with an emphasis upon usual, often absurd, relationship and forms	超现实主义
realism	an approach to artistic formulation that emphasizes the reproduction or duplication of "things as they are"	现实主义

cubism	a form of artistic organization that implies that it is possible to observe and experience all aspects and levels of an object simultaneously—as if with limitless perspective	立体主义
expressionism	the attempt of an artist to project an image on the basis of his own recreation to reality	表现主义
impressionism	an artist's presentation of an oblique look at reality, as if through a cloud or mist	印象主义
abstraction	the process of reducing a thing to its most basic or essential characteristics	抽象化处理
distortion	…	曲解
self-expression	…	自我表现
self-actualization	…	自我实现
representation (painting)	a creation that is a visual or tangible rendering of someone or something	表象、具象表现

(7) Movements

motif/motive	This is a word that is most commonly used within the dance composition speech. It refers to a small choreographic unit (a gesture, movement or phrase) that is the main reference from which a bigger choreography (or dance piece) is built and composed.	动机
motif-development	This is a procedure of a dance composition method that consists of transforming a basic choreographic motif to create a larger or whole piece of dance. Variations of the motif are done through strategies like repetition, inversion, rhythmical modifications, amplification, minimization, ornamentation, deconstruction and all imaginable compositional tools.	动机发展
suspension	a quality of movement that occurs in a moment of resistance to gravity, such as the instant in which the dancer hangs in space at the top of a leap	滞空
sustained movement	A quality of movement that is smooth and unaccented. There is no apparent start or stop, only a continuity of energy flow.	持续性动作、延伸动作
swing movement	a quality of movement established by a fall with gravity, a gain in momentum, a loss of momentum, and the repeated cycle of fall and recovery, like that of a pendulum	地心引力摆、摇摆动作
vibratory moment	a quality of movement characterized by rapidly repeated bursts of percussive movement; like jitters	震颤
arch	the extension up and back of the upper body and head	拱背
chest lift	with back on the floor, chest lifts off the floor	挺胸

contraction	tightening the abdominal, tucking the pelvis, and forming a "C" with the torso so that the shoulders are over the pelvis (Graham technique)	收缩
turnout	A position of the legs in which the feet are pointing outwards. It is an external rotation of the limb that is executed with the whole leg, including the hip.	外开
turn in	rotation of a limb away from the front of the body	回旋、内扣
abduction	Abduction of a joint moves a bone away from the midline of the body.	外展
adduction	Adduction of a joint moves a bone toward the midline of the body.	内收
mirroring	Exercising method that may be used by dancers but that is most commonly used by actors or in the training field for drama. It consists of a bodily activity for two, in which one person moves and the other follows as if s/he was a mirror. This strategy is used to develop concentration, communication, cooperation and creative skills.	镜仿法
extension	Extension of a joint is generally to straighten it.	伸展、延伸
natural gesture	movements drawn from daily life experience	自然姿态

(8) Verbal phrases as exercise

ST	TT
Kinaesthetic sensations:	动觉：
tension to relaxation	收紧或放松
how it feels to run fast	跑得快的感觉
pounding a nail	敲钉子
whipping cream	打奶泡
blowing up a balloon	吹气球
"sitting on top of the world"	"坐在世界之巅"
sailing in a strong wind	强风中航行
walking in outer space	外太空行走
riding on the rail of a kite	坐在风筝线之上
Sense-memory experiences (try to remember how it felt and relive it):	感官记忆经历（努力回忆那种感觉，并重新感受它）：
on a sticky, hot day	身处潮热的一天
locked in a small, dark room	被锁在一间小黑屋里
late at night in a strange and dismal place	深夜身处陌生凄凉的地方
the feel of sandpaper	磨砂纸的感觉
taking a cold shoulder	遭冷遇
tasting a sour lemon	尝一口酸柠檬
hot sand on your feet	脚上的热沙子

skiing down a deep snow slope	从一个雪坡上滑下
wind blowing from a mountain meadow	从草场吹来的风
diving into cool, green water	潜入又冷又绿的水中
Natural action and gesture:	**自然行为和手势：**
human and animal locomotion	人与动物的运动
bird in flight	逃走的鸟
rooster crowing	鸡鸣
workman at a lathe	机床旁的工人
leopard crouching	蜷伏的美洲豹
boy on a skateboard	滑冰的男孩
snake coiling	螺旋的蛇
woman scrubbing steps	擦洗台阶的女人
parachute jumper	跳伞运动员
tennis players	羽毛球运动员
First reaction in dramatic situations:	**突发情况下的第一反应：**
You trump your partner's ace.	你在对手强项上战胜了他。
Hurricane warning is posted.	飓风警告贴出。
You win $50,000 prize.	赢得五万美元大奖。
Messenger brings black-edged letter.	信使送来黑边信封。
House is on fire.	房子着火了。
Earthquake is beginning.	地震了。
You got an A in physics.	物理课得了优秀。
War is declared.	宣战了。
Your leg is broken.	腿断了。
The wedding date is set.	婚期定了。
Response to action words:	**对行动词汇的回应：**
melt	融化
wiggle	扭摆
bounce	弹跳
ooze	泄露
collapse	倒塌
soar	吼叫
snatch	抢走
cling	贴着
"gimme"	"给我"
flip	轻掷

jiggle	轻摇
pitter-pat	噼噼啪啪
slink	溜走
Within space limitations:	空间限制：
in a small square	小型广场
in a three-foot circle	半径三尺的圆
by a rope stretched diagonally between two pillars	两根柱子之间连着一根绳子
around a single pylon	一座指示塔周围
behind a screen	屏幕的后方
on a high ox	一头高大的牛之上
by a rope suspended from the ceiling	天花板垂下一根绳子
surrounded by three benches	由三条长凳包围
by a stepladder in a corner	角落里一把梯子旁
using both stage and audience space	运用舞台与观众席两个空间

(9) Special terms

Graham technique	A modern dance technique developed by Martha Graham, based on "contraction and release" as the motivation of all movements. It includes terms such as spiral, tilt, and pitch turn. Used in the choreography of Graham, Ailey, and Elisa Monte companies.	葛兰姆技巧
Horton technique	A modern dance technique which was developed from a balance study by Lester Horton. It includes terms such as squat, T, table, and stag. Used within the choreography of companies such as Ailey, Philadanco, and Tristler.	何顿技巧
Humphrey technique	A modern dance technique based on the concept of "fall and recovery", developed by Doris Humphrey. A predecessor and mentor to Jose Limon of Limon technique.	汉弗莱技巧
Limon technique	A modern dance technique developed by Jose Limon, which built on the concepts of Doris Humphrey and is based on the "fall, recovery, and rebound". Used within the choreography of Limon, Falco, Muller, and Lubovitch.	李蒙技巧

3.2.2　Second Principle: Flexibility

A Primer for Choreographers as a textbook that guides the students in learning the knowledge and method of choreography, concerns the faithful transfer of the foreign concepts so that the students can have the knowledge that the English readers receive the same or similar as well.

Inevitably, however, the direct translation of foreign concepts requires a certain background of education. On the one hand, domesticating certain definitions of dance terms, i.e. finding the equivalent or corresponding expressions in Chinese dance, is helpful for the students to receive and understand the information most efficiently. Foreignizing would attain the original or SL expressions of the foreign concepts that are exactly what this textbook attempts to teach. On the other hand, polysemous terms being translated will change their meaning in different collocations, such as *form*. When it goes with body, it means 造型. When it is used to describe dance works, it refers to 形式 or 结构架构; When it is put around words like *spiral,* it will be better to translate it into 形态. Let us check out more as below:

(1) Polysemy

Motive/Motif:

Such patterns grow out of the primal <u>motives</u> of man: love, hate, hope, fear, aspiration, greed, and simple animal joy.	这类动作源于人最初的<u>欲望</u>：爱、恨、希望、恐惧、抱负、贪婪或简单的动物性快感。
What do you want to do with it? What do you have to say? What is your <u>motivation</u>?	你想怎样处理它？你要说什么？你<u>创作的动机</u>是什么？
Unless the choreographer wants a shock of unheralded differences, he should consider both the <u>motivation</u> of what has happened and the implication of what will happen.	编舞者如果不想碰到料想不到的效果，就既要考虑之前动作的<u>动机是什么</u>，又要考虑它对接下来动作的影响。

Theme:

Simple manipulation of <u>theme</u>: Choose a simple four-count theme. Repeat it. Develop into a seven-count phrase. Repeat original four-count. Contrast with a new four-count. Return to original four-count movement.	**<u>主题</u>动作的简单处理：** 选择一个四拍的简单主题动作。 重复做一遍。 将其发展至七拍的句子。 再重复原先的四拍动作。 重新做一段四拍的动作。 返回原先的四拍动作。
Variations on a <u>theme</u>: Form a simple <u>movement theme</u> and rehearse it carefully so that you are sure of its components. Vary this selected movement phrase in at least five different ways (experiment with varying relationships of space, time, and dynamics). Develop another and contrasting theme and make variations on this.	**<u>主题</u>动作的变奏处理：** 编排一组简单的<u>主题动作</u>并认真排练它，一直到确定每一个部分。 以五种以上方式来改编这组主题动作（通过改编空间、时间、力量来试验）。 发展另一组动作和不同的主题，并做改编。
The resolution was a simple <u>twelve-count theme</u> performed intermittently by varying numbers of dancers, finally blending into a two-voice canon in which the unusual dynamic and spatial variables were explored.	解决方法是不同数量的舞者间歇表演一段<u>十二拍的动作</u>，最后汇合成二声部卡农形式，不寻常的动态与空间变量都可以进行探索。
Transitions, changing from one movement to another, are both a part of the <u>theme</u> that precedes and the <u>theme</u> that follows.	动作之间转换时做的过渡动作，既联系着前面的<u>主题</u>，又连着接下来的<u>主题</u>。

After the initiation of the <u>movement theme</u>, something must happen. One movement phrase is followed by another, sometimes varied, contrasted, or developed. There may be <u>theme and counter-theme</u>, rhythmic complications, or a dynamic resolution.	动作主题一旦确定，一切都顺其自然。舞句紧扣主题展开，有时会产生变化，或形成对比，或经过发展演绎。有符合主题的，也有与之相反的，有节奏上的丰富复杂，又或是动感的结尾。
Sequential forms such as AB, ABA, rondo, <u>theme</u> and variation, suite, and sonata are aids in identifying relationships.	类似 AB 形、ABA 形、回旋曲形式、<u>主题与变奏形式</u>、组曲形式和奏鸣曲形式的动作顺序，都可以帮助识别各种关系。
theme and variation theme and development theme and contrast	主题与变奏 主题与发展 主题与对比

Phrase:

All perform the same nine-count <u>movement phrase</u> simultaneously, moving in a circle for five counts, in a straight line for four counts...
    Group 1 continues as before, repeating several times.
    Group 2 waits for five counts, then starts and continues several times.
	全体舞者同时做九拍相同的<u>动作组合</u>，绕圈用五拍，并四拍在一条线上……
	
	    第一组继续保持，重复多遍。
	    第二组晚五拍开始，并重复多遍。

Simple **manipulation of theme**:
    Choose a simple four-count theme.
    Repeat it.
    Develop into a seven-count **phrase**.
	旋律的简单变换：
	    选择一个四拍的简单主题动作。
	    重复做一遍。
	    将其发展至七拍的句子。

Expression:

Movement beyond performers' ability, either in technique or <u>expression</u>	动作难度超出了演员的能力，无论是技术还是<u>表现力</u>。
Did your technique, style, or dance appearance overshadow your <u>expression</u>?	你的技巧、风格或者舞蹈的表面遮挡了你<u>想要表达的</u>？
The basis for such a choice is highly personal, because it is a means toward the expression to be made—which is in part *self-<u>expression</u>* or, more precisely, expression *through self*.	这种选择的基础是高度个人化的，因为它是一种表现方式——在某种程度上是自我<u>表现</u>，或者更准确地说，是通过自我来表现。
Movement is the most persistent experience in living—the first and last <u>expression</u> of life.	运动是生命中最持续的体验——生命最初和最终的<u>表征</u>。
Let it be remembered that while choreography is a *forming* of **expression**, it is never *mold* for it.	我们应记住，编舞是对**动作**进行"编排加工"，而绝非用于填充的"模子"。

If the choreographer is to develop an expression—his expression—he must have the courage to follow his own intent into whatever real it leads.	如果编舞者想要发展一套自己的<u>表达方式</u>，就必须大胆地跟随内心所引的方向。
A choreographer is a maker, a creator of dances. He seeks to create an expression by having dancers move according to his design.	编舞者是舞蹈的制作人和创造者。他让舞者根据他的设计来移动从而<u>有所表达</u>。
Expression in dance comes about as a result of the total act of moving—not because of any particular gesture, rhythmic trick, or good intention.	舞蹈<u>表达的含义</u>并不单是某一个手势、节奏花样，或者有好的想法就可以实现的，它要通过所有肢体动作的总和呈现。
Distortion, as a means of treating the <u>materials of expression</u>, means any deviation or extension from the natural.	曲解转化作为处理<u>动作素材</u>的一种方式，指的是不同于自然状态下的任何偏离或拓展。
The same is true of dance and its medium of <u>expression</u>—movement.	对于舞蹈和用于<u>表达</u>的媒介——动作，是一样的道理。

Form:

<u>Form</u> is the <u>shape</u>, the sequence, the organization of the action.	<u>形式</u>指的是动作的<u>造型</u>、顺序和构成。
Seldom is any one of these movement quality found in a pure form in dance. Usually, there is a <u>combination</u> of several identifiable qualities, with its own dramatic overtones.	以上这些动作特性很少以纯粹的<u>形式</u>出现在舞蹈里，通常都是由几种辨识度高的特性<u>组合</u>起来，表现其各自特别的含义。
In fact, dancers with sensitivity and concern do more than follow a dance's <u>form</u>. They also enrich the projection designed by the choreographer.	实际上，心思敏感的舞者除了按照舞蹈本身的<u>编排</u>跳，也会丰富编舞者的设计。
It is equally true that magnificent technique and brilliant <u>form</u> cannot save a dance which lacks significance.	同理，具备优秀的技术技巧和完美的<u>架构</u>，缺少意义表达也是不能构成一支舞蹈作品的。
Form a simple movement theme and rehearse it carefully so that you are sure of its components.	<u>编排</u>一个简单的动作主题，然后认真练习，直到确定每一个动作。
Scallops, or partial circles, are lyrical in form; they exaggerate points of beginning and ending.	扇形或者半圆形的路线在<u>形态</u>上充满节奏感；他们将开头和结尾夸张化处理。
The dramatic implications of the ***spiral***, with its encircling or ever-widening form, depend on the point of beginning and the scope and direction of its path.	螺旋形围绕或扩展的<u>形态</u>，通过其路线的开头、长度和方向来反映其戏剧化的意义。
Choreographers, as all other creators in the arts, are concerned with <u>content, form</u>, technique, and projection.	像其他艺术领域的创作者一样，编舞者也需要考虑<u>内容、形式</u>、技巧和影射意义。
Considering the visual <u>form</u> of the design resulting from the dancer's action in space?	思考舞者在<u>空间</u>移动时的视觉<u>形态</u>？

(2) Cultural substitution [**NB:** See "whys" after the table.]

ST	Direct Translation	Cultural Substitution
Historical, legendary, or literary events or figures:	历史、传说、文学事迹或人物：	历史、传说、文学事迹或人物：
Boston Tea Party	波士顿倾茶事件	太平天国
Carrie Nation	嘉莉·民族（旧禁酒运动）	林则徐禁烟运动
Pandora	潘多拉	妲己
Davy Crockett	大卫·克洛科特	霍去病
Paul Bunyan	保罗·布尼安	盘古开天
Paul Revere	保罗·列维尔	余则成
As the dance uses movement to evoke a dynamic image, so the title may use a poetic image to give promise of what will come. The following titles illustrate this suggestive quality:	舞蹈用动作来唤起动态的形象，舞蹈作品名称也可以用诗意的形象来预示即将发生的事情。以下标题就体现了这种暗示性：	舞蹈用动作来唤起动态的形象，舞蹈作品名称也可以用诗意的形象来预示即将发生的事情。以下标题就体现了这种暗示性：
Ruins and Visions	《废墟和幻觉》	废墟和幻觉
Dark Meadows	《黑暗草甸》	黑暗草甸
Dark Elegies	《黑暗挽歌》	黑暗挽歌
Opus 51	《作品 51》	作品 51
Root of an Unfocus	《失焦的原因》	失焦的原因
8 Clear Places	《8 个清静之地》	8 个清静之地
Totem	《图腾》	图腾
Acrobats of God	《天降杂艺》	天降杂艺
And Daddy Was a Fireman	《父亲是个消防人员》	父亲是个消防人员
Village of Three	《三个人的村庄》	三个人的村庄
With My Red Fires	《我红色的火焰》	我红色的火焰
Pillar of Fire	《火柱》	火柱
Here and Now with Watchers	《随时随地·看护人》	随时随地看护人
Tossed as It Is Untroubled	《就像一切都没发生过》	就像一切都没发生过
		中国现代舞作品（补充）： 《红与黑》　金星 《重置》　桑吉加 《流浪者之歌》　林怀民 《断章》　伍国柱 《九歌》　林怀民

[NB: Using Chinese cultural equivalents or similar events or historical figures that suit dancers in China, or providing more Chinese related examples based on each categories that would help Chinese dancers understand the background knowledge better.]

(3) Borrowed terms (*Ballet*)

French/English/Italian	Chinese	Diagram
Arabesque	阿拉贝斯克姿势 （transliteration 音译）	
attitude	雕塑势、鹤立式 （adopting the established popular translated names 约定俗成）	
corps de ballet	伴舞队、群舞 （*ditto*）	
grand jeté	大的换脚跳、 大跳、凌空跃 （direct translation 直译 & domestication or adaption 归化）	
relevé	立半脚尖 （paraphrase 释义）	

fouette	单足趾尖旋转、挥鞭转 （specification or paraphrase & domestication/ adaptation）	
fish dive lift	鱼钻水势 （diction 约定俗成）	
pas de chat	猫步（不同于模特走台步） （annotation 加注）	
pas de cheval	马步（不同于中国武术马步） （annotation 加注）	

4　Methods of Translating the Modern Dance Textbook

4.1　Transliteration

Transliteration is normally strictly limited to translating those borrowed terms in French or Italian, and special terms named after the creator of the dance technique. This is because that first, some of the French ballet terms refer to a certain posture or movement that cannot be translated within a short phrase as required in terminology; second, certain technique or movements are named after people's name that could only be translated by transliteration.

Examples see 3.2.1 (4) and (9), and 3.2.2 (3). Those terms are named after a musician, a dancer or borrowed from French.

4.2　Annotation & Illustration

There are a few terms about which readers need to have certain background knowledge about music, dance history, famous choreographers, etc. In such cases translators may need to add annotations (e.g., in footnote or endnote).

Examples:

ST	Explanation	Annotation
ABA form	ABA form is a musical term that is applied into choreography. A represents one theme, B another; ABA being two contrasting themes followed by a repeated of the first.	ABA 形式，A、B 分别表示一个主题动作，按照 ABA 的顺序依次展开。
"I'm not creative," another dancer insists, convinced that he can't choreograph like Humphrey or Tudor, so why bother?	Humphrey, Doris (1895—1958), a dancer and choreographer. He was one of the second generation modern dance pioneers in exploring the use of breath and developing techniques still taught today.	Doris Humphrey (1895—1958)，舞者与编导。第二代现代舞先驱，研究呼吸的运用与技术技巧，沿用至今。
	Tudor, Antony (1908—1987), an English ballet choreographer, teacher and dancer. He was seen as a principal transformer of ballet into a modern art. His work is usually considered as modern "psychological" expression.	Antony Tudor (1908—1987)，英国芭蕾舞者、老师与编导。他在芭蕾向现代艺术改革中扮演了重要角色，其作品被视为现代"心理"写照。

Besides annotations, illustrations of dance form, movements or posture are provided within the textbook, in order to help the readers have a better understanding of the concepts or knowledge. Both of the two methods are applied to give background information and references to fill the gaps existing between the reader and book, as well as the gaps between Chinese (dance) culture and Western (dance) culture.

4.3 Diction

Example 1

ST	TT
Dance uses energy to fill space, but it must do so within time. The elements of time include the factors of *tempo* and *rhythm,* which are of special concern to dancers.	舞蹈用"力量"来填满空间，但是这必须与"时间"相配合。时间的元素包括"节拍"和"节奏"，二者对于舞者来说都有特殊意义。

Comments: While explaining the process of choreography, some terms that are similar or slightly different are mentioned, such as *tempo* and *rhythm* in this case. Very often in daily life, these two terms in Chinese are used mostly in the same context when talking about how the music moves in pattern. But when choreographing, the slight difference that usually is ignored would be the key to differentiate two concepts and the concepts will affect the understanding of the structure of choreography. This is also why modern dance is known as more scientific, it applies logic and reason. So in this case, *tempo* refers to the speed of the music while *rhythm* the rhythmic unit of a piece of music, i.e. 拍子 and 节奏.

Example 2

　　Normally in translation, notional words are put in priority. Functional words are often ignored, Although in most cases, functional words are not as important as notional words and sometimes be omitted for the sake of brevity and fluency of expression. However, empty words undertake significant function in forming a sentence or paragraph, making the expression even vivid and dynamic if used properly, especially its grammatical function, which draws the attention of the translator.

Functional words include articles (a, an, the), pronouns (mine, his, hers, ours, yours, theirs, etc.), conjunctions (and, with, so…that…, which, when, etc.) and prepositions (by, on, of, over, in, with, against, at, etc.). In our proposed project for translation, *The Premier for Beginning Choreographers*, the most frequently used empty words are prepositions. See the table below:

ST	TT
Within space limitations:	空间限制：
in a small square	小型广场里
in a three-foot circle	半径三尺的圆里
by a rope stretched diagonally between two pillars	两根柱子之间连着的一根绳子旁
around a single pylon	一座指示塔周围
behind a screen	屏幕的后方
on a high ox	一头高大的牛之上
by a rope suspended from the ceiling	天花板垂下的一根绳子旁
surrounded by three benches	由三条长凳包围
by a stepladder in a corner	角落里一把梯子旁
using both stage and audience space	运用舞台与观众席两个空间

Comments: This is one exercise for movements within *space limitations*. Each exercise is a single phrase led by one preposition. During translating those phrases, there are two principles to follow: **one** is to make sure to translate the position of the dancer, whether it is above or under, around or behind; **the other** is to avoid redundant information that disturbs the imagination of the students, by which I mean that choreography is an activity of movement imagination. Therefore in this particular exercise, there is no need to add action words, like *stand, lie, grab, etc.* because those words are just a small part of the imagination. While considering how to move in space, they would figure out more than those ways to realize special choreography. As is shown in the table, for instance, *by a rope* is translated into *绳子旁*.

Example 3

Diction refers to the choice of vocabulary considering both the original meaning and the context the ST is in. In this exercise, it tends to train students' *response to action words*.

ST	TT
Response to action words:	对行动词汇的反应：
melt	融化
wiggle	扭摆
bounce	弹跳
ooze	泄露

collapse	倒塌
soar	吼叫
snatch	抢走
cling	贴着
"gimme"	"给我"
flip	轻掷
jiggle	轻摇
pitter-pat	噼噼啪啪
slink	溜走

Comments: As is shown above, the TT or TL expressions follow(s) a consistent pattern and is/are kept as brief as possible. The consistent pattern not only meets the requirements of textbook publishing standards, but also eases the least possibility of distraction. For instance, if you translate first five verbs as below,

SL verbs	TL verbs
melt	融化
wiggle	摇摆扭动
bounce	弹起来
ooze	渗漏出来
collapse	倒塌

It would not be difficult to feel the stagnancy lying within the expressions. And the TL phrases appear to be verbose and not pithy at all.

The translation of those systematic verbs calls for the translation of the meaning of the SL verbs. Most importantly it is to inspire the students' motive to move accordingly without posing any obstacle to the students' imagination.

There is a factor of phonological correspondence to be considered, for the students respond firstly to the sound of the action verbs not the meaning of them. For instance, *扭摆* is better than *摆动*, for the Chinese pinyin of *扭摆* (/niubai/) tends to be closer to the pronunciation of *wiggle* (/ˈwɪg(ə)l/) and therefore better than *摆动* (/baidong/). Similarly, it is better to turn *soar* (/sɔː/) into *吼叫* (/houjiao/) than into *喊叫* (/hanjiao/); to turn *slink* (/slɪŋk/) into *溜走* (/liuzou/) than into *潜逃* (/qiantao/), etc.

Response to action words:	对行动词汇的反应：
melt	融化
wiggle	扭摆
bounce	弹跳
ooze	泄露
collapse	倒塌
soar	吼叫
snatch	抢走
cling	贴着

"gimme"	"给我"
flip	轻掷
jiggle	轻摇
pitter-pat	噼噼啪啪
slink	溜走

4.4　Compensation & Specification

Example 1:

ST	TT
Expression in dance comes about as a result of the total act of moving—not because of any particular gesture, rhythmic trick, or good intention. The place where the dancer is, what he is doing as well as how he is affecting the space around him, are all important. The <u>rhythm</u>, design, and <u>dynamics</u> are all consciously manipulated and controlled. Anything not important to the total expression is a distraction, and sometimes in our concern for finding movement we forget that we must also *get rid of* movement. Dance, as language, must be formed and then edited and re-formed.	舞蹈中的表达并不单是某一个手势、节奏的花样或者有好的想法就可以了，而是通过所有肢体动作的总和来呈现的。舞者所处的位置、他所做的动作以及他怎样影响他所处的空间，这些都很重要。编舞者需要有意识地控制舞蹈<u>作品整体的节奏</u>、编排和<u>动作的强弱变化</u>。任何与作品整体表达不重要的部分都会分散注意力，有时为了找回忘记的动作还必须舍弃这些不重要的部分。舞蹈作为一种语言，必然会经历组合、编辑、重新组合。
It is difficult to talk or write about a dance, to reconstruct in words what has been designed in action, through movement sensation, idea, feeling, kinetic memory, and a host of connotations intermingled in the movement sensations they have had simply because they find no words to describe them. The language we know structures our experience. Nowhere is this more obvious than in the <u>choreographer who is limited to what he can describe verbally</u>. It is equally true of the viewer who is limited to verbal identification.	很难用语言讲述或者描写一支舞蹈，也很难通过重新组织语言来表达专门用肢体语言来传达的内容。舞蹈本身也正是因为有些情感无法用语言来表达而存在。我们掌握的有限的语言构成了我们各自的体验和感受。这一点尤其体现在编舞者身上，<u>口中话语不能将其心中所想表达出来，所以要用肢体语言来表达</u>；同理，<u>观众也受限于用语言来理解，所以通过肢体语言来感受</u>。

Comments: Either compensation or specification attempts to provide the background knowledge, in case that the readers do not know how to collect the dots, or to fill the gaps with hidden information so that the readers may find it more logical in Chinese. See the last two sentences in the ST,

Nowhere is this more obvious than in the <u>choreographer who is limited to what he can describe verbally</u>. It is equally true of the viewer who is limited to verbal identification.

In this inverted sentence, the subject is *choreographer* and *viewer.* The whole sentence seems to explain why choreographers choreograph the way they do and why viewers view the way they do. Therefore, it is not enough just to stop where the sentence is finished, but to compensate the hidden meaning unspoken out, i.e. *所以要用肢体语言来表达* and *所以通过肢体语言来感受*. In this way, the whole paragraph ends with a logical period.

As to the former sentence and its translation:

[SL sentence] The <u>rhythm</u>, design, and <u>dynamics</u> are all consciously manipulated and controlled.

[TL sentence] 编舞者需要有意识地控制舞蹈作品<u>整体的节奏</u>、编排和<u>动作的强弱变化</u>。

Comments: The direct translation of *rhythm* and *dynamics* would be surely 节奏 and 强弱变化. However, to simply say that 节奏、编排和强弱变化均有条不紊地操控着 could not reveal a clear message of *who* is manipulating and controlling, and the rhythm or dynamics of *what* subject. Therefore, those hidden information is given in the TL sentence in order to make the argument clear and to the point, i.e. *编舞者需要有意识地控制舞蹈作品整体的节奏、编排和动作的强弱变化*。

Example 2:

Movement exists in space, which, to a dancer, means <u>a potential of position and dimension</u>. Position includes the dancer's level in regard to the floor surface and the direction in which he is moving. Dimension refers to the size of the dancer's movement. <u>*Direction*</u>, <u>*level*</u>, and <u>*size*</u> are clearly relative terms. Where, for example, is forward? How high is up? Only when some standard is established can we recognize differences.	舞蹈动作存在于空间中。对于舞者来说，就意味着<u>下一个动作的位置和幅度</u>。位置包括舞者相对于地面的高度以及下一个动作的方向。幅度则表示舞者动作的大小。很明显，<u>"方向""水平高度"以及"幅度大小"</u>是相关联的。例如，向前指的是什么？多高才算是向上？只有设定一些标准，我们才能够识别其不同点。

Comments: *Dimension* refers to the length, width, height, or depth of something (*Merriam-Webster's Advanced Learner's English Dictionary*, 2012). So the translation could be 大小, 长短, 深浅, etc. However depending on the context where dance movement is the subject, it would be better to translate it into 幅度 that could better imply the body movement rather than just a descriptive word. Since the source material is for beginners to better understand how contemporary dance is made, so the translation should be both simplified and informative enough, such as *direction*, *level*, and *size*, all of which could be easily translated into 方向, 水平, and 大小. However, it is too simplified to acknowledge the connection between the words and movements. So it would be better to translate them into 水平高度 and 幅度大小, so that the beginners could conveniently understand what abstract concepts do with the choreography thanks to the translation method of *compensation*.

Example 3:

As he moves *diagonally* forward across the performing area, he gains the combined strength of the powerful diagonal plus the increasing apparent size of his figure, with its more rounded aspect. <u>This creates the appearance of "becoming" and evoke a sense of</u>	当舞者沿对角线穿过舞台时，他便因为强大的对角线和不断明显增大、丰满的立体形象而获得一种综合的力量。<u>这种情形呈现出一种"渐渐呈现"的过程，并唤起了一种愈发明确的肯定感。</u>身体的竖直

<u>affirmation.</u> It is decorative as well, in the appearance of the vertical body line and the diagonal as they bisect.	线条同对角线交叉时的效果，也具有美学意义。

Comments: Describing art, not just dance, often involves an abstract narration, a better understanding of which needs not only context but more information from translation. In this case, the ST is *This creates the appearance of "becoming" and evoke a sense of affirmation.* It seems even easier to understand in English than in Chinese. In order to provide more information in words like *becoming* and *affirmation*. The translation methods of *specification and conversion* are applied when translating an abstract description.

4.5　Foreignization and Domestication

Foreignization and domestication, two approaches or methods to be adopted, have much to do with the concept of equivalence or correspondence. The nature of equivalence in terms of translation theory remains controversial and different theories of the concept of equivalence have been discussed for last decades. Either "SL and TL texts or items are translation equivalents when they are *interchangeable in a given situation*" (Catford, 1965: 49), or "the reproduction of the message is emphasized rather than the conservation of the form of the utterance" (Nida, 1982: 13); equivalence was classified into **formal equivalence** and **dynamic equivalence**. Some other scholars categorized the different levels on which the concept of equivalence was elaborated. Baker (1991) adopted a hierarchical principle by widening its focus on *equivalence at word level, equivalence above word level, grammatical equivalence, textual equivalence: thematic and information structures or cohesion,* and lastly *pragmatic equivalence*, while from a quantitative perspective, there can be three categories. The following discussions are especially from the viewpoint of *textbook translation:*

(1) Complete equivalence

Since modern dance is an foreign art, seldom do the terminological expressions of modern dance can find their equivalents without discovering that the equivalents are in fact back-translation, such as Graham technique/葛兰姆技巧, canon/卡农, rondo/回旋曲, and fouetté turn/挥鞭转. In terms of body parts or basic dance techniques, it appears apparently to be complete equivalence: shoulder/肩膀, arms/胳膊, hip joint/髋关节, grand jété/凌空跃, etc.

(2) Incomplete equivalence, partial-/non-equivalence, or zero-equivalence

Sometimes the translation seems to be equivalent to the original text, however it turns out to be semantic compensation rather than complete equivalence. As elaborated above in 3 with a lot of musical terms like sonata, canon, cumulative rhythm, accent, etc., these are all professional musical terms. However, in modern dance, the said terms refer to the variation of movements that correspond, or otherwise, to the rhythmic feature of each musical term. Therefore, the translator adds 形式 after the direct translation in order to highlight the nature of the movement rather than merely music.

Besides, among the exercises in this textbook for beginning choreographers, there are a certain amount of examples that are closely related to the history of America where the original targeted readers are born and raised but which has little to do the targeted readers in China. So, to make the historical or legendary examples in Western culture understood to a certain degree, it is useful to call forth, more by domestication than by foreignization, similar emotions, feelings and responses about the historical, legendary or literary events or figures, as illustrated as follows:

Historical, legendary, or literary events or figures	历史、传说、文学事迹或人物	历史、传说、文学事迹或人物
Boston Tea Party	波士顿倾茶事件	太平天国
Carrie Nation	嘉莉·纳逊	林则徐禁烟运动
Pandora	潘多拉	妲己
Davy Crockett	大卫·克洛科特	霍去病
Paul Bunyan	保罗·布尼安	盘古开天
Paul Revere	保罗·列维尔	余则成

This author of the thesis is aware that the domesticated or foreignized versions in the above table make up partial-, non-, or zero-equivalence to the original, but it doesn't matter to the Chinese students learning choreography taught in *A Primer for Choreographers*. Their reaction and teaching effect in terms of culture, history, feelings, association, allusion, and emotional understanding COUNT.

For instance, "太平天国" is a Chinese peasant uprising (1851—1864) against the foreign invasion in Chinese history. It is partially correspondent to **Boston Tea Party**, which was the culmination of a resistance movement throughout British America against the Tea Act that had been passed by the British Parliament in 1773.

The other instances include "妲己" (*Da Ji*) vs **Pandora**. Da Ji is portrayed as a malevolent fox spirit in legends as well as novels who caused disaster to men, the ruler in particular, thus the fall of the dynasty. According to the myth, Pandora, a "beautiful evil" whose descendants would torment the human race, opened a jar (sometimes mistranslated as "Pandora's box", releasing all the evils of humanity—like plagues and diseases—leaving only Hope inside once she had closed it again.

"霍去病" (Huo Qubing) vs. **Davy Crockett**. Huo (140 BC—117 BC), a distinguished military general of the Western Han dynasty, is better known as a national hero of the Han nationality who fought through five Western Regions kingdoms (in or near the Chinese frontier). Davy Crockett (1786—1836) was a 19th-century American folk hero, frontiersman, soldier, and politician. He is commonly referred to in popular culture by the epithet "King of the Wild Frontier".

"盘古"(*Pangu*) vs. **Paul Bunyan**. Pangu is the creator of the universe in Chinese mythology, whereas Paul Bunyan is a giant lumberjack in American folklore. They both can show great power in their work.

"余则成" (Yu Zecheng) and **Paul Revere**. Yu Zecheng is a special intelligence agent working for the CPC, or a representative of underground CPC members chiefly during the War of Resistance Against Japan and the War of Liberation (roughly 1938—1949). Paul Revere was a prosperous and prominent Boston silversmith, who helped organize an intelligence and alarm system to keep watch on the British military. Revere later served as a Massachusetts militia officer, though his service culminated after the Penobscot Expedition, one of the most disastrous campaigns of the American Revolutionary War, for which he was absolved of blame.

From these instances both at home and abroad, we may obtain inspiration and typical cases for better translation of modern or contemporary dance terms that are not readily available in terms of TL equivalence. In this context, therefore, several approaches/methods like domestication and foreignization can be pragmatically applicable to the translation of Western-style dance terms. Semantically and functionally, they will be instrumental in promoting cross-cultural translation as a whole, especially the contact between Chinese dance culture and Western dance culture.

【案例分析】

（1）作者在翻译现代舞入门教材及其评述过程中，运用了常见的翻译原则——"忠实"原则和"灵活"原则，译例丰富多彩。有关名词术语见下文中的画线部分（下同）。

（2）作者较多地运用常用翻译技巧/方法，如"音译""注释""图解""简化""选词""补偿""具体化""异化""归化"等，对翻译案例进行了分析。

（3）作者在上述所引论文中还列出了评价翻译质量的 6 条标准/要求：

The yardsticks for evaluating the quality of translation of terminology include:

①Clarity. ...

②Consistency. ...

③Decency. ...

④Conciseness. ...

⑤Accuracy. ...

⑥Domestication. ...

（4）作者整合运用了"译"与"论"，以下目录足以说明：

3　Principles of Translating the Modern Dance Textbook

   3.1　…

   3.2　Principles of Dance Textbook Translation

      3.2.1　First Principle: Faithfulness

      3.2.2　Second Principle: Flexibility

4　Methods of Translating the Modern Dance Textbook

   4.1　Transliteration

   4.2　Annotation & Illustration

   4.3　Diction

   4.4　Compensation & Specification

   4.5　Foreignization and Domestication

◎研究与实践思考题◎

1.　细读"译与论整合之解读"。

2.　熟悉、理解、搞懂 BA/BTI 学位论文中实践与理论是如何有机结合的。

3.　结合概念与实践，整体并一一认识**46 种笔译技巧、30 种口译/导译技巧、136 种常用翻译理论/策略/原则/途径/方法**等。

4.　根据第 6 章的有关介绍以及你自己的理解，分析二维码中内容的"译论整合"。

5.　根据第 6 章的有关介绍以及你自己的理解，分析二维码中内容的"译论整合"。

6.　建议学生从本科一年级的翻译实践练习开始，进行"译与论"的整合实践型研究，一直继续到四年级撰写学位论文前后——坚持数年，必有好处。

第7章 如何研究（讲究方法）

How to Do a Practice-based Research (Methodology-oriented)

◎学习目标◎

　　翻译研究方法论的讨论乃本章重点，也是初涉研究的本科生学习、学好翻译研究的重点。学好研究方法可为毕业生更具竞争力地走向社会、走向世界打下基础。通过本章学习，学生将：

- 了解、熟悉研究方法的重要性；
- 了解、熟悉翻译研究方法的基本知识；
- 大致了解翻译研究的领域；
- 大致了解、熟悉提问式研究方法；
- 了解、熟悉翻译常用研究思路；
- 了解、熟悉翻译研究的主要理论模式；
- 了解、熟悉翻译研究变项之间的几种关系；
- 了解、熟悉并掌握翻译实践/研究论文的写作流程。

7.1 研究方法之重要性

　　科学研究的方法乃科学研究方法论的研究对象。科学研究方法论是一门思维科学，因为作为研究主体的人须在科学研究过程中运用思维形式（如概念、判断、推理等）、运用逻辑思维方法（如抽象和具体、演绎和归纳、分析和综合、比较和类比、假设和理论等）、运用非逻辑思维方法（如直觉、想象、灵感、头脑风暴）等。据此，翻译实践过程（此处特指双语/多语转换过程，当然还有语内转换、符际转换过程）就是一个思维/思考过程、一个研究过程、一个调查过程、一个学习过程；翻译研究过程同样是一个思维过程，或另一种思维过程。本章讨论的有关翻译研究的方法就是指从事翻译研究所采取的**方法、手段、途径、思路**[①]、**模式**和**规则**（操作型）等。

　　这些研究方法，最终将导致论文结论如何收尾，换言之，论文的结论该如何撰写——论文之结论也是使用方法论之结论。

　　显然，翻译研究方法（论）与翻译方法是两个完全不同的概念。对翻译研究方法（论）的熟悉、掌握及运用是写好（毕业）论文的关键所在。换言之，没有好的、有效的翻译研究方法，就难以写出高质量的、规范的、像样的论文来。

---

① 研究方法是一种"思路"；"思路"也构成一种研究方法/套路——这是笔者长期思考之观点/主张。

由于本书不是翻译研究方法（论）的专著，仅起导引作用，因此我们遵循"简洁""实用""够用""能有"的原则来介绍翻译研究方法，而且把重点放在本章的英文标题的概念上，即 practice-based research（实践研究），而非(pure) theoretical research（[纯]理论研究），这样对翻译类本科生更为合适、更为实用，也更为有效。（翻译）研究用途分为基础研究/理论研究和应用研究，我们主张本科生应把重点放在应用研究上。

BTI/BA 生如何做研究？简言之，我们建议、鼓励学生多做基于（笔译/口译）实践的研究或实践研究。考虑到翻译类学生需要运用英文思维来进行科学研究，我们尽可能在合适的地方多使用英文来讨论关涉方法论的问题（methodological issues）。以下是我们在学科研究方法论第一堂课上向学生开门见山提出的问题：

Q①What is the major difference between translation methods and translation research methods?

Q②Why are BTI students weak (or poor) in research?

Q③Why are American (under)graduates (more) creative?

Q④Why do our BTI students remain weak in critical thinking and academic judgment?

Q⑤Ideally, why should the dual-supervisory system be implemented and promoted?

Q⑥What does this chapter offer?

有关简要回答如下（仅供参考）：

A①The former concerns possible specific methods or techniques/skills (to be) used in translating/interpreting, while the latter indicates specific research methods applied to (practical & theoretical) studies of translation/practical and pure translation studies.

A②Both because they are rather/almost ignorant about research methodology and because their translation competence still remains weak.

A③Concisely speaking, it is research methodology that enables them to be creative. Thanks to, perhaps, the world's most standard and strict education in the U.S., the students know better how to integrate creativity with norms, which is best reflected in academic writing. Translation research is based on a research question or a hypothesis. How to find a solution or to prove/confirm a hypothesis is, first of all, to choose a proper methodology. Therefore, it is correct to say that in your graduate studies you need to do more methodological training, which starts from the undergraduate period in leading or key universities.

A④Few of them care or know about research methodology. Only a (very) limited number of BTI students (freshmen and sophomores, for example) are deemed critical and creative, and therefore academically able to go global. That's only one side of the coin. For the other side, still many translation teachers (including supervisors) are (rather) less conscious and less strong in research methodology. Most translation students are totally in the dark about which supervisors know methodology well or both practice and theory well.

A⑤Because many of our supervisors in Translation Major are (far) less balanced in translation ability and research ability. Given this, therefore, the dual-supervisory system would help allocate a practice-oriented supervisor (one from the translation profession/industry) and a theory-oriented supervisor (college teacher) in a proper way to a BTI student. In other words, one of the supervisors is or could be better trained in research methodology. However, it does take time due to a variety of causes.

A⑥It will offer some common knowledge about translation research methods beginning with research questions, and much more.

7.2　翻译研究方法简介

7.2.1　研究概念解读

（1）Chambers (1989):

●We define research broadly as a "systematic investigation towards <u>increasing the sum of knowledge</u>".（转引自 Williams & Chesterman, 2004: 1）

（2）Gillham (2000):

●…"research is about <u>creating new knowledge, whatever the disciplines</u>". <u>Innovation is vital if a discipline is to grow and prosper.</u> However, the definition of "new knowledge" will vary according to the level at which the research is undertaken. An essay at advanced BA level will clearly differ in scope from a doctoral dissertation. "<u>Creating new knowledge</u>" can consist <u>in summarizing new research in an emerging field or providing a very small amount of new evidence to support or disconfirm an existing hypothesis at one end of the scale, to develop a new methodology for Translation History at the other.</u>（转引自 Williams & Chesterman, 2004: 1-2）

（3）MWCD's definition (1059):

●careful or diligent search;

●studious inquiry or examination; esp: investigation or experimentation <u>aimed at the discovery and interpretation of facts, revision of accepted theories or laws in the light of new facts, or practical application of such new or revised theories or laws;</u>

●<u>the collecting of information about a particular subject.</u>

（4）Andre Chesterman：

●It (Research) involves <u>two basic cognitive processes: looking for *differences* (variation) and looking for *similarities* (patterns). Differences may also form a pattern, so that there may be similarities among the differences. Looking for differences is a process of analysis. This means breaking a concept or a set of data down into smaller units; it needs concentration, convergent intelligence. Looking for similarities is a process of synthesis, of generalization. It means looking for regularities, shared features, patterns; it needs imagination, divergent intelligence.</u>

Both these processes come together in categorization. The formation of relevant categories is indeed one of the most crucial and difficult parts of a research project. Categories are yet another form of interpretive hypothesis: you propose a category if you think it is useful, if it allows you to say something interesting, to make a valid generalization, to formulate a precise hypothesis about some part of the data.（Williams & Chesterman, 2004: 94）

（5）《现汉》（1507）：

●探求事物的<u>真相</u>、<u>性质</u>、<u>规律</u>等。

7.2.2　研究目的与贡献

Williams 和 Chesterman（2004: 2）指出：“The aim of Translation Studies research is…to <u>make a contribution to the field which increases the sum of our knowledge</u>. You can make your contribution in a number of ways:

●By <u>providing new data</u>;

●By <u>suggesting an answer to a specific question</u>;

●By <u>testing or refining an existing hypothesis, theory or methodology</u>;

●By <u>proposing a new idea, hypothesis, theory or methodology</u>.”

就**翻译理论**与**翻译实践**而言，上述两类/种研究可以解读为：“The first kind of research might <u>lead to better theories, better ways of looking at translation</u>. The second would <u>aim at improving translation quality or perhaps raising the status of translators themselves</u>. Applied research of this kind can <u>offer guidelines for better practice based on the study of successful professional translation</u>. It can also test and perhaps revise prescriptive claims in the light of evidence from competent professional practice.”（3）

7.2.3　翻译研究定义

“Translation Studies” is defined as the field of study devoted to <u>describing, analyzing and theorizing the processes, contexts and products of the act of translation as well as the (roles of the) agents involved</u>.（1）

7.2.4　翻译研究类型①

（1）途径、性质及应用视角（图 7-1）

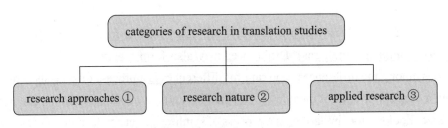

图 7-1　翻译研究的途径、性质及应用视角

---

① 笔者特地用英文做介绍。请读者（包括任课教师）自行用汉语来解读。

（2）研究途径简析（图 7-2）

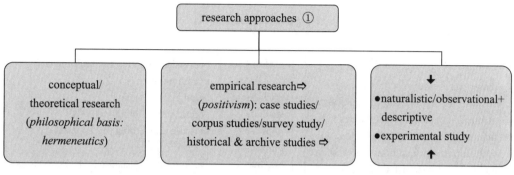

图 7-2　研究途径简析

（3）研究性质简析（图 7-3）

图 7-3　研究性质简释

定性研究与定量研究的区别见表 7-1。

表 7-1　定性研究与定量研究的区别

Perspective	Qualitative	Quantitative
ontological/TS	subjective interpretation	objective statement
epistemological	subjective experience as a whole	objective explanation based on causality
methodological	ideographic[1]	nomothetic[2]
researcher's	personal involvement and shared feeling	no researcher's involvement
relationship between researcher(s) and research object(s)	personal involvement	split
methods/technology	description in words	statistical
purpose	to confirm whether A or B exists	to confirm the quantity of A or B
content	more elastic; less structuralized	more structuralized; more definite
methods	case study; in-depth talk; group talk; observation; projective technique	investigation; meta analysis[3]; experimental study

---

① 追求特殊关系的整体了解。

② 追求普遍性关系或定律。

③ 总汇法、元分析、荟萃分析。

（4）应用研究简析（图 7-4）

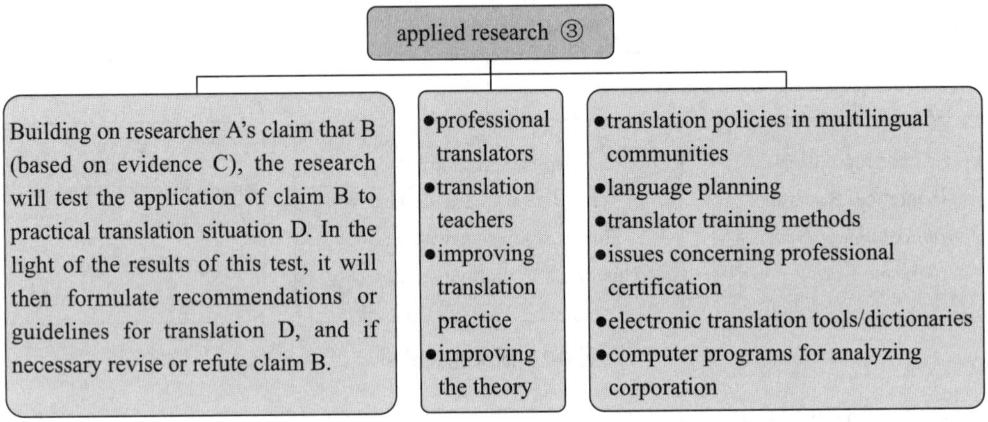

图 7-4　应用研究简析

（5）研究逻辑及常用专题研究法①（表 7-2）

表 7-2　研究逻辑及常用专题研究法

专题序号	英文名称	中文名称
1	formal logic	形式逻辑
2	deductive and inductive	演绎法与归纳法
3	qualitative and quantitative	定性分析与定量分析
4	prescriptive and descriptive	规定性研究与描述性研究
5	conceptual and empirical	概念/理论研究与实证研究
6	corpus and TAPs	语料库与 TAPs 法
7	verification and falsification	证实与证伪
8	synchronic and diachronic	共时法与历时法
9	macro and micro	宏观研究与微观研究
10	literature review	文献综述

（6）常用研究操作方法（表 7-3）

表 7-3　常用研究操作方法

操作方法序号	英文名称	中文名称	备注
1	literature review method	文献法	定性/定量
2	historical method	历时法	定性/数据驱动
3	observation	观察法	定性
4	comparision	比较法	定性
5	inductive method	归纳法	逻辑推理

---

① 按照专题分类，主要用于翻译研究与论文撰写。

（续表）

操作方法序号	英文名称	中文名称	备注
6	survey/investigation	调查法	定量/描述
7	experiment	实验法	定量/探索
8	interview	访谈法	数据驱动
9	questionnaire	问卷法	数据驱动/归纳/解析
10	other techniques	其他技术	数据驱动、分析等

7.2.5　常用研究方式

基于不同的翻译研究目的，有以下六类翻译研究方式（表 7-4）。

表 7-4　基于不同目的的常用翻译研究方式

序号	中英名称	研究方式举例
1	探索性研究 (explorative research)	导译研究：翻译学的新分支（Guide-interpreting Research: A New Branch of Translation Studies）/ 作者：陈刚[①]
2	描述性研究 (descriptive research)	从描述翻译学的角度探讨《了不起的盖茨比》两译本中的译者"主体性"——兼评翻译的"忠实性"（On the Translator's Subjectivity in the Two Versions of *The Great Gatsby* from the Perspective of DTS—With Comments on Fidelity）/ 作者：许维腾[②]
3	预测性研究 (predictive research)	归化口笔译在跨文化交际中仍将占主导地位（Domesticating T/I Still Prevails in Cross-cultural Communication）/ 作者：陈刚[③]
4	解释性研究 (explanatory research)	以目的论视角审视英译中文小说的文体翻译——以《色·戒》为例（On Stylistic Translation of Chinese Fiction from the Perspective of *Skopostheorie*—A Case Study of *Lust, Caution*）/ 作者：李竹[④]
5	评估性研究 (evaluative research)	性话语的解构与重构：以《查太莱夫人的情人》中译本为例（Chinese Translations of *Lady Chatterley's Lover* from the 1930s to the 2000s）/ 作者：吴奕霏[⑤]
6	行动研究 (action research)	推荐译写三原则在公示语翻译中的运用（"Three Transwriting Principles" Recommended for Translating Public Signs）/ 作者：陈刚（2021: 190-257）

7.3　常用翻译研究领域

民间有"英雄无用武之地"的说法。的确，不了解翻译的研究领域，即使有了研究方法，也不知道在哪里运用，你的"研究功夫"就无处施展。

[①] 见陈刚（2013）或搜索国际学术 Weekly Digest。
[②] 作者为南京大学英语专业本科毕业生，保送浙江大学攻读翻译学方向研究生（其导师是本书作者）。
[③] 该作者论文的原始标题，正式论文发表见陈刚（2006）。
[④] 作者为浙江大学英语专业本科毕业生。
[⑤] 作者为浙江大学翻译专业本科毕业生。

在此有必要对常用的翻译研究领域做一介绍。由于是针对翻译类本科生学士学位论文撰写，而非翻译学（科）研究，我们仅分两个主题加以简介。

7.3.1 霍氏译学图及其扩展

美籍荷兰翻译理论家詹姆斯·霍姆斯（James Holmes）是现代翻译研究的奠基人，熟谙美国和荷兰两种语言及文化。他的研究不以驳斥其他的知识体系为基础，而是在他自己的领域中打造出独立的学术新天地，提出了翻译学科的成立"宣言"，为"翻译学"立名，并提出了著名的译学图。任何学科要建立，必须有：①相对统一的名称和术语；②公认的学科结构和研究范围。1972 年，霍姆斯在哥本哈根举行的第三届应用语言学国际大会的翻译讨论会上宣读的著名论文《翻译研究的名与实》（"The Name and Nature of Translation Studies"），可谓建立了翻译学科的蓝图。他采用"翻译研究"/"翻译学"（Translation Studies）作为这一学科的标准名称，采用"翻译"（translation）作为标准术语；还提出了译学图，满足了上述第②项条件。图 7-5 是霍氏的译学图。

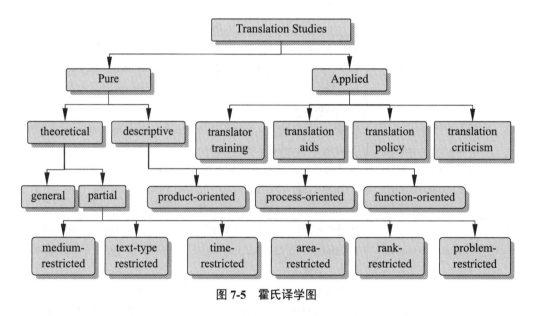

图 7-5　霍氏译学图

其中，应用翻译学又可作如图 7-6 的划分或扩展。

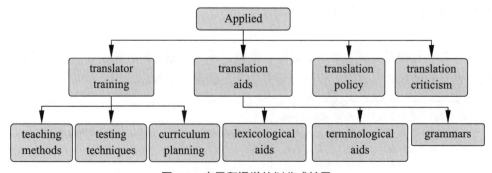

图 7-6　应用翻译学的划分或扩展

霍姆斯把翻译学分为纯翻译学（Pure Translation Studies）和应用翻译学（Applied Translation Studies）两大系统。

1. 纯翻译学可分为：

（1）理论翻译学（theoretical）

①通用翻译理论（general）

②局部/专门翻译理论（partial）

a. 特定手段/媒介研究（medium-restricted）

b. 特定文本/文本类型（text-type restricted）

c. 特定时间/翻译时间（time-restricted）

d. 特定领域/翻译语对（area-restricted）

e. 特定语层/翻译层级（rank-restricted）

f. 特定问题/具体翻译问题（problem-restricted）

（2）描述翻译学（descriptive）

①产品导向研究（product-oriented）

②过程导向研究（process-oriented）

③功能导向研究（function-oriented）

2. 应用翻译学可分为：

（1）翻译教学/翻译培训（translator training）

①教学方法（teaching methods）

②测试技术（testing techniques）

③课程设置（curriculum planning）

（2）翻译辅助（translation aids）

①词汇辅助（lexicological aids）

②术语辅助（terminological aids）

③语法（grammars）

（3）翻译政策（translation policy）

（4）翻译批评（translation criticism）

虽然给翻译研究分了类，但是霍姆斯认为纯翻译学和应用翻译学这两个分支之间的关系是辩证的、相互渗透的（参考陈刚，2011: 522-525）。

从上述"译学图"的简述，我们可以清楚地发现，翻译学的理论框架起码还有不少需要、值得增补/扩展的方面或领域。已有学者和感兴趣者提出了自己的"科目"并著述，其中 30 项翻译（实践）研究扩展领域见表 7-5。

表 7-5　翻译（实践）研究扩展领域

序号	SL 名称	TL 名称	提出者
1	翻译（学）史	the history of translation & translation studies	A. Chesterman、A. Lefevere、D. Robinson 等

（续表）

序号	SL 名称	TL 名称	提出者
2	翻译研究方法论	research methodology of TS	穆雷、陈刚、韩子满等
3	哲学思维	philosophical thinking	刘宓庆
4	纯理翻译学（或"meta 理论"）	meta theory	范守义
5	translation and the recipient culture	翻译与接受者文化	S. Bassnett
6	translation and linguistics	翻译与语言学	S. Bassnett
7	translation and poetics	翻译与诗学	S. Bassnett
8	口译职业道德；译者的职责和要求	code of professional ethics; the responsibilities and requirements for the translator	AIIC、谭载喜等
9	翻译伦理（学）	translation ethics	L. Venuti、A. Pym、J. Williams & A. Chesterman 等
10	翻译信息工程	translation information project	刘宓庆
11	翻译工程	translation project	杨自俭
12	多视角研究(语言学、符号学、文化学、社会学、文艺理论、系统论、控制论、信息论、思维科学、心理学、美学、知识学、译者行为批评等)	research from multi-perspectives	范守义、杨枫、周领顺等
13	（应用翻译学）应用技巧（笔译、口译、机器翻译等）	skill-oriented research in translating, interpreting and MT	范守义
14	（应用翻译学）翻译手段（与范守义"应用技巧"的提法不同）等	method-oriented research in full translation, partial translation, and trans-editing & trans-writing	陈刚
15	翻译管理（包括学术管理、行政管理和市场管理三大块，涉及学科管理、译者管理、翻译机构管理等）	translation management(不同于翻译项目管理)	陈刚
16	（应用）翻译策略	practical translation strategy/strategies	方梦之、陈刚等
17	公示语(信息+召唤+表情文本)英文译写（操作）原则及方法	principles and methods of transwriting of public signs (informative + vocative + expressive texts)	陈刚等

（续表）

序号	SL 名称	TL 名称	提出者
18	旅游—导译行业/领域 DTI 研究、其他领域 DTI 研究	research on DTT-DGI (doctor of tourism translation & guide-interpreting)	陈刚、中央编译局+天外、任东升等
19	导译职业/工种研究	profession/job-specific research in guide-interpreting	陈刚
20	专门翻译研究（诸如涉外旅游翻译、导译、会展、新闻等特殊领域）	research on specialized translation like tourism translation, guide-interpreting, MICE translation, news translation, etc.	陈刚、滕超、张健、许明武等
21	口笔译与对外传播或全球旅游等跨学科研究	interdisciplinary research, like one integrating T&I with external communication or global tourism	陈刚等
22	翻译服务（指有偿服务）	translation service	同业（王立非等）
23	影视翻译	AV translation	海外及国内学者
24	LSP (language service provider/ professional)	语言服务提供者/语言服务专业人才	海外学者
25	科技翻译	translation for science and technology	方梦之等
26	生态翻译学/翻译生态学	eco-translatology/translation ecology	胡庚申、许建忠等
27	国家翻译实践	state translation practice	任东升等
28	变译	translation variations	黄忠廉等
29	译介学	medio-translatology	谢天振
30	国家领袖及党政文献翻译	translation of State leaders' works and CPC & national government documents	中国外文局专家（国内外）

（多项内容参考陈刚, 2004: 110-111）

　　上述"译学图"或"译研图"——翻译（学）研究图及其扩展领域给翻译类学生提供了提纲挈领的研究指南。由于翻译学的跨学科性质，译学图的细分扩展给初次搞翻译研究的学生做了初步的、标题性的介绍，为 BTI/BA 毕业生在一个相对较新和尚未完全开发的研究领域指明了前进的道路。

　　译研图及其扩展领域有系统的分类划分，这有助于对翻译及其中介/动因作用下的过程、语境、结果进行描写、分析和理论阐述。授课老师或学生读者自己完全或基本有潜力/能力搞明白这些译研类别的内涵。

7.3.2　十二大翻译研究领域

　　为便于读者直接进入翻译（实践）研究的具体领域，根据 Williams 和 Chesterman（2004: 6-27），笔者特归纳、总结、简化了以下英文版翻译研究的十二大领域（twelve major translation research areas/subject areas），并根据研究新手及中国学生特色补充、提供了更为具体的研究领域、方面、层面，乃至研究主题、研究专题等（分类与原有引文有差异，读者应同时比较、参考表 7-5）。请通过二维码阅读"表 7-6　十二大翻译研究领域"。

7.4　提问式研究方法案例

常用的翻译研究方法有很多，根据学生的实际情况，我们还是从毕业论文目录、写作大纲或必备的章节小标题等"研究问题"（research questions/problems）讲起。换言之，按照笔者的学术造词（coinage/coined term），这种研究方法可采用引入法来命名，即"提问式"研究方法（ask-questions research method）。

7.4.1　研究问题概念解读

所谓**研究问题**，<u>就 BTI/翻译专业学位论文而言</u>，是论文作者在翻译项目进行过程中发现或找到的、需要攻克的难题（translation/research problems to be tackled），或者是有应用价值并值得加以研究的翻译实践问题或具有实践研究价值的翻译理论/策略/原则/方法/技巧等问题（practice-based research questions to be studied）。<u>就 BA/翻译学术学位论文而言</u>，是论文作者依照科学方法要解决的翻译理论和/或翻译实践问题（theoretical and/or practical questions to be researched）。

就此，Williams 和 Chesterman 有一段精彩的论述："The research process is like a dialogue with Mother Nature, or with 'reality'. We ask questions, and try to understand the answers we discover. As the dialogue progresses, we understand more and more (or at least, we think we do). <u>One of the secrets of research is learning how to ask</u> good questions. Questions then lead to possible answers, and then to claims and hypotheses."（2004: 69）

在整个翻译活动或翻译研究过程中，研究问题起着"纲举目张"的作用。与此同时，研究问题以问题的形式（即提问形式）对论题做进一步阐释，这有助于论文作者以清晰的思路进行研究设计（research design），并根据精心设计的问题对论文进行谋篇布局。

7.4.2　研究问题逐步确定

就撰写学位论文而言，确定研究领域、选择研究话题、提出研究问题这三者之间关系密切，甚至就是（接近）同一回事。这个过程是一个从笼统到具体（from general to specific）、从模糊到清晰（from vague to clear/focused）、从发散到集中（from divergent to convergent）的不断缩小范围（narrowed-down）的过程。

作文课上，老师布置作业时会统一给一个题目，即话题/主题，或给若干个题目，供学生选择。如果老师不给作文题，学生自己就得找一个——找一个自己感兴趣的话题，自己熟悉的话题，自己写得好的话题。表 7-7 为翻译研究话题十大来源，表 7-8 为翻译研究话题初选三大特点，表 7-9 为翻译研究话题范围缩小步骤举例。

表 7-7 翻译研究话题十大来源

Ten major sources for research topics

- personal experience
- peer groups (network with friends to discuss areas of interest in TS)
- topics in China- and/or Chinese-based English news like *China Daily*, Xinhua News, etc.
- one of your translation/interpreting course syllabuses
- academic journals on translation or foreign language research in China and beyond
- bibliography for translation textbooks or monographs available (to you)
- online & printed lists of periodical literature
- encyclopedias
- librarians
- web search

表 7-8 翻译研究话题初选三大特点

Three important characteristics for research topic selection

- It is of <u>interest</u> to you.
- There appears to be a lot of information <u>available</u> on this topic.
- You have the <u>background</u> or <u>expertise</u> to understand and write about the information you'll be reading.

（参考 Buffa, 1997: 11）

表 7-9 翻译研究话题范围缩小步骤举例

范围缩小步骤	翻译研究话题范围	备注
1	旅游翻译研究	a broad **category** chosen—a *comprehensive* topic
2	导译研究	the **scope** narrowed—a division of tourism translation (research)
3	汉英导译研究	the **subject area** further narrowed down (to)
4	汉英导译词研究	the **subarea** of the subject
5	莫高窟导译词研究	the **focused part** of the subarea

7.4.3 BA 学位论文研究方法案例①

步骤	论文题目/研究问题
1	**To finalize the thesis title (+ subtitle)—bilingual titles (+ subtitles)** 许渊冲四首英译中国古诗的描写性案例研究 ——翻译规范探讨与目标读者反应测试② A Descriptive Case Study on Xu Yuanzhong's Four Translations of Classical Chinese Poems

① 该案例展示确定翻译研究问题之步骤，适合 BA 学位论文的撰写。
② 论文作者为浙江大学英语专业本科毕业生（翻译方向）。

—Testing Translational Norms, and Target-Reader's Response

【备注】确定论文题目（即研究话题）：探讨研究许渊冲先生古诗英译的规范及读者反应，涉及描写案例研究、翻译规范研究和读者反应研究，既属于概念/理论分析/研究，又属于实证分析/研究。

2	**To read the relevant literature—working bibliography**

(1) Baker, Mona (ed.) *Routledge Encyclopedia of Translation Studies* [M]. London: Routledge, 1998.

(2) Bassnett, Susan. Transplanting the Seed: Poetry and Translation [G]. In: S. Bassnett and A. Lefevere. *Constructing Cultures: Essays on Literary Translation*. Shanghai: Shanghai Foreign Language Education Press, 2001.

(3) Birch, Cyril. *Anthology of Chinese Literature, Volume I* [M]. New York: Grove Press, 1965.

(4) Even-Zohar, I. Polysystem Studies [J]. *Poetics Today*, 1990(1): 9-26.

(5) Graham, Angus. *Poems of the Late Tang* [M]. London: Penguin Classics, 1965.

(6) Hamill, Sam. *Crossing the Yellow River: Three Hundred Poems from the Chinese* [Z]. Rochester: BOA Editions, 2000.

(7) Han, Yanhui. A Comparative Study on Thematic Structure in Yin Jiu (V) by Tao Yuanming and Its English Translation [D]. Southwest Jiaotong University, 2011.

(8) Holmes, James, Lambert, J. & van den Broek, R. (eds.). *Literature and Translation: New Perspective in Literary Studies* [C]. Leuven: Acco., 1978.

(9) Holmes, James. *Translated! Papers on Literary Translation and Translation Studies* [C]. Amsterdam: Rodopi, 1994.

(10) Lefevere, André. *Translating Poetry: Seven Strategies and a Blueprint* [M]. Assen/Amsterdam: Van Gorcum, 1975.

(11) Lefevere, André. *Translation, Rewriting and the Manipulation of Literary Fame* [M]. London: Routledge, 1992.

(12) Lowell, Amy & Ayscough, Florence. *Fir-flower Tablets: Poems Translated from the Chinese* [M]. Boston: Houghton Mifflin, Co., 1921.

(13) Miall, David. & Don, Kuiken. Aspects of Literary Response: A New Questionnaire [J]. *Research in the Teaching of English*, 1995(29): 37-58

(14) Owen, Stephen. *An Anthology of Chinese Literature: Beginnings to 1911* [M]. New York: Norton & Company, 1996.

(15) Rexroth, Kenneth. The Poet as Translator [G]. In: W. Arrowsmith & R. Shattuck (eds.). *The Craft and Context of Translation*. New York: Angkor Books, 1964.

(16) Savory, Theodore. *The Art of Translation* [M]. London: Jonathan Cape, 1957.

(17) Schlepp, Wayne. *Translating Chinese: A Poem by Ts'ui Hao* [M]. North Harrow: Middlesex P. Ward, 1964.

(18) Toury, Gideon. *Descriptive Translation Studies and Beyond* [M]. Amsterdam & Philadelphia: John Benjamins, 2012.

(19) Waley, Arthur. *A Hundred and Seventy Chinese Poems* [DB/OL]. London: Constable and Co. Ltd., 1962. [2014-12-21]. http://www. gutenberg.org/files/42290/42290-h/42290-h.htm.

(20) Williams, R. J. *Mapping the Invisible: Orientalist Mythologies in the Translation of Chinese Poetry* [D]. Utah State University, 2001.

(21) 陈奇敏. 许渊冲唐诗英译研究——以图里的翻译规范理论为观照[D]. 上海外国语大学, 2012.

(22) 丛滋杭. 得意忘形　求同存异——读许渊冲译《汉英对照唐诗三百首》兼谈韵体译诗优势[J]. 浙江树人大学学报（人文社会科学版）, 2009(4): 92-96.

(23) 党争胜. 中国古典诗歌在国外的译介与影响[J]. 外语教学, 2012(3): 96-100.

(24) 丁娟. 从"三美论"评析《如梦令》的许渊冲英译本[J]. 语文学刊（外语教育与教学）, 2009(11): 83-86.

(25) 冯丽霞. 许渊冲英译中诗在大学英语学习者中的接受调查[J]. 黑龙江史志, 2009(7): 119-120.

(26) 葛瑞汉. 中国诗的翻译[G]//张隆溪. 比较译学论文集. 北京：北京大学出版社, 1982.

(27) 孔慧怡. 译诗应否用韵的几点考虑[J]. 上海外国语大学学报, 1997(4): 42-44.

(28) 林文韵. 英译古典诗词的隐喻转化策略——许渊冲先生译文评析[J]. 鸡西大学学报, 2013(6): 69-70.

(29) 马红军. 从文学翻译到翻译文学[M]. 上海：上海译文出版社, 2006.

(30) 聂珍钊. 英语诗歌形式导论[M]. 北京：中国社会科学出版社, 2007.

(31) 任诚刚. 许渊冲古诗词韵译的多样性[J]. 海外英语, 2014(22): 150-154.

(32) 谭业升. 论翻译文本对比分析的描写翻译学方法[J]. 外语与外语教学, 2006(12): 48-51.

(33) 王程程. 谈许渊冲的"三化"对意美表达的作用[J]. 湖北广播电视大学学报, 2011(9): 108-109.

(34) 王凤霞. 从许渊冲诗歌翻译看文化转基因的再现——以许渊冲先生所译《游东田》为例[J]. 西华大学学报（哲学社会科学版）, 2008(1): 101-103+112.

(35) 王厚平. 美学视角下的文学翻译艺术研究[D]. 上海外国语大学, 2010.

(36) 王靖怡. 汉诗英译的押韵研究——以许渊冲译《唐诗三百首》绝句为例[D]. 大连海事大学, 2012.

(37) 王力. 诗词格律概要[M]. 北京：北京出版社, 2011.

(38) 王丽萍. 许渊冲翻译美学思想探微——从"三美"角度分析《诗经》英译本[J]. 海外英语, 2011(2): 121-122.

(39) 王运鸿. 描写翻译研究及其后[J]. 中国翻译, 2013(3): 5-14.

(40) 熊婧. 从《漱玉词》看许渊冲韵体译诗之不足[J]. 群文天地, 2011(20): 55-56.

(41) 徐日宣, 潘智丹. 从许渊冲法译唐诗看译诗理论中"音美"的传达[J]. 外语与外语教学, 2011(1): 58-61.

(42) 许渊冲. 翻译的艺术[M]. 北京：五洲传播出版社, 2006.

(43) 许渊冲. 文学与翻译[G]. 北京：北京大学出版社, 2003.

	(44) 许渊冲. 中诗英韵探胜——从《诗经》到《西厢记》[M]. 北京：北京大学出版社, 2010.
	(45) 杨青. 简论许渊冲的中诗英译[J]. 大连民族学院学报, 2003(3): 85-87.
	(46) 朱明海. 许渊冲翻译研究：翻译审美批评视角[D]. 上海外国语大学, 2008.
	(47) 张智中. 许渊冲与翻译艺术[M]. 武汉：湖北教育出版社, 2006.
	(48) 张智中. 如诗入诗，自成一家——许渊冲先生古典诗词英译的语言风格[J]. 安徽理工大学学报（社会科学版）, 2005(2): 33-37.
	【备注】阅读相关文献：上边所列的 48 条中英文参考文献是作者在撰写论文过程中确定 6 个主要研究问题时所引用和/或参考的有关文献（包括某项全部或部分）。没有认真地阅读文献，作者很难提出并确定下一步的研究问题，尤其是 "好问题"。
3	**To formulate research questions—specific research questions**
	① What are XYZ's <u>preliminary norms</u>, and <u>two main sets of considerations</u> <u>related to</u> <u>directness of translation</u> and <u>translation policy</u>?
	② What are the <u>operational norms</u> in XYZ's translation process of four verse translations?
	③ What are the <u>initial norms</u> and how are they reflected in the general cultural inclination in XYZ's four translations?
	④ What is the <u>general evaluation</u> of XYZ's four verse translations made among young English-speaking readers, most of whom are university students?
	⑤ What are <u>their evaluation and comments on the rhyme and rhythm</u> of XYZ's four translations?
	⑥ What is <u>the most possible theme</u> they have perceived from each verse translation?*
	【备注】确定研究问题：具体所涉问题见上面加了底线的关键词。此外，论文作者就 "研究问题" 之⑥有一英文脚注（引用者特在关键词下加了底线）："The Author has <u>narrowed down the scope of the research</u> since it is almost impossible to conduct a questionnaire survey on all XYZ's verse translation."

【BA 学位论文案例简析①】

（1）确定研究问题之要义——学会提问。根据 Williams 和 Chesterman（2004: 69）："<u>At first, the questions are often a bit vague and general, but gradually they become more focused as the research topic is more clearly defined</u>. One reason for <u>reading the relevant literature</u> is to <u>discover good questions</u>. Eventually, you should be able to <u>formulate a specific question or *research problem*</u>. This <u>final focus</u> is <u>usually something that gradually emerges from your work, as you proceed</u>. <u>Don't worry if it does not appear obvious at the start; just keep on asking questions and exploring, drawing mind maps for yourself, and then new maps</u>…"

（2）提出具体问题之基础——阅读文献。针对这 48 项参考文献（浙江大学外语学科本科生毕业/学位论文撰写所要求阅读参考文献的最低数量是 10 篇/部，其中中英文各 5 篇/部），我们分成三类来分析：

①有关理论框架、研究方法主题：10 项参考文献；

---

① 该案例分析（1）同样适用于接下来的案例以及所有的类似案例。

②有关译诗理论及诗歌常识主题：31 项参考文献；

③有关中国古诗英译及译诗主题：7 项参考文献。

（3）确定研究问题之原则——聚焦范围。查看 6 个研究问题，我们不难发现这 6 个问题聚焦于以下几个关键词语：

①XYZ's preliminary norms；

②directness of translation；

③translation policy；

④the operational norms in XYZ's translation process；

⑤the initial norms；

⑥the general evaluation of XYZ's four verse translations。

7.4.4　BTI 学位论文研究方法案例

步骤	论文题目/研究问题
1	**To finalize the thesis title (+ subtitle)—bilingual titles (+ subtitles)** 论现代舞教材翻译之忠实与灵活 ——以翻译《专业编舞入门》为例① On Faithfulness and Flexibility in Translating —the Modern Dance Textbook *A Primer for Choreographers* 【备注】确定论文题目(即研究话题)：探讨研究《专业编舞入门》的翻译，涉及两大翻译原则——"忠实"与"灵活"。
2	**To read the relevant literature—working bibliography** ●**Publications** (1)　蔡基刚. 准确是教科书翻译的基本准则[J] 上海科技翻译, 1999(1). (2)　陈刚. 翻译学入门[M]. 杭州：浙江大学出版社, 2011. (3)　冯双白. 中国舞蹈史及作品鉴赏[M]. 北京：高等教育出版社, 2010. (4)　冯双白, 等. 中国舞蹈大辞典[Z]. 北京：文化艺术出版社, 2010. (5)　辜正坤. 外来术语翻译与中国学术问题[J]. 北京大学学报（哲学社会科学版）, 1998(4). (6)　金秋. 舞蹈创作法[M]. 北京：学苑出版社, 2005. (7)　梁爱林. 术语资源质量评估研究[J/未发表]. 惠州学院, 2014. (8)　孟令霞. 从术语学角度看术语翻译[J]. 中国科技翻译, 2011(2). (9)　欧建平. 舞蹈知识手册[M]. 上海：上海音乐出版社, 2001. (10) 欧建平. 现代舞术语辞典[Z]. 上海：上海音乐出版社, 2002. (11) 朱立人. 芭蕾术语词典[Z]. 上海：上海音乐出版社, 2003. (12) Au, S. *Ballet and Modern Dance.* [M] London: Thames & Hudson Ltd, 1997. (13) Baker, Mona. *In Other Words: A Coursebook on Translation* [M]. Beijing: Foreign Language

---

① 论文作者为浙江大学 BTI 毕业生。

Teaching and Research Press, 2000.

(14) Catford, J. C. *A Linguistic Theory of Translation* [M]. Oxford: Oxford University Press, 1965.

(15) Nida, E.A. & Taber, C.R. *The Theory and Practice of Translation* [M]. Shanghai: Shanghai Foreign Language Education Press, 2004.

●Online citations

(16) http://www.contemporary-dance.org/dance-terms.html [accessed 2015/05/11].

(17) http://www.contemporary-dance.org/ [accessed 2014/12/10].

【备注】阅读相关文献：上边所列的 17 项中英文参考文献（包括纸质和网上资料）是作者在撰写论文过程中确定两个主要方面的研究问题时所引用和/或参考的有关文献。这些文献有助于作者在首次翻译舞蹈入门教材过程中提出具有实践价值的问题。

3	**To formulate research questions—specific research questions**

The research questions are chiefly in two aspects:

One is how to better translate modern dance terms, including those with choreographic elements and space explorations, geometric terms, borrowed words, etc.

The other is to explore the flexibility in translating polysemy, abstract or functional words, and those with cultural difference.

【备注】确定研究问题：具体所涉问题见上边加了底线的关键词语。其中，"how to better translate..." 指如何（更）忠实地翻译现代舞词汇（含术语）等。在审读作者论文时发现：要把英文中的现代舞术语译成具有专业水准的汉语，其原则、策略的确是，也首先是"忠实"与"灵活"。

【BTI 学位论文案例简析】

（1）确定研究问题之要义——学会提问①。

（2）提出具体问题之基础——阅读文献。针对这 17 项参考文献，我们分成三类来分析：

①有关翻译原则、教科书类主题：7 项参考文献；

②有关舞蹈专业理论及知识主题：9 项参考文献；

③有关其他专题和百科知识主题：1 项参考文献。

（3）确定研究问题之原则——聚焦范围。查看两个基本方面的研究问题，论文的研究问题聚焦于以下几个关键词语：

①how to better translate modern dance terms, including those with choreographic elements and space explorations, geometric terms, borrowed words, etc.；

②(how) to explore the flexibility in translating polysemy, abstract or functional words, and those with cultural differences.

综上，关于 BA/BTI 学位论文研究方法的案例都涉及最为基本、最为常用的"提问

---

① 该案例分析（1）详见【BA 学位论文案例简析】之（1）。

式"研究方法。至于这些提出的研究问题最终是如何得到一一解决的，可谓存在多种多样的方案和方法（solutions/answers）。由于展示这些方案和方法需要引用论文中很大的篇幅才能讲得清楚，因此书中不得不对此做出必要的省略。BTI 论文中是如何回答所提出的研究问题的，详见第 6 章。

为方便读者"窥斑见豹"，我们仅就 BA 论文中如何将研究问题和研究方法结合起来，做如下引用。

【BA 论文回答研究问题的部分选段】

5.4.1　Readers' Response Survey

The last question in this study is to find out whether the acceptability-oriented translation norms followed by XYZ are helpful in fulfilling the expected effect of intercultural communication. Chesterman (1997: 90) indicated that readers would have expectations of the translation in grammatical reasonability, acceptability, texts, style, etc. Therefore, readers' response survey is actually the final one for a descriptive study.

5.4.2　Illustration I

小雅·采薇 Home-going after War

General Impression			Rhyme & Rhythm		
Excellent	4	13.8%	Excellent	2	6.9%
Good	12	41.4%	Good	10	34.5%
Fair	11	37.9%	Fair	13	44.8%
Poor	2	6.9%	Poor	4	13.8%

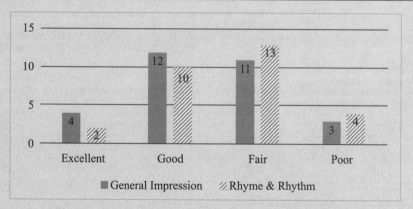

Over half of participants considered this translation as "Excellent" and "Good", and less half thought so in the sound pattern. The participants stated that they liked those short four-syllable lines, which sounded very exotic, even though some of them didn't sounded like poetic language but telling a story. One spoke highly of "willows shed tear", which reminded him of "people wipe tears" when she imagined seeing wickers waving.

Theme		
Intolerable grief / Sorrow / Hardship on the way	13	44.8%
War-weariness	8	27.6%
Homesickness / Longing to go home	6	20.7%

Bitterness of loneliness	1	3.4%
Old and poor	1	3.4%
Unclear	0	

The comprehension of the theme was more diversified and accurate. Grief, war-weariness, and longing for home were all right answers. Possible reasons were as follows: First, "grief" directly appeared in the translation; second, the introduction mentioned this poem was about a "soldier serving his country in the war… on the far northern frontier"; Third, Xu changed the title to "Home-coming from War".

Attitude to "o'erflow"		
Positive comment	2	6.9%
Neutral comment	7	24.1%
Negative comment	12	41.4%
Blank	8	27.6%

One of the only two participants, who gave positive comments, thought it was "amazing" for a Chinese translator to think of "an archaic word". However, almost 3/5 of the participants who made comments, were negative. The following two comments were very representative: "I can get it, but sounds weird." "It doesn't make the translation an old style English poem." These comments reflected the said target readers' disapproval of omitting consonant in the word, which is actually "very common in English poems" (聂珍钊, 2007: 11).On the other hand, two mentioned the reasons why they gave no comment: one he didn't know this word, the other had no idea why he used an abridged "o'erflows", though he could guess. This can explain why more than 1/4 of participants left it blank, thus reflecting the fact that many participants aren't familiar with English poetic rhythm.

…

5.4.6 General Evaluation

General Impression		Rhyme & Rhythm	
Excellent	18.95%	Excellent	15.53%
Good	36.20%	Good	27.53%
Fair	32.75%	Fair	38.73%
Poor	11.16%	Poor	14.65%

About 55% of target readers held positive attitude to XYZ's translations, and nearly 90% readers basically accepted them as acceptable translations. In the sound pattern, the acceptance was respectively lower, especially among the readers who checked it "excellent" and "good". Concerning the theme, most readers could catch the point of the poems, and that owed much to the brief introduction after each translation. XYZ's rhymed translation was very likely to be acceptable for a fair amount of target readers, even though the free translation of classic Chinese poetry dominated at home and abroad. Such results brought justification into the norms Xu followed in his translations, and proved that his translations can fulfill a certain expectation for introducing classic Chinese poetry and culture into the West.

7.5　翻译常用研究思路简介

研究思路构成一种研究方法，即你将或你该如何开始或进行你的研究。

按照翻译研究路径或路线图，有关整个过程是：

　　　questions ➜ [answers ➜] claims ➜ hypotheses

虽然 claim 和 hypothesis 是近义词，但还是有区别的。前者指 "a statement that sth. is true although it has not been proved and other people may not agree with or believe it"（主张/观点；宣称；断言），后者指 "an idea or explanation of sth. that is based on a few known facts but that has not been proved to be true or correct"（假说，假设）。[①]

根据 Williams 和 Chesterman（参考 2004: 69-71），改用中国背景的例子，有一些 **initial questions**（IQ/初始阶段的研究问题）值得推荐，涉及意义或定义。有关思路和发展过程，即有关思考的方式方法如下：思考问题时需要紧紧围绕的要素，如原则、尺度、特征等，可包括 "七大性"——可行性、时效性、逻辑性、针对性、计划性、多元性、操作性。

7.5.1　初始阶段研究思路

IQ01
What does X mean? How can X best be defined?

AN01
Answering this question might involve conceptual analysis, a kind of philosophical approach to clarifying a complex idea, such as "equivalence". This question could also be paraphrased: **How can X be interpreted or best understood**? This then prompts a follow-up question: <u>interpreted by whom</u>? This in turn might lead to a <u>survey</u> of what previous scholars had thought, or to a series of <u>interviews</u> or even a <u>questionnaire study</u>.

其他问题涉及基本数据问题（basic data questions）：

IQ02
What can I find out about X?

AN02
This kind of introductory question leads to <u>preliminary exploratory research</u>. For instance: ...

IQ03—04
●What was happening on the interpreting scene in the Chinese mainland in the late 1970s?
●I wonder how professional guide-interpreters actually worked in the 1980s.

随着研究计划的成熟，这两个问题会变得更为具体：

IQ05—06
●Which new form of interpreting began to take shape?
●What role did guide-interpreting play from the early 1980s?

---

① 有关两个词的解释、翻译，参考 OALD。

于是便发生了描写性问题（descriptive questions）：

IQ07—09

- What is this new form of interpreting actually like, compared to the traditional forms of interpreting?
- What is the key role that guide-interpreters have played from the early 1980s to the present?
- How is tour interpretation different from text interpretation?

当研究计划继续推进时，研究问题则变得愈加具体：

IQ10—11

- How has the guide-interpreter dealt with names of scenic spots?
- What specific methods does the guide-interpreter use to translate historical names?

其实，还有其他研究问题与因果（causes and effects）有关系：

IQ12—16

- Why is the translation of the said tour narration like this, with so many errors?
- Why are there so many more written or formal expressions in the G-I's narration than I would have expected?
- Why was this travel brochure translated and not that one?
- How do the English tourists react to this new translated narration?
- Why do so many British tourists react like that?

7.5.2　观点阶段研究思路

随着研究的不断进展，你会慢慢地形成一种/一些概念，这些概念有助于你思考基本的研究问题。你也慢慢开始建构有关研究问题的可能的答案。当然，有关答案是建立在数据、分析、综述等基础之上的。不过，这些答案可能仅仅是初步性质的，会逐步达到"健全"的程度，最终，你就能够构建漂亮的答案，即（专业）观点或（学术）主张，并有事实依据和逻辑论证的支撑。于是，你的这些观点或主张是对有关研究领域的贡献。如果你提不出任何新的观点或主张，你的研究工作就如同他人思想的一种总结或一些事例的罗列（参见 Williams & Chesterman, 2004: 71）。

下一步思路，则是如何对你的观点/主张进行论证（substantiate your claim），进行验证和评估（test and evaluate）。

【典型案例解说】

假设你发现某导游词的英译文问题较多，很有重译的必要，即将同一篇导游词或同一个源语文本（source text/ST）重译成同一种目标语（target language/TL）。此时，你不妨在重译前和重译中向自己提出一些问题，并且不断充实自己的观点，提出自己的主张。用英文思考的有关问题及观点/主张如下（参考 Williams & Chesterman, 2004: 71-72）：

Steps	Questions to consider	Explanation/Claim
1	How does this particular retranslation seem different from the first translation?	Your initial impression, which you will then methodically test.

2	What do I mean by a retranslation, as compared to a revision?	⇨**Claim**: This is how to define the distinction...
3	Do other translations of the same ST exist, in the same TL? Who were the translators? Who commissioned the translations? Why? Why were they published?	⇨**Claim**: These are relevant new facts.
4	Can I make any generalizations about the various differences I notice between the first translation and this retranslation?	⇨**Claim**: The initial topic of the thesis after my generalizations is given below: On **Simplification** and **Amplification** for Re-translating "Potala Palace" and "Shaolin Temple" in a **Cross-Cultural** Way
5	How can I explain these differences? Is there maybe any general principle underlying them? Is there a translator's preface or publisher's note that gives any clues?	⇨**Claims** about explanations...
6	If I were the only retranslator, could I be able to do a better job?	⇨**Claim** (made by my supervisor): This MTI candidate is competent to do an excellent job, namely, to offer a much better retranslation, together with the thesis.
7	Some scholars have claimed that retranslations tend to be closer to the original than the first translations: is this claim (*known as the* **retranslation hypothesis**) supported by my data?	⇨**Claim** (made by my supervisor): The said claim or **retranslation hypothesis** would be supported by the candidate's new target text as illustrated below.
8	How do I test this claim? How can I define "closer" in some way that I can reliably measure? (I can't measure everything, after all!)	⇨**Claim**: This is a good way to measure closeness...
9	In what specific ways do I measure or make a comparative study of the old version (TT1) and the new version (TT2)?	⇨**Claim**: Considering the translation errors/problems in TT1, the candidate will measure TT1 against "simplification" and "amplification" in a "cross-cultural" way, the most appropriate translation techniques (*to be*) applied in TT2.
10	Are my results (TT2) *tenable* or even *creative*? Do my results suggest that the retranslation hypothesis needs to be *modified* somehow, *refined*? Or even *rejected*?	⇨**Claim** about the hypothesis...

在上述 10 步/阶段验证和评估过程中，第 7 步/阶段出现的 retranslation hypothesis（重译假说/复译假说）指 "a claim about a particular general characteristic of retranslations. In the philosophy of science, specific claims are often called hypotheses"（Williams & Chesterman, 2004: 73）。

再根据上述 10 个阶段的问题及观点主张、有关解释，我们试着来回答这些问题。

Steps	Questions to consider	Answers to be tested
1	How does this particular retranslation seem different from the first translation?	This retranslation differs from the first translation in cross-cultural awareness and professionalism, which call for different translation techniques.
2	What do I mean by a retranslation, as compared to a revision?	The retranslation done by me means basically full retranslation, while revision means lexical and semantical improvement and correction.
3	Do other translations of the same ST exist, in the same TL? Who were the translators? Who commissioned the translations? Why? Why were they published?	No other translations of the same ST exist in the same TL.
4	Can I make any generalizations about the various differences I notice between the first translation and this retranslation?	Based on my generalizations, I found many differences between the first translation and this retranslation. To solve these differences or to improve the first translation (TT1) fully, I made the initial topic of the thesis by highlighting the keywords that have proved general weaknesses in TT1: On **Simplification** and **Amplification** for Re-translating "Potala Palace" and "Shaolin Temple" in a **Cross-Cultural** Way
5	How can I explain these differences? Is there any general principle underlying them? Is there a translator's preface or publisher's note that gives any clues?	There are some general principles for guiding the retranslation and specifying translation errors in TT1, which include linguistic, cultural, pragmatic and text-specific errors. The practical guidelines for retranslation is to make good he maximum use of two basic translation techniques—simplification and amplification for the sake of syntax and CSI.
6	If I were the only retranslator, could I be able to do a better job?	Yes, I could. I have done a large quantity of C-E translation. I have won an award in China's national translation contest.
7	Some scholars have claimed that retranslations tend to be closer to the original than the first translations: is this claim (*known as the* **retranslation hypothesis**) supported by my data?	Yes, this claim (retranslation hypothesis) is generally supported by my retranslation (TT2), which can prove much better/much more effective in terms of cross-cultural communication.

8	How do I test this claim? How can I define "closer" in some way that I can reliably measure? (I can't measure everything, after all!)	I will test the claim by conducting a comparative study of TT1 and TT2. I will define "closer" as "(of retranslation) more similar to the ST in sense and to TT2 in style, tone, taste, idiomaticity, poetics, TL-orientedness or TL culture-orientedness".
9	In what specific ways do I measure or make a comparative study of the old version (TT1) and the new version (TT2)?	I will measure TT1 against the yardsticks of "simplification" and "amplification" in a "cross-cultural" way, the most appropriate translation techniques (*to be*) applied to TT2. This is followed by an explanation based on comparative case studies.
10	Are my results (TT2) *tenable* or even *creative*? Do my results suggest that the retranslation hypothesis needs to be *modified* somehow, *refined*? Or even *rejected*?	The results or retranslation hypothesis are tenable, and need to be modified in some way. TT2 proves to be as creative as the retranslation is both idiomatic and professional.

为了更好地展示 BTI（乃至 MTI）学位论文真实的一面，以说明如何提出作者自己的**学术主张/观点**或**假设**，这里特地引用了论文题目以及论文中的一小部分。

On **Simplification** and **Amplification** for Re-translating "Potala Palace" and "Shaolin Temple" in a **Cross-Cultural** Way[①]

...

These two source texts (ST) and their target texts (TT) the Author's supervisor chose for the thesis present a considerable challenge by cultural problems and translation. Firstly, both the STs and the TTs abound with cultural-specific expressions at lexical, syntactic and textual levels. Secondly, religious contents are especially dominant in both types of texts. To translate them well is no easy job at all, while to revise and re-translate the first TTs (TT1) effectively is far more difficult. This Author has been required to do a professional job in this translation project by completing two major tasks, namely, providing a revised translation/re-translation of his own and making theoretical and technical comments on the new or second TTs.

1.2　Research Questions

There are a couple of crucial questions to be addressed in this thesis.

Question 1 (Q1): Why does the original translation (TT1) fail to be an effective cross-cultural communication?

Question 2 (Q2): How can amplification and simplification techniques be professionally used in revising and re-translating so that English-speaking tourists can better appreciate the "great wonders" of the East?

Question 3 (Q3): How can wording and information be better organized to express the text-specific ideas both economically and effectively?

---

① 作者为浙江大学英语专业 BA 毕业生和 MTI 毕业生。

1.3 Problems to be Tackled

It is clear that there are a host of translation problems in the two TTs. Firstly, there are mistranslations at the lexical level, because of either wrong transliterations or misinterpretations of the objects described in the ST. In other cases, the expressions adopted are less or much less proper ones. Secondly, to put across source-language (SL) narrations filled with a large number of proper nouns, historical figures, copious descriptions, exotic philosophies and detailed stories, the translator should have keen cross-cultural awareness of these cultural matters and acquire the technical know-how about cross-cultural translation. In other words, it doesn't work at all to faithfully reflect every detailed piece of information in the translated text. Instead, the translator has to be specifically clear about what to omit and what to add in the entire process of translation. Unfortunately, there are too many problems waiting to be tackled in revising TT1 and/or re-retranslating the STs.

1.4 Methodology

1.4.1 Amplification and Simplification as Translation Methods

Given the significant differences between the Chinese culture and the English one, trans-editing is necessary in tackling cross-cultural translation problems. In other words, the translator has to choose the right bits of information, piece them together, and present them seamlessly to the target readers/visitors. Ranking among the most commonly used translation techniques, amplification and simplification must be adopted wisely in the trans-editing process. By looking at both techniques, the Author suggests that they are applicable in a wide spectrum of tourism translation, ranging from oral speeches to written texts.

Amplification, as a translation method, is commonly used to make up for what is insufficient both linguistically and culturally in the TT. This method or strategy can be applied at the lexical, syntactical, contextual and rhetorical levels for respective purposes.

In many cases, the amplification technique is adopted to reveal cultural connotations of CSIs, or a phenomenon in cases when formal equivalence falls short of the communicational goal.

The simplification technique is another practical strategy in dealing with tourism translation. Given grammatical, rhetorical and cultural differences in the Chinese and English languages, the translator has to be aware of unnecessary words and/or expressions in the TT.

More often than not, Chinese T/G narrations abound with detailed descriptive texts and expressive comments while its English counterparts tend to be of a relatively simple and direct style. The reduction of superfluous words, repeated references or redundant descriptions, and other unnecessary detailed information will contribute to a concise, smooth and tourist-oriented translation which will not be labor-lost for translators and guide-interpreters.

Based on a specific context, simplification is usually made possible by omission, restructuring as well as other techniques.

To sum up, amplification and simplification combined in this particular re-translation project will serve as two major methods for the improvement of both tour narrations.

1.4.2　Cross-cultural Translation Competence

The lack of cross-cultural awareness coupled with professionalism is a major source of inappropriate/improper renderings or mistranslations in the selected narrations.

The concept of culture can be defined in varied ways. Nida, for instance, defines it as "the totality of beliefs and practices in a society" (Nida, 2001: 78). In Newmark's view, culture is "the way of life and its manifestations that are peculiar to a community that uses a particular language as its means of expression" (Newmark, 2002: 94).

As Vermeer (2000: 29) pointed out, transcultural action or communication across culture barriers has to take account of cultural differences with regard to behavior, evaluation and communicative situations. A competent translator, or rather, a professional translator for tourism, should be alert to cultural and linguistic pitfalls. These pitfalls may refer to major types of cultural differences that are categorized into historical and regional ones as well as the differences in values and in thought pattern, which will be further reflected in the case studies section.

1.4.3　Comparative Case Studies

The thesis conducts comparative case studies in its main body.

Overall, it follows a simple problem-finding, problem-solving and assessment procedure centering on the use of amplification and simplification techniques. A detailed analysis is given to identify the translation problem before offering an improved version, which is followed by sufficient reasoning and assessment. The thesis classifies representative cases into five major categories, which respectively emphasize the use of amplification and simplification in:

1. the translation of names and titles;

2. the translation of culturally-loaded terms;

3. the translation of poems, lyrics and couplets;

4. the translation of narrative texts;

5. the translation of descriptive texts.

Relevant translation theories and philosophies are referred to when necessary to support each case.

7.5.3　假说阶段研究思路

假说的提出，是在观点/主张提出之后。根据《现汉》，所谓"假说"通"假设"之第三个义项，指"科学研究上对客观事物的假定的说明，假设要根据事实提出，经过实践证明是正确的，就成为理论"（《现汉》第 628 页）。本小节中的"假说"大都译自或源于《路线图》第 5 章（Williams & Chesterman, 2004）中的 hypothesis，故保留"假说"这一说法。至于"假设"，有原文 claim 作为依据。

"严格讲来，假说是永远不能被证明其真实性的，或被确认为是真实的。"（Williams & Chesterman, 2004: 81）假说是对研究问题做阐释性、描述性、解释性、预测性的回答，是对研究问题的深化。"科学不是靠堆积真理而发展的，而是靠提出越来越好的假说而前进的。"（81）假说主要分为四种，每种假说与某一特种研究问题相联系。

（1）阐释性假说（interpretive hypothesis）

1）英文定义：something can be usefully defined as, or seen as, or interpreted as, something else; i.e. that a given concept is useful for describing or understanding something（73）。

2）概念解读：任何阐释努力对概念研究、实证研究等都很重要。阐释性假说在翻译理论研究、翻译实践研究、概念分析、意义阐释、定义建构、各种分类等方面起积极作用，"阐释性假说是所有概念分析的基础"（74）。

3）举例说明：<u>有关导译的研究可以被称为"**导译研究**"或"**导译学**"。顾名思义，导译包含两大层面的意思，即"导"和"译"，但二者之间密不可分，与单纯意义的"导（游）"和"（口）译"不能相提并论</u>（陈刚，2013）。

（2）描述性假说（descriptive hypothesis）

1）英文定义：all instances (of a given type / under given conditions) of phenomenon X have observable feature Y（Williams & Chesterman, 2004: 75）。

2）概念解读：①a universal, unrestricted claim（无限制性之普遍性/一般性假设）。在实证研究中，描述性假说对某一条件的一般性质或总体特征提出某一假设。换言之，这种假设是可以进行实证检验、验证的，具有普遍性/一般性特点。②a less general claim（限制性之普遍性/一般性假设）。这种假设是有条件的，即为条件式的普遍性/一般性假设。引用专家的话语，"the descriptive claim is less than general, but it is still a generalization" "descriptive hypotheses aim to generalize, not to explain"（75, 76）。描述性假说用于描述性研究问题，分为无限制假说翻译研究和有限制假说翻译研究两种。前者如研究 translation universals（翻译共性/翻译普遍性/翻译普遍现象），后者如 particular translation types or text types（特种翻译类别或特定翻译文本类别等）。

3）举例说明：①<u>**导译**从改革开放的 1978 年开始全面发展，它实际已经成为跨专业、跨行业、跨学科的，隶属于翻译学的一个新分支。导译研究的重要性早已摆在学术界和行业领域面前，对专业导译人员的培养也早已成为旅游行业的重中之重</u>（陈刚，2013）。②本科毕业论文《许渊冲四首英译中国古诗的描写性案例研究》是这样开展研究的：根据图里的翻译规范理论，本文对许渊冲翻译的四首中国古诗进行了案例研究，并重构了蕴含于译文之中的预备规范、操作规范和初始规范。其后，<u>通过在以英语为母语或第二语言的大学生中进行的目标读者反应调查，得出结论：许渊冲的韵体翻译很有可能为相当数量的目标读者所接受，并在一定程度上实现了将中国古典诗歌引入西方世界的期望。本文证明了许渊冲四首译诗中可接受性导向的翻译规范的接受度，也证明了中国当代译者翻译中国古典诗歌的能力。本文探索了在中国古诗翻译领域，描写性案例研究与读者反应调查相结合的研究方式，这种方式可以使描写翻译研究变得更加客观而有说服力</u>。[①]
③<u>cross-cultural translations</u> from Chinese to English tend to <u>simplify sentence structures</u>（详见浙江大学图书馆毕业生论文资料，题目是"On <u>Simplification</u> and <u>Amplification</u> for Re-translating 'Potala Palace' and 'Shaolin Temple' in a <u>Cross-cultural</u> Way"）。

---

① 引自浙江大学英语专业本科生毕业论文（本章已选用该论文部分内容，用于"7.4.3　BA 学位论文研究方法案例"）。

（3）解释性假说（explanatory hypothesis）

1）英文定义：a particular phenomenon X is (or tends to be) caused or influenced by conditions or factors ABC（Williams & Chesterman, 2004: 76）。

2）概念解读：解释性假说探讨、分析已经发生的翻译现象，找出这种现象发生的潜在条件，从而做出清晰合理的解释。这种方式常用来研究某种翻译文本/结果、方式、行为、策略、原则、技巧等为何具有某项特征（a particular feature of a translation）。换言之，为何 A 译文优于 B 译文，翻译策略 X 强于翻译策略 Y，如此等等。

3）举例说明：旅游是一种典型的文化活动和跨文化交际。但是，跨文化意识的缺失、专业性的薄弱极易导致这种跨文化交际出现故障——而跨文化意识和专业素养正是旅游翻译不可或缺的两大要素。本节（2）描述性假说 3）举例说明之③中提及的论文详细地分析了《走遍中国——中国导游词精选（综合篇）》一书中《布达拉宫》和《少林寺（一）》两篇文章的英译，突出强调导游词翻译中"以旅游者为导向"的重要意义。该文作者还提供了上述两篇文章的全新译文，通过词、句和篇章层面的对比研究，重点考察如何将"增译"和"简化"这两种常用翻译技巧有效应用于导游词中的名称/头衔、文化负载词、楹联、诗歌、歌词以及描述性和叙述性段落的汉英翻译中。

（4）预测性假说（predictive hypothesis）

1）英文定义：conditions or factor ABC will (tend to) cause or influence phenomenon X（77）。

2）概念解读：这种假说始于表因的条件，结束于对结果（现象）的预测，能用来验证解释性假说是否成立。"某译本中出现某些问题，造成客户退稿，你可能由此预测：如果这些问题出现于任何译本，客户都会退稿。"（77）

3）举例说明：论文题目是《归化口笔译在跨文化交际中仍将占主导地位——导译经验与〈鹿鼎记〉英译样本研究》。具体阐述如下：相当多的中国翻译研究者认为：向外国读者译介中国文化，应采取"异化"策略，而且这是一种主要趋势。其实这是对跨文化翻译的大量事实视而不见的一种盲目。导译之长期丰富的第一手跨文化交际的专业经验表明，目前中国翻译界推崇的"异化"翻译，在专业实践中往往事与愿违，甚至是徒劳的。对近年推出的金庸小说《鹿鼎记》英译本的样本研究也同样表明，"归化"翻译，而非"异化"翻译，还将是一种主要趋势和整体策略。口笔译中总体采用可行的"归化"策略之主要因素是基于对口笔译实践的客观描述——包括口笔译的功能/目的与译者翻译观、口笔译实践中的决策、翻译规范/标准等——所得出的，但真正能使跨文化翻译产生较好效果的更为深层的原因却是文化相异性的可接受性在于这种相异性之归化/本土化。而通常只有这样，异国文化才有较大的可能或更容易被移植到目的语文化体系中。然而，"归化"处理后的《鹿鼎记》能否赢得英文读者，并不完全在于是否选择"归化"策略或译文水平之高低，而是在于作品所表现的主人公和文化在目的语文化系统中能否得到认同。如果归化译本难以为读者所接受，那么异化译本只能是"望'异'兴叹"了。

7.5.4　假说区别简释与验证

（1）假说区别简释

上述四种假说的区别在于提出假设的方式不同，建构假说的方式不同，各自回答的问题不同（见表 7-10）。就后三种假说而言，Williams 和 Chesterman 指出："The difference between descriptive and explanatory or predictive hypotheses is sometimes a matter of how the hypothesis is formulated, within a given research project. If you are studying the retranslation hypothesis… you could either take it as a universal descriptive hypothesis (all retranslations have this characteristic) or as a predictive one (if a previous translation exists, I predict that this new translation will have this feature, because I think the existence of a previous translation, plus perhaps the translator's familiarity with it, will have this kind of creative effect). In both cases, you could proceed to test the hypothesis on your data."（2004: 77）

表 7-10　阐释性/描述性/解释性/预测性假说简释

假说分类	英汉名称	简释
1	interpretive hypothesis（阐释性假说）	①事物 X 为何（被定义为/被看作/被解读为何）；②概念 A 能用于描写或理解概念 B 事物；③X 在哪些方面区别于事物 Y。
2	descriptive hypothesis（描述性假说）	①现象 X 具有可观察到的特征；②事物 X、事物 Y、事物 Z 具有什么普遍特征。
3	explanatory hypothesis（解释性假说）	①现象 X（容易）由条件 ABC 或因素 ABC 而产生；②现象 X（容易）受到条件 ABC 或因素 ABC 的影响；③现象 X 在某一过程中受哪些因素影响而形成。
4	predictive hypothesis（预测性假说）	①条件 EFG 或因素 EFG 将/容易产生或影响现象 P；②条件 EFG 或因素 EFG 对 P 施加影响会导致什么结果。

（2）假说验证

1）何为好的假说。好的假说或观点/主张（good hypothesis/claim）必须是能够自圆其说并经得起验证的。要证明假说是合理的，必须对其合理性提出论证理由。如果假说仅被暂时证实，还需要通过观测等途径进行进一步的验证（testing）。如果假说被证伪，就有必要对该项假说进行修正，并进行新的验证。

2）验证操作。假设的验证过程可分为两个步骤：（可）操作步骤；验证步骤。

①（可）操作步骤，指使假说验证可操作化（operationalizing）。换言之，将抽象的概念具体化，使其验证时具有可观察的具体指标，具有清晰的操作程序。[①]

【案例】

假说：(This thesis[②] tried to justify) the possibility of XYZ's rhymed translation outperforming the English translation of classic Chinese poetry done by English and American scholars.

---

① 以下写作部分路径参照有关专著（Williams & Cheterman, 2004；穆雷, 2012）。

② 选自浙江大学英语专业（翻译方向）本科生毕业论文中问卷调查之部分内容。

分析：（a）必要性——该研究属于汉译英文学翻译范畴，研究对象是由 XYZ 英译的（几首）中国古诗。该研究旨在通过实证方法（问卷调查）提出假说，因而假说的操作化很有必要。（b）过程——假说中涉及两个概念：一、the *possibility* of XYZ's *better* rhymed translation；二、the English translation of classic Chinese poetry done by English and American scholars。于是需要对这两个概念进行操作化处理。

操作化：（a）界定概念，列出维度——XYZ's rhymed translation；the English translation of classic Chinese poetry done by English and American scholars。（b）选定指标——XYZ's English translations of four ancient Chinese poems；the English translations of the same four ancient Chinese poems done by the English and American scholars the thesis author has chosen。

至此，论文作者便可以通过问卷调查的形式直接对上述指标进行评估和测量。

②验证步骤，指实际验证（actual testing），有不同程度的可验证性（various degrees of testability）。实证假说的最高要求就是证伪，最低要求则是可以验证（testable）。从实证研究的视角出发，不能验证的假说或观点/主张是不值得做验证的，最多算是推测/猜测（speculation）。有的假说（如阐释性假说）不能直接验证，但还是可验证的，因为这种假说旨在以最佳方式方法解读/理解某一事物，实际上不能被证伪；它并不阐明因果关系和描写事物特征，而是预测某些特征、关系之有用性（usefulness），即在应用中检验其功能。一句话，阐释性假说是验证有用性的，否则将会被淘汰。Williams 和 Chesterman 举了一个很有说服力的例子："For instance, suppose you claim that it would be a good idea to teach translator trainees to think in such-and-such a way about translation: to think of translation in terms of, say, creative performance. This claim (an interpretive hypothesis about how best to understand translation) has testable consequences if we assume that *if* translators think in this new way, then their translations will be somehow different, perhaps better. That is, their translations will have different profile features—and we can then go ahead and test for the presence of these features, in comparison with translations produced by trainees who had *not* been expressly taught to think about translation in this way."（2004: 80）

Williams 和 Chesterman 提供了验证假说的四大标准（four criteria）——ACID tests：

- **A** for added value in general: new understanding；
- **C** for comparative value, in comparison with other hypothese；
- **I** for internal value: logic, clarity, elegance, economy；
- **D** against data, empirical evidence。

验证的项目包括：

- **A**scertain that the hypothesis does indeed add to our understanding of the phenomenon: it brings something new; it is not trivial; it is genuinely interesting；
- **C**heck it against other competing hypotheses: in what respects is it better than others?
- **I**s it logical, elegant, parsimonious (economical), with no unnecessary concepts or assumptions? Is it plausible?
- **D**oes it accurately represent the empirical evidence? Does it account for the facts? Does it cover a wider variety of data? Is it more general than competing hypotheses?

严格地说，没有一种假说可以被证明是正确的，或确认为正确的。"Science does not proceed by piling up truths, but by developing better and better hypotheses, which may well approximate closer and closer to being accurate descriptions or explanations of reality. An empirical test may support a hypothesis, or corroborate it; or it may not support it; or it may falsify it. In Translation Studies the results of a single test are seldom conclusive, one way or the other." "Hypothesis-testing often pertains to the *scope* of a claim. Unrestricted claims are maximally general, such as those proposing translation universals. But most hypotheses specify a narrower scope of application." (80, 81)

在应用上述 ACID 验证原则的同时，还要采用其他方法与途径对假说反复检验。通常，毕业论文作者可以采用实际观察、问卷调查、科学实验等方法收集经验数据，并通过统计、分析等对假说进行验证。其结果有三种：其一，假说被证实；其二，假设被部分证实；其三，假设被证伪。

以下通过问卷调查法展示如何进行某一假说论证，即如何试图 "justify the possibility of XYZ's rhymed translation outperforming the English translation of classic Chinese poetry done by English and American scholars"。

【问卷调查（questionnaire）案例】①

Part I

Questionnaire
Participant profile
●Name＿＿＿＿＿＿＿＿＿＿＿＿＿＿＿＿＿＿
●Age ＿＿＿＿＿＿＿＿＿＿＿＿＿＿＿＿＿＿
●Education＿＿＿＿＿＿＿＿＿＿＿＿＿＿＿＿
●Major field of study＿＿＿＿＿＿＿＿＿＿
●Nationality＿＿＿＿＿＿＿＿＿＿＿＿＿＿
●Email address＿＿＿＿＿＿＿＿＿＿＿＿

Part II

Definitions of some concepts
Classical Chinese poetry (***ku-shih***, 古诗): The normal formal style is for uniform line lengths of 4, 5 or 7 syllables (Chinese characters), with lines in syntactically-paired couplets. Parallelism emphasizing thesis or antithesis is frequently found but is not an obligatory feature. Rhymes generally occur at the ends of couplets, the actual rhyme sound sometimes changing through the course of the poem.
Rhyme: A rhyme is a repetition of similar sounds (or the same sound) in two or more words, most often in the final syllables of lines in poems and songs (e.g. bright-light).
Rhythm: The measured flow of words and phrases in verse as determined by the relation of long and short or stressed and unstressed syllables.

---

① 本书作者根据浙江大学 BA 生毕业论文问卷调查样本做了简化及表格化处理，其中包括文字、技术处理。

Part III

【General questions】

1. How often do you read English translation of classical Chinese poetry?

Very often	Often	Sometimes	Ocassionally	Rarely

2. How do you like those translations of Chinese poetry?

Excellent	Good	Fair	Poor	N/A

3. Those English versions of Chinese poetry you read were translated by _____.

American	British	Chinese	Chinese-American	N/A

4. Please name a few translators of Chinese poetry, whatever nationalities they are.

(Leave it blank if not applicable.)

5. Typical classical Chinese poems are mostly metered and end-rhymed. Most of the poems consist of lines of the same number of Chinese characters (5 or 7), and some verse are antithetical. You expect their English translations to be _____. *(Please check all that apply.)*

- in a poetic form
- in a prose form (or free verse)
- rhymed
- unrhymed
- literal
- creative
- imagery-oriented
- faithful to the original rhyme scheme
- faithful to the original rhythm (e.g. *stress*)
- _____ *(other features if not listed above)*
- Reasons: _____

6. In your opinion, those most satisfactory publications of Chinese poetry should include _____. *(Please check all that apply.)*

- the original text
- Chinese Pinyin
- Wade-Giles Romanization
- word-for-word translation
- thorough notes
- introduction, interpretation & commentary
- Chinese calligraphy
- watercolor illustration
- CD with professional recitals
- _____ *(other suggestions if not listed above)*

7. In your opinion, the ideal translators of classical Chinese poems are _____. *(Please check all that apply.)*

- English-speaking translators who are experts in both Chinese and poetry
- Chinese-speaking translators who are experts in both English and poetry
- English-speaking translators and Chinese-speaking translators in collaboration
- Chinese-American translators who are experts in both languages and poetry
- Others *(please specify)* _____

Part IV

【Evaluation of four published translations】（限于篇幅，仅举一例）

Poem Two

Fishing in Snow

by Liu Tsung-yüan

From hill to hill no bird in flight;

From path to path no man in sight.

A lonely fisherman afloat

Is fishing snow on lonely boat.

1. What is your general impression of this translated version?

Excellent	Good	Fair	Poor

2. How do you like its sound patterns (rhyme & rhythm, etc.)?

Excellent	Good	Fair	Poor

3. Based on your feeling, what is the theme idea of the poem? (*leave it blank if unclear*)

_____

_____

4. The third line in the original poem would be "single boat, coat, hat, an old man" if translated word-by-word. Someone criticized the translation for its omission of images. So, what do you think if the last two verses are translated into:

    A single boat, coat, hat, old angler,   (A lonely fisherman afloat)

    Alone fishing in a cold snow river.   (Is fishing snow in lonely boat.)

[NB] angler: a person who catches fish as a hobby

Much better	Better	Fair	Worse

Comments (*if any*) _____

_____

_____

Brief comments, suggestions for improvement, or anything you want to say about this poem, poet, etc.

_____

_____

[Background knowledge] Liu Tsung-yüan (773—819) was one of the four great pastoral poets of the Tang Dynasty, who was exiled to the remote Southwestern China, where he wrote this masterpiece. Almost every word is concrete and makes an image, e.g., the first couplet begins with "a thousand mountains" and "ten thousand paths" which form a contrast not only with the bird and the footprint also the single boat and the lonely fisherman so that the scenic beauty is accentuated.

Part V

Conclusion

...

XYZ's rhymed translations are very likely to be acceptable for a fair amount of target readers, and fulfill a certain expectation for introducing classic Chinese poetry and culture into the West. The results justify the acceptance of the norms in Xu's translations among a certain number of young Western university students whose mother tongue is English or who are fluent in English, and the capability of the contemporary Chinese translator in the translation of classical Chinese poetry.

From this Author's perspective, Xu's rhymed translation is quite a wise choice. To outdo the influence of Western English translators is very difficult because it is hard for Chinese "inverse translator" to master the mainstream in Western poetics and the native ability of language. However, Xu's translation strategies reflect his advantages in the accurate comprehension and the pursuit of phonological beauty, which are the deficiencies in most Western English translators. Because of the limited length, this thesis only conducts a descriptive study on the four translations of XYZ. Besides, the participants in the reader's response survey seem less persuasive due to the limited quantity of first-hand data. Moreover, this thesis's application of Toury's theories on the socialization of translator, the translation laws and its probabilistic nature is quite scattered, and due to the Author's scope of knowledge, many related problems have not been discussed or not fully discussed. In future descriptive studies on XYZ's translation of classic Chinese poetry, much endeavor should be made on the practical survey of effect of acceptance among target readers, and other perspectives in descriptive study, based on case studies on a relatively large number of Xu's translations.

7.6 翻译研究的主要理论模式、7.7 翻译研究变项之间的几种关系、7.8 翻译实践/研究论文写作流程均为扩展阅读内容，详见二维码。

◎研究与实践思考题◎

1. 研究方法的重要性体现在哪些方面？

2. 翻译方法与翻译研究方法有相同之处吗？

3. 翻译研究类型和常用翻译研究方法各有哪些？

4. 常用翻译研究领域有多少，内容主要包括哪些，还有需要扩展的地方吗？

5. 何为"提问式研究方法"？你自己能否提供案例？

6. 你清楚什么是翻译常用研究思路吗？请分别谈谈你自己的认知。

7. 充分了解"对比模型""过程模型""因果模型"，各写一个相关的典型案例。

8. 何为"变项"和"变量"？它们之间的关系如何？何为翻译研究的"变项"/"变量"？它们之间的关系如何？请举例说明。

9. 请总结翻译实践/研究论文写作流程，并自己尝试写作。

10. 论文结论写作有哪些要素？请分析以下两个毕业论文结论段案例。

①BA 论文结论段：

Conclusion[①]

From the perspective of Katharina Reiss's translation theories, the author tries to look into ST "LOCOG Plays PR Card", and find out its text type and translation strategy. The analysis is organized in a systematic way, from review of News and ST, proceeding to introduction of Katharina Reiss's text typology and translation methodology theories. And the final part elaborately combines the former parts together to apply theoretical knowledge to translation practice of ST. The detailed reflection of ST is made at lexical, syntactical and textual levels to elaborate what the translation difficulties are and how Reiss's theories help the translator to solve these problems. Concerning the special structure of news, the author gives special attention to the headline and sub-titles of ST. In terms of lead and body, the author discusses the translation of Chinese idioms, subject conversion and long sentences in particular. Regarding the informative features of ST, The translator weighs accurate transmission of news facts and information over maintaining stylistic forms, aesthetic effects, etc. In addition, the author also raises questions to the limitations of Reiss's theories in order to indicate the need for further discussion. Throughout the reflective comments, the translator delivers precisely the information using the most concise and simplest words and expressions.

There is still much room for improvement of the present study, owing to the limitation of the author's understanding about news and Reiss's theories. As to the prospect of further study, more study can be done in the drawbacks of Reiss's theories and the comprehensive combination of other Functionalists' thoughts. The author hopes that new perspective and new efforts can be added to news translation and Functional theories of translation.

---

②BTI 论文结论段：

Conclusion[②]

6.1 Major findings

Massive readings of academic articles and books of this field are necessary as the first step in the translation of an academic monograph for it may help in the familiarization of the discourse style and terminology, which on the other hand may further contribute to the comprehension of the source text and prevent mis-translation to a large extent. As for me, I think translation is based on comprehension. "Two-time reading/interpretation" (陈刚, 2003) and intralingual translation would be helpful in grasping the full meaning of the ST objectively and comprehensively. This is exactly what Prof. Gile mentioned in his book the comprehension equation (C = KL + ELK) that comprehension consists the interaction between both existing knowledge and extralinguistic knowledge. There is no need to worry if a translator is unfamiliar with certain text. All he/she should do is to make more effort in the understanding and familiarization of the

---

① 该论文结论选自华东师范大学翻译系本科生毕业论文。

② 该论文结论选自浙江大学翻译专业本科生毕业论文。

subject in terms of linguistic features and the content as well. It is the same case with the translation of long sentences. The most important step after comprehension is to divide the sentence into meaningful segments and reorganize them logically under the theoretical framework of the *skopostheorie*, conforming to the linguistic convention of the target language.

All in all, major strategies used to guide this translation project could be summarized as follows:

(1) Maintenance of the lexical, syntactical and grammatical equivalence in the spirit of intertextual coherence;

(2) Interaction between linguistic knowledge and extra-linguistic knowledge with logical analysis of the context in the spirit of intratextual coherence;

(3) The integrated use of various translation techniques in terms of different situations determined by the *skopos* rule.

6.2 Limitations and suggestions

It is the first time I have ever encountered with an academic monograph of interpreting, which has imposed significant influence on my future translation practice. Limitations of this translation project largely resulted from the unfamiliarity with academic monograph of translation studies. Specifically, it has something to do with the insufficient extralinguistic knowledge of this text. I had to read relevant papers and books of translation studies for this project first, which was inevitably non-proficient and thus led to some rigid expressions in target language, especially in the handling of technical terms without established equivalence in Chinese and of long sentences with complex structures.

Translation is a step by step process, which is gradual, repetitive and progressive. I read the ST twice to get a general idea of the style, the content and the purpose of this text before starting the translation. After finishing the first draft, there were the second, the third and the forth draft. It is not only a process of translation, but also a process of developing a deeper understanding of the ST. Much attention should be paid to the sentence structure as well so as to prevent mis-translation.

In this case, suggestions for further translation practice of such texts will be to read more academic monograph or journals of translation studies bilingually, namely to develop a better understanding of the source text before engaging in the translation. There is still a long way to go in the translation field. I have to read more and learn more from others work and my own practice.

第8章 如何引注（注重规范）

How to Cite (Academic- & Bibliographic-oriented)

◎学习目标◎

　　参考文献是（学位）论文不可或缺的组成部分。如何找寻有价值的参考文献并加以规范运用，往往困扰着不少初涉论文撰写的本科生（乃至硕士生）。学生对何为参考文献知之甚少，这常常导致不应有的学术失范（而发达国家大学对学术诚信把关甚严）。此外，BTI/BA 生可能转读社会科学或自然科学专业，或者毕业后在国内外读研深造，因此，熟悉有关学术规范有利无弊。本章有助于学生：

- 了解、熟悉文献的基本概念；
- 了解、熟悉参考文献的概念、功能及作用；
- 了解目录学的点滴知识；
- 了解引注和规范的有关概念；
- 了解并熟悉 MLA、APA、CMS、ICMJE 及"国标"；
- 通过案例详细了解、熟悉有关的 MLA Style 和"国标"；
- 通过案例详细了解、熟悉有关文献检索的应知应会。

8.1　文献引注概念

　　这个标题涉及诸多概念：文献、参考文献、目录学、引注（引/注）、规范等。了解这些概念对选择、利用现有文献进行研究颇有助益，而且，使用什么级别的文献对判断自己的论文价值也颇有益处。在阅读本节时，读者不妨根据自己的需求，与"8.3　文献检索 ABC"进行交叉阅读。

8.1.1　文献概念解读

　　根据《现汉》，**文献**指"有历史价值或参考价值的图书资料：历史～｜科技～"。根据《文献著录总则》（GB/T 3792.1—1983），文献指"记录有知识的一切载体"。它与"文件"是同义词。该词出现于孔子的《论语》（约前 540—前 400）[①]，可以用英文 document、literature、historical data、sources 等来表示。它还可以根据载体分为印刷型文献（printed documents/literature/data）、微缩型文献（micro documents/literature/data）、声像型文献（audio/video documents/literature/data）、电子文献（electronic documents/literature/data）和数据文献

---

① 参照"汉典"（http://www.zdic.net/c/7/13c/301680.htm）。

（digital documents/literature/data）；根据文献内容的学科属性分为哲学文献（philosophy documents/literature；documents/literature in philosophy）、社会科学文献（social science documents/literature；documents/literature in social sciences）、人文科学文献（arts documents/literature；documents/literature in arts and humanities；documents/literature in humanities）、自然科学文献（natural science documents/literature；documents/literature in natural sciences）、综合科学文献（integrated science documents/literature；documents/literature in integrated science）和专科文献（subject documents/literature；documents/literature in subject areas）等。

1．文献级别

根据文献内容、性质和加工情况可将文献分为：零次文献、一次文献、二次文献、三次文献。

（1）**零次文献**（source documents/source literature/source data/original documents, data, and records）是指未经加工出版的手稿、数据原始记录等文件。换言之，记录在非正规物理载体上的未经任何加工处理的**源信息**叫做零次信息，比如书信、病例、论文手稿、笔记、实验记录、会议记录等，这是一种零星的、分散的和无规则的信息。它具有原始性、新颖性、分散性和非检索性等特征，如口头文学、（通过）邮件（提供的）译文、傅雷翻译手稿、钱锺书日记、译文问卷调查、现场口译、口译笔记、授课讲义（lecture notes）、课堂笔记（classroom notes）、（即兴）导游词、论文答辩的 PPT 自述文本等。

（2）**一次文献**（**一级文献/原始文献**，primary sources/documents）指以作者本人的工作经验、观察或者实际研究成果为依据而创作的具有一定发明创造和一定新见解的原始文献，如期刊论文、研究报告、专利说明书、会议论文、学位论文、技术标准等。一次文献具有以下特点：其一，文献内容有独创性，是作者本人的工作经验、观察或者实际研究成果，该种文献内容具有先进性和新颖性，反映了有关领域的最新研究成果；其二，文献内容叙述具体、详尽，可供研究；其三，文献数量庞大，分散在各种期刊、媒体、会议论文集、图书、连续性出版物、特种文献之中，所以寻找困难。

具体而言，一次文献包括图书①、期刊、报纸、会议文献、学位论文、专利文献、政府出刊物、产品样本、科技报告、标准文献、档案等。图书的范围很广，它包括名著、专著、教科书、科普通俗读物、资料性工具书等，如专著 *Translation Studies* (Susan Bassnett)、教科书 *In Other Words: A Coursebook on Translation* (Mona Baker)、名著《物种起源》（达尔文；原著全名 *On the Origin of Species by Means of Natural Selection, or the Preservation of Favoured Races in the Struggle for Life*）、期刊《中国翻译》等。

（3）**二次文献**（**二级文献**，secondary sources/documents）是对一次文献进行加工整理后的产物，即对零散无序的一次文献的外部特征如题名、作者、出处等进行著录，或将其内容压缩成简介、提要或文摘，并按照一定的学科或专业加以有序化处理而形成的文献形式，如目录、文摘杂志（包括简介式检索刊物）等。它们都可用作文献检索工具，能比较全面、系统地反映某个学科、专业或专题在一定时空范围内的文献线索，是积累、

---

① 注意对"图书"的正确定义及解读，因为它可以是一次文献、二次文献或三次文献。

报道和检索文献资料的有效手段。

二次文献具有以下特点：其一，浓缩性。二次文献是对原始文献内容的浓缩，所以，它是情报工作的重要工具。成为一种信息文体，是随着科技、文化的发展，为适应信息的急剧增加而出现的。其二，汇集性。二次文献经过情报工作者加工。把有关内容汇集在一起，能比较全面地反映某个学科、专业或专题在一定时空范围内的文献线索。其三，系统性。由于二次文献是经过情报工作者加工的，因此，它能系统地反映某个学科、专业或专题在一定时空范围内的最新研究成果。其四，报道性。它传递科技信息，又具有文献检索功能。

二次文献作为一种信息文体，以提供一次文献内容梗概为目的，其基本作用就是提供密集的科研信息，便于研究人员获取原始文献，提高检索效率，使研究人员花费较少的时间和精力，获得较多、较全面的原始信息和原始情报，有利于提高科研工作效率，还有利于信息交流。二次文献种类很多，有书目、题录、简介、文摘等。它们都可用作文献检索工具，如《中国出版年鉴》、《全国报刊索引》（月刊）、*The New Encyclopaedia Britannica* (MICROPAEDIA Ready Reference and Index)、《中国社会科学学术论文、学位论文活页文摘》、《中华翻译文摘》（罗选民主编）、《西方翻译理论著作概要》（文军、穆雷主编）等。

（4）三次文献（三级文献，tertiary sources/documents）指对有关的一次文献、二次文献进行综合、广泛、深入的分析研究之后编写出来的文献。这类文献常被称为"情报研究"的成果，包括综述、专题述评、学科年度总结、进展报告、数据手册、进展性出版物以及文献指南等。这类文献的特点是浓缩性、指引性、针对性、参考性。充分利用这类文献，可以在短时间内了解所研究课题的研究历史、发展动态、水平等，以便能更准确地掌握课题的技术背景，如《麦克米伦百科全书》（原版及汉译版）、《新华词典》、《汉英翻译词典》、*Murray's Handbooks for Travellers*、*World Almanac* (140th Anniversary Edition)、*China Travel Kit Series*、数据库①等。

与此类似，也有把情报分成一次情报、二次情报、三次情报的。

2. 文献级别价值简析②

（1）零次文献是原始资料，是最为宝贵的。当我们评判某一译员当时是否译得不妥，原则上是要看现场的录像和录音的。

（2）不同的学科对一次文献的定义会有（所）不同。作家/作者（writer）对某一信息的级别不得而知，这样的文献不能算是一级文献；但历史学家却在缺乏一级文献的情况下将其用作一级文献。因此，这种一级文献属于 artifact（人工制品）——是历史研究者在研究过程中制造出来的文献，如资料、录音、录像等。就新闻学而言，一级文献可以是直击者（a person with direct knowledge of a situation）或是这位直击者亲笔的证据材料（document）。

（3）"事后诸葛亮"（accounts written after the fact with the benefit of hindsight），即追

---

① 如果将零次文献（加工后）直接输入数据库，该文献可以属于一次文献。
② 根据维基百科简述并做简短评论。

述回忆的文献，一般属于二级文献，但也可以是一级文献，这要看如何使用。例如，研究某一回忆录——就其作者及其书中所述人物（如男女朋友）而言——可以被认为是在研的一级文献；但是，就其作者所成长的文化环境而言，这个回忆录只能算是二级文献。

（4）一级文献还是二级文献，是一个相对的概念和词，取决于特殊、具体的历史语境和研究的对象。

（5）对学术写作来说，文献分级的一个重要目的是确定学术研究价值的独立性和可靠性。

（6）The Lafayette College Library 给一些学科对一级文献的定义做了归纳：

1）人文科学，一级文献可以定义为在研期间所制造的文献，或在此之后对研究反思所制造的文献。

2）社会科学，一级文献的定义可扩展为数字数据（numerical data），特指用于人、事件及其环境之间关系的分析。

3）自然科学，一级文献可以定义为原始发现的报告或原始思想的报告。这些文献报告经常以研究论文的形式出现，这类论文可归入"方法与结果"栏目。

（7）下列 8 个英文问题常被用来判别是否为一级文献：

1）What is the tone?

2）Who is the intended audience?

3）What is the purpose of the publication?

4）What assumptions does the author make?

5）What are the bases of the author's conclusions?

6）Does the author agree or disagree with other authors of the subject?

7）Does the content agree with what you know or have learned about the issue?

8）Where was the source made?

（8）一级文献的优劣转换。

1）研究历史者，应尽量使用一级文献。

2）一级文献要避免降格为二级文献，因为每位新的作者都有可能歪曲先前作者所引用的文献，还会就所引文献做倾向性描写。

3）一级文献未必一定比二级文献更具权威性、有效性，一级文献存在被扭曲的现象——观点的扭曲和人为的扭曲。然而，这些一级文献可以在第二级别得到更正。具备严谨学科研究方法论（methodological accuracy）的历史学家经常能够发挥这样的功效。

4）作为博客日志的一级文献（a primary source such as a journal entry or the online version, a blog）仅反映一家之言，未必正确、完整或真实。目击者或参与者也许有意无意地误解了有关事件或歪曲了有关报道。政府也会因出于宣传考虑或特殊的目的对自己的新闻报道做出"调整"。一级文献常因被负面使用而招致事实上之歪曲；律师也常利用被歪曲的证据去支持或反击控方/原告或辩方/被告。

5）一级文献造假。典型例子之一是，造假者通过一些人为的阴谋，借着欺诈与伪造等手段，成功地加强了教皇的地位和权势，从而达到了卑鄙的目的——这个赝品被称为《君士坦丁御赐教产谕》（"Donation of Constantine"）。此外，早在 20 世纪 80 年代，愚弄了全世界新闻界的 60 卷《希特勒日记》，其造假者居然是英国历史学家休·特雷弗–罗珀（Hugh Trevor-Roper）。他因研究希特勒成名，但又因 1983 年误证伪造的《希特勒日记》为真品而名誉扫地。一些"误证"的文献（false provenance）已经被"珍藏"在英国国家档案馆。

6）正如一级文献和二级文献的定义因主观解读和语境而异，二级文献与三级文献之间的"转换"也会因不同情形而异。换言之，这两种级别的文献会重叠、交叉。学者们会依据研究课题，视某些参考文献、词典、百科全书等为三级文献或二级文献。

7）根据联合国国际科学信息系统模式，二级文献包括参考文献/书目目录，而三级文献是一级文献的综合。

3. 文献级别之间的关系

四种不同级别文献之间的关系虽然是"静态"的、相对固定的，但有些级别的文献之间的关系的确是动态的。有关解释可参见"2. 文献级别价值简析"。再比如，"数据库"属于"三次文献"/"三级文献"，但我们将"零次信息"——比如书信、病例、论文手稿、笔记等——（经加工）直接输入数据库后，它属于"一级文献"，还是"三级文献"呢？有鉴于此，笔者将四个级别文献之间的基本关系进行了梳理，如表 8-1 所示[①]。

表 8-1　四个级别文献之间的基本关系

SD	⇨	PD	⇨/⇄	SeD	⇨/⇄	TD
source documents		primary documents		secondary documents		tertiary documents
SOURCE DOCUMENTS			⇦			TERTIARY DOCUMENTS

对上述表格的解读是：

● SD 是 PD 的素材；

● PD 是文献的基本形式，是检索供研究的主要对象，是 SD 和 TD 的基础；

● SD 是检索 PD 的工具，但二者之间的关系是可以互相转换的；

● TD 是在综合、分析、归纳、整理 PD、SeD 的基础上形成的，它往往从新的高度揭示相关的 PD，或者说在更高层级上系统地再现 PD，并返回 PD；

● TD 与 SeD 构成（可能的）转换关系；

● SD ⇨ PD ⇨ SeD ⇨ TD，是一个对知识信息由分散到浓缩，从无序到有序的创造、加工、提炼过程，是一个从基本的信息源到按照专题进行分类加工的结构化和系统化的规程。

8.1.2　参考文献概念解读

按照《信息与文献——参考文献著录规则》（GB/T 7714—2015）的定义，参考文献是指："对一个信息资源或其中一部分进行准确和详细著录的数据，位于文末或文中的信息源。"根据《中国学术期刊（光盘版）检索与评价数据规范（试行）》和《中国高等学

---

① 参考《翻译研究方法概论》（穆雷，2011）第十二章部分内容及维基百科后有所加工、进展及解读。

校社会科学学报编排规范（修订版）》的要求，很多刊物对参考文献和注释做了区分。根据《学术出版规范——注释》（CY/T 121—2015），注释是"对学术作品的某些内容所作的说明"，其中"内容注"指"对正文中相关内容进行解释、校订、补充和扩展的注释"，列于文末并与参考文献分列，或置于当页页脚。

按照国家标准来解读，参考文献属于名词、术语：其一，指"**文后参考文献**"——为撰写或编辑论著而引用的有关文献资料；其二，指"识别题名"——国际连续出版物数据系统（ISDS）认可的某种连续出版物唯一的名称。

"文后参考文献"可以用英文 bibliographic references、bibliography、references 来表示。根据 MWCD，bibliography 意指"the works or a list of works referred to in a text or consulted by the author in its production"；reference 意指"one referred to or consulted as: (1) a source of information (as a book or passage) to which a reader or consulter is referred; (2) a work (as a dictionary or encyclopedia) containing useful facts or information"。根据 LDCE，bibliography 意指"a list of writings on a subject, esp. a list of all the written materials used in the preparation of a book or article, usu. appearing at the end"。

从上述概念介绍中不难解读出，参考文献包含值得参考的有用事实或信息，这正是指**参考文献的功能与作用**。

首先，作为论文不可或缺部分的参考文献，不仅是论文写作的规范要求，也能为作者的论点提供有力的论据，同时增加论文的学术信息量，具有学术/信息价值。其次，参考文献注明了被引理论、观点、方法、数据的来源，反映了论文真实的（学理）依据，没有参考文献的论文，实属缺乏专业、学术工作的严谨性和继承性，也是无法在论文开题报告答辩中获得通过的。再次，引用必要的规定数量的参考文献，除了是对他人科研成果的尊重，也为指导教师、论文评审专家等鉴别论文价值水平提供了重要信息。最后，参考文献为生生交流、师生交流等学术活动提供了与论文有关的文献题录，便于检索，以达到共享信息资源和推动学术进步的作用。

8.1.3　目录学概念解读

根据维基百科，**目录学**是图书馆学的一门分支学科，研究文献目录工作的一般原理及形成和发展的一般规律。班固（32—92）撰写《汉书·叙传》，始有"目录"之名。刘向、刘歆父子整理图书，著有《别录》《七略》，开中国目录学之先河。而早在公元前 5 世纪，希腊喜剧诗人已经开始使用书目（bibliography）一词[①]。被称为 bibliographical (bibliographic) studies 或者 study of bibliography 的"目录学"最早于 1797 年被《大英百科全书》第 3 版收录，从此目录学作为一个术语，进入了西方学科体系。

目录学的分支学科有普通目录学、专科目录学、比较目录学、版本目录学。我们撰写毕业/学位论文所用到的 bibliography，与"专科目录学"（subject bibliography）关系最为密切。

---

① 参照：程焕文. 他山之石，可以攻玉——关于中西目录学的几点比较研究. 晋图学刊，1998(3): 10.

8.1.4 引注和规范概念解读

引注即"引用本事或其他著作做注释"。清代才女陈婉俊《唐诗三百首补注》"凡例"曰:"是编引注之义有二,即引本事以证之者为正注,至寻源遡流博采他书以相证者为互注。"从学术引注的视角看问题,本书应使用英文 cite/citation/quote/quotation。

(1) cite 一词的出现,不迟于 15 世纪,意指"to quote by way of example, authority, or proof"(MWCD)。该词一词多义,必须用"引用""引证""引注""引文""援引""例证"等词来全面表达。

(2) quote 一词的出现,也不迟于 1582 年,意指"to speak or write (a passage) from another usu. with credit acknowledgement; to repeat a passage from *esp.* in substantiation or illustration; to cite in illustration"(MWCD)。该词也是一词多义,必须用"引用""引述""引证""援引"等词来全面表达。

因此,读者在阅读本部分内容时,请务必时刻用英文思维,即用 cite 来考虑问题,因为仅用汉语中的单一表达法,无法全面、综合概括作者的意图和语境意义。

学位论文的引注(academic citation),需要遵循学术规范和注释规则(citation norms)。国际上,最为著名、常用的引注规范是 MLA style、APA style、Chicago style 和 Vancouver style。中国则有最新版的国家标准《信息与文献——参考文献著录规则》(GB/T 7714—2015)和《学术论文编写规则》(GB/T 7713.2—2022)。[①]

(1) MLA(Modern Language Association, 美国现代语言协会)制定的论文指导格式。

● 有关总体简介:MLA is a reference tool used in subject areas for the Humanities. It provides extensive guidelines on how to formulate a topic, format a research paper, cite parenthetical texts and compile a list of works cited in English as well as other foreign languages. Other useful capabilities include documenting online sources, writing a quote from an e-mail received or incorporating abbreviations in your list of references. There is also in-depth discussion on plagiarism.

● 有关 MLA Formatting and Style Guide 的简介:MLA style is most commonly used to write papers and cite sources within the liberal arts and humanities. This resource, updated to reflect the *MLA Handbook for Writers of Research Papers* (7th ed.) and the *MLA Style Manual and Guide to Scholarly Publishing* (3rd ed.), offers examples for the general format of MLA research papers, in-text citations, endnotes/footnotes, and the Works Cited page.

(2) APA(American Psychological Association, 美国心理学会)出版的《美国心理协会刊物准则》。

● 有关总体简介:APA style is most commonly used to cite sources within the social sciences. This resource offers examples for the general format of APA research papers, in-text citations, endnotes/footnotes, and the reference page.

● 有关 Types of APA Papers 的简介:There are two common types of papers written in

---

① 关于 MLA、APA、CMS 和 GB/T 7714—2015 的介绍分别参考有关英文和中文线上/下资料。

fields using APA Style: the literature review and the experimental report. Each has unique requirements concerning the sections that must be included in the paper.

（3）CMS 格式（*The Chicago Manual of Style*，《芝加哥格式使用指南》）。

●有关总体简介：*The Chicago Manual of Style* is an **American English style and usage guide** published continuously by the University of Chicago Press since 1906. Today, it is used widely in many academic disciplines and is considered the standard for US style in book publishing.

●有关"语法迷"对 Chicago style 之语法规则的赞誉：Grammar enthusiasts celebrate "Chicago style" rules, such as whether to put the title of a book in italics (Chicago style says yes, whereas AP style recommends quotation marks), or whether to use a serial comma—also known as an "Oxford" comma (Chicago style: yes; AP style: no). However, the editors at the University of Chicago Press acknowledge that rules are often context-dependent, and sometimes need to be broken. The *Manual* is thus also respected for its flexibility.

（4）Vancouver 格式（*Vancouver Style*，《温哥华格式》）。

●有关总体简介：1978 年 1 月，国际上一些医学期刊的编辑在加拿大温哥华召开会议，制定了向其刊物投稿的稿件格式要求。这些编辑后称"温哥华小组"，其制定的稿件格式也被称为"温哥华格式"（Vancouver style）。后来，温哥华小组不断扩大并演变成国际医学期刊编辑委员会（International Committee of Medical Journal Editors, ICMJE），温哥华格式也演变成为其规范文件 *Uniform Requirements for Manuscripts Submitted to Biomedical Journals*（《向生物医学期刊投稿的统一要求》，最新的为第 5 版），并于 1979 年最早提出英文科技论文写作的通用 IMRAD 模式（一种常用的写作结构，为 Introduction、Methods、Results、And、Discussion 的首字母缩写）。国际医学期刊编辑委员会对该规范文件进行了数次修订，其内容不断丰富，不仅仅是格式的要求，也包含了诸多其他的内容，甚至以专门文件进行阐述。目前我国及世界上大多数国家的科技期刊都采用温哥华格式著录参考文献。温哥华格式也是我国国家标准文献《信息与文献——参考文献著录规则》（GB/T 7714－2015）中推荐的两种著录格式之一，即顺序编码制。

●有关制定规范的目的：ICMJE developed these recommendations to review best practice and ethical standards in the conduct and reporting of research and other material published in medical journals, and to help authors, editors, and others involved in peer review and biomedical publishing create and distribute accurate, clear, reproducible, unbiased medical journal articles. The recommendations may also provide useful insights into the medical editing and publishing process for the media, patients and their families, and general readers.

（5）GB/T 7714—2015——《信息与文献——参考文献著录规则》。

●有关总体简介：GB/T 7714—2015 是 2015 年 12 月 1 日实施的一项中华人民共和国国家标准，归于全国信息与文献标准化技术委员会。该标准规定了各个学科、各种类型信息资源的参考文献的著录项目、著录顺序、著录用符号、著录用文字、各个著录项目的著录方法以及参考文献在正文中的标注法。该标准适用于著者和编辑著录参考文献，而不是供图书馆员、文献目录编制者以及索引编辑者使用的文献著录规则。

●有关修订背景简介：随着信息化的高速发展以及我国期刊国际化进程的加快，"获取和访问路径"的著录成为电子资源必备项，数字对象唯一标识符（DOI）方兴未艾，这些昭示着大数据时代文献记录、传播以及查找路径的变化，学界对参考文献的著录相应也提出了更多要求，而 2005 版明显滞后，很有必要及时进行修订。

（6）GB/T 7713.2—2022——《学术论文编写规则》。

●有关总体简介：本标准描述了撰写和编排学术论文的基本要求和格式规范；适用范围包括一切反映自然、社会和人文等的科学体系的学术论文；采用本标准进行学术论文编写宜采取严肃性和灵活性相结合的原则。本标准对 GB/T 7713—1987 中的学术论文编写内容进行了必要的检查、更新，进而形成单独的学术论文编写规则，代替 GB/T 7713—1987 中的学术论文编写格式部分。

●有关实施日期：2023 年 7 月 1 日起实施。

（7）AI 工具使用规范。

●有关背景简介：复旦大学发文①规范毕业论文 AI 使用，包括禁止用于方案设计、正文生成、语言润色等。浙江大学亦有相关规定，详细规则需咨询本科生院、外国语学院及指导教师。《浙江大学学术道德规范》的核心原则是：要求学术成果必须体现学生的独立思考和原创性，禁止任何形式的学术不端行为（剽窃、伪造、篡改等）。据此，若使用 AI 工具生成内容需声明并保证核心创意的原创性。未声明使用 AI 工具可能会被认定为"学术失范"，将面临论文重审或处分。

●有关实施时间：与时俱进，从撰写毕业论文起。

8.2　文献引注范例

文献引注范例可以用英文 style guide 来表达。考虑到毕业生撰写学位论文的语言是英文，考虑到撰写论文须遵循的引注 style 主要来自美国，又同时考虑到我们的大学生更应该具有国际视野，本章会用必要的篇幅介绍英文文献引注规范及其范例。与此同时，《信息与文献——参考文献著录规则》也是学生应该了解、掌握的（该著录规则总共二十几页，很多问题可以通过自学、练习解决）。

8.2.1　引文规则及案例

(1) Citations② (引证)

Throughout your [thesis], you will be citing the different works you have used in your research. As we've stated before, <u>careful citation is the key to avoiding plagiarism</u>. Your note cards will help you to avoid using information without giving credit. There are three ways for

---

① 2024 年 11 月 28 日，复旦大学率先发布《复旦大学关于在本科毕业论文（设计）中使用 AI 工具的规定（试行）》，对人工智能工具在本科毕业论文（设计）撰写过程中的使用进行了详细规范。

② 本小节英文部分主要引自 *Research Paper Smart*（Buffa, 2003）之 Chapter 4（本书作者仅做了少量文字调整，并给部分重要文字添加了下画线）。其中外加英文引文均有出处说明，以示区别。这也是一种规范及范例。

you to use information that you've researched:

1) **Direct quotation (直接引文/引用)**. In this form, you are taking any piece of writing and putting it word for word in the body of your [thesis].

Martin Buber believed that "The relationship between religion and reality prevailing in a given speech is the most accurate index of its true character."

2) **Paraphrasing (释义)**. When you are paraphrasing, you are taking the direct quotation and putting it in your own words.

Martin Buber believed that we could judge any era's character by the way it related religion and reality.

3) **Summary (概述)**. When you summarize, you take a whole section of material and give a short synopsis of it.

(2) Quotations (引用)

… Many beginning writers fall into the trap of overusing quotations. Be careful: Too many quotes will make your thesis look unoriginal, or like you are simply trying to fill space. Effective quotation, like anything, depends on judicious use.

First, let's run through the rules of how to use a quotation in the body of your [thesis].

Rule #1 (规则一)

You must quote *exactly*. After all, this is a quotation, not a paraphrase. If you must leave out a few words from the middle of your quote, use the ellipsis (three dots with a space before and after each…) to indicate that words have been removed. Sometimes you must change a word or two to clarify a quote pulled out of context or make it blend more smoothly into the body of the [thesis]. Any word that has been changed from the original or added for clarity must be bracketed: [ ].

You have an obligation, however, to retain the integrity of the original document. This isn't a movie poster: Pulling the word *tremendous* out of a quote that reads "this movie was a tremendous failure" isn't ethical in the academic world. Use the ellipses and brackets carefully and with respect.

Exact quote (完整引用):

"If there is one word on which we can fix, which will suggest the maximum of what I mean by the term 'a classic,' it is the word *maturity*." (T. S. Eliot, "What is a Classic," *On Poetry and Poets*. [1948; New York: Farrar, Straus & Giroux] 54)

Incorporating a phrase from the quote into your text (部分引用):

T. S. Eliot writes about the term "classic," with the suggestion that the reader focuses on one word, "the word *maturity*."

Words omitted with writer's additions (作者增益):

When Eliot defines the word "classic," he offers the following caution: "If there is only one word on which we can fix… it is the word *maturity*."

Words changed (改变引语):

"If there is one word on which we can fix, which will suggest the maximum of what [Eliot means] by the term 'a classic,' it is the word *maturity*."

【细节注释】

①If the omitted words come at the end of the sentence, you have to incorporate a period into the ellipsis. Use four dots, with no space before the first or after the last. We will use the following quote:

"Those who arrived from West Indian nations were usually legal, but the quotas for other Western Hemisphere countries were too low to handle the increasing numbers of émigrés." (Alana J. Erickson, " 'I Don't Want Her in My Home': Bias against African-American Domestic Servants, 1910—1980," *Race and Reason* 1996—1997)

Erickson writes that "Those who arrived from West Indian nations were usually legal...."

②If you have a citation in parentheses after the ellipsis at the end of the quote, put the period after the citation:

Erickson writes that "Those who arrived from WEST Indian nations were usually legal..." (31).

③You do not need the ellipses if you are just taking a phrase from the quote:

Erickson notes that this particular group was "usually legal."

Rule #2 (规则二)

If you have four lines or fewer of quotation, just incorporate them into the body of your [thesis]. If, however, the quote runs to more than four lines, you should indent the quote, ten spaces (one inch) in from the left margin. When you indent in this way, do not use quotation marks. If you are quoting a single paragraph, no further indentation is needed. If you are using more than one paragraph, use three-space indentation for each paragraph on top of the ten-space indentation.

Rule #3 (规则三)

If you are quoting poetry that is four lines or less, separate the lines with slashes:

Robert Frost laid claim to that feeling when he wrote, "But I have promise to Keep, / And miles to go before I sleep, / And miles to go before I sleep."

If the quote runs longer than four lines, indent as you did for a prose quote:

Samuel Coleridge's poem "Kubla Khan" was written after a dream induced by an opiate he had taken:

> In Xanadu did Kubla Khan
>
> A stately pleasure-dome decree:
>
> Where Alph, the sacred river, ran
>
> Through caverns measureless to man
>
> Down to a sunless sea.

8.2.2　参考文献的格式

（1）总体原则

Buffa 指出："There are many different ways to reference your citations. Most academic institutions require or accept MLA (Modern Language Association) style documentation[①]. While the traditional style (sometimes called "Chicago Style") uses footnotes to cite specific texts, MLA style cites a text in parentheses right in the body of your [thesis]. This eliminates the need for footnotes. The reader can then refer to the Works Cited list at the end of your [thesis] to get the full citations (author, title, etc.) You will find, in general, that most professors are simply looking to see that you have used an accepted method for citing documents, and that you are consistent in that method."（2003: 145）

（文后）参考文献/书目的英文表达法有若干种：Bibliography、List of Works Cited、Literature Cited、References Cited 或 Works Cited。也有论文指导教师要求学生编制 Annotated Bibliography，即要求学生就每条参考文献写若干句（2—5 句）简介。

然而，撰写论文还需要参考的很多文献未必一定引用，因此学生须编制 List of Works Consulted 或 References Consulted。

不管你采用哪种参考文献格式，有几项原则是须共同遵守的：

①Bibliographies are always arranged in alphabetically by author.

②If there is no author credited, use the title of the work, alphabetizing by the first main word (excluding the articles *a*, *an* or *the*).

③If your research is vast, your professor may ask you to divide the works-cited list by chronology or subject matter. You will certainly be told if you are expected to arrange bibliography in other than a standard way.

④The list should always be at the end of your [thesis]. Always begin on a new page— don't start it on the last page of your writing. If you have any notes or table, the bibliography will follow those. The page numbers should follow the page numbers of your document. Don't start new page numbers for the bibliography, or leave out page numbers.

⑤The title *List of Works Cited* or *Bibliography* should be centered at the top of the list, one inch from the top of the page. Each entry should begin at your right margin; intent five spaces if the entry is longer than one line. The list should be double-spaced throughout.

⑥You will note that we italicize titles in the entries that follow. Just to reiterate: italicizing and underlining titles of various works are usually interchangeable; check to see whether your professor has a preference.（146-147）

（2）具体案例（文后参考文献著录）

请通过二维码阅读。

---

① 翻译学科（在中国归属人文学科）原则上使用 MLA Style，亦可参考 Chicago Manual Style，而非 APA Style（主要用于社会科学领域）或 Vancouver Style（主要用于医学、自然科学、工程技术等领域）。但在国内学术杂志上发表论文，更多地应遵循中国国标《信息与文献——参考文献著录规则》（GB/T 7714—2015）。——作者注

（3）具体案例（文内参考文献引用）

以下介绍文中参考文献的引用与格式，由"脚注""尾注""夹注"三部分组成，重点是后者，即"夹注"，又称"文内引注"，属于"In-text Citation: MLA Style"。

我们要了解 documentation for the footnotes，endnotes 及 embedded citations。使用哪种格式，有老师或学生的"好恶"之分，专家建议"check your instructor's preference"（Gibaldi, 2001a: B.1）。Buffa 也指出："Most of the time that is dictated by the professor. MLA style uses embedded citations and most professors favor it. Ask your professor which is the preferred method for your paper."（2003: 176）

1）脚注。*Footnotes* make reference to the document at the bottom (or foot) of the page. (176)

2）尾注。*Endnotes* are just like footnotes, except all the documentation is at the end of the paper, not at the foot of each page. (176)

注意，Most professors prefer footnotes to endnotes, but always ask. (176)

【案例1】From 1543 through the eighteenth century, water in England gained importance for agriculture and transportation.[1]

在页脚或正文后，相关的脚注或尾注是：

[1] Romain L. Klassen, "Brief History of Real Estate Appraisal and Organizations," *The Appraisal Journal*, vol. 44 (July 1976), p. 378.

3）夹注/文内引注。*Embedded citations* are probably the easiest for students. The citation is not referred to, but simply follows the information you are referencing, in parentheses. (177)

【案例2】From 1543 through the eighteenth century, water in England gained importance for agriculture and transportation (**Klassen 378**).

由于"脚注"和"尾注"属于 Chicago Manual Style，我们先介绍"夹注"/"文内引注"。表 8-3 是关于常用/常见"夹注"的好处、规则和要求（参照 MLA 格式）（177）。表 8-4 是 MLA 与 GB/T 7714—2015 文内参考文献引用案例及解释。

表 8-3　"夹注"的"好处""规则""要求"

夹注好处	①Embedded citations (used in MLA style) are nice and simple: No messy op.cits. or ibids. ②The idea of parenthetical references is to keep the flow of the paper as smooth as possible.
夹注规则	In the embedded citation, instead of a raised number, just follow the area where you wish to make your citation with a parenthetical reference.
夹注要求	①Use whatever you began your bibliographic reference with as the reference for the citation. ②If you have mentioned the author and referenced the work in your writing, you do not need a citation unless you are referring to a specific section. ③For example, "Mill's utilitarian philosophy was well known." would not need a citation to Mill's *Utilitarianism*. If you have mentioned the author in the quote or paraphrase, you need only make reference to the page to which you are referring. Sometimes there is no specific page reference—you may be summarizing and therefore referring to a whole document or section. In that case, you need only put the author's name.

表 8-4　MLA 与 GB/T 7714—2015 文内参考文献引用案例及解释

文献条目示例	编排格式解释
【案例 3—4：Citation by a page reference】 ●Lomax tells us that over thirty such organizations exist **(30)**. ●While this may be true, Kierkegaard felt that this would never be proved **(39)**.	文中已有作者名，故仅注明页码。
【案例 5—6：Citation by the author's last name and page reference】 ●The message was brought by a new messenger **(Finch 34)**. ●While this may be true, some felt that this would never be proved **(Kierkegaard 39)**.	夹注含姓+页码。
【案例 7：Citation after the quotation mark, before any other punctuation】 ●Stern felt that rare books can be "a link with the past, yet...marvelously current and contemporary" **(427)**.	引文信息的位置在引号之后，其他标点符号之前。
【案例 8—9：Citation by the volume number followed by colon and page number】 ●The reason Bradley felt it was true was clear to all around him **(6: 456)**. ●After all his hard work was finished, Kissinger went into private practice **(Phelps 5: 67)**.	括号中的数字指多卷本著作的卷/册及页码。 如果 the multi-volume work 的作者没有在引文中提及，须补充。 句号要放在括号之外。
【案例 10—13：Works listed by title only or by title plus more】 ●International espionage was as prevalent as ever in the 1990s **("Decade")**. ●That idea was popular even as far back as the nineteenth century **(*Annals* 5: 67)**. ●We can read in volume five of *Annals of America* that this was true **(67)**. ●In *Annals of America*, we can read that this was true **(5: 67)**.	夹注中仅提供文章题目（中的首字）。 若文献（如书）名未在引文中提及，须在括号中注明，外加卷号、页码等。 若文献名未在引文中提及，使用其缩略形式（a shortened version of the title），除非文献名已经足够短。缩略书名时，使用第一个主要单词，这样便于读者在"参考文献"中查询。 句号要放在括号之外。
【案例 14：Two or more works by the same author】 ●We could see that he was no longer able to play at that point **(Winthrop, *Farewell* 55)**	如果一名作者同时有两本及以上的作品被引用，须按照以下顺序：use the author name, followed by a comma, a shortened version of the title and the page reference。

（续表）

文献条目示例	编排格式解释
【案例 15：Reference to a reference】 ●It was then that Lilienthal, in his confirmation hearings for head of Atomic Energy Commission, said that "[his] convictions are not so much concerned with what [he is] against as what [he is] for; and that excludes a lot of things automatically" **(qtd. in Ravitch 295).**	若从一文集或（诗、词、曲、画、歌）选集中引用其中一文献，在括号中使用"qtd. in"，再加上"夹注"——此案例指作者姓+页码。
【案例 16：Classic books, plays, and poems】 ●The reference in *Moby Dick* was clear **(Melville 7; ch.1).**	如果你引用的文献有若干种版本，你可以提供更多的信息，如章、节（《圣经》或小说）或场（如话剧）等。此外，还可以在页码、分号后提供你认为有必要的信息。 本例中，Melville 指 Herman Melville（赫尔曼·梅尔维尔，世界文学名著《白鲸》[*Moby Dick*]的作者）；"7"指小说页码；"ch.1"指"第一章"。
【案例 17：More than one reference/reference to several works】 ●Several works have substantiated that theory **(Williams 67; Smith 7; Julia 6: 78).**	如果需要从"参考文献"中引用一部以上文献，应用分号把这几部文献引文信息分开。 要避免夹注中的项目文字过长，否则会打断文章本身。
【案例 18：Scientific citation】 ●The mitochondria were found to tumble rather than scoot towards the pathogen **(Smith 1996).**	纯科学引文，一般在括号中注明作者姓+日期/年份即可。页码可以不注。就科学文章而言，所引文献的出版时间比页码更为重要。 如果你没有把握，请教你的教授。
【案例 19—20：Works written by the same author and published by the same year】 ●... (Newmark, 2001a) ●... (Newmark, 2001b)	如果某作者的两部作品在同一年出版，夹注时仅提供出版年份还不能将不同的引文区分开来，所以须加以注明，如本例中的"2001a"和"2001b"。
【案例 21—22：Authors with the same last name】 ●… (G. Bush 50) ●… (G. W. Bush 50)	如果遇上文献作者的 last name 相同，分别加上他俩 first name 的缩写。如果他俩的 first name 的缩写也相同，把两个 first name 全部拼写出来；如果全部拼写出来的 first name 还是一样，使用他俩的 middle name。于是，George Bush（乔治·布什）维持不变（习惯称谓），而他的儿子则是 George W. Bush——乔治·W. 布什。应避免使用非正式的称谓，如"老布什"或"小布什"，来达到所谓区分的目的。
【案例 23：Interview】 ●As Reverend Simon points out, ... **(interview).**	如果引用访谈中的内容，照此办理即可。

（续表）

文献条目示例	编排格式解释
【案例 24：Quotations】 ●"Be true! Be true! Be true! Show freely to the world, if not your worst, yet some trait whereby the worst may be inferred!" Nathaniel Hawthorne (242) impresses upon his readers this singular statement in order to "relieve the darkening close of a tale of human frailty and sorrow" (56).	对"quotations"夹注，在有该引文作者（此处是美国著名小说家霍桑——Nathaniel Hawthorne）的情况下，只需（分别）提供作品中的具体页码即可。
【案例 25：Edition and year of publishing】 ●根据新版的《现代汉语词典》（**第 7 版，2016**），"职业"和"专业"在作为形容词这一属性词时，是同义词。	迄今《现代汉语词典》已经出了 7 个版次（edition），截至 2022 年 8 月总印次达 768 次。当引用该词典时，应注明是第几版，外加哪年出版。
【案例 26：Indirect source (in the Chinese context)】 ●尽管人类从事翻译活动已有数千年的历史，但以培养翻译人才为目的的专业化/职业化翻译教学却只有大约七十年（**参见 Delisle，引自 Baker, 2004: 361**）。	汉语中提及的间接引语"以培养翻译人才为目的的专业化/职业化翻译教学却只有大约七十年"，是参考了源自加拿大翻译学者 Jean Delisle 的话，但引用者却间接引自 Mona Baker 编写的《翻译研究百科全书》（2004 年出版）第 361 页。可谓"间接之间接"引注。有关间接引文的英文出处之文献详细信息，在文后"参考文献"中可找到。

（4）具体案例（脚注与尾注）

Buffa 指出："If you're <u>using Chicago rather than MLA style</u>, you will <u>use footnotes or endnotes instead of embedded citations</u>"（2003: 182）。可见，脚注和尾注属于 Chicago Style 的"专利产品"。

【案例 1】

假设你引用美国学者专家 William Ophuls 的 *Ecology and the Politics of Scarcity*，这一文献条目在文后参考文献列表中应是：

Ophuls, William. *Ecology and the Politics of Scarcity*. San Francisco: W. H. Freeman and Company, 1977.

该书第 100 页有一段话如下：

"In sum, geothermal power has a significant potential, but only extreme optimists foresee this form of energy constituting more than 20 percent of supply."

在你的论文中，你用了这样一句话：

Even though geothermal power has the possibility of being a significant energy source, most feel that it could not be more than 20 percent.[1]

你应把这行话作为引文处理，如使用脚注。由于这是你论文中的第一个脚注，所以

使用阿拉伯数字"1",并将此上标。脚注格式如下:

¹ William Ophuls, *Ecology and the Politics of Scarcity* (San Francisco: W. H. Freeman and Company, 1977), 100.

【案例2】

脚注与参考文献条目(a bibliographic entry)之间有什么不同?脚注中:其一,作者名和文献名后使用逗号,而非句号;其二,作者名非逆序排列;其三,专著出版信息置于圆括号内;其四,页码紧跟在括号后。尾注亦照脚注办理。下画线表示有区别之处。

文献条目	Thomas, W. J., ed. *A Collection of Early English Prose Romances*. London: Pickering, 1858.
脚注/尾注	² W. J. Thomas, ed., *A Collection of Early English Prose Romances* (London: Pickering, 1858), 212.

【案例3】

文献条目	American Bar Association. *A Portable Guide to Federal Conspiracy Law: Developing Strategies for Criminal and Civil Cases*. Chicago: PPM of the American Bar Association, 1997.
脚注/尾注	³ American Bar Association, *A Portable Guide to Federal Conspiracy Law: Developing Strategies for Criminal and Civil Cases* (Chicago: PPM of the American Bar Association, 1997), 3.

【案例4】

文献条目	Matthews, John. Foreword. *The Encyclopedia of Arthurian Legends*. By Ronan Coghlan. Shaftesbury, Dorset: Element, 1991. iii-iv.
脚注/尾注	⁴ John Matthews, Foreword, *The Encyclopedia of Arthurian Legends*, by Ronan Coghlan (Shaftesbury, Dorset: Element, 1991), p. iii.

【案例5】

文献条目	"Confessions of an Erstwhile Child." *The New Republic*. 15 June 1974: p 11.
脚注/尾注	⁵ "Confessions of an Erstwhile Child," *The New Republic*, 15 June 1974: 11.

【案例6】

文献条目	Bryden, M. P. "Attentional Strategies and Short-Term Memory in Dichotic Listening." *Cognitive Psychology* 2 (1971): 99-116.
脚注/尾注	⁶ M. P. Bryden, "Attentional Strategies and Short-Term Memory in Dichotic Listening," *Cognitive Psychology* 2 (1971): 99-116.

【案例7】

文献条目	Blumenthal, Sidney. "The Cold War and the Closet." Rev. of *Whittaker Chambers*, by Sam Tanenhaus. *The New Yorker* 17 Mar. 1997: 112-117.
脚注/尾注	⁷ Sidney Blumenthal, "The Cold War and the Closet," rev. of *Whittaker Chambers*, by Sam Tanenhaus. *The New Yorker* 17 Mar. 1997: 114.

【案例8】

文献条目	*Citizen Kane*. Dir Orson Welles. Perf. Orson Welles, Joseph Cotton. Mercury, RKO, 1941.
脚注/尾注	⁸ *Citizen Kane*, dir Orson Welles, perf. Orson Welles, Joseph Cotton, Mercury, RKO, 1941.

【案例 9】

文献条目	"Bosnia and Herzegovina." *The New Grolier Multimedia Encyclopedia*. Rel. 6. CD-ROM. Online Computer Systems, Inc., 1993.
脚注/尾注	[9] "Bosnia and Herzegovina," *The New Grolier Multimedia Encyclopedia*, rel. 6, CD-ROM (Online Computer Systems, Inc., 1993).

【案例 10】

文献条目	Hobbes, Thomas. *Leviathan, or the Matter, Forme, and Power of a Common Wealth, Ecclesiastical and Civil*. Based on Eds. of 1651 and 1839. Pittsboro, N.C.: InteLex Corp., 1994? Online. Columbia University Digital Lib. Collec. Internet. 31 Mar. 1997. Available https://dx.doi.org/10.7916/D82J6HK8.
脚注/尾注	[10] Thomas Hobbes, *Leviathan, or the Matter, Forme, and Power of a Common Wealth, Ecclesiastical and Civil*, based on Eds. of 1651 and 1839 (Pittsboro, N.C.: InteLex Corp., 1994?) online, Columbia University Digital Lib. Collec., Internet. 31 Mar. 1997, available https://dx.doi.org/10.7916/D82J6HK8.

【案例 11—12】

重复引用同一文献	如果你引用同一文献，你不必再次将引注全文抄录。MLA 规则允许使用简化形式，即作者的姓（last name）+页码。如果需引用同一作者的两部或多部著作，使用所引著作题目的缩略形式，之前是作者姓氏。
脚注/尾注	●[11] Helms 56.（比较：陆谷孙 50） ●[12] Helms, *Fearless* 67.（比较：陆谷孙，新英汉 50）

【案例 13—20】

拉丁文缩写	如果一次以上引用同一出处的文献，应使用拉丁文缩写： ●Ibid. (*ibidem*) meaning "in the same place." ●Op. cit. (*opera citato*)—"in the work cited." ●Loc. cit. (*loco citato*)—"in the place cited."
脚注	●[13] Stephen Knight, *Forma and Ideology in Crime Fiction* (Bloomington, Indiana: Indiana University Press, 1980), 45. ●[14] **Ibid., 55.** ●[15] Dilys Winn, *Murder Ink: The Mystery Reader's Companion* (New York: Workman Publishing, 1977), 44. ●[16] **Knight, op. cit., 77.** ●[17] Betty Rosenberg, *Genreflecting: A Guide to Reading Interests in Genre Fiction* (Littleton, Colorado: Libraries, Unlimited, 1982), 143. ●[18] **Loc. cit.** ●[19] **Ibid., 49.** ●[20] **Winn, op. cit., p.66**

【案例 21—28】

解释	作为脚注/尾注，还有一种"解释"形式，但不为 MLA 所推荐。务必跟你的教授确认。
脚注	• [21] This is the first footnote reference for the book *Form and Ideology in Crime Fiction* by Stephen Knight. The writer is referencing material used on page 45. • [22] This is a reference to the same book as the previous note, Knight's *Form and Ideology in Crime Fiction*, but for a different page, page 55. • [23] The first reference to the book by Dilys Winn, *Murder Ink: The Mystery Reader's Companion*; the note refers to material on page 44. • [24] This refers back to the Knight book referenced in note 1, for page 77. • [25] This is the first reference to a third source, Rosenberg's *Genreflecting: A Guide to Reading Interests in Genre Fiction*, page 143. • [26] Loc. cit. refers to the Rosenberg work in the previous note: same book, same page. • [27] Ibid. refers to the previous note as well—the Rosenberg book—but a different page, page 49. • [28] This refers back to the Winn book, page 66.

【案例 29—33】

内容注释	脚注和尾注能发挥增加论文内容的功能，包括解释、评论、强调、指引等。值得提醒读者的是，如果在整篇文档中使用尾注，而又希望将内容脚注与正在评论的文本放在同一页上的话，请使用星号（*）在页面底部标注内容脚注。
举例	• [29] This particular incident was later dramatized in the Truman Capote novel *In Cold Blood*. • [30] The author acknowledges the assistance of the research department in this cause. • [31] Please refer to Table A in the addendum. • [32] While the case was never solved. There was much speculation on the part of the police department that Jones was guilty. • [33] These principles are explained in *Doing Honest Work in College*, chapter 1.

【案例 34—35】

脚注和尾注形式	脚注和尾注都是有形式要求的。比如，我们可以发挥 Word 文档里的有关功能，依样画葫芦。再如，不要将脚注/尾注的顺序编号放在句子中间。又如，在句子和脚注编号之间没有空格；脚注编号之后不跟句号。（根据 MLA 规范，案例 35 是错误形式，但在实际运用的汉语语境中，案例 35 是可接受的。——作者注）
举例	• [34] 正确形式：The claim was fostered by the notion that the allegations were false.[1] • [35] 错误形式：The claim was foster by the notion[1] that the allegations were false.

【案例 36—37】

脚注和尾注形式	脚注内单倍行距，脚注之间双倍行距。页面底部的注释应在第一行缩进 5 个空格（或 2 个汉字空格键），次行顶格；引文中的脚注数字与其在同页文中的对应数字一样，为上标形式（中文语境中的脚注未必），后面没有句号。页面正文与脚注部分之间应保持双倍行距。最为简便易行的做法是使用电脑中的 Word 功能。

举例	•[36] Lynn E. Birge, *Serving Adult Learners: A Public Library Tradition* (Chicago: American Library Association, 1981), 97. •[37] Charles H. Busha and Stephen P. Harter, *Research Methods in Librarianship* (San Diego: Academic Press, Inc., 1980), 169.

如果使用尾注，应在整篇文档中连续编号，并在正文之后用 NOTES（全部大写）标注新一页注释，标注位置应居中，距离页顶 1 英寸（2.54 公分）。尾注应使用双倍行距，与参考文献类似。与脚注不同的是，引注顺序编号不必上标：第一行从边距缩进 5 个空格，后跟一个句点、两个空格，接着开始尾注。

8.3　文献检索 ABC

8.3.1　文献特征

（1）内容，与文献构成一对多或多对一的模糊关系，如关键词（keywords）、分类号等。

（2）外表，与文献构成一对一的精确关系，如题名、责任人、序号、专利号、文献识别码等。

根据中国学术期刊检索与评价数据规范，国家期刊出版格式要求在中图分类号的下面应标出文献标识码（document code）。《中国学术期刊（光盘版）检索与评价数据规范》规定的分类码的作用在于对文章按其内容进行归类，以便于文献的统计、期刊评价、确定文献的检索范围，提高检索结果的适用性等。同时，我们在此将《信息与文献——参考文献著录规则》（GB/T 7714—2015）中对参考文献的五种主要分类（包括文献类型和文献载体标识代码，含电子文献类型标识）介绍给读者，具体如下：

●A. 专著：普通图书、学位论文、会议文集、技术报告、标准、汇编、古籍、多卷书、丛书等。

●B. 连续出版物：期刊、报纸等。

●C. 析出文献：专著中析出的文献（普通图书中析出的文献、会议文集中析出的文献等）、连续出版物中析出的文献（期刊中析出的文献、报纸中析出的文献等）。本硕博论文中常见的参考文献就是从会议文集等专著、期刊等连续出版物中析出的文献，因为我们大部分时候只是参考某某会议、某某期刊的某篇论文。

●D. 专利文献：专利申请书、专利说明书、专利公报、专利年度索引等。

●E. 电子文献：电子书刊、数据库、电子公告等。

英文的文献类型代码应与中文的文献类型代码相对应：

●A——专著、论文集中的析出文献，档案；	●C——论文集，会议录；
●C/OL——网上论文集/会议录；	●CD——光盘（CD-ROM）；
●CM——美图；	●CP——计算机程序；
●CP/DK——磁盘软件；	●D——学位论文；
●D/OL——网上学位论文；	●DB——数据库；

- DB/MT——磁带数据库；
- DK——磁盘（disk）；
- EB——电子公告；
- G——汇编；
- J/OL——网上期刊（文献）；
- M/CD——光盘图书；
- MT——磁带（magnetic tape）；
- N/OL——网上报纸（文章/文献）；
- P——专利；
- R——报告；
- S——标准（文献）；

- DB/OL——联机网上数据库；
- DS——数据集；
- EB/OL——网上电子公告；
- J——期刊（文献）；
- M——普通图书；
- M/OL——网上图书；
- N——报纸（文章/文献）；
- OL——联机网络；
- P/OL——网上专利（文献）
- R/OL——网上报告；
- S/OL——网上标准（文献）；

- Z——其他（未说明的文献类型，如词典、百科全书、译作/著）。

需要注意的是：对于非纸张型载体的电子文献，当被引用为参考文献时需在参考文献类型标识中同时标明其载体类型。该规范建议采用双字母表示电子文献载体类型，如上述电子文献类型标识：磁带——MT，磁盘——DK，光盘——CD，联机网络——OL，并以下列格式表示包括了文献载体类型的参考文献类型标识：

[文献类型标识/载体类型标识]

- [DB/OL]——联机网上数据库（database online）；
- [DB/MT]——磁带数据库（database on magnetic tape）；
- [M/CD]——光盘图书/专著（monograph on CD-ROM）；
- [CP/DK]——磁盘软件（computer program on disk）；
- [J/OL]——网上期刊（journal online）；
- [EB/OL]——网上电子公告（electronic bulletin board online）。

以纸张为载体的传统文献在引作参考文献时不必注明其载体类型。

8.3.2　检索常识

（1）工具：分为目录型、文摘型、索引型。

（2）语言：分为分类语言、主题语言。前者指图书分类号、专利分类表等；后者指主题词等。

（3）方法：分为常规法、追溯法、综合法。常规法包括顺查法、倒查法、抽查法等。追溯法指利用原始文献后所附的索引、注释或参考文献等线索，扩大信息来源之方法。综合法的使用路径是：选择特定条件下的主题 A（如旅游语言的社会语境翻译）⇨检索到 10 篇⇨选择其中一篇 B⇨利用 B 文后的参考文献用追溯法扩大检索线索。

（4）途径：分为著者、序号、分类、主题。著者指个人作者或机构作者；序号指文献的序号（如专利号、文摘号、索引号等）；分类指中图分类法（基本部类分为五大类部：马列毛邓、哲学、社会科学、自然科学、综合性图书；基本大类分为 22 个，其中 H 类是语言、文字，I 类是文学——与语言文学和翻译的关系最为密切）；主题指主题词。其他检索途径包括引文、刊名、文摘、机构等，都可以综合、单独用来检索所需文献。

（5）类型：主要分为搜索引擎、数字图书馆和网络数据库。

1）搜索引擎：百度、360、必应、谷歌、INFOGALACTIC 等。

2）数字图书馆：中国数字图书馆、中国国家图书馆、北京大学图书馆、清华大学图书馆、浙江大学图书馆、南京大学图书馆、书生之家数字图书馆、超星数字图书馆等。

3）网络数据库：CNKI（中国知网）、维普、万方、CALIS（中国高等教育文献保障系统）、EBSCO（之 ASP、BSP）、ProQuest（美国）、CASHL（中国高校人文社会科学文献中心）、各高校特色数据库、各单位及个人的自建数据库、各发达国家和地区的政府网及高校网、国内外各大出版社网站、国内外各大国际旅行社网站、UNESCO 网站等。

◎研究与实践思考题◎

1. 何为文献和参考文献？

2. 何为引注和引注规范？

3. 何为参考文献格式？

4. 熟悉各种文献特征，实践各种检索方法、途径。

5. 网搜、下载并细读《信息与文献——参考文献著录规则》（GB/T 7714—2015），了解、熟悉"国标"。

6. 网搜 MLA Style，了解有关 MLA formatting and style guide。

7. 网搜 APA Style，了解有关 Popular Style Guidelines。

8. 网搜 Chicago Manual of Style 17th Edition，了解有关 Chicago Style。

9. 网搜 The Purdue OWL: Citation Chart，了解有关 MLA、APA 和 CMS 之间的基本异同。

10. 自行对 GB/T 7714—2015 与 MLA、APA 和 CMS 之间的异同做一比较了解。

第 9 章　如何致谢与声明（知法守礼）

How to Acknowledge & Declare (Law- & Courtesy-oriented)

◎学习目标◎

本章介绍（学位）论文撰写进入收官阶段的有关内容。与前面各章比较，这些内容看似简单多了，但意义非凡，不可或缺，因为它们涉及学生的（学术）行为规范和法礼观念，所以既是"法"，也是"礼"。通过本章学习，学生可以：

● 明白论文中"致谢"之概念及其重要性；

● 了解并学会如何用英文撰写"致谢"；

● 了解、熟悉中英文版本论文独创性声明的各自特点；

● 了解、熟悉中英文版本论文版权声明的不同行文；

● 了解、熟悉关键内容合并于一体的毕业论文（设计）承诺书。

9.1　如何致谢

9.1.1　致谢概念解读

撰写毕业/学位论文，"致谢"/"鸣谢/感谢"（acknowledgments）是不可省略的一部分。西方大学学生撰写毕业论文有"致谢专页"——Acknowledgements page。该页用来感谢直接和间接帮助、指导、鼓励毕业生完成论文撰写、获得学位的个人、机构及学校组织。根据 Slade，"[The] acknowledgements section contains expressions of appreciation for assistance and guidance. The help given by advisers and readers does not require written acknowledgement, but the recognition of generosity with time and knowledge is a courtesy that is widely appreciated. Acknowledgements should be expressed simply and tactfully." "Permissions that you have obtained for quotations may be presented in the Acknowledgements or on the copyright page. When permissions are granted as a special favor, they are best placed in the Acknowledgements."（2000: 42）

在西方学术界，撰写"致谢"有着严格的规范或规定。原则上，措辞应简明、真诚；值得致谢者应该在此一一提及。一般来说，按照提及顺序，需致谢的个人及单位顺序如表 9-1 所示（仅供参考），但并非要求严格如此排序，应该感谢多少人、感谢哪些人、感谢哪些机构或单位、如何致谢等等，完全是作者个人的选择。

表 9-1　需致谢的个人及单位排序

Serial No.	Thanks to be rendered to	What have been done
1	the supervisor(s)/tutor(s)/ mentor(s)/adviser(s)	primary/first supervisor and secondary/assistant supervisor who has/have done the most
2	the teacher(s)	who taught you related courses (that helped you) and gave you advice and more on your research
3	the classmate(s)	who offered you suggestions and more on your research
4	particular person(s)	who helped you collect data and do proof-reading or even revision
5	sources/institution(s)	for financial support (*if any*)
6	those/institution(s)	that kindly permitted you to use their research instruments or other materials like photos, diagrams, figures, charts, and tables
7	anyone	who once helped you one way or another
8	family and friends	who gave you both/either physical and/or mental support

9.1.2　致谢写作要求

用英文撰写"致谢"不是很难，因为有样本（sample）可供参考，但也未必简单，因为存在的问题也不少。有关问题见表 9-2。

表 9-2　致谢写作问题

致谢写作问题（按英语字母顺序排列）	简要说明
abstract	过于抽象——缺具象感
exaggerated	过于夸张——缺事实感
(*simply for*) formality	过于官样——缺真情感
general	过于笼统——缺真实感
lengthy	过于冗长——缺简洁感
over-modest	过于谦逊——缺诚实感
(*too*) simple	过于简单——缺真诚感

要避免致谢写作中出现的上述 7 种常见问题，只需在心底里记住并用准确的语言表达以下几个关键词的内涵，就会给读者"暖暖"的人情味和真正的学术味：

- academical
- brief
- concise
- conventional
- formal
- sincere
- specific

这"ABCCFSS"应体现在具体的撰写之中。

（1）本科 BA 毕业论文致谢案例

Acknowledgements[①]

Upon completion of this thesis, I wish to sincerely express my gratitude to those who have helped me during the period.

I owe my deepest gratitude to my chief supervisor Professor ×× of the Translation Department. It was Prof. ××'s course that first showed me the way to the door of translation, and his textbook offered me the first glance of Xu Yuanzhong's translations. This thesis would not have been possible without Prof. ××'s support, encouragement, insightful instructions and guidance. He made his support available to me in numerous ways: from punctuations to basic structure, and his strictness and discipline are witnessed by his students every year.

My thanks also go to my assistant supervisor Dr. ×××, who kindly gave me instructions when I had a thesis proposal oral defense.

Finally, special thanks go to my family and friends for their kindly encouragement and unconditional support. Thesis writing has been much happier with them by my side.

（2）本科 BTI 毕业论文致谢案例

Acknowledgements[②]

It has been rewarding to write my BTI thesis for the last months. First of all, I would like to extend my sincere gratitude to my supervisor Prof. ××. He patiently guided me with his extensive knowledge of translation theory and practice. His keen interest in dance and trust in my potential encouraged me throughout the whole process. I am greatly indebted to him for his always caring, academic expertise, and long-term vision. Without his support and patience, this thesis would not have got off the ground and I would not be able to discover more about the spark of connection between Dance and Translation.

I would also like to extend my thanks to Dr. ××× for his pertinent suggestions and encouragement. His opinions helped me better understand my research direction and improve my thesis from every detail. I feel grateful to ×××, dance teacher of Zhejiang University and visiting scholar in Ohio State University, who first introduced me the dance textbook for translation and generously shared with me her knowledge of modern dance. A special tribute should go to ×××, Chinese-German Choreographer, ××, professional modern dancer and all the other friends with dance-related background. Their opinions helped me gain a deeper understanding of dance and broadened my horizon on art communication.

I also thank the School of International Studies, Zhejiang University for providing me with lots of academic resources and studious atmosphere. They have proven valuable to my research and produced a far reaching influence on my attitude towards academics and my view on learning for life.

Last but not least, I owe an immense debt to my parents, who have been supportive all the way along.

总而言之，上述两个"致谢"案例符合规范要求，不论从西方惯例还是从东方惯例（或中国惯例）的视角判断，均符合"**双 A 标准**"——**Appropriate & Acceptable**。

---

① 选自浙江大学本科英语专业毕业论文的真实文稿，文中错误与不足在所难免。
② 选自浙江大学本科翻译专业毕业论文的真实文稿，文中错误与不足在所难免。

9.2　如何声明

一篇/部合格的毕业论文必须是独创的，具有版权的。正规的做法，作者应该并必须对论文的独创性和论文的版权或论文版权转让提出书面声明。

9.2.1　论文独创性声明

学位论文独创性声明是有规范格式和写法的。英文版的论文独创性声明有其自身的特色。由于要求 BTI/BA 生用英文撰写毕业/学位论文，我们特地参考了若干英国及欧洲大陆名校（如剑桥国际、帝国理工、苏黎世联邦理工等）的论文独创性声明等类似文本，同时参考国内高校的特殊情况，设计出简洁的论文独创性声明英文文本（我们不是很提倡使用所谓的中英/英中"平行文本"或"对应文本"，因为存在语言、文化、惯例、排版、形式和内容等方面的诸多差异），见表 9-3、表 9-4 及其必要说明。

表 9-3　Statement of Originality

Statement of Originality

Student declaration:

I confirm that the thesis presented in the submission is all my own work. I have not copied or based my work on any samples or exemplars to which I had access. Any work taken from another source has been appropriately referenced and acknowledged. All data and findings in the work have not been falsified or embellished.

I understand the University's policy on plagiarism and that the work may be screened electronically for plagiarism.

Full name (*signature*)＿＿＿＿＿＿＿＿＿＿＿＿＿＿＿＿＿＿＿＿＿＿

Student number＿＿＿＿＿＿＿＿＿＿＿＿＿＿＿＿＿＿

Place and date＿＿＿＿＿＿＿＿＿＿＿＿＿＿＿＿＿＿＿＿＿＿＿＿＿＿

Title of the thesis＿＿＿＿＿＿＿＿＿＿＿＿＿＿＿＿＿＿＿＿＿＿＿＿＿＿

＿＿＿＿＿＿＿＿＿＿＿＿＿＿＿＿＿＿＿＿＿＿＿＿＿＿＿＿＿＿＿＿＿＿

Teacher declaration:

I verify that I have supervised sufficient work to enable me to say with confidence that this is the candidate's own work. The work has been fully checked and these checks included looking for:

● copying from any sample/exemplar materials;

● copying from other students;

● the possibility of a third person writing the work.

I also confirm that the thesis regulations on the role of the teacher have been observed.

Full name (*signature*)＿＿＿＿＿＿＿＿＿＿＿＿＿＿＿＿＿＿＿＿＿＿

Teacher reference number_____

Place and date_____

_____

This statement must be filled out, signed and attached to your student work.

表 9-4　Declaration of Originality

Declaration of Originality

This is to certify that the copy of my thesis, which I have presented for consideration for my BTI/BA degree, embodies the results of my own course of study and research, has been composed by myself and has been seen by my supervisor before presentation.

表 9-3 有以下几个特点：学生和导师有文字表述不同的独创性或原创性声明（即声明不是合二为一），并分别签字；签名地点需填写；明确使用 "(the University's policy on) plagiarism"（剽窃）一词，并指出 "the work may be screened electronically for plagiarism"。国内在原创性声明中（一般）不具体使用"剽窃"一词，但本科高校早已启动"论文查重"程序。"查重"是汉语的委婉表达，实则指检测论文的抄袭率和原创度。发达国家高校中，很多原创性声明版本行文具体、详细，篇幅较长，（不少）采用表格形式。

表 9-4 的格式选自英国世界知名高校的学位论文开始页，行文简洁明了，仅代表学位申请者本人，也是一种（个人）特色。

必须指出的是，原创性声明意味着对任何"非原创"做法之否定。复旦大学、北京大学、清华大学、上海交通大学、浙江大学等都已经对论文使用 AI 工具做出规定。若使用 AI 生成内容未明确标注，可能会被视为"未声明来源的引用"，违反了学术诚信，还可能被查重系统（如知网、万方等"AI 查重"/AI checker 模块）标记为"非原创"，触发学术审查。

9.2.2　论文版权使用授权声明

学位论文的版权的重要性，体现在知识产权保护法中。论文作者在将自己的论文版权正式转给母校、出版社或其他单位与个人之前，该论文属于其作者本人，并且受到法律的保护。

考虑到学术论文具有"利他功能"，毕业生会被要求或主动填写"学位论文版权使用授权书"。

版权声明或版权使用授权书有规范格式和写法。以下各提供一种简明中文版与简明英文版的论文版权使用授权声明（及说明）。各位毕业生应使用各自学校提供的版本。

（1）学位论文版权使用授权声明（中文版）（表 9-5）

表 9-5　学位论文版权使用授权书

学位论文版权使用授权书

　　本学位论文作者完全了解＿＿＿＿**大学** 有权保留并向国家有关部门或机构送交本论文的复印件和电子文本，允许论文被查阅和借阅。本人授权＿＿＿＿**大学** 可以将学位论文的全部或部分内容编入有关数据库进行检索和传播，可以采用影印、缩印或扫描等复制手段保存、汇编学位论文。

（保密的学位论文在解密后适用本授权书）

学位论文作者签名：　　　　　　　　　　　　导师签名：

签字日期：　　　年　　月　　日　　　　　　签字日期：　　　年　　月　　日

（2）学位论文版权声明（英文版）（表 9-6）

表 9-6　学位论文版权声明

Copyright Declaration

　　The copyright of this thesis rests with the Author and is made available under the University's thesis regulations. Researchers are free to copy, distribute or transmit the thesis on the condition that they attribute it, that they do not use it for commercial purposes and that they do not alter, transform or build upon it. For any reuse or redistribution, researchers must make clear to others the license terms of this work.

　　表 9-5 参考了本校及其他重点高校（曾经使用）的不同版本，重新设计、行文而成。表 9-6 选自英国世界知名高校的学位论文开始页，本书作者仅对行文做了少量调整，而没有采用简单的对等翻译方法，将"学位论文版权使用授权书"处理成 Authorization Letter for Thesis Copyright Use。

　　上述英文版声明本身没有像"Thesis author"/"Supervisor""Signature""Date and place"等文字，使用者可以自行增加。

9.2.3　论文承诺声明

　　以浙江大学为例，毕业生在其论文（设计）编写格式做到符合《浙江大学本科生毕业论文（设计）编写规则》要求的前提下，须签署《浙江大学本科生毕业论文（设计）承诺书》并遵守承诺。学生在毕业论文（设计）工作中须恪守学术诚信，遵循学术准则，尊重和保护他人知识产权等合法权益。学生如有学术不端行为，经调查核实，毕业论文（设计）成绩记载为"违纪"，并按学校相关管理规定处理。其实，"论文独创性声明""学位论文版权声明"或"学位论文版权使用授权书"已经体现了论文作者必须讲诚信、守承诺等关键内容。国内有些高校的做法是在不同的声明书上签名，有些高校则将有关重要内容合并于一个声明书中。浙江大学目前就是采用了后一种做法，见表 9-7。

表 9-7　浙江大学本科生毕业论文（设计）承诺书

浙江大学本科生毕业论文（设计）承诺书

　　1. 本人郑重地承诺所呈交的毕业论文（设计），是在指导教师的指导下严格按照学校和学院有关规定完成的。

　　2. 本人在毕业论文（设计）中除了文中特别加以标注和致谢的地方外，论文中不包含其他人已经发表或撰写过的研究成果，也不包含为获得 <u>浙江大学</u> 或其他教育机构的学位或证书而使用过的材料。

　　3. 与我一同工作的同志对本研究所做的任何贡献均已在论文中做了明确的说明并表示谢意。

　　4. 本人承诺在毕业论文（设计）工作过程中没有伪造数据等行为。

　　5. 若在本毕业论文（设计）中有侵犯任何方面知识产权的行为，由本人承担相应的法律责任。

　　6. 本人完全了解 <u>浙江大学</u> 有权保留并向国家有关部门或机构送交本论文（设计）的复印件和电子文本，允许本论文（设计）被查阅和借阅。本人授权 <u>浙江大学</u> 可以将本论文（设计）的全部或部分内容编入有关数据库进行检索和传播，可以采用影印、缩印或扫描等复制手段保存、汇编本论文（设计）。

作者签名：　　　　　　　　　　　　　　　　导师签名：

签字日期：　　　年　　月　　日　　　　　　签字日期：　　　年　　月　　日

◎研究与实践思考题◎

1. 清楚认识学位论文中"致谢"之概念。
2. 细读、了解、熟悉论文中有关"致谢"部分的内容及意义。
3. 熟悉用英文撰写论文"致谢"的具体要求。
4. 熟悉、了解中英文版本论文独创性声明的不同元素和不同写法。
5. 熟悉、了解中英文版本论文版权使用授权声明的不同元素和不同写法。

第10章　如何答辩（迈向成功）

How to Defend (Results-oriented)

◎学习目标◎

论文答辩是本科生毕设工作五大环节中举足轻重的环节。本章讨论的所谓答辩，包括开题报告答辩和毕业论文答辩两大关键环节。学生"卡"在这两个环节（或其中之一）上的不在少数。答辩对答辩者提出了综合性的挑战，涉及专业、学术、情感、心理、管理等全方位。本章帮助学生明白：

●何为开题答辩（不进则退）；

●何为中期检查（及时纠错）；

●何为论文答辩（毕业关键）；

●何为答辩意义（质量完善）；

●何为答辩准备（自我挑战）；

●何为答辩程序（循规蹈矩）；

●何为答辩策略（诚心诚意）；

●何为答辩评定（自我鞭策）；

●何为论文提交（仍需努力）。

10.1　答辩概念

本科毕业/学位论文答辩实则是有关论文工作五大环节中最为重要的环节。其他环节包括选题、开题、论文（设计）实施（含论文检测/查重）、中期检查等。就答辩而言，它包含两层意思，或者涉及两个环节或阶段的任务。其一，论文开题报告答辩；其二，学位/毕业论文答辩。第一阶段的任务过不了关，就意味着你还不能（不被允许）进入第二阶段，即开始着手正式撰写论文。同理，若中期检查（碰巧）不过关，也要暂停论文撰写。

所谓**"中期检查"**是指上述有关论文工作五个环节中的第四个环节，即在第三环节开题答辩和第五环节论文答辩之间的一个不可轻视或忽视的环节。各院（系）根据毕业论文（设计）工作进度安排，组织中期检查工作，检查内容包括但不限于选题情况、任务书落实情况、过程管理情况等，及时发现存在问题，提出整改措施。学校组织有关人员对中期执行情况进行抽查。这些都是学校明文规定的。

就时间段而言，在冬学期结束前基本完成开题答辩；在春学期第 6 周开始前基本完成中期检查。

10.1.1 开题报告答辩概念

开题报告答辩（thesis proposal defense/oral proposal defense）分为开题报告（[thesis] proposal）和答辩（proposal defense）两部分，实际上就是对学生学位论文（设计）初期、规划阶段的成果进行相对全面的审核的一种形式。开题报告确定了论文（设计）的整体原理是否具有可行性（feasibility），换言之，开题报告犹如项目建议书（project proposal）或项目可行性研究报告（feasibility study report）。

有关开题报告的内容和答辩，详见第 3 章。这里，再就该环节内涵及一些"要点"简述如下（这些都是本书提出的较为理想的建议，本校或其他学校在实操中会有所不同，标准、要求甚至会更高）。

（1）BA/BTI 学位论文开题报告答辩环节内涵

学生根据毕业论文（设计）任务书要求，在指导教师指导下开展文献综述、外文翻译和开题工作，撰写论文文献综述和开题报告，在院（系）或翻译专业自己规定的时间内参加答辩，完成开题。

各院（系）成立开题答辩委员会，下设答辩组。答辩组人数以 3—5 名为宜（答辩组多的话，每组 3 名成员即可），成员应由中级及以上专业技术职称的教师担任，答辩组组长应由高级职称教师担任，可聘请外单位副高级及以上职称人员参加答辩工作。

开题报告答辩结束后，答辩组根据学生的开题材料及答辩情况，对学生开题工作给出评价并评定成绩，并明确是否同意学生进入论文（设计）实施环节。

（2）开题答辩需/须涉及的常见问题

①为什么选择这个题目？

②研究这个题目的意义和目的是什么？

③研究问题/翻译难题是什么？使用什么方法来解决？

④论文全文纲要（基本框架/结构）如何？

⑤论文各部分之间的逻辑关系如何？

⑥在研究/翻译过程中，发现了哪些新的见解？又是如何认识的？

⑦文献综述有代表性吗？与时俱进吗？

⑧理论框架跟"问题/难题"和"解题"关联度大吗？有立论依据吗？

⑨与论文正文密切相关的问题有哪些？

⑩若要开始撰写论文，还存在哪些不足或困难？

（3）开题答辩技巧及须知

①10—15 分钟的自述报告（PPT presentation）。

②题目、摘要一定要使人耳目一新，起码是最为恰切的。

③要"说"，不要"讲"，即要"说课"，而非"讲课"。

④忌"照本宣读"，论/述论文写作动机、缘由、研究问题/翻译难题以及新发现。

⑤论/述言简意赅，突出重点、主题。

⑥避免主题不明、内容空泛、平淡无料、东拉西扯。

⑦注意仪表仪态，要淡定大方。

⑧多带些佐证（参考书籍、图表等），届时据理力争。

⑨沉着冷静，做好笔记，虚心听取专家的各种意见。

⑩答辩论证，尽心尽力；存在问题，及时处理。

（4）开题答辩质量判断

●理论创新——

①新概念的提出或重新界定？　　　　②新现象、新事实的揭示？

③新观点的提出？　　　　　　　　　④旧观点的新表述？

⑤新体系的提出和/或建立？

●实践创新——

①源语文本首译？　　　　　　　　　②源语文本重译？

③优质复译译文？　　　　　　　　　④翻译新策略/原则的提出？

⑤翻译新方法/技巧的论证？

（5）英文再现开题+答辩重点

●The thesis proposal defense

①**Thesis proposal**: purpose and overview

②Proposal format: as *specified* in Chapter 3

③Format requirements: as *specified* in Chapter 3

④Proposal development: as *specified* in Chapter 3

⑤**Proposal defense**: as *programmed* in Chapter 3 and reality

⑥**Form completion**: plan of research form completion

（6）BA/BTI 学位论文开题报告评估标准（表 10-1、表 10-2）

表 10-1　BA 学位论文开题报告评估标准

	评估项目	肯定	基本肯定	不足	否定
书面文本	①选题依据；理论意义；实践意义				
	②预期成果之创新性/特色/有益性				
	③毕业生水平与选题难度之匹配				
	④研究方案之合理性				
	⑤论文写作时间表之合理性				
	⑥开题报告整体及个体①之学术性				
口头报告	⑦表述清楚，条理清晰，层次分明				
	⑧选题理据，概念解读，综述水平				
	⑨答辩之逻辑性；论证之严密性				
结果	是否同意开题				

---

① "整体"指整篇 BA 开题报告；"个体"指各有关组成部分（如题目、摘要、文献综述、参考文献等）。

表 10-2　BTI 学位论文开题报告评估标准

	评估项目	肯定	基本肯定	不足	否定
书面文本	①选题依据；实践意义；指导意义				
	②预期成果之创新性/特色/有益性				
	③毕业生水平与选题难度之匹配				
	④翻译/研究方案之合理性				
	⑤论文写作时间表之合理性				
	⑥开题报告整体及个体①之学术性				
口头报告	⑦表述清楚，条理清晰，层次分明				
	⑧选题理据，试译水平，试评水平				
	⑨答辩之逻辑性；论证之严密性				
结果	是否同意开题				

10.1.2　学位论文答辩概念

　　学位/毕业论文答辩（oral thesis defense/oral defense）是一种有组织、有准备、有计划、有鉴定的比较正规的审查论文的重要形式。为了搞好论文答辩，在举行答辩会前，校方/院方/系方/所方、答辩委员会、答辩者等三方都要做好充分的准备。在答辩会上，答辩委员会（成员）要极力找出答辩者（即毕业生）在其论文中所表现的水平是真是假。而答辩者（即毕业生）不仅要证明自己的论点是"对"的，而且还要证明老师的论点是"错"的（此处特指学生要勇于答辩，善于答辩，以理服人）。

　　根据美国西北大学副教授 Chris Riesbeck②，我们就论文答辩的相关概念来认真看看英文思维的回答。

　　（1）何为论文答辩（What is a thesis defense）？

　　A thesis defense has two parts: a thesis and a defense. The second mistake many students make is not knowing what their thesis is. The third mistake is not knowing how to defend it. (The first mistake will be described later.)

　　（2）何为学位论文（What is a thesis）？

　　Your thesis is "a position or proposition that a person (as a candidate for scholastic honors) advances and offers to maintain by argument" (*Webster's 7th New Collegiate Dictionary*). "I looked at how people play chess" is not a thesis; "people adapt memories of old games to play new games" is. Similarly, "I wrote a program to play chess" is not a thesis; "playing chess requires a database of actual games" is. A thesis has to claim something.

　　（3）何为（论文）答辩（What is a defense）？

　　A defense presents evidence for a thesis. What kind of evidence is appropriate depends on

---

①　"整体"指整篇 BTI 开题报告；"个体"指各有关组成部分（如题目、摘要、翻译实践、理论评述等）。

②　参见 https://users.cs.northwestern.edu/~riesbeck/defense.html。

what kind of thesis is being defended.

Thesis: process X is a feasible way to do task Y

One defense for this kind of claim is an analysis of the complexity, or completeness, or whatever, of the theoretical algorithm. In computer science, the more common defense is based on empirical results from running an experiment. A good defense here means more than one example, and answers to questions such as the following. What are the capabilities and limits of your experiment? How often do the things that your experiment does come up in the real world? What's involved in extending it? If it's easy to extend, why haven't you? If your example is a piece of a larger system, how realistic are your assumptions about input and output?

（4）何为答辩前常犯的第一个错误（What is the first mistake that students likely make concerning thesis defense）？

If you're bright, educated, and have worked hard on a topic for more than a year, you must have learned something no one else knew before. The first mistake that students make is to think that a thesis has to be grander than the theory of relativity. A thesis should be new and interesting, but it doesn't have to change the foundations of all we believe and hold dear.

（5）论文答辩难吗（Is thesis defense difficult for you from the very beginning）？

Don't try to come up with a thesis first, and then investigate it. Start by exploring some task domain. Take some initial ideas and push them hard for a year or so. Now, stop and think about what you've done and what you've learned. Among your accomplishments and experience, there will be several good candidate theses. Pick one. Test it out on your advisor and other faculty members. Test it out on other students. Is it a claim that you can describe clearly and briefly? Is it a claim that anyone cares about? Is it a claim that people don't find perfectly obvious, or if they do find it obvious, can you convince them that it could easily be false.

Once you've refined your claim into a good thesis, now you can determine what kind of defense is appropriate for it and what more you need to do. This is where the hard part comes, psychologically, because to create a defense for your thesis, you're going to have to attack it harder than anyone else. What happens if the thesis fails? Negate it and defend that! In a year or so of focused research, you should be ready for a real thesis defense.

See how easy it is, once you know how?

10.2　答辩意义

10.2.1　确保毕业质量

真正意义上的大学本科毕业生（文科），除了要获得本科学历证书（academic certificate/diploma of undergraduate），还要获得（文科）学士学位证书（BA degree diploma/certificate），即要获得"双证"（学历、学位证书）。换言之，这位本科毕业生不仅修完了所有本科课程，还通过了学位论文的答辩，即该毕业生具备了本专业的专业、学术能力和资历

（qualifications）。同理，BTI 也是具备了相应的学历和学位证书的毕业生（undergraduate diploma holder；BTI degree holder）。所谓论文答辩，其**目的**是看该论文是否符合学位论文的基本要求或底线要求；其**内容**涉及论文之"身内"和"身外"；其**语言**是论文写作语言。显然，这个**真正意义**意味着以下几个要点：

（1）考察综合学识。论文答辩是对书面形式论文考察的关键环节，不仅要考察已经"固化"了的论文内容，还要或更要考察"动化"的综合专业知识及能力、学术知识及能力、专业技能及其他能力等。

1）对论文内容本身的考察。就 BA/BTI 而言，涉及笔译/口译的实践、翻译的基本/常用理论、专门知识、百科知识、专业化、职业化、专门化、地方化、技能化等。

2）对论文内容之外的有本专业关联度的能力以及其他相关能力、技能的考察。就 BA/BTI 而言，涉及与本论文内容似乎"无关"其实"相连"的翻译理论与实践——**other related translation/interpreting theories and practice**，涉及直接的、动态的口头表达能力、风格、方式等——**delivery**（关联演讲基本功、语音基本功、语法基本功、思辨基本功、临场应变基本功、心理素质基本功等）。这几个方面是全面、综合考察一名（优秀）毕业生不可或缺的，虽然不是或未必是考察的重点，但却是论文答辩过程中自然而然展现出来的，甚至还可以反映答辩者的本质水平或能力，反映作者论文的真与伪。

（2）验证论文真伪。学位论文可谓一种 take-home examination，因此容易产生抄袭现象。论文抄袭可以通过审读论文本身发现、通过查重发现，而在面对面的现场答辩过程中，更容易得到论文真伪之验证及（再）确认。

1）验证有利于对论文做出客观、准确的判分。有些"抄袭"并非严重到涉及（学术）道德本质问题，现场验证更利于实事求是地判分。

2）验证有利于维护学术之权威性，也有利于提高论文质量。有些"抄袭"涉及本质问题，属于严重学术失范，必须对论文作者予以严肃处理，因为真正的学术精神是不能被玷污的，学术之权威性应是神圣不可侵犯的。与此同时，通过验证，论文答辩者会从中了解、找到、重新发现自己论文中还存在的诸多问题。

3）验证出题的四个视角。

①检验真伪——围绕论文的真实性拟题——这是检验论文真假的有效办法。

②探测水平——围绕论文主要内容拟题——这是检验学生水平高低的有效办法。

③弥补不足——围绕论文中的薄弱环节——这是检验论文存在不足的有效办法。

④电子查重——针对论文主要组成部分——这是较为科学的检验学术不端的办法。

10.2.2　确保自我完善

学位论文中出现（诸多）问题在所难免。由于 BA/BTI 学位论文答辩委员会是由本专业较高水平的教授（高教系列）、专家（翻译系列）、行家（特殊领域口笔译）组成的，因此，two heads are better than one。这些成员在提问中一定会对毕业生的论文提出不少宝贵的意见和建议，对学生及其导师都是有益无弊的，最后有利于论文的论述更为全面，论文的分析更为深入，论文的外观更为漂亮，论文的作者更为完善。

同时，论文答辩还会给毕业生带来其他方面的诸多好处（benefits）：

①答辩是学生增长知识、交流信息的一个良好的学术互动过程；

②答辩是学生全面展示自己的勇气、雄心、才能、智慧、风度和口才的难得机会；

③答辩是学生向答辩组成员和有关专家学习、求教的良好机会；

④答辩是学生学习、锻炼辩论艺术的一次特殊机会。

10.3　答辩准备

10.3.1　院系准备工作

对于院系（或翻译专业）来说，答辩前的准备，主要是指做好答辩前的组织工作（包括论文查重）：

（1）审查学生资格。审查学生参加毕业论文答辩的资格（根据教育部及各校自己的具体规定办理）。

（2）论文匿名送审。安排校内外专家匿名评阅学位论文，换言之，就是答辩前盲审和末位审核工作[浙江大学等"双一流高校"要求相关学院（系）制定和完善相应工作的实施细则，并向教务处备案]。

（3）论文查重外审。浙江大学等高校要求各学院（系）加强对本科生的学术诚信教育，严格实行毕业论文（设计）查重和抽检。学校将根据教育部《本科毕业论文（设计）抽检办法（试行）》的通知精神，加强毕业论文（设计）的外审力度。

（4）全员论文查重。学校提供统一的论文检测平台，院（系）负责组织落实毕业论文（设计）检测工作，产生论文检测报告，用于辅助学术规范指导。**论文查重**旨在规范学术诚实和严谨的风格，制止剽窃的不公平行为。其具体操作，就是把写好的论文通过与论文检测系统资源库的比对，得出与各大论文库的相似比，即检测抄袭率，以检测论文的原创度，以及是否存在抄袭等学术不端行为。有关查重的主要内容简介如下：

1）浙江大学本科生院就毕业论文（设计）管理工作正式发文，要求加强对本科生的学术诚信教育，严格实行毕业论文（设计）查重和抽检。

2）论文（设计）查重检测统一使用中国知网（http://check.cnki.net/pmlc/），运用技术手段对论文质量进行初步筛查。查重结果作为学生毕业论文（设计）学术规范检查的重要参考，查重后产生的查重检测报告、重复率须在各院本科教学科备案。每位学生只可检测一次（存有弹性）。如需修改后重新检测，应于结题答辩前联系院（系）本科生科，查重率在 10% 以下方能进入答辩。

3）论文（设计）查重检测要求（目前暂定要求）：

①在规定的期限内完成查重检测。

②检测的具体操作指南有书面说明（略）。

③查重内容包括信息齐全的论文封面、致谢、中英文摘要、目录、论文正文、参考文献、附录（若有）等。检测系统对格式正确的封面、目录、参考文献这类内容自动识

别后忽略不做检测，其他内容包括致谢、附录等都做检测。

④查重率在 10% 以下的为通过，根据检测报告做适当修改。

⑤查重率在 10%—20% 为修改后通过，需要指导教师督促修改并确认。

⑥查重率在 20% 以上的为不通过，需要重大修改后再次查重。

⑦论文重复率未达到标准，但经答辩组判断可以答辩的，视为通过，但需由本人和/或指导教师提交书面情况说明，经答辩组确认后交本科教学科备案。

⑧学生需重视查重后的论文修改，并将查重的文本复制检测报告单（全文标明引文）和检测报告单（全文对照）及时发送给自己的指导教师。

（5）组织答辩委员会或答辩组。进行毕业论文答辩，必须成立答辩委员会或答辩组，该委员会或组的功能是审查和公正评价毕业论文、评定毕业论文成绩，并以正式的组织形式作为学位论文质量之重要保证。该委员会或组还需配备一名秘书，秘书的职责是客观如实地做好答辩记录，填写本科生毕业论文（设计）现场答辩记录表。

答辩委员会或答辩组一般由 3—5 人组成，其中至少一人应具有高级职称（可聘请外单位副高级及以上职称人员参加答辩工作）。初级职称的教师不担任答辩委员会或答辩组成员。答辩委员会主席或答辩组组长应由一位学术水平较高的成员担任，负责答辩委员会或答辩组会议的召集工作。该项工作主要包括拟订毕业论文成绩标准；答辩结束后，根据学生毕业论文（设计）及答辩情况对学生论文（设计）工作给出评价并评定成绩。

（6）答辩组审核材料。答辩组要审核学生论文（设计）答辩材料，审核不通过的，不予答辩。学生论文（设计）答辩材料可包括毕业论文（设计）指导教师评价意见、论文检测报告、论文（设计）及相关工作成果等。

（7）布置论文答辩会场地。要重视毕业论文答辩会场地的布置，以营造论文答辩会的良好气氛、确保答辩者的现场情绪。

（8）分送答辩论文。答辩委员会或组成员确定以后，原则上应在答辩会举行前半个月（起码不少于一周）把要答辩的论文分送到答辩委员会或组成员手里。在答辩时，答辩专家会提出什么问题，提出多少问题，是答辩者最为关心的。

我们的忠告是：专家的提问防不胜防，做好自己的功课为上策。这是因为诸多论文之间存在着较大的个体差异，所以答辩专家提出的问题也就必然是因人而异的。而且，即使是同一篇论文，不同的专家提问的重点、视角也会有所不同。有鉴于此，论文答辩者在准备答辩时，还是应把重点放在对自己论文的全面、重点及个案的把握上（详见本章其他有关部分），不要花大心思去猜题、"押宝"。

10.3.2　准备自述报告

在答辩开始时，学生要向论文答辩委员会简要地自述论文的主要内容，自述时间一般有 10、15、20 分钟几种安排；自述手段通常采用 PPT 形式；自述内容原则上包括：

①论文的题目、摘要；

②选题的缘由、依据、目的、意义、学术/实用价值等；

③论文的研究问题，或者翻译实践难题；

④本课题的理论/实践创新，或者研究特色/翻译项目的创新点/攻关难点；

⑤研究方法，或者翻译策略/方法等；

⑥典型案例及理论阐述，或者译例分析及理论诠释；

⑦最终结论；

⑧参考文献。

10.3.3　准备专家提问

学生在完成自述任务后，必须回答论文答辩委员会的提问，一般是有关论文内容的3—5 个问题，通常涉及：

●论文选题；	●文献研究；	●理论框架；
●翻译实例；	●高清逻辑；	●论据论证；
●价值所在；	●突然袭击；	●……

事实上，答辩专家的提问是有一定的范围并遵循一定的原则的。

①只涉及学术问题。答辩专家一般不会也不能提出与论文内容毫无关系的问题（特殊情况除外），这是专家拟题的大范围。

②重点放在质量方面。为确保论文的真正品质，专家会在上述这个大范围内，就"检验真伪""探测能力""弥补不足"三个方面提问（详见"10.2.1　确保毕业质量"）。

③提问所遵循的原则：

●理论视角——应有一个涉及基础理论知识及其运用。

●实践视角——应有一个涉及口笔译实践问题及难题。

●难度视角——应有难易适中的问题，或有针对性的高难度问题。前者应针对普通答辩者提出，后者应针对答辩成绩可能为优秀或良好的答辩者提出（对优秀论文作者的提问，难度必须大，甚至一个接着一个；对良好论文作者的提问，难度可以较大）。

●结合视角——应有点面结合、深广相连的提问。

●形式视角——应有各种形式的提问。

下列设计的问题在原则上会对答辩者有所启发，并对答辩本身产生良性循环：

●Why did you choose this topic?

●Who assigned to you the translation task as a main part of your thesis?

●In one sentence, what is the main claim/point/argument of your thesis?

●What is your thesis statement?

●Academically, what are the rationale and significance of your research/translation project?

●Why did you choose Translation Practice Report as your thesis?

●How did you put this theory/theoretical approach into your Translation Internship Report?

●What companies did you serve as a part-time escort interpreter?

●Why did you write the abstract so long/short?

●Have you chosen the keywords carefully?

●What are the research questions you are going to answer?

●How did you answer your second research question?

●What are the representative translation problems you are going to address?

●What real problems did you often find hard to tackle in trans-editing Xinhua news stories?

●How can you tell that your re-translation is better?

●Based on your limited interpreting practice, in what way can you convince us of your note-taking qualifications as a (professional) conference interpreter?

●What major translation/interpreting problems in this specialized area (trade/tourism/legal affairs/foreign affairs/MICE) did you manage to solve? And how?

●How can you prove that your survey of translation service is valid or acceptable?

●What is your theoretical framework for cross-cultural interpretation?

●Why did you rely on Translation Theory/Method A rather than Translation Theory/Method B?

●Why did you make use of this (research) methodology?

●Is your research a conceptual one or empirical one? Did you do a good job?

●What conclusion did you reach after the comprehensive/critical review of literature?

●Please clarify what you mean by this statement on this translation issue.

●How does your translation project contribute to knowledge in your domain/filed/ subject area(s)?

●What made you choose sports/financial/TCM/music/dance materials for your translation task?

●How has your conception of this research on domestication/foreignization changed over time?

●What have you learned about conducting research in this specialization?

●Were you unable to complete any aspect of this translation task as originally conceived?

●Which part of the translation/thesis did you most enjoy?

●What would you translate/interpret differently if you had to do it all over again?

●Do you plan to continue the research on Arthur Waley's translation of Chinese poetry?

●Which versified translation do you prefer, XYZ's or Giles'?

●What limitations do you have about your practical translation/interpreting research?

●How did you manage to solve the typical translation problems encountered in your long translation (translation task)?

●In what aspects can you prove that your re-translation is better?

●Have you found any/some/many errors concerning your bibliography?

●Are you clear enough of the basic academic norms the thesis author is required to follow?

●Do you know something necessary about citing, writing conventions, and paper format in your BTI thesis?

●Have you ever read MLA (, APA, Chicago Manual,) and GB/T 7714—2015 (carefully)?

10.3.4　做好心理准备

答辩过程中，学生的心态、情绪控制对确保论文答辩顺利进行关系密切。一些有效的做法建议如下：

- 树立信心；
- 充满信心；
- 端正态度；
- 明确目的；
- 事先排练；
- 事先设想；
- 答辩策略；
- 放缓节奏；
- 心理暗示[①]；
- 莫怵评委；
- 倾听提问；
- ……

10.4　答辩程序

这里的答辩程序指狭义的毕业论文答辩流程，详见表 10-3。

表 10-3　毕业论文答辩流程

答辩流程	答辩流程内容
1	**开场环节**：答辩委员会主席（答辩组组长）宣布答辩规程、纪律、答辩人姓名、答辩顺序、论文题目等信息（可结合 PPT 展示）；介绍答辩委员会或组成员、秘书等。
2-1	**自述环节 1**：答辩人 A 自述（10—15/20 分钟，结合 PPT 展示）。
2-2	**答辩环节 1**：答辩专家提问（不少于 3 个问题），答辩人回答、辩护（结合各种展示）。
2-3	自述环节 2：答辩人 B 自述（10—15/20 分钟，结合 PPT 展示）。
2-4	答辩环节 2：答辩专家提问（不少于 3 个问题），答辩人回答、辩护（结合各种展示）。
2-5	自述环节 3：答辩人 C 自述（10—15/20 分钟，结合 PPT 展示）。
2-6	答辩环节 3：答辩专家提问（不少于 3 个问题），答辩人回答、辩护（结合各种展示）。
3	**现场环节**：（open defense）可以安排并允许/欢迎旁听答辩的师生提问。
4	答辩人休会、退席。
5	**讨论环节**：答辩委员会开会讨论，就答辩人的答辩情况、论文质量、现场表现以及指导教师对论文的评语等进行细致讨论，若有必要还可以参阅匿名评审专家的意见。委员会主席执笔撰写论文评语，集体通过对论文的评语，并以无记名投票方式对论文是否最后获得通过进行表决，并做出决议。决议须经过三分之二的答辩委员会委员通过，方可生效。
6	**宣布环节**：答辩委员会主席或答辩组组长宣布答辩会复会，宣布论文的评阅和表决结果。
7	**结束环节**：毕业/学位论文答辩会结束。

---

① "心理暗示"特指自我暗示你在这方面的研究是做得最好的、你的译文几乎万无一失、不怕任何刁钻的提问等。

10.5　答辩策略

有关论文答辩的原则性要求和宏观忠告，已经在"10.3　答辩准备"部分做了比较细致的介绍。本节将就具体的注意事项或经验之谈再做一些必要的补充（不含有重要理论创新、实践创新的论文答辩之策略，因为说法、思路有质和量的不同），总计18项。

（1）准备好备用PPT——陈述完整版，包括题目、致谢、摘要（含关键词）、目录、研究目的及意义、研究问题/翻译难题、研究方法、文献综述、理论框架、案例讨论、最终结论、参考文献等；可自述时间长度20分钟；作为备用；要有层次感；（几乎）不能有语病。

（2）准备好自述PPT——自述答辩版，包括题目、致谢、摘要（含关键词）、研究目的及意义、研究问题/翻译难题、研究方法、理论框架、案例讨论、最终结论、参考文献等；可自述时间长度10分钟；作为展示；要有层次感；（几乎）不能有语病。

（3）事先模拟排练——在安静或吵闹的环境下反复排练，做到几乎能够背诵。语音语调不理想或不善于公共演讲的学生，更要多花气力，不断"彩排"训练。

（4）事先选好服装——用于答辩穿着，只要干净、得体即可。

（5）注意自身修养——答辩时注意有礼有节。

（6）注意劳逸结合——答辩前夕要有充足的睡眠，确保答辩时精力充沛、头脑清晰。

（7）自述声音、节奏——声音要饱满、响亮/适中，节奏中速，以防卡壳。

（8）文本自述方式——参照10分钟长度的PPT文本自述，不要（完全）照本宣科，根据事先准备好的纲要、文字去"说"（即"说课"），而非去"讲"（即"讲课"），这样容易带出"精华""亮点"来。

（9）致谢领先——对自己的导师表示感谢，天经地义，应该先于论文自述之前；有时你的论文匿名评阅专家对论文的改进提出过宝贵的意见，更应该首先表示致谢。

（10）带够资料——答辩时应带上论文答辩时（可能）有用的资料（印刷本、电子版、手抄版），还应包括图片、音频、视频等多媒体文献。这样多媒体穿插，答辩生动、形象。

（11）带上纸笔——用于答辩环节记录专家们的提问及有用的话语。

（12）态度诚恳——学生尊重师长，不言而喻，尤其在论文答辩时，更要表现新时代翻译专业学生的礼貌风范。

（13）不耻下问——在答辩时特指一旦听不明白专家提问，不要急于回答、不懂装懂，一定不要怕"丢面子"，而要礼貌地请求专家再重复一下问题，确实听不懂的时候，再虚心求教。

（14）勇于承认——对自己论文中的大小错误，或对自己研究/翻译中的学术问题/实践问题，一旦被指出，要襟怀坦白，勇于承认。小问题固然不最后影响答辩通过，本科生/研究生水平有限也在所难免，但遮遮掩掩，讳莫如深，还"狡辩"不断，态度不端正，就有失一名学生起码的为人与为学的礼貌及规范了。

（15）虚实得当——搞学术，不是谈生意。前者要务实，后者可以虚实结合。答辩时，可以避免论及"虚"，即自己没有把握的地方和观点。然而一旦被发现，就应虚心承认，表示当场求教以及答辩后研究跟上，切忌玩"虚"的，因为学生的"虚"很容易暴露，结果适得其反——这就是"实"，即实实在在做人、做事。

（16）答辩语言——使用非母语英语答辩，难度不言自明。尽可能使用规范的语言、学术语言（尤其是术语），若能运用得体的 colloquialism，意味深长的 allusion，经典的 quotation，并目光移动，辅以体态语言（paralinguistic features），风趣幽默，则可加分。务必使用第一人称。如果表达力不强，不要刻意而为之，注意语言简明扼要，以免"言多必失"。

（17）答辩时控——自述时间和答辩时间都是有限制的，所以，自述不要超时而被叫停；答辩时除非答辩专家特别强调要求展开论述，一般都不必要展开过细。直奔主题，去掉枝节，简单干脆，言简意赅。Good timing 的人计划性强，准备充分，势必有加分因素。

（18）返璞归真——说千道万，答辩之策略、对策、技巧、窍门，如此等等，都是"应景之作"。说其有用，毕竟有其实用性/适用性；说其无用，毕竟是因人而异/程度各异。专业学习、学术研究是需要脚踏实地的，唯有返璞归真，细水长流，戒骄戒躁，苦练笔译口译，苦读翻译理论，注意平时点滴积累，不断提高自己的专业水平、综合素质及职业能力，一步一个脚印，才能企及专业、学术之高峰。

10.6　答辩评定

毕业论文答辩过程结束后，答辩委员会或答辩组将根据论文本身的质量和答辩者的现场表现，经过集体评议，评定学生的成绩，并写出评语。

最终成绩包括论文成绩和答辩成绩两部分。以下是论文及答辩成绩的评定标准[①]，仅供参考。

（1）BA 学位论文答辩评定标准（表 10-4）。

表 10-4　BA 学位论文答辩评定标准

评估项目		肯定	基本肯定	不足	否定
书面文本	①选题依据；理论/实践意义				
	②研究问题之合理性及可解性				
	③文献综述之评论性				
	④理论框架与研究方法之合理性				
	⑤案例讨论及研究结果之可接受性				
	⑥研究成果之特色/创新性/有益性				
	⑦参考文献之规范性				

---

① 一般各高校都有自己的评定标准（成文的或非成文的），此处笔者自己的研究成果仅供参考。

（续表）

	评估项目	肯定	基本肯定	不足	否定
口头报告	⑧表述清楚，条理清晰，层次分明				
	⑨选题理据，概念解读，综述水平				
	⑩答辩之逻辑性；论证之严密性				
结果	是否同意通过				

（2）BTI 学位论文答辩评定标准（表 10-5）。

表 10-5　BTI 学位论文答辩评定标准

	评估项目	肯定	基本肯定	不足	否定
书面文本	①选题依据；实践/理论意义				
	②翻译难题/研究问题之可解性				
	③理论框架与研究方法之解释性				
	④译文之准确性、专业性、艺术性				
	⑤案例讨论及研究结果之可接受性				
	⑥翻译/研究成果之特色/创新性/有益性				
	⑦数据分析及参考文献之规范性				
口头报告	⑧表述清楚，条理清晰，层次分明				
	⑨选题理据，译文解读，诠释水平				
	⑩答辩之逻辑性；论证之严密性				
结果	是否同意通过				

10.7　论文提交

答辩后毕业论文的提交，虽然已是整个论文撰写、答辩的最后环节，但仍是一个细致且未必轻松的阶段。

（1）修改定稿

就工作程序和学术严谨而言，学生有义务和责任根据答辩委员会提出的意见（有书面意见）对论文进行修改。这里涉及三个问题：一是行动问题——学生是否根据修改意见进行了修改；二是能力问题——学生是否有能力按照专家意见进行修改；三是原则问题——导师是否严格把关（学生不修改或修改不到位，不予以通过）。换言之，翻译专业对尚未定稿者，不予以毕业放行，或者等论文修改达标后再发给毕业证书和学位证书。此外，本校不定期组织教学督导组对全校的毕业论文（设计）进行抽查，不定期抽调部分院（系）毕业论文（设计）送外校复评，论文（设计）抽查和复评结果返回相关院（系）。这种把关只会加强，不会放松。

（2）成绩评定

毕业论文（设计）成绩由文献综述、开题报告、外文翻译、论文（设计）答辩等部分组成，一般文献综述占 10%、开题报告占 15%、外文翻译占 5%、论文（设计）及答辩占 70%（成绩评定采用百分制）。论文（设计）及答辩部分成绩可根据论文（设计）工作成果、学生的工作态度及出勤情况、指导教师评价、答辩情况等予以综合评定。学院（系）或翻译专业都制定了毕业论文（设计）成绩的具体考核标准。

（3）上交环节

论文经答辩委员会或答辩组讨论答辩成绩合格，结合答辩委员会或答辩组专家意见修改，并经论文指导教师评阅后确认可以正式定稿的同学（含全日制在校本科生、留学生、双学位学生），需上交及上传毕业论文正式稿（定稿）的电子版（注意事项参看"上传环节"），同时上交纸质版。

上交论文要符合编排要求：封面（中外文题目）、题名页、承诺书、摘要（中英文）、目录、论文正文部分材料、开题报告（含文献综述）。翻译/英语专业都有具体的论文格式要求标准可参照。

（4）上传环节

毕业论文完整版（符合编排要求）正式稿（电子版）需/须于规定时间段内上传至现代教务系统（针对本校学生）。上传论文前，学生务必确认论文题目是否需要修改；若需要修改毕业论文题目，可参看具体操作指南（略）完成修改。该论文题目最终将导入学生成绩单并上交档案馆。

（5）上交环节

毕业/学位论文正式稿（纸质版）需要上交。这有利于学习和交流。

（6）其他说明

要认真对待毕业论文上传、上交工作。如不按照规定上传、上交毕业论文电子版、纸质版，将不发放毕业证书和学位证书。未通过毕业论文答辩的同学，须待答辩通过、论文定稿后，完成上述要求。

根据浙江大学本发〔2018〕3 号文件，毕业论文还涉及档案保存和涉密管理问题：

第一，本科生毕业论文（设计）全套资料成果及其他相关材料等由院（系）保存，保存期限不低于五年；毕业论文（设计）电子版由学校档案馆保存。

第二，从事涉密毕业论文（设计）的本科生在进行开题报告前，接触涉密论文（设计）的人员（论文评阅人、答辩委员会委员等）在接触涉密论文（设计）前均须与学校委托负责人（指导教师）签署《浙江大学本科生涉密学位论文申请暨保密协议书》。毕业设计封面右上角须标明为涉密论文。毕业论文（设计）上传教务系统时须明确为涉密毕业论文（设计）；保密期限（一般为两年）届满的，自行解密；解密后的涉密毕业论文（设计）按照无密级毕业论文（设计）进行管理。

◎研究与实践思考题◎

1.　明白开题报告答辩的概念、意义和方法，同时重视中期检查环节。

2. 熟悉开题答辩可能涉及的常见问题，试着一一自我回答。

3. 熟悉开题答辩技巧和须知，试着在同学之间互练互评。

4. 了解 BA/BTI 论文开题报告评估标准。

5. 了解学位论文答辩概念，细读 Chris Riesbeck 关于论文、答辩等方面的解答。

6. 了解论文答辩的意义，认真对待盲审，确保一次过查重关；通过毕业论文的撰写及答辩，努力做到全方位的自我完善。

7. 了解何为答辩准备（涉及院系方、自述报告、专家提问、心理生理等）。

8. 了解/细读本章设计的 40 个英文问题，选择跟自己相关的问题并做好必要的准备。

9. 了解论文答辩程序，准备自己的答辩策略。

10. 根据 BA/BTI 学位论文答辩评定标准，准备好自己的 presentation & delivery。

手 册 篇◆◆

For Easy Reference

I. 学术规范与操作（Academic Norms & Operations）

【作者按】本书重点推荐使用 MLA style、《信息与文献——参考文献著录规则》（GB/T 7714—2015）和《学术论文编写规则》（GB/T 7713.2—2022）。

MLA style 专著（Gibaldi）在 21 世纪再版多次，学生可从校图书馆借阅，也可以上网查询有关不断更新的电子文献（http://www.mla.org/style）。国家标准《信息与文献——参考文献著录规则》（GB/T 7714—2015，2015 年 5 月 15 日发布）是迄今的最新版本，还有国家标准《学术论文编写规则》（GB/T 7713.2—2022）的最新版本，也很容易从网上搜索、下载。详见"第 8 章　如何引注（注重规范）"。

II. 拒绝剽窃（Anti-plagiarism Advice）

【作者按】拒绝剽窃或避免剽窃的要旨是细致了解、严格遵循有关的学术规范。重中之重是从一开始就诚实守信，崇尚并遵循学术道德。学校要营造重视学术规范的氛围。我国拟立学位法：如有利用人工智能代写学位论文等行为，或被撤销学位证书。

1. 剽窃概念解读

剽窃译自 plagiarism，源自拉丁文 plagiarius，意为 "kidnapper"（绑架；劫持）。根据 *MLA Style Manual and Guide to Scholarly Publishing*： "plagiarism refers to a form of intellectual theft that has been defined as 'the false assumption of authorship; the wrongful act of taking the product of another person's mind, and presenting it as one's own'." "In short, to plagiarize is to give the impression that you wrote or thought something that you in fact borrowed from someone, and to do so is a violation of professional ethics."（Gibaldi, 2001b: 151）

还有一种对 plagiarism 比较通俗的定义："the unauthorized use or close imitation of the language and thoughts of another author and the representation of them as one's own original work; something used and represented in this manner."（*The Random House Unabridged Dictionary*，引自 Buffa, 2003: 92）

2. 剽窃两大表现

剽窃具体表现在两大方面，一个涉及他人，一个涉及自己。

其一，剽窃他人（思想、文字等）。"Forms of plagiarism include the failure to give appropriate acknowledgement when repeating another's wording or particularly apt phrase, paraphrasing another's argument, and presenting another's line of thinking. You may certainly use other persons' words and thoughts, but the borrowed material must not appear to be your creation."（Gibaldi, 2001b: 151）

其二，自我剽窃。"Another issue related to plagiarism concerns not outside sources but the author's own earlier writing. Whereas reprinting one's published work, such as having a journal article appear in a subsequent book of essays, is professionally acceptable—as long as appropriate permission is secured and complete bibliographic information about the original publication accompanies the reprint—professionals generally disapprove if previously published work is reissued, whether verbatim or slightly revised, under another title or in some other manner that gives the impression it is a new work. Although not the same as plagiarizing someone else's writing, this practice nonetheless qualifies as a kind of self-plagiarism and constitutes another type of unethical activity."（152）

3. 剽窃行为定性

剽窃是一个道德问题，而非法律问题。Gibaldi 指出："Plagiarism is a moral and ethical offense rather than a legal one. Most instances of plagiarism fall outside the scope of copyright infringement, a legal offense. Plagiarism remains an offense even if the plagiarized work is not covered by copyright law or if the amount of material used and the nature of the use fall within the scope of air use; copyright infringement remains a legal offense even if the violator acknowledges the source."（151-152）

4. 剽窃处罚后果

"The penalties for plagiarism can be severe, ranging from loss of respect to loss of degrees, tenures, or even employment."（152）

Slade 也同样指出："Whether intentional or unintentional, plagiarism can have serious consequences—not only academic, in the form of failure or expulsion, but also legal, in the form of lawsuits. Plagiarism is taken seriously because it violates the ethics of the academic community."（2000: 55）

5. 学生剽窃四大原因

其一，欧美观点。"They honestly believe that no one will know they didn't come up with the material on their own."（Buffa, 2003: 91）

其二，欧美观点。"They don't realize that they are plagiarizing. This is probably the more common reason for plagiarism."（91）

其三，笔者观点。故意而为之，不管是否被发现，甚至一而再，再而三地剽窃。

其四，笔者观点。剽窃者所处环境或氛围所致，大家都习惯成自然了。高考可以作弊（如代考），剽窃算得了什么呢？此外，老师一来不管；二来也没有水平发现；三来即使管，也是不严格的，如睁一只眼闭一只眼，甚至还会"保密""包庇""隐瞒"等。

6. 如何看待有意剽窃

根据 Buffa，学生务必 "Keep in mind that your professors are extremely well-read in a variety of academic journals. While it may seem improbable to you that 'anyone really reads this stuff,' let us assure you that people do—the kind of people who are grading your papers. Teachers are trained to recognize a passage that stylistically doesn't match the rest of your paper. If you lift something and plunk it into the middle of your own writing, chances are good that it will stick out like a sore thumb."（91）

7. 如何看待无意剽窃

Buffa 特别指出：" <u>most schools won't take into account what your intentions were</u>. While we summarize the rules for what you must cite, use this as a general guideline: <u>If in doubt——cite!!!</u> "（91）

8. 如何避免剽窃

（1）避免剽窃参考准则（92-95）（表 11-1）[①]

表 11-1　避免剽窃参考准则

Some Useful Guidelines to Follow

- **You must give credit to:**

    Any direct quotation.

    Any indirect or paraphrased ideas from other sources.

    A sequence of ideas or information; for example, a table or an interesting presentation of a topic.

    Any opinion, theory or judgement formulated in one of your sources.

- **You *don't* need to give credit to:**

    Facts. This means that you don't need to document a fact that "everybody would know." Anything that can be looked up in a standard reference book is free for the taking. For example, you wouldn't need to give a reference for the scientific name of an animal.

    Old sayings, well-known Biblical scriptures, or familiar quotations such as *a cat has nine lives* would not need a citation.

- **You may use your own material again. If, however, you are going to try to use the exact same paper for more than one course, you should probably check your school's policy.**

- **You may not hand in other students' papers and claim them as your own.**

- **When you take notes, use a special method to distinguish your own ideas from your source's ideas. You may use a different color pen, or bracket your own ideas.**

- **You must put quotation marks around a quote, even if it is one or two words long. If you are going to paraphrase, make sure your paraphrase from the earliest drafts of your paper. If you copy something directly with the idea that you'll paraphrase it later, you may forget and inadvertently plagiarize.**

- **Don't become intimidated when you are reading source material. Your teachers don't expect you to have the polished style of a published author. They will probably be more suspicious than impressed if you hand in a perfect-sounding paper that isn't your own. You are expected to sound like a student.**

- **When in doubt——cite. It is better to give credit for something that you didn't need to credit than to take credit for something you had no right to.**

[①] 直接引用英文原文准确、有效。笔者特选择引用 Buffa 的 Guidelines，浅显易懂，适合学生读者。

●Once you get in the habit of writing research papers, you will become more sophisticated about when and where to cite sources. At first, you may feel as though you are citing too much, but that's probably okay. ... Although a research paper relies on outside sources, always remember that it is your own voice that will distinguish it. Your professors are not looking for a string of quotes and rehashed ideas.

（2）避免剽窃举例说明（表 11-2）[①]

表 11-2　避免剽窃举例说明

Quoting Without Plagiarizing	
Joe Blow was a happyman, who often walked down the road whistling and singing.	Sentence in the book *Joe Blow: His Life and Times*, by Jay Scrivener.

What's Right	
"Joe Blow was a happyman, who often walked down the road whistling and singing."	**Correct:** Full quote is inside quotation marks, followed by citation to *Joe Blow: His Life and Times*. Besides, **footnote superscript** was used to show when that sentence was cited.
●According to Scrivener, Blow "often walked down the road whistling and singing." ●"Joe Blow was a happyman," writes Scrivener.	**Correct:** Each partial quote is inside quote marks, followed by citation. The partial quotes are not misleading.
According to Scrivener, Blow was "a happyman," who often showed it by singing tunes to himself.	**Correct:** Partial quote is inside quotation marks; non-quoted materials are outside. The paraphrase (about singing tunes to himself) accurately conveys the original author's meaning without mimicking his actual words. Citation properly follows the sentence.
Joe Blow seemed like "a happyman," the kind who enjoyed "whistling and singing."	**Correct:** Two partial quotes are each inside quotation marks; nonquoted materials are outside. Citation properly follows sentence.
Joe appeared happy and enjoyed whistling and singing to himself.	**Correct:** This paraphrase is fine. It's not too close to Scrivener's original wording. The citation acknowledges the source.

What's Wrong	
Joe Blow was a happyman, who often walked down the road whistling and singing. **(no citation)**	**Wrong:** It is plagiarism to quote an author's exact words or to paraphrase them closely without both quotation marks and proper citation. **Acknowledge your sources!**

---

① 选自美国学校常用案例，笔者改用表格形式展示，并向 C. Lipson 和 C. Simpson 谨致谢忱。

Joe Blow was a happyman, who often walked down the road whistling and singing.	**Wrong:** These are actually Scrivener's exact words. It is plagiarism to use them without indicating explicitly that it is a quote. It is essential to use quotation marks (or block indentation for longer quotes), even if you give accurate citation to the author. This example is wrong, then, because it doesn't use quotation marks, even though it cites the source.
Joe Blow was a happyman and often walked down the road singing and whistling. **(no citation)**	**Wrong:** Although the words are not exactly the author's, they are very similar. (The words "singing" and "whistling" are simply reversed.) Either use an exact quote or paraphrase in ways that are clearly different from the author's wording.
Joe Blow was a happyman. **(no citation)**	**Wrong:** There are two problems here. First, it's an exact quote so it should be quoted and cited. Second, even if the quote were modified slightly, Scrivener should still be cited because it is his personal judgment (and not a simple fact) that Joe Blow is happy.
Joe Blow often walked down the road whistling and singing. **(no citation)**	**Wrong:** Same two problems as the previous example: (1) exact words should be both quoted and cited, and (2) Scrivener's personal judgment needs to be credited to him.
Joe Blow appeared to be "a happy man" and often walked down the road whistling and singing.	**Wrong:** Despite the citation, some of Scrivener's exact words are outside the quotation marks. That creates the misleading impression that the words are original, rather than Scrivener's. This is a small violation, like going a few miles over the speed limit. But if such miscitations occur often or include significant portions of text, then they can become serious cases of plagiarism.
"Joe Blow was an anxious-man, who often ran down the road."	**Wrong:** The quote is not accurate. According to Scrivener, Joe Blow was not anxious; he was "happy." And he didn't run, he "walked." Although this misquotation is not plagiarism, it is an error. You should quote properly, and your work should be reliable. If such mistakes are repeated, if they are seriously misleading, or, worst of all, if they appear to be intentional, they may be considered academic fraud. **(Plagiarism is fraud, too, but a different kind.)**
Joe Blow "walked down the road" quietly.	**Wrong:** The words inside the partial quotation are accurate, but the word following it distorts Scrivener's plain meaning. Again, this is not plagiarism, but it does violate the basic principle of presenting materials fairly and accurately. If such mistakes are repeated or if they show consistent bias (for example, to prove Joe Blow is a quiet person or hates music), they may be considered a type of academic fraud. At the very least, they are misleading.

（3）避免剽窃补充说明

上述有关"Joe Blow"的举例说明，重点放在单句上。若引文涉及段落、章节，或者引用他人的思想等，原理与单句引用如出一辙。具体做法如下：

●使用解释性引注（explanatory citation）。事先或在开始部分就做一说明，可以用脚注或尾注。如可以这样表达："My analysis in this section draws heavily on George Chen's work, particularly his 'A New Sub-branch of Translation Studies' (Chen, 20××: 210-215)."或者，也可以改为使用相似的评述性文字，同时告知读者你在引用 George Chen 的文献。

●使用文内引注（in-text citation）。出现一次，引注一次，出现两次，引注两次，以此类推。

●使用解释性脚注（descriptive footnote）。解释略。

●使用解释性尾注（descriptive endnote）。解释略。

●使用解释性话语（paraphrase）。避免与原文过于接近，如要避免有几个字/词与原文相同的现象发生，又如要避免解释性话语中仅仅替换了两三个同义词。这些都会被判为剽窃，即使你不是有意而为之。总之，解释性话语必须看起来、读起来与原文不同，也避免使用其他作者的优美文字来作为解释性话语。

●使用解释性增益（explanatory amplication）。借用他人思想须引注，引注原则与借用他人文字一致。换言之，"Cite borrowed ideas as well as borrowed words."

●使用综述性文字（summarizing）。经综述原文后，文字会少很多。为避免剽窃，务必将有关思想/内容的出处加以注明。换言之，"To avoid plagiarism, one must acknowledge the source of the ideas. Borrowed ideas must be acknowledged as well as borrowed words."[①]但要防止"歪曲"或"篡改"他人的思想。你可以同意或者不同意别人的观点，然而，要力图避免因综述别人的思想观点而造成原意走样。

●使用四大引文系统格式。即 MLA 格式、APA 格式、Chicago 格式以及国家标准。就翻译学而言，学生要熟悉、了解、学会 MLA 格式和国家标准（GB/T 7714—2015）等。

III. 经验之谈（Coaching Tips）

【作者按】毕业论文之撰写，是一个好奇的开局（a curious beginning），是一个坚持的过程（a persistent process）、一个付出的过程（a devoted process）、一个快乐的过程（a pleasant process）、一个有益的工程（a rewarding project），最后是一个幸福的结局（a happy ending）、一个圆满的终局（a complete and successful culmination）。

从开始，到结尾，在每个重要环节，有许多值得与各位同学分享的经验之谈（rules of thumb/coaching tips），这些经验之谈一定会使你受益良多。

表 11-3 是笔者提供给大家的"要诀"（know-what & know-how），言简意赅，点到为止。

---

① 参考 Plagiarism Overview—The Christ College of Nursing and Health Sciences。

表 11-3　论文撰写全过程"要诀"

（1）态度第一	（2）如何开始
●脚踏实地 ●坚持到底	●选择你感兴趣的话题 ●选择与论文相关的课程 ●选择需要写论文的课程 ●选修论文相关领域的高级课程 ●了解你专业以外的相关领域 ●收集与论文相关的观点
（3）如何发展	（4）选择导师
●不断添加有关论文的主题思想 ●给自己读过的论文和专著做"批注"、写"评述" ●记录你感兴趣的研究问题 ●记录会丰富论文话题的思想 ●时常温故知新，剔除意义不大的思想或建议	●在大三下或大四上选定指导教师 ●在低年级不妨选择自己"心仪"的老师为意向导师 ●选择与你比较"合拍"的导师 ●选择你兴趣领域的专家做导师 ●选择熟悉你专业方向的做导师 ●主动与导师面谈
（5）面谈内容	（6）好的问题
●介绍你的专业方向 ●介绍你的兴趣领域 ●介绍你选修的课程 ●介绍你的课程论文 ●介绍你的研究问题① ●介绍你的准备情况 ●确定下次见面日期	●真正吸引你的 ●你想深入探讨，但尚难以回答的 ●你有能力加以研究的 ●你的时间、能力及导师有助于你研究的 ●暂且说不出论文主题，不妨先将其分成三至五个话题或问题（通过与导师讨论之后可以将范围缩小） ●与导师初步或大致确定你的论题和/或翻译课题 ●将你的论文暨研究问题/翻译课题切分成几个可操作的段落或研究问题/翻译章节，并分别设定完成任务的最后期限
（7）好的格式	（8）文献收集
●各校都有规定的论文格式，选择你中意的论文版本（特指你的学长、学姐的BTI/BA 论文版本）作为模式（如长度因素等） ●选择新版 MLA style 和新版国家标准（结合本校规定）	●文献阅读要先于论文撰写 ●列表收集阅读文献 ●从一流学科杂志中寻找 ●从学科专著、教科书中寻找 ●从二、三级文献中寻找 ●从有关书籍的脚注、尾注和参考文献中寻找 ●从学科专业书评、文献综述、学术专著中寻找

---

① 好的论文通常源于好的研究问题和引人入胜的或激动人心的、挑战性的难题。

	●从名著名译、翻译范本、译文对比研究中寻找
	●从你感兴趣的学科专业领域中寻找源语文本
	●从一些杂书、（学术和非学术）公众号中搜寻
	●在不断的文献寻找过程中增减、完善参考文献
（9）文献读写	（10）避免剽窃
●通读（几乎全部）文献，选读（有关）文献，细读（重点）文献，（在电脑上）记录读书笔记	●严格遵循学术规范进行参考文献或其他必要信息的脚注、尾注、文内引注以及文后参考文献著录
●对读不懂、解不透的难题，务必搞清楚，坚持不懂就问的虚心态度	●表述他人的意见，使用自己的话语，不要模仿原文，但要注明出处
●围绕论文主题，按照时间性、全面性、评论性要求撰写综述	●借用他人的观点，不管你是否同意，都要注明出处
	●注意 quote 和 paraphrase 之间的严格差别。如果是前者，注意学术规范；如果是后者，避免与原话完全相同
	●引用他人的思想与引用他人的话，同样必须注明出处
	●切勿歪曲他人的观点或话语
（11）文献笔记	（12）正常约见
●陈述文献的主要观点	●与导师确定正常约见日期
●陈列文献的次要观点	●确定见面频率、最佳时间
●点明论点论据及论证	●事先该如何准备书面材料
●记录自己的简要评述	●讨论文献并听取导师意见
●抄录有益于你的思想	●讨教使用文献的层级问题
●备份自己的读书笔记	
（13）确定选题	（14）开题报告
●第一个月确定论文选题	●应有一个好题目
●选题务必具有可操作性	●应有论题重要性
●缩小范围必须合理恰当	●应有研究的途径
●普通论文讨论一般选题	●应提出重要问题
●优秀论文讨论重大选题	●可以暂时不回答
●平时关注重大话题讨论	●要认真修改开题
	●修改有利于论题清晰
	●修改使研究问题准确
	●修改使研究途径正确
	●参加开题报告讨论会
	●讨论会全面提升开题
（15）研究方法	（16）研究计划
●应符合两大标准	●说明研究材料
●能针对研究问题	●说明研究方法
●能配合研究技巧	●说明理论框架

	●研究计划要不断改进
	●案例研究要讲清为何使用案例法而非其他
	●案例研究要讲清为何要使用这些特殊案例
	●研究案例未必典型或常态，可以独特非常
	●所选案例要具有典型性、有难度、有门槛
（17）论文论题	（18）论文题目
●背景阅读后初步写下一个自然段或几句话的论题陈述	●好的题目不仅切题，还反映论题视角
	●论题可以不断修改，直至满意
●不断修订、改进论题，使之最后真正成为论文的论题	●论题是否可行，看看能否三言两语讲明白
（19）论文撰写	（20）有效写作
●起步可以先预写，涉及对笔记和评述的梳理	●语言明白、易懂、自然、学术
	●以主动语态为主
●预写在原有笔记的基础上再扩展，并加以逻辑串联	●删除多余的话语
	●论文题目要醒目、切题、抓人
●预写五步骤：分几大章、逻辑衔接、合并同类、对号入座、逻辑顺序	●摘要应突出研究目的、重点、方法、结论
	●绪论首段要开宗明义
●开写首章为绪论，次章方法论，中间是理论，接着乃论证，最后要结论	●绪论末段要给出路线图
	●每节要有描写性小标题
●边写边改，参考样例，联系自己，不断改进，充实论文	●每节首段要点明本节内容及重点
	●节与节之间要衔接合理，过渡自然
●初稿到定稿，不少于三稿；五稿为终稿，算是水平高	●每段应以主题句开始
	●例证、故事、图表、经典，引人入胜
●八稿十稿确保优秀，既毫不夸张，也充满希望	●检查拼写、语法、标点、格式、规范、各层标题等
	●观点鲜明是重中之重
●没有导师的有效修改，通常论文质量难以提高	●最后章节要突出研究之成果、论点之正确、成果之意义及研究之局限
●学生写几遍草稿，导师就应修改几遍	●反复修改是确保论文高质的唯一办法
●师生邮件往来互动，必要时再次面谈	●每完成一个章节便可进行编辑、修改
●写作基本步骤是 prewriting ⇒ drafting/draft writing ⇒ rewriting ⇒ repeated revision ⇒ finalization ⇒ submission for external examination/review ⇒ revision for oral defense	●（英文）加工修改涉及两大范围，一是词、句、段；二是论文设计、章节安排及其逻辑关系
	●电子文本修改与纸质文本修改相结合
	●了解、熟悉 MLA style，以及 APA style、Chicago style、Vancouver style，遵循国家标准（如 GB/T 7714—2015 和 GB/T 7713.2—2022）
	●撰写对指导教师以及其他对你（论文写作）有帮助的老师、专家、同学、亲友的致谢（Acknowledgements）

IV. 论文案例（Case Illustrations）

【作者按】开卷有益。细读、学习已经毕业的 BA & BTI 生（有代表性）的学位论文，乃至 MA & MTI 生（有参考价值）的学位论文，不仅能获得关于用英文独立（内含原创性）完成 BTI/BA 学位论文的必不可少的感性认识，而且能在较为全面了解、熟悉如何谋篇布局（包括选题、定题、撰写摘要、选择关键词等），如何进行翻译实践及其研究，如何进行文献综述、理论思考及方法论运用，如何进行参考文献引注等方面获得深度的理性认识。BTI/BA 生学习了有典型意义的 BTI 和 BA 学位论文+MTI 和 MA 学位论文[其中序号（10）MTI 生的毕业论文既是优秀的专业学位论文，也是优秀的学术学位论文；序号（4）和（5）BTI 论文则是具有专业学位+学术学位特色的论文；序号（9）MA 论文亦是类似情况；序号（1）和（7）论文是典型的学术学位论文；序号（8）论文是典型的 MTI 论文，其作者已担任联合国全职翻译多年]之后，可以产生高屋建瓴的获得感，对写好本科毕业论文有利无弊，对今后继续深造（如攻读 MTI/MA）会更有前进、向上的目标。

因篇幅关系，书中不宜长篇介绍学生的论文，只能分专题介绍。这里特别介绍 10 名学生的学位论文（全文或有关重要部分），主题丰富，重点不同，视角各异，特色鲜明，涉及 BA、BTI、MA、MTI 等四种类别（获取论文途径见后）。

1. 10 部学位论文

（1）BA 论文（学术学位论文）："On Chinese-English Translation of Journalistic Texts from the Perspective of Functionalist Text Typology—A Case Study of Chinese-English Translation of 'LOCOG Plays PR Card'"（《功能派文本类型学指导下的汉英新闻稿翻译——以新闻稿 "伦敦奥组委大打公关牌" 汉英翻译为例》）。

（2）BTI 论文（专业学位论文）："On Faithfulness and Flexibility in Translating the Modern Dance Textbook *A Primer for Choreographers*"（《论现代舞教材翻译之忠实与灵活——以翻译〈专业编舞入门〉为例》）之 "Part II　Translation of the selected texts from *A Primer for Choreographers*"。

（3）BTI 论文（专业学位论文）："On Language Function-oriented Translation Principles and Methods of the Translation of *Picture Yourself Playing Cello: Step-by-Step Instruction for Playing the Cello*"（《语言功能视角下的大提琴教材翻译原则与方法研究——〈"图" 说大提琴——零起点演奏教程〉翻译案例探讨》）。

（4）BTI 论文（BA+BTI 特色论文）："On the Translation of Imagery in Du Fu's Poems into English: A Case Study of Du's Poems Selected from *300 Tang Poems*"（《论杜甫诗歌中的意象英译——以〈唐诗三百首〉选录的杜诗为例》）。

（5）BTI 论文（BTI+BA 特色论文）："A Study of Translation Strategies of Culture-specific Items in Subtitles of the English Cultural Documentary *Secrets of the Manor House*"

（《论英语文化纪录片〈英国庄园的秘密〉——字幕中文化专有项的翻译策略》）。

（6）BTI 论文（BTI+BA 特色论文）："A Study on the Translation of *Basic Concepts and Models for Interpreter and Translator Training* (Chapter 8) from the Perspective of the *Skopostheorie* and the Comprehension Equation"（《从目的论和理解公式视角论〈口笔译的基本概念与模型〉第八章的翻译实践》）

（7）MA 论文（学术学位论文）："A Comparative Study on the Translations of Hanshan's Poems by Gary Snyder and Arthur Waley—Translating as a Form of Textual Traveling"（《从文本旅行角度比较研究斯奈德和韦利的两个寒山诗翻译版本》）。

（8）MTI 论文（专业学位论文）："On Simplification and Amplification for Re-translating 'Potala Palace' and 'Shaolin Temple' in a Cross-cultural Way"（《跨文化视角下〈布达拉宫〉与〈少林寺〉重译中的简化与增译问题研究》）之 "Part Two　Translation Project"。

（9）MA 论文（学术学位论文）："Towards Standardizing English Translation of Chinese Medical Terms: Principles and Methods"（《试论中医术语英译标准化：原则与方法》）。

（10）MTI 论文（MTI+MA 特色学位论文）："On the Contextual Translation of the Sixth Chapter of *The Language of Tourism: A Sociolinguistic Perspective*"（《论〈旅游语言：社会语言学视角〉第六章的语境翻译》）之 "Part Two　Translation Project"。

2. 获取以上论文途径

（1）论文全文见《翻译论文写作与答辩指南》（陈刚, 2015a: 746-768）

（2）
●论文题目、翻译实践部分见《翻译论文写作与答辩指南》（陈刚, 2015a: 768-781）；
●论文全文（纸质版、电子版）于浙江大学图书馆获取。

（3）论文全文（纸质版、电子版）于浙江大学图书馆获取。

（4）同上。

（5）同上。

（6）同上。

（7）
●论文题目、摘要、关键词、目录、第 4 章等见《翻译论文写作与答辩指南》（陈刚, 2015a: 808-846）；
●论文全文（电子版）见知网（CNKI）；
●论文全文（纸质版、电子版）于浙江大学图书馆获取。

（8）
●论文题目、翻译实践部分见《翻译论文写作与答辩指南》（陈刚, 2015a: 846-855）；
●论文全文（电子版）见知网（CNKI）；
●论文全文（纸质版、电子版）于浙江大学图书馆获取。

（9）
●论文题目及第 1、4、5、6 章等见《翻译论文写作与答辩指南》（陈刚, 2015a: 855-886）；
●论文全文（电子版）见知网（CNKI）；

● 论文全文（纸质版、电子版）于浙江大学图书馆获取。
（10）
● 论文全文（电子版）见知网（CNKI）；
● 论文全文（纸质版、电子版）于浙江大学图书馆获取。

V. 口译研究建议（**Suggestions for Interpreting Research**）

【作者按】BTI/BA 生想撰写口译主题的毕业/学位论文的不在少数，最终写得好的（即与笔译主题论文相比较而言）却不多，这里有指导教师的问题，但更多的则是本科生自身的问题所致，如缺乏足够的实践量、学习口译本体理论和跨学科理论有困难等。以下，特根据本书作者多年的实践积累和不断的观察、研究（包括指导学生撰写口译主题的毕业论文的切身体会）[①]，与学生读者分享适合 BTI & BA 生的一些有待成熟、完善的问题、建议及思考。请通过二维码阅读。

[①] 笔者指导过本科生、研究生（含高校教师在职研究生）撰写口译主题的学位论文。虽然这些论文写得都不错（个人分别给予优秀—B+的评分），但均不具备代表性意义供 BTI & BA 生参考。

主要参考文献^①
（Bibliography）

边春光. 出版词典[Z]. 上海：上海辞书出版社，1992.

陈刚. 西湖诗赞（英文版）[M]. 杭州：浙江摄影出版社，1996.

陈刚. 旅游翻译与涉外导游[M]. 北京：中国对外翻译出版公司，2004.

陈刚. 归化翻译与文化认同——《鹿鼎记》英译样本研究[J]. 外语与外语教学，2006(12): 43-47.

陈刚. 旅游英汉互译教程[M]. 上海：上海外语教育出版社，2009.

陈刚. 旅游英语导译教程[M]. 上海：上海外语教育出版社，2010.

陈刚. 翻译学入门[M]. 杭州：浙江大学出版社，2011.

陈刚. 导译研究——翻译学的新分支[J]. 华侨大学学报（哲学社会科学版），2013(4): 133-140.

陈刚. 旅游翻译[M]. 杭州：浙江大学出版社，2014.

陈刚. 翻译论文写作与答辩指南[M]. 杭州：浙江大学出版社，2015a.

陈刚. 文学多体裁翻译[M]. 杭州：浙江大学出版社，2015b.

陈刚. 旅游英汉互译教程（2.0 版）[M]. 上海：上海外语教育出版社，2021.

陈刚，杜志峰，李瑶. 基础影视翻译与研究[M]. 杭州：浙江大学出版社，2013.

陈刚，阮绩智，等. 高级商务口笔译：口译篇[M]. 杭州：浙江大学出版社，2007.

陈刚，滕超. 会展翻译研究与实践[M]. 杭州：浙江大学出版社，2012.

陈刚，滕超，孔飞燕. 英汉法律互译：理论与实践[M]. 杭州：浙江大学出版社，2008.

陈刚，伍锋，何庆机，等. 应用文体与翻译：理论与实践[M]. 杭州：浙江大学出版社，2008.

陈刚，吴波，朱健平，等. 新闻翻译：理论与实践[M]. 杭州：浙江大学出版社，2011.

陈刚，徐锡华，伍锋，等. 高级商务口笔译：笔译篇[M]. 杭州：浙江大学出版社，2007.

从丛，李咏燕. 学术交流英语教程[M]. 南京：南京大学出版社，2003.

让·德利尔. 翻译理论与翻译教学[M]. 孙慧双，译. 北京：国际文化出版公司，1988.

方梦之. 中国译学大辞典[Z]. 上海：上海外语教育出版社，2011.

傅道彬. 文学是什么[M]. 北京：北京大学出版社，2002.

葛剑雄. 历史学是什么[M]. 北京：北京大学出版社，2002.

顾曰国. 论文项目设计（*Practical Project Design*）[M]. 2 版. 北京：外语教学与研究出版社，2002.

胡军. 哲学是什么[M]. 北京：北京大学出版社，2002.

梅里亚姆·韦伯斯特公司. 韦氏简明写作手册（*A Merriam-Webster Concise Handbook for Writers*）[M]. 北京：世界图书出版公司，1996.

---

① 限于篇幅，这里仅列出主要的 50 项参考文献，其余以脚注形式列出。敬请有关学者/读者谅解！

斯蒂芬·F. 梅森. 自然科学史[M]. 上海：上海人民出版社，1977.

穆雷. 翻译研究方法概论[M]. 北京：外语教学与研究出版社，2011.

凯蒂·普赖斯. 成为乔丹：我的自传[M]. 陈刚，喻旭燕，译. 哈尔滨：哈尔滨出版社，2006.

邱泽奇. 社会学是什么[M]. 北京：北京大学出版社，2002.

王铭铭. 人类学是什么[M]. 北京：北京大学出版社，2002.

王佐良. 新时期的翻译观[A]//杨自俭，刘学云. 翻译新论. 武汉：湖北教育出版社，1994.

文秋芳. 应用语言学研究方法与论文写作[M]. 北京：外语教学与研究出版社，2004.

周宪. 美学是什么[M]. 北京：北京大学出版社，2002.

Baker, Mona (ed.). *Routledge Encyclopedia of Translation Studies* [M]. Shanghai: Shanghai Foreign Language Education Press, 2004.

Bassnett, Susan & Andre Lefevere. *Constructing Cultures: Essays on Literary Translation* [M]. Shanghai: Shanghai Foreign Language Education Press, 2001.

Beidler, Peter G. *Writing Matters* [M]. Chengdu: Sichuan University Press, 2004.

Boyd, Amanda et al. *Writer's Encyclopedia* [M]. 3rd ed. Cincinnati: Writer's Digest Books, 2000.

Buffa, Liz. 兰登书屋英语研究报告高手[M]. 长春：长春出版社，2003. (Buffa, Liz. *Research Paper Smart* [M]. New York: Princeton Review & Random House, 1997.)

Delisle, Jean et al. 翻译研究关键词[Z]. 孙艺风，仲伟合，编译. 北京：外语教学与研究出版社，2004.

Devlin, Brian. *International Standards for Students' Writing* [M]. Beijing: Tsinghua University Press, 2004.

Gentzler, Edwin. *Contemporary Translation Theories* [M]. Rev. 2nd ed. Shanghai: Shanghai Foreign Language Education Press, 2004.

Gibaldi, Joseph. *MLA Handbook for Writers of Research Papers* [M]. 5th ed. Shanghai: Shanghai Foreign Language Education Press, 2001a.

Gibaldi, Joseph. *MLA Style Manual and Guide to Scholarly Publishing* [M]. 2nd ed. Shanghai: Shanghai Foreign Language Education Press, 2001b.

Newmark, Peter. *Approaches to Translation* [M]. Shanghai: Shanghai Foreign Language Education Press, 2001a.

Newmark, Peter. *The Textbook of Translation* [M]. Shanghai: Shanghai Foreign Language Education Press, 2001b.

Nida, Eugene A. *Language, Culture, and Translating* [M]. Shanghai: Shanghai Foreign Language Education Press, 1993.

Slade, Carole. *Form and Style: Research Papers, Reports and Theses* [M]. 10th ed. Beijing: Foreign Language Teaching and Research Press, 2000.

Williams, Jenny & Andrew Chesterman. *The Map: A Beginner's Guide to Doing Research in Translation Studies* [M]. Shanghai: Shanghai Foreign Language Education Press, 2004.